'A highly ingenious solution to the mystery of Jane Grey's thirteen-day usurpation of the throne. Ives's research skills are formidable and will make this book essential, if provocative reading.'

John Guy

'Eric Ives has provided the first full-scale account of one of the most surprising sequences of events in the politics of Tudor England. It is an engrossing tale, here presented in incisive style by a scholar who has an instinctive grasp of how to bring the surprises back to life.'

Diarmaid MacCulloch,
author of *Reformation, Europe's House Divided*, and
A History of Christianity: The First Three Thousand Years

'A Tudor mystery is brilliantly solved, and the story of one of England's most dangerous crises is thrillingly told . . . This book, which takes us as close to the truth of these events as is possible, will convince scholars who thought that they knew the story already, and delight general readers.'

Susan Brigden,
Lincoln College, Oxford

To my many friends who have grappled with
The Reign of Edward VI

LADY
JANE GREY
A Tudor Mystery

ERIC IVES

WITHDRAWN

(W)WILEY-BLACKWELL

A John Wiley & Sons, Ltd., Publication

This edition first published 2009
© 2009 Eric Ives

Blackwell Publishing was acquired by John Wiley & Sons in February 2007. Blackwell's publishing programme has been merged with Wiley's global Scientific, Technical, and Medical business to form Wiley-Blackwell.

Registered Office
John Wiley & Sons Ltd, The Atrium, Southern Gate, Chichester, West Sussex, PO19 8SQ, United Kingdom

Editorial Offices
350 Main Street, Malden, MA 02148-5020, USA
9600 Garsington Road, Oxford, OX4 2DQ, UK
The Atrium, Southern Gate, Chichester, West Sussex, PO19 8SQ, UK

For details of our global editorial offices, for customer services, and for information about how to apply for permission to reuse the copyright material in this book please see our website at www.wiley.com/wiley-blackwell.

The right of Eric Ives to be identified as the author of this work has been asserted in accordance with the UK Copyright, Designs and Patents Act 1988.

Library of Congress Cataloging-in-Publication Data

Ives, E. W. (Eric William), 1931–
    Lady Jane Grey : a Tudor mystery / Eric Ives.
       p. cm.
Includes bibliographical references and index.
    ISBN 978-1-4051-9413-6 (hardcover : alk. paper)
    1. Grey, Jane, Lady, 1537–1554. 2. Great Britain–Kings and rulers–Succession–History–16th century. 3. Queens–Great Britain–Biography. I. Title.

DA345.1.D9I94 2009
942.05′3092–dc22
[B]
                                                            2009005159

A catalogue record for this book is available from the British Library.

Set in 10.75/13.5pt Galliard by SPi Publisher Services, Pondicherry, India
Printed and bound in Singapore by Fabulous Printers Pte Ltd

I   2009

CONTENTS

ILLUSTRATIONS

FIGURES

Map

PREFACE

JANE Grey, the rightful queen of England, was deposed on 19 July 1553 and beheaded on 12 February 1554. This may not be what the text books say, but it is the conclusion offered by this study. The book is not a conventional biography. Jane Grey did not live to see seventeen and the successive crises which destroyed her lasted, each of them, for only a fortnight. It is, rather, 'a mystery', a detective story, in English parlance, 'a whodunnit'. It asks how it was that in 1553 England came suddenly and desperately close to civil war and why those involved behaved as they did. It surveys the facts, discusses the options, suggests where the evidence leads, and weaves the discussion around as much as can be known of the remarkable girl who in right was the fourth of the Tudor monarchs and the first of the Dudley line. As with the solutions offered to every 'mystery', it is for the jury of readers to be persuaded or otherwise.

The notion of 'a mystery' determines the structure of the book. It looks first at the available evidence and then assesses each of the protagonists in turn. Next the complexities of the key decisions are unravelled. The narrative of Jane's thirteen-day reign follows and finally the focus switches back to the sixteen-year-old and the last six months which elevated her to martyrdom.

In the course of what has been a tortuous investigation I owe a debt of gratitude to many archivists and librarians, notably Philippa Bassett (University of Birmingham), Andrea Clarke (British Library), Bridget Clifford (Royal Armouries), Tanya Cooper (National Portrait Gallery), Michael Frost (Inner Temple Library), Wayne Hammond (Williams College, Mass.), Sonje Marie Isaacs (the Lady Jane Internet Museum), Alexandra Kess-Hall (University of Zurich), Sheila O'Connell (British Musuem), Michael Page (Surrey History Centre), Jayne Ringrose (University of Cambridge), Susan Tomkins (Beaulieu), Naomi van Loo (New College,

Oxford University) and Martin Killeen (University of Birmingham). I am also indebted to discussions with and generous help from Diarmaid MacCulloch and many other scholars and critics, particularly Benjamin S. Baum, Dermot Fenlon, Christopher Foley, Meg.Harper, Susan Ives, Leanda de Lisle, Nicholas Orme, Inga Walton and Barry Young. Not least, this book owes much to Tessa Harvey and her colleagues at Wiley-Blackwell. Finally the dedication bears tribute to the students who, over the years, have joined me in wrestling with 'the mystery' of 1553.

TITLES AND OFFICES

IN the years covered by this study, titles and office-holders changed. What follows lists the principal identifications; see also the index.

Admiral		*see:* Dudley, John [I]; Seymour, Thomas; Fiennes, Edward
Brandon, Charles	1514–45	duke of Suffolk
	1539–45	lord great master and president of the council
Brandon, Frances	1533	marchioness of Dorset
	1551–9	duchess of Suffolk
	1555–9	Lady Stokes
Canterbury, Archbishop of	1533–55	*see:* Cranmer, Thomas
Chancellor	1544–7	Thomas Wriothesley
	1547–52	Richard Rich
	1552–3	Thomas Goodrich
Clinton, Lord		*see:* Fiennes, Edward
Cranmer, Thomas	1533–55	archbishop of Canterbury
Darcy, Thomas	1550–1	vice-chamberlain of the household
	1551	Lord Darcy of Chiche
	1551–3	lord chamberlain of the household
Dorset, marchioness of		*see:* Brandon, Frances
Dorset, marquis of		*see:* Grey, Henry
Dudley, John [I]	1542	Viscount Lisle
	1543–7, 1549–50	admiral
	1547	earl of Warwick
	1547–50	lord great chamberlain
	1550–3	lord great master and president of the council
	1551	duke of Northumberland

Paulet, William	1539	Lord St John
	1546–50	lord great master and president of the council
	1550	earl of Wiltshire
	1550–72	lord treasurer
	1551–72	marquis of Winchester
Protector		*see:* Seymour, Edward [I]
Radcliffe, Henry	1542–57	earl of Sussex
Radcliffe, Thomas	1542	Lord Fitzwalter
	1557–93	earl of Sussex
Russell, John	1539	Lord Russell
	1542–55	lord privy seal
	1550–5	earl of Bedford
Russell, Francis	1550–5	Lord Russell
	1555–85	earl of Bedford
Salisbury, countess of	1514–39	Margaret Pole
Secretaries of state	1543–7	William Paget
	1544–57	William Petre
	1550–3	William Cecil
	1553	John Cheke
Seymour, Edward [I]	1536	Viscount Beauchamp
	1537	earl of Hertford
	1547–9	lord protector
	1547–52	duke of Somerset
Seymour, Edward [II]	1547–52	earl of Hertford
Seymour, Thomas	1547–9	Lord Seymour
	1547–9	admiral
Southampton, earl of		*see:* Wriothesley, Thomas
Suffolk, duke of		*see:* Brandon, Charles; Grey, Henry
Sussex, earl of		*see:* Radcliffe
Vice-chamberlain of the household		*see:* Darcy
	1551–3	John Gates
Winchester, bishop of	1531–51, 1553–5	Stephen Gardiner
Winchester, marquis of		*see:* Paulet
Wriothesley, Thomas	1544–7	chancellor
	1544	Lord Wriothesley
	1547–50	earl of Southampton

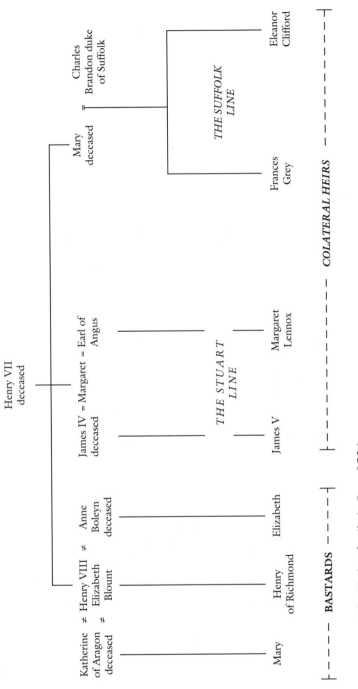

Figure 1 The Tudor family in June 1536

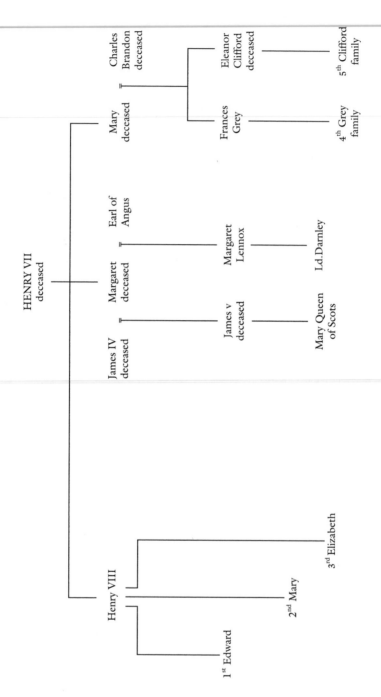

Figure 2 The succession according to Henry VIII's will

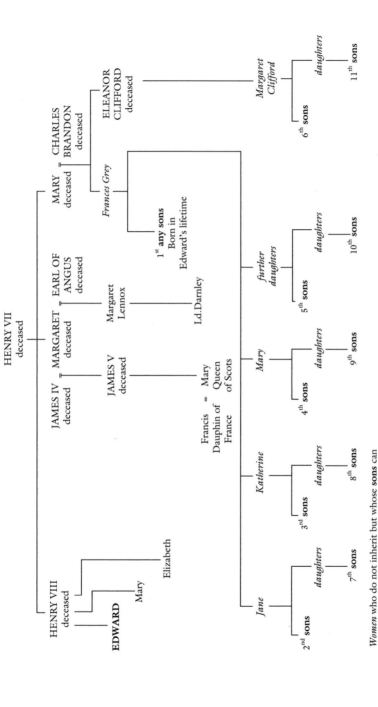

Figure 3 Edward VI's 'deuise', VERSION ONE

Women who do not inherit but whose **sons** can *Mary* and *Elizabeth* are debarred by illegitimacy

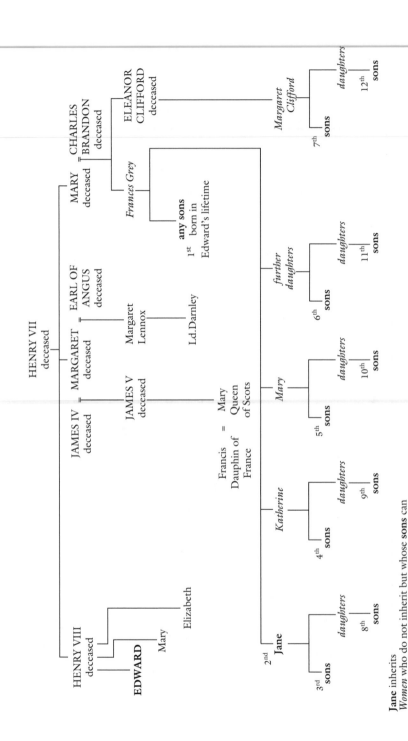

Figure 4 Edward VI's 'deuise', VERSION TWO

Jane inherits
Women who do not inherit but whose **sons** can
Mary and *Elizabeth* are debarred by illegitimacy

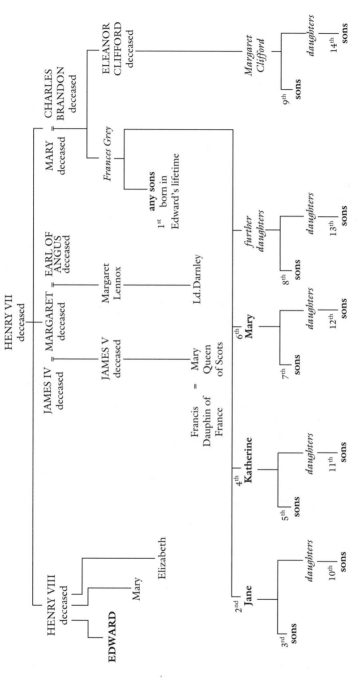

Jane, Katherine and **Mary** inherit, their daughters do not
Women who do not inherit but whose **sons** can
Mary and *Elizabeth* are debarred by illegitimacy

Figure 5 Edward VI's 'declaracion', 21 June 1553

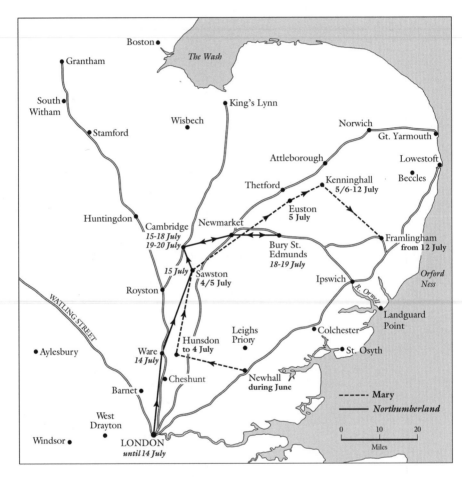

The movement of forces, July 1553

PROLOGUE

O N the evening of Sunday 11 February 1554 Jane Grey sat writing in the gentleman-gaoler's house in the Tower of London. She was sixteen. Slightly built, 'prettily shaped and graceful' but short enough to require platform shoes, Jane had brown eyes, hair nearly red, and a fair complexion with freckles.[1] She was also frighteningly precocious; her scholarly reputation was talked of as far away as Zurich. But that evening she was not composing one of her elegant Latin missives to a foreign scholar. Jane was saying farewell. In twelve hours she would be dead, beheaded on the scaffold she had watched being built on the other side of Tower Green. Except for its horrifying finality, her death would be a piece with the whole of Jane's previous life. From birth she had been treated as an object to be passed around to the advantage of first one Svengali and then another. Now she was to be disposed of finally at the behest of her cousin, the ageing Queen Mary I, the daughter of Henry VIII and Katherine of Aragon.

Jane had by then been in the Tower for seven months, but not originally on Mary's instructions. On Monday 10 June 1553 Jane had been escorted to the royal apartments next to the White Tower with pomp and ceremony as, following the death of her cousin Edward VI the previous Thursday, leading magnates of the realm united to proclaim her queen. Taking over the fortress was a symbolic act of possession required of all incoming English monarchs. All that remained was Jane's coronation. But ten days later the Tower changed into a prison, ten days which had seen Mary displace her in a wholly unexpected political coup.

That, of course, is not the way in which the events of 1553 have been remembered. Over the centuries there has been almost a tacit agreement to play down Jane Grey's revolt as 'not quite English', a piece of naked self-seeking in contrast to morally acceptable rebellions which are driven by principle, by genuine grievances or by loyalty to a 'king over the water'. The name by which Jane Grey is universally remembered says it all: 'the nine days queen' – not so much because she ruled for nine days (the more correct figure is thirteen), but because her reign was a proverbial 'nine days wonder'. Yet when Edward died, Jane's succession had looked secure. Nobody in the know gave Mary any chance at all; even the envoys of her cousin and supporter, the emperor Charles V, had concluded that 'her promotion to the crown will be so difficult as to be well-nigh impossible'.[2] Jane's backers held all the cards. They controlled the machinery of government; the whole of the political establishment was sworn to her, so too the royal guard; the Tower (the nation's armoury) was held in her name, the navy similarly. We have to turn tradition on its head and recognize that it was not Mary but Jane who was the reigning queen; her so-called 'rebellion' against Queen Mary was, in reality, the 'rebellion of Lady Mary' against Queen Jane. Mary's achievement was unique in the century and a half which separates the fifteenth-century wars of York and Lancaster from the seventeenth-century Civil War of king and parliament. It was the single occasion when the power of the English crown was successfully flouted. She alone of all the challengers succeeded in taking over government, capital and country, and in so doing ousted an incumbent ruler who had all the state's resources behind her. Had Mary failed as was expected, Jane Grey would have been the fourth monarch of the Tudor line and her rival, yet one more illegitimate contestant in the competition for the English throne which had been going on since 1399.

Of course, no sooner had Mary won than the country became unanimous that she was and always had been the legitimate heir to her brother. History is always written by the winners. In popular memory, the story of Lady Jane Grey and the rebellion of 1553 has become one of the great mythic dramas of English history. When the curtain rises, Edward VI is centre stage, two months short of his sixteenth birthday, coughing away his life, tortured in equal portions by disease and Tudor medicine. Who is to succeed him? Enter Edward's half-sister Mary, Henry VIII's elder daughter and the young king's 'rightful' heir. Also enter Mephistopheles, John Dudley, duke of Northumberland, Edward's chief minister, dragging with him the teenage Jane Grey whom he has forced to marry his son Guildford. Determined to oust Mary in favour of this daughter-in-law and his son her husband, the duke is willing to endanger everything the Tudor kings have achieved in rescuing England from the lawlessness and political collapse of the Wars of the Roses. Around the duke is a gaggle of noble sycophants cowed into supporting him, but from the wings comes the chorus, common folk, loyal-hearted Englishmen, who surge on to the stage, win Mary the crown and bring the curtain down on the duke's machinations. Right triumphs. England's future is saved, and Jane and Guildford, innocent victims, go to the Tower and death.

The script for this drama virtually wrote itself. When Mary won, those who had backed Jane – who, as we shall see, included virtually the whole of the English political establishment – had to find a fall guy. It was in everyone's interest to depict the crisis as the evil action of one overbearing individual. When the earl of Arundel arrived to arrest Northumberland, the duke reminded Arundel that he had only acted to implement properly authorized decisions for which the earl and the rest of the council were equally responsible. The reply was the most cynical brush-off in Tudor history: 'My lord, you should have sought for mercy sooner.'[3] Nor did Dudley's reputation benefit from any rehabilitation. With the English elite vying with each other to express loyalty to the Tudor line, there was every reason not to ask how the duke had seen things. It was not in the interest of his family to say anything either. 'The axe was home' and the overriding concern of the Dudleys was to escape the family ruin which went with condemnation for treason. Within months, Jane's surviving brothers-in-law were out of the Tower, jousting before Mary and her husband Philip, on the road to restoration.[4] Nothing changed even when Elizabeth's accession effectively brought back the Dudley ascendancy of 1553 – minus the duke. With those brothers-in-law, Robert and Ambrose, secure in the new queen's favour and on the way to earldoms, with their sister Mary the most intimate of Elizabeth's companions and with William Cecil, the duke's erstwhile henchman, her most trusted adviser, it was a case of 'least said soonest mended'. Not that all consciences were clear. Cecil spent twenty years devising excuses for his behaviour in 1553![5]

The effect of this collective *omertà* has been to discourage interest in the actual crisis of July 1553. The case has become progressively colder. Overwhelmingly, concern has been diverted to Jane's personal tragedy. Furthermore, the evident importance of both the progress of religious reformation under Edward and of the attempt under Mary to reverse that progress has made the fortnight that intervened between the one and the other appear insignificant. Commenting on the episode the great Restoration judge, Matthew Hale, spoke for the majority. It was 'only a small usurpation ... which lasted but a few days and soon went out.'[6] In consequence the crisis of 1553 today offers the components of a detective story, both a 'whodunnit' of the early genre – concerned with ways and means – and the emphasis on character and psychology of more recent writing. Certainly the episode was not simple. Many things and many people came into conflict – the provinces with the centre, the general populace with the political elite, the new Protestant religion with the old religion of Rome, the will of the dying Edward with the political calculation of men around him, legitimist loyalty to Mary against Northumberland's loyalty to Edward VI, the brilliantly effective duke against men whose hatred of him conjured effectiveness out of nothing. The episode poses question after question. That it was also a struggle between two women, Mary and Jane, seems almost incidental. Mary Tudor herself played a key role in her victory; Jane Grey was the least influential figure in the crisis. On Sunday 9 July 1553 Jane was informed that she was queen of England, on Thursday 19 July Jane was told that she was not, and she had as little say in the one as the other. The victorious Mary recognized as much. She left Jane and her husband in the Tower, in isolation and obscurity. Only by a subsequent turn of events Jane knew nothing about was she awaiting the headsman on that Sunday in February 1554.

PART I

THE SCENE

1

THE YEAR OF THREE SOVEREIGNS

IN England, 1553 had opened with hope. The crises which had darkened recent years seemed to be receding. The 1552 harvest had been good; prices, though high, had of late been weakening; debasement of the coinage had been stopped and the currency was stable; the pound had recovered its international value; royal debt was under control; law and order was back and the epidemic of 'the sweat' had eased. Fundamental problems remained, notably the inadequate revenue, but even here modest steps towards reform were in hand. Abroad, England had successfully avoided entanglements and the two 'big beasts' of Europe – France and the Habsburg empire – were once more at each other's throats. Best of all, the country had a young and vigorous king on the verge of manhood – some three months past his fifteenth birthday. At that particular time Edward was at Greenwich enjoying the Christmas season. The festivities were lavish, with the Lord of Misrule descending on the court with a large cast of assistants and an elaborate programme for appearances at Greenwich and in London.[1] On New Year's eve the lavish programme included a juggler, a mock joust on a dozen hobby horses and a Robin Hood sequence; on Twelfth Night there was a play, 'The Triumph of Cupid'.[2] No expense was spared; overall it cost nearly £400. Whether Edward took part is not clear, but evidently he enjoyed himself because a further play was ordered for February. One unexpected absentee from court was John Dudley, duke of Northumberland, the minister who had presided over much of the nation's recovery thus far. He was confined to his Chelsea home by, as he put it, 'extreme sickness' and a hope for some 'health and quietness'.[3] The country's other duke, Henry duke of Suffolk, probably spent the twelve days of Christmas with his family, including his eldest daughter Jane Grey. This could have been at their Leicester home at Bradgate but possibly, as in 1550–1, with their Willoughby cousins at

Tilty in Essex, perhaps with theatricals again provided by the earl of Oxford's players and others.[4] Barely twenty-five miles from Tilty was Hunsdon, the principal home of Henry VIII's daughter, the Princess Mary, though whether any of the Greys visited her that year is not known.[5] What Mary must certainly have had on her mind was the ceremonial visit to court she was due to make in a few weeks. Nothing, nationally or personally, gave warning that, before the year was out, Edward and Northumberland would be dead, Jane a prisoner in the Tower and Mary the acknowledged queen of England.

The first indication that all might not be well came on 6 February when Mary arrived to visit her brother and found he was confined to bed with a feverish cold. She had to wait until the 10th to see him.[6] The condition was dismissed as a chill – Edward was a healthy youth – but it was enough to cause the postponement of the play which had been called for 'by occasion that his grace was sick'.[7] Throughout the month the king's condition continued to give concern, even putting in doubt his fitness to attend the meeting of parliament due on 1 March.[8] Precisely what the trouble was is unclear. Medical opinion at the time eventually diagnosed tuberculosis, the disease which was believed to have killed his illegitimate half-brother, the duke of Richmond, seventeen years earlier. Modern diagnosis – in so far as the symptoms can be identified – is more cautious and has suggested that the presentation of the illness could indicate that the cold led to a suppurating pulmonary infection which developed into septicaemia and renal failure, a condition incurable before modern anti-biotics.[9] In the event Edward improved sufficiently to make it only neces-sary to transfer the opening formalities of the parliament to Whitehall Palace, and by 31 March he was well enough even to preside over the tiring, two-hour-long dissolution ceremony.[10] In the second week in April he was allowed out, first to walk in St James's Park and then to travel to Greenwich.[11] Very probably it was during this illness that Edward began to speculate about the succession. It would be some years before he would marry and there was no certainty of a child arriving at the earliest oppor-tunity. His father had to wait for a son until he was 46. Who should succeed if he died before becoming a father? The result was that Edward worked out what he called 'my deuise [device] for the succession'.[12] This survives as a rough draft in the king's own handwriting, and specifies how the crown should pass if he died without children of his own and how royal power should be exercised in a minority, depending on the age of the prospective heir. Although Jane Grey's marriage to the duke of North-umberland's son Guildford Dudley must have been arranged early in

1553, she figures in the 'deuise' as only one of the prospective mothers of a possible successor.

Edward's health improved somewhat and in early May the ministers were excitedly exchanging news of his recovery.[13] Whether this was one of the remissions characteristic of tuberculosis we cannot know, but it did not last. The French ambassadors saw the young king in mid-May and noted how weak he was and how persistent his cough.[14] A secret case conference was held on 28 May, and the doctors gave Northumberland their professional assessment that Edward would not survive beyond the autumn.[15] The duke of Northumberland must certainly have feared that Edward's condition was terminal. As the boy's chief minister he was, in the words of the earliest English account of the events of 1553–4, 'the man best aware of and acquainted' with the king's condition.[16] But fearing and knowing are different. Now a change of monarch was inevitable and imminent. According to Henry VIII's will and a parliamentary statute of 1544, if Edward died childless, the crown was to go to his half-sisters, first Mary and then Elizabeth, but as hope in the king's recovery ebbed away, all this was revised.[17] On 12 June, the senior judges and crown lawyers had an audience with the king at which Edward gave them instructions to put in legal form the provisions in his 'deuise', but with a crucial amendment which made Jane Grey his immediate heir. After some debate and revision, a patent naming Jane as the next queen was completed and signed on 21 June. Edward's death fifteen days later was kept a secret – or, rather, a badly kept secret – while the details of the succession were attended to.

Mary, however, was quicker off the mark. Hunsdon was twenty-eight miles from London, so when warned that her brother was near death she was able to get away rapidly to the security of her substantial estates in East Anglia. There on Saturday 8 July she had herself proclaimed queen, and sent out letters calling on local Catholic gentlemen to rally to her side. Thus, when on Monday 10th the councillors in London were preparing to proclaim Queen Jane, a letter arrived from Mary calling on them to proclaim her. Despite this Jane was proclaimed queen that afternoon and escorted to the Tower with traditional ceremony. A few hours after Edward's death, Robert Dudley – Northumberland's fourth son – had been sent with a few hundred men in a vain attempt to detain Mary, but with the princess asserting her right to the crown, more urgency was now vital. The council sent Mary a firm reply, calling her to order, and plans were put in hand. By Friday 14 July Northumberland was able to set out with limited forces but intending to rendezvous with reinforcements at Cambridge before marching on Framlingham which Mary had made her base. He moved from Cambridge on the morning of the 18th but his promised reinforcements did not arrive. By then Mary's supporters in the Thames Valley had been able to muster sufficient force to make the councillors in London worry about their own skins. On 19 July the end came. At Bury St Edmunds Northumberland abandoned his advance against Mary, while in London the council jettisoned Jane Grey to the enormous relief and jubilation of the city. On 20 July the duke himself proclaimed Mary queen.

Through all this Jane Grey remained in the Tower with her husband, first a sovereign then a prisoner. On 25 July the duke was brought there under guard along with three of his sons, his brother Andrew and five prominent supporters; another nine followed shortly, including Jane's father, the duke of Suffolk, although he remained under arrest for only three nights. Trials began on 18 August, first Northumberland with his eldest son, the earl of Warwick, and also the Marquis of Northampton; the next day, Sir Andrew Dudley, the Gates brothers, Sir John and Sir Henry, and Sir Thomas Palmer. All seven were condemned, but only the duke, John Gates and Palmer were to die. However, on the day announced for the execution, the sentence was postponed for twenty-four hours to allow the duke and the others to take the sacrament according to the Catholic rite and one by one announce to a picked audience that they had come back to the true church. As the duke put it, 'he had erred from the true Catholic faith fifteen years and had been a great setter forth of the ill doctrine now reigning which he sore lamented'.[18]

The crown only got round to trying Jane Grey three months later, along with her husband Guildford, Thomas Cranmer, archbishop of Canterbury, and two more of Northumberland's sons, Ambrose and Henry. On 13 November each was found guilty and sentenced to death, but that was understood to be largely a formality. The expectation was that Cranmer would be dealt with by the church machinery and that the others could hope eventually to be pardoned. The trial of the other son involved, Robert Dudley, was delayed even longer; he was not condemned until 22 January 1554. By then, however, a new and quite distinct conspiracy was afoot, triggered by Mary's determination to marry Philip, king of Spain. Known now as Wyatt's Rebellion, it drew in the duke of Suffolk, and five days after Wyatt's surrender Jane and Guildford were beheaded. Her father went to the block on 23 February.

For each of those involved – Edward, Jane, Northumberland, Mary – the events of 1553 were wholly unexpected, and this raises historical problems. There is not only the need to explain how and why each behaved as she or he did in those immediate events, but also to square that behaviour with the previous history of that individual. Postulating a sudden rush of blood to the head or an action entirely out of character is not convincing. Historical tradition is another problem. The simple fact is that the Edward, Jane and Northumberland of history are the Edward, Jane and Northumberland of 1553 – one a supposedly abused child, one a virgin saint beloved of the Victorian schoolroom, and the third an English Machiavelli. By contrast, thanks to the alleged disasters of Mary's subsequent reign, 1553 has counted too little in her favour; nothing ever became a Tudor better than Mary's conduct that July. The events of the year also raise wider questions. As we have seen, Jane's accession was not just endorsed by Northumberland but by the overwhelming majority of the governing elite. Such men were political survivors. They must have been aware that in switching from Mary to Jane they were taking a deliberate gamble. When the duke was on the point of leaving to capture Mary, he reminded his fellow councillors that

> I and these other noble personages and the whole army go forth ... upon the only trust and faithfulness of your honours, whereof we think ourselves most assured ... which trust and promise if ye shall violate, hoping thereby of life and promotion, yet shall not God count you innocent of our bloods, neither acquit you of the sacred and holy oath of allegiance made freely by you to this virtuous lady the queen's highness.

The reply was: 'My lord, if you mistrust any of us in this matter your grace is far deceived; for which of us can wipe his hands clean thereof? And if we should shrink from you as one that were culpable, which of us can excuse himself as guiltless?'[19] Nobody can have been under any illusion about the risk. Thus, if, as Matthew Hale claimed, the attempt to put Jane on the throne was 'only a small usurpation ... which lasted but a few days and soon went out', we are faced with irrationality – men behaving like lemmings after lives spent successfully negotiating the uncertain and murky thickets of Tudor politics – and politics under Henry VIII![20]

The events of 1553 also raise issues of detail. The first is the date of the decision to crown Jane rather than Mary. When the princess paid her visit to court in February she was, so the imperial ambassador reported, 'more honourably received and entertained with greater magnificence ... than ever before during the present king's reign'. Northumberland stood with the councillors at the outer gate of the palace and they 'did duty and obeisance to her as if she had been queen of England'.[21] They then escorted her to the presence chamber and through to the sick room where Edward entertained his sister with 'small talk, making no mention of [the contentious issue of] religion'. Unless a very double game was being played, this looks very much as if no councillor had any doubt that Mary was 'the second person in the kingdom', i.e. the heir presumptive. If so, at the start of February, no move to replace her by Jane had been contemplated, let alone made. Evidently the decision was made in the four months between that visit and Edward's orders to the royal lawyers in June. Along with the question 'when' goes the question 'who'. As we shall see, Edward overbore the objections of his lawyers by force of his personal authority, but that tells us nothing of the origination of the scheme. Tradition may give the answer 'Northumberland', but on what justification?

A further question is suggested by a letter from Charles V to his ambassador in London, dated 11 July. It refers to 'the carefully prepared course of action that Northumberland is working out with, as you suspect, the help of France'.[22] Yet nothing seems less like a 'carefully prepared course of action' than the actions of the duke or the privy council in June and July 1553. Neither took any steps to neutralize Mary in advance of the king's demise. Indeed, far from keeping her under surveillance, they furnished the princess with medical reports of the progress of her brother's illness. Nor was anything done to conceal the imminent change of monarch. Few people can have misinterpreted the publication on 19 June of an order of prayer for Edward's recovery, 'meet to be used of all the king's true subjects'.

> O almighty and most merciful Lord ... look down with thy pitiful eyes upon thy servant Edward our king ... and as thou didst most favourably deliver King Hezekiah from extreme sickness and prolongest his life for the safe-guard of thy people the Israelites ... so we most entirely appeal to thy great mercies graciously to restore the health and strength of thy servant our sovereign lord.[23]

Not much was done either to keep confidential the intended change in the order of the succession. Sixteenth-century diplomats followed the principle of reporting everything, be it fact or be it rumour, and the imperial ambassador had for months expressed a pathological suspicion of Northumberland's intentions. However, by 15 June he had facts, and we can assume that if he knew, Mary knew.

In contrast to conciliar inaction, the prompt action of Mary both to put herself out of reach and to be ready to claim the throne argues for considerable pre-planning. All that held her back was the need not to act prematurely. To claim the crown before Edward was dead would have been treason. But the council had no such constraint. So why, given the ample warning, was London not ahead of the game? When Henry VIII died, his executors had custody of Edward within hours and the interval between his father's death and the young king's proclamation was some fifty-seven hours, even though Edward had first to be fetched from Hertford, twenty-five miles away. It took a day more to proclaim Jane, and she was no further than Chelsea.[24] Mary built up her forces with speed. The need for troops caught the council in London flat-footed. Even with a danger which apparently was foreseen – Charles V sending a force from Flanders to support or rescue Mary – preventative action was tardy. On 4 July the necessary ships were reported to need a week to be ready to sail.[25]

All this argues preparation on the part of Mary and a total lack of preparedness by those supporting Jane, even though hope for Edward had been abandoned days earlier. If Northumberland had been ready and so able to arrive at Bury St Edmunds a week earlier than he did, Mary's handful of supporters would have been swept aside and Jane would have won. And that deduction returns us to the whodunnit of character and motivation. Nothing in Mary's past would have argued for her display of vigour. Nothing in Northumberland's would suggest a ditherer. And the others?

2

In Search of Jane Grey

W HEN N. H. Nicolas published a 'memoir' on Jane Grey in 1825, he remarked on the difficulty of the task.

> It is an error of frequent occurrence in biography to suppose that the early years of those who attain celebrity must exhibit some traits of a peculiar nature, and hence every schoolboy feat or childish expression which if the individuals had remained in obscurity would have received no more notice than it deserved, is presented in the most vivid colours as the prognostications of that genius or courage which rendered them in after life the subject of public consideration.[1]

Two centuries later the situation is only a little easier. A Tudor teenager who died at the age of sixteen is very unlikely to have left much trace on the historical record, and still less if female. Even if an aristocrat, that girl will hardly trouble today's archivists beyond possible mention of negotiations over putative marriages. Finding a single surviving letter or a mention in someone else's account book is finding gold. For Jane Grey there is a little more, but only a little.

The immediate frustration in the case of Jane Grey is that we have only one detailed report of her appearance, in the letter of a Genoese merchant who observed her entry into the Tower on 10 July. He described her as

> very short and thin, but prettily shaped and graceful. She has small features and a well-made nose, the mouth flexible and the lips red. The eyebrows are arched and darker than her hair, which is nearly red. Her eyes are sparkling and reddish brown in colour. I stood so near her grace that I noticed her colour was good but freckled. When she smiled she showed her teeth which are white and sharp. In all a gracious and animated figure.[2]

The comment of the French ambassador, Antoine de Noailles, was positive, but hardly informative – 'virtuous, wise and good looking', 'well made'.[3] Roger Ascham the famous educator waxed lyrical about the conversation he had with her, but only noted that she smiled.[4] In an elegy for her published in 1560, Sir Thomas Chaloner, who was active in public life and had known Jane, likened her to Venus: 'If he had seen her face, a suitor might have shamelessly burned with passion.'[5] Chaloner, however, was writing in Latin verse (for which he was renowned), with all the conventions that implied. Richard Grafton, another who would have known her, described Jane as 'that fair lady whom nature had so not only beautified, but God also had endowed with singular gifts'.[6] On the other hand, in 1616 Francis Godwin wrote that she was 'handsome' but not remarkable, and this probably repeated a comment of his father, Thomas Godwin (1517–90) who became the Elizabethan bishop of Bath and Wells.[7] Still, even the Catholic tradition which reached the Italian Girolamo Pollini was 'very attractive'.[8]

Having so little verbal evidence to go on makes it very difficult to establish a likeness for Jane with anything like authority. An engraving by Willem and Magdalena de Passe was published as *Jana Graya* in 1620.[9][plate 5] The sitter wears a distinctive jewel and this led to a full-length portrait of a woman wearing the jewel being also identified as Jane.[10] This was despite a difference in the face mask and Jane being far too young at the conjectured date of the painting, c.1545. It is now known that the particular jewel was owned by Katherine Parr, Henry VIII's last wife, so the identification of the full-length has been revised.[11] However, the fact that the sitter in the de Passe engraving wears one of Katherine's jewels need not rule out the identification as Jane. She spent some eighteen months in Katherine's household and could easily have been lent the jewel for a sitting. Willem and his sister were originally from Utrecht, but were based in London and clearly worked from an existing painting which is known in two later copies.[12] Alternative likenesses have also been widely canvassed, but all raise problems. One is a miniature of about 1550, attributed to Levina Teerlinc, an artist in Tudor royal service from 1546 to 1576.[13] Previously proposed as the young Princess Elizabeth, the sitter wears a gold brooch mounted with a black classical head and behind it a bunch of acorns and a spray of yellow flowers. [plate 6] The claim is that these are 'gillyflowers', and a carving in the Tower of London symbolising the Dudley brothers does have Guildford represented by a gillyflower. Hence, it is argued, the miniature should be linked to the marriage of Jane and Guildford in May 1553. Against this, the

flowers of the miniature are not the gillyflowers of the Tower carving and
are as likely to be cowslips, while the acorns have yet to be explained.[14] As
for the jewel, although Jane did have one similar, in that instance the head
was carved from agate, not jet.[15] What finally rules out the sitter as Jane is
the inscription 'A° XVIII' which would make her a year too old.[16] Another
painting which has been advanced is an anonymous three-quarter length
from the 1550s by Hans Eworth.[17] [plate 9] The one substantive clue to
identity is the embossed 'D' on the sitter's girdle book, leading to the
suggestion that again the painting was produced to mark Jane's marriage.[18] However the sitter is hardly a sixteen-year-old, and the interval
between the announcement of Jane's marriage in April and her imprisonment in July is too brief for a painting to be finished, and thereafter no
Dudley was in any position to pay for completion.[19] There are, furthermore, alternative candidates among the Dudley women – the duke's wife
Jane and their two daughters or even the touching possibility of their
daughter-in-law, Ambrose Dudley's wife whose sudden death affected the
duke deeply.[20]

A persuasive likeness of Jane is offered by three paintings, one formerly
in the collection of Lord Houghton and exhibited in 1866 as 'Jane Grey',
[plate 1] the second a panel painting (the 'Streatham' portrait) acquired by
the National Portrait Gallery in 2006 [cover], and the third, an inferior
version (whereabouts unknown).[21] The NPG panel dates from the 1590s
and thus must be a copy of an earlier original, but it carries the legend 'The
Lady Iayne' and the sitter's costume is congruent with the 1550s. The face
in the Houghton portrait is perhaps better executed, but details show it is
not the source of the NPG picture. Alternative sitters of rank can be
suggested – Jane Radcliffe who married Lord Montague, and Jane Seymour, daughter of the duke of Somerset – but they died in 1552 and 1561
respectively, and why should a number of likenesses of them or any other
Jane from the 1550s be being produced a generation later? Jane Grey, on
the other hand, was a Protestant icon. Portraits of Jane's sisters, Katherine
and Mary survive [plates 3 and 4] and although family likenesses lie in the
eye of the beholder, they may give conjectural support to the Streatham/
Houghton image.[22]

A likeness of Jane which, if located, would be conclusive is a full-length
owned in 1590 by John Lord Lumley and described as '*of the Lady Jane
Graye, executed*'.[23] Lumley was born *c*.1533 and could have met Jane
but he became the son-in-law and heir of Henry Fitzalan, earl of Arundel,
who was Jane's uncle by marriage and intimately associated with her
story.[24] Lumley paintings carry a cartellino (label), and although no

full-length of a possible Jane is known to exist, a half-length Lumley portrait of a young female sitter of the mid-century is in a private collection [plate 2] and was formerly at Northwick Park.[25] Detailed inspection and comparison with the Streatham/Houghton pictures has not been done, but a single sitter does, superficially, not seem impossible. Searching for Jane also brings in a cluster of paintings of an auburn-haired young woman, full faced, usually in sober black, wearing a ruff, and a fur tippet. [plate 7] For many years identified as Jane, more recent opinion has swung towards the young Elizabeth.[26] A quite different likeness is presented by a painting formerly at Wrest Park in Bedfordshire. [plate 8][27] It is painted on a panel which can be dated to *c.*1541, so, whether Jane or not, the portrait was very possibly completed in her lifetime. The identification *Jane Grey* goes back at least to 1681 and two later versions belonged to the family of Jane's uncle John (the sole male of the family to escape execution).[28] The only clue to the sitter is the posy at her throat, violets, lavender and a gillyflower or pink (of the variety found in the Tower of London carving).[29] This raises the possibility that it does represent Jane after her marriage. In that case the costume becomes of particular interest because it is unusually plain and wholly lacking in adornment which suggests that it could have originated in a likeness taken when she was a prisoner in the Tower.[30] In its present condition – it has been much over-painted – the sitter is unlikely to be the same as in the Streatham/Houghton or in the Northwick Park *Jane*, but in an engraving of the Wrest Park likeness which appeared in 1681 the comparison is closer.[31]

Authenticity is even more important when it comes to Jane's letters. Some are unquestionably by her. There is an early letter thanking Thomas Seymour, Lord Sudeley, and three Latin letters forwarded by third parties to Henry Bullinger at Zurich.[32] Then there is a letter to her father and a message to Sir John Brydges, the lieutenant of the Tower, in Jane's own handwriting on the margins of the prayer book that she carried to her execution. It is now one of the treasures of the British Library.[33] Seven other pieces attributed to Jane are known only in printed copies. They come from her months of imprisonment in the Tower and cannot automatically be taken as genuine. The longest is a letter to 'an apostate' – in fact the Greys' former chaplain, Thomas Harding, who on the accession of the Catholic Mary had abandoned his previous Protestantism. Also lengthy is an account of the discussion Jane had with John Feckenham, a Benedictine monk sent to convert her before she was executed. The others are a personal letter to her sister Katherine, reports of the speech she made from the scaffold, a second letter to her father, a prayer written 'in the time of her trouble' and a remarkable piece attributed to Jane in hostile Catholic sources.

Of these by far the most important is the last because, if genuine, it is the only first-hand evidence we have about Jane accepting the crown. Substantial in length – over 1,000 words in translation – it first appears in an account written in 1554 by a papal official and future cardinal, Giovanni Francesco Commendone, and other sources (again Catholic) confirm that it circulated at an early date.[34] Commendone introduced the piece by saying that 'before her death, Jane wishing to account to the world for her proclamation and how it had taken place without her fault or agreement made the following statement'.[35] What follows, however, is not a scaffold speech but a detailed personal account by Jane of her part in the events which followed Edward's death. This immediately invites disbelief because no prisoner confined in the Tower of London was in any position 'to account to the world' other than from the scaffold. After the early notices the letter disappears, but in 1591 a similar text attributed to Jane surfaces in the *Storia Ecclesiastica della Rivoluzione d'Inghilterra* which Fra Girolamo Pollini published in Bologna in 1591 and in an enlarged edition in Rome in 1594.[36] This text is beyond doubt cognate with the text reproduced forty years before, and Pollini might be thought simply to be following Commendone. He certainly made much use of the work of an Oxford cleric, Nicholas Sander, who devoted his life to the Counter-Reformation assault on England, and Sander knew the cardinal.[37] Pollini, however, claims to have used a text obtained from London and in his second edition he also discusses the origin of the piece.[38]

> These are words that according to some she said in the hour of her death to the population. But according to others, this was a letter that she wrote to the Queen Mary when she was in the Tower, [after] her people proclaimed her queen for the first time [i.e. in July 1553]. At that time, hearing the execution of the sentence against the duke of Northumberland, and knowing very well the dangers and judgement of her life in which she found herself because of her people, even if it was not her fault for that, in any case she showed herself to be a wise and prudent young lady by asking forgiveness to the queen for the sin she was accused of, informing her majesty about the truth of the events.

The first explanation is, of course, the one given by Commendone but Pollini himself inclined to the second, 'since I came into possession of this manuscript through people worthy of trust, who had at the same time a copy in London, under the form of a letter to the Queen dated August 1553 when the queen forgave her for her first mistake, by finding her not guilty.' A letter of explanation and confession to the queen is the one written appeal from Jane that would have been allowed, the August date is what one would expect, and remarks made by Mary to the imperial ambassador on the 13th indicate that she had received such a letter.[39]

Existence and content are, of course, different and if it were not for Commendone and others recording the letter soon after Jane's death, Pollini's reference to a copy being extant in London after such a long interval and communicated to him by 'people worthy of trust' would raise major doubt. His contacts can only have been English recusants who may seem unlikely custodians of the apologia of an alleged Protestant martyr nearly forty years earlier. What, however, can explain their unexpected conduct is the ongoing battle between Catholic and Protestant. From the Protestant side of the confessional divide John Foxe used the *Acts and Monuments* [the *Book of Martyrs*] to imply by association that Jane was a martyr and that she and Guildford were innocents, victims of Rome.[40] The text which was copied for Pollini disproves that. On Jane's own admission she was imprisoned for political offences, not religious conviction. Indeed, as Pollini says specifically, Mary forgave Jane: 'being rather more benevolent and against bloodshed and much more keen on charity and politeness than bowing to revenge and severity'. Only later did rebellion make it 'necessary for justice, duty and the quietness of the kingdom' to put Jane to death.[41] It is no small irony to conclude that this most important item in the Jane Grey canon survived as recusant ammunition to defend 'Bloody Mary'.

If analysis vindicates Jane's letter to Mary – somewhat surprisingly – the opposite is true of the letter to her father that is not from Jane's prayer book. At first sight it seems to fit both the occasion and the circumstances. It was thanks to his attempted rebellion that Jane was to be executed and the letter begins:

> Father, although it hath pleased God to hasten my death by you, by whom my life should rather have been lengthened; yet I can so patiently take it, as I yield God more hearty thanks for shortening my woeful days, than if all the world had been given unto my possession, with life lengthened at my own will.[42]

What more natural than to place the blame where it belonged? But would Jane have written like this? The style and format is not the style and format of the genuine autograph message in her prayer book. Far from addressing

Suffolk as 'father', this begins 'The Lord comfort your Grace' and ends 'Your Grace's humble daughter'.[43] And when was the supposed letter written? It refers to her father's imprisonment and thus must be after the duke of Suffolk's arrival in the Tower, that is on Saturday/Sunday 10/11 February.[44] Yet only a matter of hours later Jane wrote the genuine letter to the duke in her prayer book. Two letters in such rapid succession is certainly enough to raise a query. The letter also presumes some communication between Jane and Suffolk's gaolers – 'I am well assured of your impatient dolours, redoubled manifold ways, both in bewailing your own woe, and especially, as I hear, my unfortunate state' – but is this likely, given that Suffolk arrived in the Tower only hours before? Also the letter surfaced at least ten years after Jane's death, so that Foxe could only include it in the second (1570) edition of *Acts and Monuments*, and without a comment on provenance. The text continues with sentiments which are appropriately Protestant, but again, is it Jane? '[Y]et my dear father (if I may without offence rejoice in my own mishaps) me-seems in this I may account myself blessed, that washing my hands with the innocency of my fact, my guiltless blood may cry before the Lord, Mercy to the innocent!' On the scaffold she said: 'The fact against the queen's highness was unlawful, and the consenting thereunto by me: but touching the procurement and desire thereof by me, or on my behalf, I do wash my hands thereof in innocency before God, and the face of you Christian people.'[45] But are the letter and the speech distinct or does the letter derive from the speech? Significantly Jane on the scaffold did not cry for God's mercy because she was innocent. She admitted her sins but declared her confidence in the Protestant gospel of salvation by faith alone. The letter also seems less a private message to a father than an early exercise in imaginative reconstruction when it goes on to say:

> And yet, though I needs acknowledge, that being constrained, and as you wot well enough, continually assayed, in taking upon me I seemed to consent, and therein grievously offended the queen and her laws: yet I do assuredly trust, that this mine offence towards God is so much more the less (in that being in so royal estate as I was) mine enforced honour blended never with mine innocent heart.[46]

And why 'thus, good father, I have opened unto you the state wherein I at present stand'? Did the duke need telling? None of this is conclusive, but enough to suggest that the alleged letter to her father may very well not be what it purports to be.

Suspicion might also appear to rest on Jane's letter to Thomas Harding and on the account of her debate with John Feckenham. The government was intent on restoring Catholicism and these items were highly subversive, so how could they have escaped Tower security? But they clearly did because both texts were circulating barely a month after her execution. In a letter smuggled out to Bullinger and dated 15 March, a John Banks (part of the Grey circle) sent news of Jane's death and Latin translations of the Feckenham dialogue and the letter to Harding and also the scaffold speech and the letter to Katherine Grey.[47] Clearly he had publication in mind but Bullinger vetoed the idea for fear of exasperating Mary's government still further. However, James Haddon, once a chaplain to Jane's father, did assure Bullinger that although parts of Banks's account were suspect because 'he has gathered them from common report and being himself too in some measure biased by his zeal', when it came to 'what regards the Lady Jane herself, and what is said in her name, (as for instance, her exhortations to a certain apostate, and her discourse with Feckenham), I believe and partly know, that it is true, and did really proceed from herself'.[48] Thanks to Banks and this comment by Haddon, the authenticity of the Feckenham and Harding pieces and, by association, the Katherine Grey letter and the scaffold speech is beyond question. Sympathizers in England had less reason to be cautious about publishing. In 1554 there appeared *An Epistle of the Ladye Iane, a righte virtuous woman to a learned man of late falne from the truth*, conjecturally from the press of John Day, a prolific Protestant printer who in October 1554 was arrested on suspicion of publishing material hostile to the Marian regime.[49] In the same year or the next came *Here in this booke ye haue a godly Epistle made by a faithful Christian*.[50] This can be linked to Anthony Scoloker, another Edwardian printer of radical religious texts.[51] Clearly, from the moment of her execution, 'Jane Grey' became powerful propaganda. Each pamphlet contains an English text of the Feckenham discussion and the letter to the 'apostate' which Haddon had warranted, plus the letter to Katherine and the speech from the scaffold which Banks had translated for Bullinger.

Foxe's *Acts and Monuments* later gave wide circulation to all four documents, but these earlier texts are highly significant. *An Epistle* states that the Feckenham discussion was printed 'even word for word, her own hand being put thereto' and ends 'By me Jane Dudley', indicating that the copy the printer was setting had been signed by Jane. *Here in this Booke* has 'which she wrote with her own hand' and closes with 'she subscribed thus, Jane Dudley'.[52] In other words, the respective printers were claiming to set from copy which was or was taken from Jane's own autograph. Moreover, there are differences between the two printings and between the printings and the text Foxe produced, and this establishes that three English texts of the Feckenham dialogue were in circulation, two at least within months of Jane's death.[53] Foxe, moreover, has an opening exchange between Jane and Feckenham which is not found in the texts that claim to be autograph. This could be imaginative invention, but it appears that Feckenham made at least two visits to see Jane, and Foxe may have conflated them for editorial reasons.[54] Furthermore, what Jane is supposed to have said does gets some support from the biography of Jane written by her Italian tutor, Michelangelo Florio.[55]

Jane's letter to Harding is less easy to pin down. The earlier printings omit material which appears in *Acts and Monuments* but this could be because Foxe was using a different text or because he (or someone else) had edited and elaborated the text for publication.[56] There is pace in the earlier material which makes it tempting to suspect that it too derives from an autograph, in this case written in the heat of the news of Harding's apostasy:

> [*Here in this Booke*] When I call to mind the fearful saying of our Saviour Jesus Christ that ... I cannot but marvel at thee and lament the case that thou sometime wast the lively member of Christ but now a deformed imp of the Devil ...[57]

> [*Acts*] So oft as I call to mind the dreadful and fearful sayings of God that ... I cannot but marvel at thee and lament thy case: that thou which sometime wast the lively member of Christ but now the deformed imp of the devil ...[58]

Foxe may also have corrected Jane's theology:

> [*Here in this Booke*] Fight manfully, come life, come death, thy quarrel is good undoubtedly, and the victory is ours.[59]

> [*Acts*] Fight manfully, come life, come death, the quarrel is God's. And undoubtedly the victory is ours.[60]

In both the earlier and subsequent texts of the Harding letter, Jane's contempt for her lapsed spiritual mentor is splenetic:

> Thou sometime wast the lively member of Christ but now a deformed imp of the Devil; sometime the beautiful temple of God but now the stinking and filthy kennel [gutter] of Satan; sometime the unspotted spouse of Christ

but now the unashamed paramour of Antichrist; sometime my faithful brother but now a stranger and an apostate; sometime a stout Christian soldier but now a cowardly runaway ... wicked man, the sink of sin, the son of perdition ... white-livered milksop.[61]

Some Victorians simply refused to believe that Jane wrote this. How could this model of young womanhood have so abused an older man and a cleric?

The hint that more than one English text of Jane's letters was extant is confirmed by her letter to her sister. The texts in *Here in this Booke*, *An Epistle* and *Acts and Monuments* each have varying titles and varying endings.[62] However, *An Epistle* and *Acts and Monuments* do agree that the letter was written at the end of Jane's Greek New Testament and this suggests a possible route by which authentic texts from Jane's time in the Tower could have evaded government surveillance. That this was the case can be demonstrated from another message in Jane's extant prayer book. It is a conventional greeting from Guildford Dudley to his father-in-law but because it talks of 'long life in this world' it must antedate the final catastrophe. Since Jane carried the book to the scaffold, unless the message had been inserted between the boy's marriage to Jane and Mary's coup, it must have travelled out of the Tower to the duke and in again on at least one occasion.[63] Additional items from Jane's imprisonment came to light early in Elizabeth's reign. The first (1563) edition of the *Acts and Monuments* includes 'A certain prayer of the Lady Jane in the time of her trouble', and, as we have seen, Foxe completed the canon of prison writings in 1570 with what purports to be 'A letter of the Lady Jane sent unto her father'.[64] The remaining text which appears in all three English sources is the speech Jane made to the crowd at her execution, something which custom dictated. Everything suggests that she spoke extempore, so it is clearly important to identify a reliable account of what she said. Despite minor differences, *Here in this Booke* gives essentially the version published by Foxe in 1563, and both texts take the story beyond Jane's speech and describe the actual execution.[65] The version in *An Epistle of the Ladye Iane* ends more abruptly and clearly comes from a different source.[66] Nevertheless the sentiments put in Jane's mouth are the same, though in a different order. This suggests two observers coming away with independent but essentially congruent recollections.

3

JANE GREY IN CONTEXT

THE 1553 succession crisis in England was the talk of Europe, but in all the contemporary comment, the person who receives least attention is Jane Grey herself. In some sources she is not even mentioned, and when she is the reporting is decidedly lopsided.

Three things explain the distortion. First, personal interest in Jane was largely for her scholarly achievement. On any account this was remarkable both for her years and for her sex. Add the admiring comments of her tutors and her tragic death, and later centuries had a myth ready made. Even A. F. Pollard, the father of modern Tudor history, could describe her as 'an almost perfect type of youthful womanhood'.[1] A second reason is that much of what we know has come down to us as through the fierce prism of religious controversy, and this is even more the case once Jane reaches the limelight. As we have seen, from that point most of her writing is polemical or evangelistic or both, and if this is read superficially, Jane can appear as the toughest of jehadis. The final reason is that Jane became a victim of posterity. Immediately on her death she became a martyr for the Protestant faith so that hagiography colours nearly every recollection of her and very many subsequent assessments.[2]

Jane Grey's political importance lay in what others made, or thought could be made, of her royal potential. The raw evidence is found first in government material. Some of this remains in the National Archives, but the most important items were retained by the officials involved or subsequently plundered by antiquaries and so are now found in repositories far and wide. Thus the evidence of the earliest marriage plans for Jane is in the papers of the Cecil family at Hatfield and the crucial documents which transferred the crown to her are divided between Corpus Christi College, Cambridge, and the Inner Temple. The only substantial collection of private material which throws light on Jane is the 12,000 surviving letters received by Henry Bullinger, the religious leader at Zurich, who in many ways became the hub of a network of mid-century reformers.[3] As well as Jane's three Latin letters, and one from her father, the two of them are mentioned in over one hundred more.[4]

The nearest we have to a continuous commentary on the events of the summer of 1553 is provided by the reports of foreign ambassadors accredited to England. Their despatches may not always be correct, but certainly were intended to be truthful. The two principal embassies were those from the French king Henry II and from the Holy Roman Emperor, the Habsburg Charles V. The Habsburg archive is the larger and more structured of the two. It needed to be. Despatches had not only to reach Charles wherever he was in his huge empire, but relevant provincial governors and ministers had to be kept informed as well, most notably his sister in Brussels. The job of a sixteenth-century ambassador, as explained by the Venetian ambassador to England during the 1553 crisis, consisted 'chiefly in three things: in the diligent execution of the communications received by them, in sending detailed and speedy advices of what occurs in the courts where they reside, and in acquainting [the state] on their return with whatever may be worth knowing.'[5] Ideally, reports were supposed to be sent every few days, with a situation résumé each month and a written debrief on returning home. Actual practice was less prescribed, but Charles V's ambassadors came close to the text book ideal. In the four months May to August 1553, the imperial ambassadors sent thirty-three reports to Charles V, many of them lengthy.[6] In May, June and August they wrote on average every four or five days; in the critical month of July, every other day. The value of this coverage is obvious, but it has to be used with caution. Ambassadors were not neutral observers; the news they collected reflected their preoccupation with the interests of their home governments. That was the lens through which they saw and interpreted everything. For Charles V's envoys in England this meant focusing first on keeping England and France apart, second on ensuring that the vital North Seas trade remained free from problems, and third on giving moral support to Mary just in case she might prove useful. As well as the perspective of ambassadors being restricted, so were their sources. Ordinary English people were cautious with foreigners – gossip was not encouraged – and in any case Charles's men rarely spoke the language. Nor did they venture much beyond reach of the various royal palaces so their ability to get news was substantially limited to court and council and to commercial contacts in and around London. Moreover, under Edward and Jane many courtiers kept their distance, and in formal meetings with privy councillors both parties had agendas, some hidden, some not. These factors, for example, explain why in July 1553 Charles V's envoys were hopelessly wrong about Mary's chances but excellently informed about Edward's sick room because they had secured an informant there.[7] Once Mary had triumphed, Charles's representatives were in a radically new position. Not only were official sources more open but unofficial contacts were more forthcoming, although still very often with an ulterior motive. Reports to the emperor therefore become more informative and reliable, although the downside for the historian is that the ambassadors – particularly Simon Renard, the long-term resident – very nearly become participants in English affairs, not observers.[8]

In the period before the collapse of Jane's government, the French ambassador was much closer to English ministers than his imperial counterpart and in consequence his reports might be expected to be more useful. However, that is not always the case. France was no dispersed empire. The focus of its coherent territory was Paris and the hundred miles or so around, and the French king was normally accessible enough to make it possible to send messages by cross-Channel travellers, a safer method than letters which might be intercepted.[9] The greater ease of communications also meant that the French tended to handle particularly important business by a special envoy. For example, on 28 May 1553, negotiations took place between the privy council and a high-ranking official from the French king Henry II, but we only know the meeting was important because cryptic references in later letters say so.[10] Nothing was ever put on paper. Yet despite such factors, the French ambassador in England still wrote weekly to the king or his chief minister and in July 1553 every four days.[11] Henry II was as concerned as Charles V to prevent England taking the 'wrong' side in international relations. Of course, once Mary (and therefore Charles) had won, the French envoy swapped roles with the imperial ambassador and he now effectively became the *persona non grata*.

There was a third diplomatic presence in mid-century England, the city state of Venice, a major power in sixteenth-century Europe. Its ambassadors had a lower profile than either the imperial or the French and were particularly concerned with commerce. However, their letters and the *Relazioni* which retiring ambassadors presented to the Venetian Senate have the great advantage of substantial neutrality which the representatives of the powers certainly lack. Thus Giacomo Soranzo, the ambassador in post during the crisis and until May 1554, could say of the duke of Northumberland's execution that 'the friends of England must lament the loss of all his qualities with that single exception (his last rashness)'. He also provides the frankest description of Mary.[12]

Ambassadors reported in an official capacity, but in the mid-century several Englishmen kept a private record of events, or, rather, such events as caught their particular attention. One of the best-informed was the herald Charles Wriothesley. His position on the edge of public life allowed him to compile a very comprehensive record from 1533 to 1559, although it does become less authoritative after his cousin Thomas Wriothesley, earl of Southampton, died in July 1550.[13] For a citizen's eye view of events there is the chronicle previously compiled at the Franciscan Friary outside Newgate and kept up after the house was dissolved.[14] A more personal record which covers the crisis of 1553–4 is the so-called 'Diary' kept by the London undertaker Henry Machyn. It combines a eye for the news-worthy with a professional interest in important funerals.[15] All three of these English sources cover the 1553 crisis but more valuable by far is an untitled anonymous manuscript which was published in 1849 as *The Chronicle of Queen Jane and of Two Years of Queen Mary and especially of the Rebellion of Sir Thomas Wyatt.*[16] The manuscript lacks its first pages, others are missing and so too a conclusion, but it is nevertheless invalu-able.[17] The writer resided in the Tower of London – in many respects the epicentre of the 1553 crisis – and seems to have made deliberately com-prehensive notes with a view to producing an overall account of events.[18] Most important, the writer gives verbatim accounts of conversations he listened to and, in the case of Jane Grey, reported on an occasion when he dined with her. That he was in a position to do so indicates that the author ranked as a gentleman, and the best guess is that he was an official of the royal mint which was located in the Tower. John Stowe, who used the manuscript, implied that his name was 'Rowland Lea', but this is probably a mistake for Richard Lea, a London goldsmith and assay-master.[19]

Lea was evidently taken with Jane Grey, and that response comes over in accounts by other people who met her. The best-known is by Roger Ascham in his famous book *The Scholemaster* where he recounted a con-versation he had with Jane when he visited Bradgate in August 1550, 'the last talk that I ever had, and the last time ever I saw, that noble and worthy lady'.[20] More extensive is the biography of Jane which was written by Michelangelo Florio who had taught Jane Italian: *The History of the life and death of the illustrious Lady Jane Grey, lately chosen and proclaimed queen in England, and of the events of her reign since the death of Edward VI.*[21] It was not published until 1607 but the text indicates that it was written six years after the martyrdom of Hooper, Ridley and Cranmer,

i.e. 1561/2. It thus dates from seven years of Jane's own execution, following which Florio had left England and become a pastor in Switzerland.[22]

Clearly the memoirs of Jane's Italian teacher should be of the first
importance, but the book presents problems.[23] Why did it take sixty
years to be printed and then at Middelburg on the island of Walcheren,
by a printer with no links to Italy, and how did the manuscript get there?
The answer lies not in the printer but in the editor and publisher, a
humanist and merchant named Johann Radermacher. He came originally
from Aachen, but spent much of his career in London – eighteen years in
all – and he left in 1580. Radermacher was clearly passionate about things
Italian. He had contact with the Italian Church in the city and built up a
substantial collection of works in Italian.[24] Florio had belonged to the
church, so that the obvious assumption is that Radermacher obtained the
Historia through his Italian contacts in England and took it with him
when he finally left for the Low Countries. He states in a preface that the
text was in Florio's own hand and had been found in the 'house of
mourning' after the death of a patron (unnamed).[25] That is puzzling
because a text intended for an English sponsor would have been in
Latin, not Italian, so it is more probable that Florio wrote the book for
Italian readers, and sent a copy from Switzerland to some member of the
Italian community in London among whose effects it was found.[26] If this
is the case, the failure of Florio to carry on and publish can be explained by
his death in the 1560s. Radermacher's further delay is best explained by
commercial considerations. There were few bookselling links between
Holland and the Italian market and the risk only became worth taking
when in the 1590s there was an upsurge in Italian interest in things
English.[27] Unfortunately the authenticity of Florio is not matched by its
value as a source. Its principal interest is in Jane's reforming credentials.

The 1553 crisis is also covered in a number of historical accounts
published in the course of Elizabeth's reign. There was a great deal of
borrowing between them but three are of particular interest because the
authors had observed events at first hand. Richard Grafton (c.1511–73)
printed Jane's proclamation and was excluded from the general pardon
announced at Mary's coronation.[28] His commercial rival John Stowe
(1524/5–1605) is important because he may well have reproduced
some of the lost section of Lea's Tower Chronicle.[29] His almost exact
contemporary, Raphael Holinshed (1525–1580?) appears to have had
personal contact with Grey's father.[30] England's mid-century upheavals
also attracted considerable interest in the rest of Europe and a number of
eyewitness or partly eyewitness accounts appeared to meet that demand.

The only one from a Protestant perspective was written by a schoolmaster from Lübeck with the Latinized name of Petrus Vincentius. He was visiting London's German community in July 1553 and was present throughout the crisis. He left after 8 August but before Northumberland's execution on the 22nd. His *Historical Account of Events which occurred in the kingdom of Britain in July AD 1553* achieved wide coverage. Editions in both Latin and German were published in 1553 (probably Marburg or Wittenberg), in German at Leipzig in 1554, in Latin at Basle in 1574 and was again in 1673.[31] It contains minor details otherwise unknown, such as the two casks of wine which the German merchants supplied for Londoners to celebrate Mary's success, but the chief importance of the book is that it is one of the earliest to give currency to the black legend of Northumberland's villainy, even stating that he poisoned Edward because the boy was beginning to criticize him.[32] From the side of the Princess Mary, several accounts of the 1553 crisis have survived. The earliest was complete by 1 September 1553, only six weeks after Mary's triumph.[33] It was written by Antonio de Guaras for the duke of Alburquerque who had served as an ambassador to Henry VIII. De Guaras was a Spanish merchant long resident in England, effectively the Spanish consul, and he was in London throughout the crisis. His account of events in East Anglia is necessarily what was reported to him, but he witnessed as many of the events in London and Westminster as he could. He appears to have got into Westminster Hall for Northumberland's trial and he says that he heard the duke's speech from the scaffold 'from being very near him'. Another account of the crisis from a foreign perspective is that prepared by Giovanni Francesco Commendone, a papal secretary sent by Julius III to congratulate Mary and sound out the possibility of a restoration of Catholicism.[34] He arrived in London on 8 August and was back in Rome by 8 September so much of his account is necessarily second hand; indeed, it continues until Mary's coronation and marriage which happened when Commendone was back in Europe.[35] Nevertheless, his account makes it clear that he made a major attempt to assemble the facts from those involved and also set up arrangements to keep information flowing after he had left England.[36] Commendone, indeed, may be the main source from which Europe gained its information about the crisis in England. He had been much assisted in his mission by Giacomo Sorenzo, the then Venetian ambassador, and after the ambassador's return to Venice an account which is very close to Commendone's was published there by a Luca Contile.[37] Two years later a further version was published in Ferrara, somewhat amended, with the author said to be Girolamo Raviglio Rosso, a diplomat from the court of Ferrara who came to England after the crisis to convey congratulations to Mary and Philip of Spain on their marriage.[38] So considerable was Italian interest in the 1553 crisis that another printing of Rosso (reset) appeared in 1591, as did the *Storia Ecclesiastica della Rivoluzione d'Inghilterra* by an Italian Dominican, Fra Girolamo Pollini. Published in Bologna, this was a lengthy account of ecclesiastical happenings in England from the reign of Henry VIII, and the second enlarged edition was published in Rome three years later.[39]

A cleric who was in London at the time and wrote about the crisis was Etienne Perlin. His *Description des Royaulmes d'Angleterre et d'Escosse* was published in Paris in 1558.[40] He was, however, very muddled about those involved and what is of principal interest is his reaction to England and the English. His comment on witnessing Northumberland's execution was that the executioner was lame and wore a white butcher's apron and that 'in this country you will scarcely find any nobleman, some of whose relations have not been beheaded. For my part (with reverence to my reader) I had rather be a hog driver and keep my head, for this disorder falls furiously on the head of great lords.'[41] A much longer account of events in England was prepared by Hugues Cousin, a member of Charles V's entourage, but it is effectively a condensation of ambassadorial reports and is of little value.[42] The most important of the sources from Mary's side is a Latin manuscript from the pen of Robert Wingfield, effectively completed between May and July 1554 and entitled 'De Rebus Gestis Mariae Anglorum Reginae Commentariolus' ['A Short Treatise of the Deeds of Mary, Queen of England'].[43] Wingfield was the son of a distinguished Suffolk lawyer and Speaker of the Commons, and lived at Brantham Hall four miles from Ipswich. Framlingham was less than twenty miles away and Robert was part of a large nexus of family and neighbours prominent in the support of Mary. As a result, Robert both knew most of the players on her side and was able to report some events as an eyewitness. Then to complete his delight, Mary spent two nights at his Ipswich house on her victorious way down to London.

PART II

THE PROTAGONISTS

JANE GREY

4

A DAMNABLE INHERITANCE

TACITUS tells the story of the Roman emperor Tiberius who was determined to wipe out the whole family of his rejected servant Sejanus, only to discover a young daughter who was protected by the legal prohibition on executing a virgin. The girl was thereupon raped, crying all the time 'What had she done? She would never do it again. Could not she be whipped for it like any other child'.[1] Parentage too cursed Jane Grey, and she was another innocent.

This damning inheritance came through her mother Frances, daughter of Henry VIII's younger sister, Mary, by her second marriage.[2] Born in July 1517, Frances was one of the only three Tudor children then alive in England. There was Princess Mary, the daughter of the king and his wife, Katherine of Aragon, and Frances's brother Henry, both born the year before. This made the new baby fourth in line to the throne, following Princess Mary, her own mother and then her brother. That brother died young – so briefly elevating Frances to third in line – but in 1522 came the birth of another brother, again Henry. True, all the while there was a possible complication – Henry VIII's elder sister Margaret and her surviving son James Stuart. But he was the king of Scotland and she had long been resident north of the border.

Frances's father was Charles Brandon, the younger grandson of a Suffolk knight who became Henry VIII's closest friend and boon companion and as such shot up to the dukedom of Suffolk in 1514. His subsequent marriage to the king's sister Mary had been one of the century's most romantic episodes. Her first husband, the decrepit king of France, had died after only three months – worn out, people said, by the demands of his new bride – and Charles was sent over to escort her home. However, when he arrived the widow effectively shanghaied him into marriage, an act of sisterly independence which faced her brother the king with a fait accompli. Frances was, thus, Henry VIII's niece and the daughter of his closest friend, but despite this her prospects were not all golden. Before he married Mary, Charles Brandon had had a somewhat convoluted marital history and this had left him with five children older than Frances to launch in society, to say nothing of her brother Henry. So, despite closeness to the crown, financial stringency cost Frances the finest match in the kingdom – to the heir of the duke of Norfolk. Instead she had to make do with the less prestigious but still wealthy Henry Grey, marquis of Dorset, although he was a difficult catch to land because he was already betrothed to Katherine Fitzalan, the daughter of the earl of Arundel.[3] Thus in order to marry Frances, Grey had to repudiate his betrothed – whether of his own free will or by persuasion is not clear – and 4000 marks (£2666.66) had to be guaranteed to sort out the financial liabilities; the king himself provided the first instalment.[4] Grey – named 'Henry' after the king, and like him a grandson of Edward IV's queen Elizabeth Woodville – was six months older than his bride and they married in 1533, nearly five years before he attained his majority, and not easy years since his father-in-law tried to renege on his obligation to support the young couple.[5]

In those five years, the Tudor family went through upheaval after upheaval. Days after the Grey wedding, Anne Boleyn was crowned queen and Katherine of Aragon demoted to the status of dowager princess of Wales. Three weeks later Frances's mother died. Then in September Elizabeth, the daughter of Henry and Anne Boleyn, was born. In the following March, parliament omitted Katherine of Aragon's daughter Mary from the succession and in the same month Frances's brother died. In 1536 Katherine of Aragon died, Anne Boleyn was executed and legislation declared both Mary and Elizabeth illegitimate and so out of the succession.[6] Nothing was said about Frances, but this catalogue of change effectively made her heir to the throne – always assuming that the Stuarts were ruled out and Henry did not reinstate one or both of his daughters. Of course once Prince Edward was born in October 1537, Frances fell back to conjecturally second in line, but that remained her position for nearly seven years. In that time she had several children of her own, but only two daughters had survived infancy: Jane born in 1537 and Katherine born in 1540.[7] Then from 1544 circumstances changed again. First, at Henry VIII's behest, parliament accepted that Mary and Elizabeth could succeed to the throne after Prince Edward while at the same time repeating that they were illegitimate.[8] Again nothing at all was said about Frances – indeed, the statute left it to the king to announce in his last will or by letters patent who was to inherit if each of his children died childless. Frances nevertheless could have assumed that she was back to being fourth in line, as in 1517. If so she was brutally enlightened in December 1546. Henry's last will and testament laid down that if none of his children left an heir, 'the imperial crown ... shall wholly remain and come to the heirs of the body of the Lady Frances our niece, eldest daughter to our late sister the French queen, lawfully begotten.'[9] Her children would inherit, but she could not.

For Frances Grey this was a blatant slap in the face, always the brides-maid and now the bride's mother, but for her eldest daughter Jane it was literally the kiss of death. With her second brother already dead, she would be the beneficiary – or victim – of the will. A month later Edward did succeed to the throne and Jane became third in line to the throne after Mary and Elizabeth. But if Edward were to die childless and if anyone decided to challenge the right of his bastardized sisters to succeed to the crown, Jane was a puppet ready to hand.

Despite their Dorset title, the Greys were a Leicestershire family. Their principal residence was at Bradgate Park, seven miles from the county town.[10] Henry and Frances had moved there in 1530 on the death of his father Thomas Grey, into what was a new house – or, rather, a house begun by his grandfather and still in process of being completed.[11] [plates 10 and 11] Some ruins remain, but the mansion proper was destroyed in the eighteenth century; in 1790, John Byng described it as 'long since burnt'.[12] William Burton, writing in the reign of James I, had described Bradgate as 'a fair and beautiful house', although in the 1540s John Leland recorded it as a lodge.[13] Such evidence as there is on the ground suggests that the building Jane knew was more the latter. As 'courtier' houses went it was not in the top league. It was built in fashionable brick in the latest style – a civilian mansion, not a fortified manor house – but its footprint was barely three-quarters that of Compton Wynyates, the house of William Compton, Henry VIII's erstwhile groom of the stool, and less than half that of Cowdray, built by William Fitzwilliam, the earl of South-ampton.[14] An engraving of the early 1700s by Johannes Kip shows an imposing if somewhat sprawling residence with formal gardens, but much of what he depicted was undoubtedly seventeenth-century addition and only the western block (minus the rectangular porch) is any evidence of the house as Jane Grey knew it.[15] Nichols writes of a square design with four corner turrets but the site today suggests that the house had a main block facing south with wings east and west.[16] Unfortunately excavation is unlikely to add anything to our knowledge of Bradgate since the ruins were substantially 'reconstructed' in the early decades of last century. Engravings published by Nichols show the ruins a century earlier. Its tiltyard, terrace and gardens have also been lost, but one feature which can in part be traced is the excellent supply of water which the Greys commissioned for drinking and sanitation and to power a mill.[17] It was the brainchild of Henry Grey's schoolmaster, a Robert Brook.[18] However, the real attraction of the lodge was its position in some of the best hunting country in England. The house itself was in the middle of a deer park, six miles in circumference. To create it Henry's father had entirely cleared away the village of Bradgate. Beyond the park were more of what Leland called the family's 'good parks and lands', Groby Park, Loughborough Park, Burleigh Park and much of Charnwood Forest. There were also several valuable slate quarries.[19]

Whether Jane Grey was born at Bradgate we do not know. Tradition, of course, has no doubt, but it is clear that what is now called 'Lady Jane's Tower' had nothing to do with her.[20] Again according to tradition, she was born in October 1537. The year does seem to be correct, although in April 1550 a German scholar, John of Ulm, writing from Oxford, said she was then about 14, and in December Roger Ascham put her age as 15.[21] The issue, however, is settled by a letter written by her tutor John Aylmer between March and early October 1551, which is quite specific that Jane was *just* 14.[22] The most probable date for the Aylmer letter is May 1551, so making Jane nearly six months older than Prince Edward.[23] A date in the spring would also agree with the report that at the time of her death in February 1554 she was then in her seventeenth year.[24]

Jane was born when her parents were still young – twenty and twenty-one – hardly in the public eye, and we have no information about her early years.[25] Indeed, even taking into account the subsequent histories of her parents, it is not easy to arrive at fair estimates of the family she was born into. The Grey clan seems to have been more cohesive than many aristocratic families.[26] Jane's father had two brothers – Lord Thomas and Lord John – and they were often to be found at Bradgate. Thomas was the decisive one. When Henry was faced with trouble in Leicestershire in the summer of 1549 he asked for Thomas to be sent to him, only to be told that John Grey had asked for their brother to be sent with troops to reinforce him in France.[27] Another frequent visitor to Bradgate was Henry Willoughby of Wollaton who had married Jane's aunt Anne. The Grey brothers made return visits and also to the second Willoughby house at Middleton in Warwickshire, but it is not clear if the women travelled as frequently. Another destination was the home of George Medley at Tilty in Essex, and in this case it is clear that Jane did go. She came with her mother and sisters in November 1549, and the following month she spent a further week there.[28] George Medley was the Greys' half-brother, and the families became even more involved when Anne Willoughby died in January 1548 and Henry her husband eighteen months later during Ket's rebellion, leaving three orphans under age.[29] George Medley became the guardian of the two younger children while Jane's father bought the wardship of the heir and acted as supervisor of Henry's will; in that capacity Grey had to arbitrate between Medley and the orphans' cousin, Sir Hugh Willoughby, the explorer. Purchasing a wardship was not cheap and when Sir Fulk Greville came forward with an attractive offer for the boy, Medley had to make Grey a counter-offer at no less than £1000. Presumably this simply compensated Jane's father for his outlay.[30] No friction was involved; George Medley would be one of the nine last-ditch supporters of Henry Grey, who were indicted with him in 1554.[31] Another Essex house which Jane visited was at [Saffron] Walden. Here lived her aunt Elizabeth, the widow of Thomas Audley, Baron Audley and former lord chancellor. Jane paid at least one visit in company with her parents and Lady Audley reciprocated.[32] The most interesting of these visits was made by Frances Grey and her three daughters to the Princess Mary late in 1549. They travelled from Tilty which suggests that the probable destination was Hunsdon, just across the border in Hertfordshire.[33] Frances and the princess seem to have been close, something which continued even after the disasters of 1553 and 1554.[34]

One tantalising possibility is that the young Frances was one of the court ladies who sat to Hans Holbein the younger (1497/8–1543). He certainly worked for the family. The drawing now at Windsor captioned 'The Lady Marchioness of Dorset' is of her mother-in-law Margaret Grey who lived until 1541.[35] The two were known as 'the young' marchioness and 'the old' marchioness.[36] Another of the Windsor drawings is labelled 'The Dutchess of Suffolk', which Frances became in 1551. [plate 13] When Holbein returned to England in 1531/2, the title belonged to her mother, Henry VIII's 35/36-year-old sister Mary (1496–1536), but although possible, she seems an unlikely sitter.[37] Mary was normally called 'Queen of France', a style dating back to her marriage to Louis XII, and for some of the time when Holbein could have taken her image she was terminally ill, and probably not at court.[38] An alternative possibility is Frances Grey's stepmother, Katherine Brandon, née Willoughby, the widow of her father Charles Brandon, duke of Suffolk. The apparent age of the sitter is no guide because Katherine was in fact two years younger

than Frances. The inscriptions on the drawings are not contemporary but
are said to have been provided by Edward VI's tutor Sir John Cheke, and
Cheke knew both Frances and Katherine.[39] If, therefore, Cheke made the
identifications before Frances became a duchess in November 1551, the
drawing is definitely of Katherine. However, if, as has been suggested, the
identifications were added between 1555 and 1557, Katherine was in exile
and the only duchess of Suffolk at court was Frances.[40] The identification
'The Dutchess of Suffolk' might, therefore, apply to her.

Over the centuries Jane's mother Frances has been regularly abused:
'buxom, hard-riding', 'ambitious', 'cunning and predatory', 'a restless
and permanently dissatisfied schemer', 'harsh, grasping and brutal', 'arrogant and energetic'.[41] Readers have been regaled with stories of an indecent haste to remarry after her husband's execution, even outdoing
Hamlet's mother Gertrude in being delivered of a still-born baby within
eight months. Adrian Stokes, her second husband, was no King Claudius
either. Probably the son of a minor Leicestershire gentleman, he had risen
in Frances's employment to the position of her master of horse. On
hearing the news, Princess Elizabeth is supposed to have said, 'What, has
that woman married her horsekeeper?'[42] William Camden wrote that
Frances 'herself forgetting the nobility of her lineage, married Adrian
Stokes, a mean gentleman to her dishonour'.[43] Other historians have
bolstered this denigration with critical remarks made (as we shall see) by
Jane Grey herself and by asserting that the duchess bullied her daughter
into accepting the throne.[44] Opinions have been particularly influenced by
a double portrait allegedly of Frances and Adrian, attributed to the
Flemish artist Hans Eworth.[45] The woman in it appears like nothing so
much as a female Henry VIII. Pasty-faced, stout, double-chinned and
bejewelled, very appropriately the king's niece and a most unlikely mother
for a blue-stocking daughter.
    Happily for Frances but not for myth, the portrait is a false lead. Despite
centuries of attribution, modern research has established that the sitters
are not Frances and Adrian Stokes but Mary Nevill, Lady Dacre and her
son Gregory Fiennes.[46] Elizabeth's jibe is equally apocryphal, as also
Frances's rush to the altar. Her second marriage actually took place in
1555. Her choice of an obscure husband has to be revalued, too. Even
Camden conceded that Frances made it 'for her security', that is, it
allowed her to escape a second husband being forced on her from the
political elite.[47] But although Stokes was an MP, and wealthy enough to
give Frances a fine monument in Westminster Abbey, marrying him was a

significant abasement for Henry VII's granddaughter.[48] When she and her husband went to law against the bishop of Exeter, the judges threw the case out because she was described as 'duchess'. They roundly declared that 'If a duchess or such marries a gentleman or esquire, by this she loses her dignity and the name she had before', and they quoted the rule of the heralds that 'if a noble woman marries a commoner, she ceases to be noble'.[49] True, polite society continued to respect Frances, but two days before her burial in December 1559, Elizabeth felt it necessary to indicate that she had been of royal stock by granting an augmentation of arms to be displayed at the ceremony.[50] A possible clue to the willingness of a king's granddaughter to pay the considerable price of becoming Mistress Stokes is Frances's renewed childbearing. The last nine years of her marriage to Henry Grey had been barren, but she soon became pregnant by Stokes.[51] 'All lost for love'? That there was an element of that in her second marriage is certainly suggested by Frances's last will and testament which left Stokes all her goods and a life interest in much of her property.[52] And the barrenness after 1545 could also suggest that in the final years of her marriage to Henry Grey the couple had not been close. Against this, in August 1552 the duke rushed from court on receipt of news that Frances's life was in danger.[53] A possible point of friction could have been Princess Mary. Frances remained close to her cousin and might have felt unable to come out boldly in support of Henry's public promotion of reform. On the other hand Frances was in the reformist camp. According to a later story, she and her cousin Eleanor Clifford had been under the influence of the martyr Anne Askew, and she was on visiting terms with that most enthusiastic Protestant, Katherine dowager duchess of Suffolk; also in choosing Stokes as her second husband she chose a keen reformer.[54]

Why Henry VIII excluded Jane Grey's mother from the place in the succession to which birth entitled her can only be conjectured. Perhaps it was something personal. Could Henry simply not envisage Frances on the throne, even though he would accept her children? Or was Grey the problem? He was a vital consideration given the universal assumption – which Henry seemed to have shared – that when a woman inherited a throne, her husband would become king. (Elizabeth's remarkable success as a virgin queen lay in the future.) Henry Grey is regularly damned by modern historians – W. K. Jordan labelled him 'that most stupid of peers', 'surely the most empty-headed peer of England' – but the contemporary record suggests something more complicated.[55] As we shall see, he was educated. He was no fool. When he was 21, a survey described positively only seven of England's nineteen earls, marquises and dukes, and he was one. In contrast to 'of little discretion', 'without wit' or in the earl of Derby's case, 'young, a child in wisdom, half a fool', the verdict on Dorset was 'lusty, with many friends, of great power, with little or no experience, well learned and a great wit'.[56] No-one was closer to the king. Henry VIII's grandmother was his great-grandmother, and Dorset was the only nobleman with a wife who was a Tudor and children with Tudor blood in them. When the king chose sixteen men to be his son's privy council, all of them except the archbishop of Canterbury were socially less prestigious than Henry Grey. Yet not only was he omitted, he was not even named as one of twelve others charged with assisting the councillors. Given that in court ceremonial he certainly was not insignificant, should we conclude that he deserved the reputation which later generations gave him: 'a man for his harmless simplicity neither much misliked nor much regarded'?[57] Or was the problem simply youth and inexperience – when Henry VIII died Grey was still only 29, ten years and more the junior of all the privy councillors.[58] By 1544 the king had, in fact, begun to use him. In the assault on Boulogne he did lead the infantry and in 1546 he was assigned command of the 'forward' in a proposed (but aborted) invasion of France. That this was intended to be a further test is indicated by command of the 'rearward' being assigned to his contemporary the earl of Surrey who was very much on probation.[59]

Any reason to ignore Grey evaporated with the accession of Edward VI on 28 January 1547. Wealthy, his wife a Tudor, his daughter third in line, Dorset's status could simply not be ignored by the Regency Council. He was elected KG on 18 February following the ceremony in which the councillors awarded themselves new honours (said to have been planned by Henry VIII).[60] These included the dukedom of Somerset for Edward Seymour, earl of Hertford, the elder of the young king's uncles, and a barony for the younger brother Thomas, while John Dudley, Viscount Lisle, became earl of Warwick. Grey was also in ceremonial demand. As chief mourner he presided at Henry VIII's funeral; at the coronation he carried the sceptre and then served as high constable for the ensuing banquet.[61] He was also drawn into politics as friction developed within the council. The obvious person to act as chairman was Edward Seymour, so the council appointed him protector of the realm and governor of the king's person; indeed, it may have been following instructions left by the old monarch. Technically, however, the functions of protector and governor were distinct, and despite replacing Dudley as lord admiral, Thomas Seymour was deeply offended at the two most senior positions going to his brother. Precedent was certainly against that. In Henry VI's minority, a century before, the two had been held separately, and in the more recent minority of Edward V, Richard of Gloucester, the young king's paternal uncle, had become protector and his maternal uncle, Antony Woodville, earl Rivers, had had custody of the king. Since Gloucester had then proceeded to murder Rivers and usurp the throne, it might appear that there were good reasons to have both functions in a single person's hands but Thomas began an eighteen-month campaign to compete with the protector.[62] What made the dispute over the offices of protector and governor worse and more personal was that Thomas immediately renewed the courtship of Henry VIII's widow, Queen Katherine Parr, a suit he had had to abandon – to her regret – when Henry VIII had come wooing in 1543.[63] With indecent haste – and without the approval of the privy council – Thomas and Katherine married. And to cap it all, an unseemly dispute erupted between the former queen and Somerset's duchess over their respective precedence. Thomas Seymour never gave up, and his most loyal supporter was Jane Grey's father.

5

JANE THE PERSON

FROM the very start Jane Grey was a key factor in Thomas Seymour's campaign.[1] He and Henry Grey were already friends but, as Jane's father would explain later, 'immediately after the king our late master's death' (i.e. after 28 January 1547) he was visited by John Harington, one of Seymour's gentlemen, and urged to place Jane in Thomas's household.[2] In itself such a suggestion was not remarkable. The English landed classes were accustomed to place their children in the households of their equals or, still better, their superiors, the sixteenth-century equivalent of a boarding or a finishing school. For the children, the object was to learn etiquette and proper behaviour, but even more to attract patronage for a future career and especially the chance to make an advantageous marriage. For the 'foster parent', the practice enhanced their status and influence and offered the potential to make money by brokering a suitable match. In 1547 Jane was already ten. The Greys had no male heir and Jane, as their eldest daughter, would be very well placed to bring to a future husband a claim to the Dorset peerage. There was, moreover, Jane's recently hugely increased status, thanks to Henry VIII's will. She would obviously quote high on the marriage market and for Seymour to invest early was a shrewd move. Control of Jane could be financially highly profitable and there were never enough prizes to satisfy anxious parents. Thomas, however, had more in mind. As Harington pointed out to her father, his master was an uncle of the king, in a position to do Grey 'much pleasure' provided he would 'enter a more friendship and familiarity with him'. In particular, 'he durst assure me that the Admiral would find the means she should be placed in marriage, much to my comfort'. When Dorset asked who was the prospective bridegroom, 'Marry', quoth Harington, 'I doubt not but you shall see him marry her to the king; and fear you not but he will bring it to pass, and then you shall be able to help all the friends you have' – that is, be in a position to make a huge profit. Henry Grey took the bait and within the week had a face-to-face meeting with Seymour where he was made 'such fair promises that I sent for my daughter who remained in his house from that time'.

Securing Jane Grey was only one element in Thomas Seymour's schemes to secure the recognition he felt entitled to. The protector seems to have dismissed Edward as a nine-year-old child, but Thomas – who was by far the more personable of the brothers – recognized that, though young, the king was politically and socially important. He therefore made the most of every opportunity to earn royal favour and, almost as important, to gain the support of Edward's closest servants who staffed the privy chamber. The protector got wind of this and there were changes at court, so Thomas turned his attention to parliament which was due to meet in November 1547, saying that 'he meant to get some authority that way which he thought otherwise he could not attain'.[3] He attempted to secure a letter from Edward backing his request, mustered the support of several other peers, including Jane's father, and threatened 'to make the blackest parliament that ever was in England'.[4] The details of the crisis which ensued are not clear, but it seems that Thomas Seymour set out to exploit flaws in Edward Seymour's position. The original appointments as protector and governor of the king's person had been made on the authority of Henry VIII's will, an authority backed by two acts of parliament. However, in March 1547, the will had been replaced by letters patent issued in the name of the young Edward – so depriving the protectorate of parliamentary protection. What is more, the patent had given Somerset additional powers which effectively turned the protectorate into a regency and so put the duke in a position, as his brother asserted, 'to give away Calais'. Finally, the March 1547 provision infringed royal authority by granting these powers to the duke until the king reached the age of eighteen – that is to September 1555. The protector's response was to introduce a bill into parliament putting his position beyond question, but he was hard-pressed to get it through. Instead of being read three times in each house of parliament, the bill was read three times in the Lords, then rewritten and read again, sent to the Commons with provisos added and read there four times before coming back for approval in the upper house.[5] With Jane's father as his staunchest ally, Thomas Seymour fought all the way, insisting 'that he would never consent or agree that the king should be kept as ward till he come to the years of eighteen', and in the end Somerset had to give way.[6] He did secure statutory confirmation of the protectorate, but only by conceding that in future he would hold the post so long as it pleased the king. This was a major weakening in his authority. It meant – in brute reality – that he would remain in power only as long as he could prevent a rival getting hold of Edward.

If, as her father indicated, Jane was sent to Seymour Place in February 1547, Thomas Seymour was then almost certainly still a bachelor. Contemporaries, however, saw no sexual implication in the sale of children and in any case the Greys were probably well aware of Seymour's intention to marry Katherine Parr – it was hardly a secret. Jane, so Dorset said, remained 'in [Seymour's] house from that time continually unto the death of the queen', but while there is no direct evidence, that appears to mean that after the marriage Jane became part of the former queen's entourage.[7] The eighteen months which Jane spent under Katherine's influence may well have been eye-opening.[8] A personable woman with a way with children, Katherine had herself been well educated – she read Petrarch and Erasmus for pleasure – and her intellectual sympathies must have appealed to Jane. Katherine was the first English queen to publish, anonymously at first and then under her own name.[9] She loved fine clothes and jewels, was keen on music and a good dancer but was equally interested in gardens. It has also been argued that she was a significant patron of painting, architecture and *objets d'art*.

It was while Jane was living with Katherine that her husband began his flirting and erotic horseplay with that other guest, the fourteen-year-old Elizabeth.[10] That story is very well known through the revelations which came out when he was arrested in January 1549. Kate Ashley, her governess, deposed that:

> At Chelsea, incontinent after he [Thomas Seymour] was married to the queen, he would come many mornings into the said Lady Elizabeth's chamber before she was ready, and sometimes before she did rise. And if she were up he would bid her good morrow and ask how she did, and strike her upon the back or on the buttocks familiarly ... And if she were in bed he would put open the curtains and bid her good morrow and make as though he would come at her, and she would go further into the bed so that he could not come at her.[11]

The queen dowager at first made light of this but in May 1548 the princess moved to an establishment of her own with Katherine's promise ringing in her ears to warn her 'of all evils that you should hear of me'.[12] How much of this behaviour Jane knew about we cannot tell. Elizabeth was four years her senior and there is no evidence of any interchange between the two. Nevertheless one must assume that Jane at least heard stories. By then

Katherine Parr was five or six months pregnant and in early June the household, including Jane, moved to Sudeley Castle for the confinement.[13] With Elizabeth gone, Jane was now the ranking lady in the household where at the end of August a daughter was born, not the 'little knave' Katherine and Thomas had hoped for.[14] Then, within days, and ruinously for Thomas, Katherine succumbed to childbed fever. She was buried at Sudeley with Jane Grey as chief mourner at the funeral, with a maid of honour holding up her train.[15]

The immediate thought of the grief-stricken Thomas was to break up the household as soon as possible and he wrote to Dorset offering to return Jane to her parents 'whenever you would send for her'.[16] However, within days he had changed his mind. On 17 September he wrote to Dorset saying that he had decided to maintain Katherine's entourage and wanted to keep Jane until the two of them had been able to talk matters over: 'My lady, my mother will be as dear to her as though she were her own daughter and I shall continue her half-father and more, and all that are in my house shall be as diligent about her as your self would wish accordingly.'[17]

At first Jane's parents were less than encouraging. Dorset replied on 19 September asking for his daughter back. Since Seymour now was 'destitute of such one as should correct her as a mistress and monish her as a mother', her own mother's 'oversight' had become vital.[18] Frances Grey wrote the same day reinforcing the request for Jane's return, although at the same time she promised to take Seymour's advice on 'the bestowing of her whensoever it shall happen'.[19] Clearly she did not want to lose Seymour's interest. Jane did, in fact, go home, but Seymour did not give up. He maintained the size of his household 'in hope of my Lady Jane, her return' and put the Dorsets under pressure.[20] First Harington brought a letter and an even harder sales pitch. He said that Jane was 'as handsome a lady as any in England and that she might be wife to any prince in Christen[dom], and that, if the king's majesty, when he came to age would marry within the realm, it was as likely he would be there, as in any other place'. In Seymour's household, 'she were as like ... to have a greater and better turn than he would think; and that he durst not tell what it was; and that being kept in my lord's house, who was uncle to the king, it were never the worse for her; and that my lord would be right glad if the king's majesty could like any in his house'.[21] Seymour then visited the marquis in person, gave even clearer assurances that Jane would marry Edward and for the first time talked money. No profit would come from Jane until she was old enough to marry, but to soften up Dorset, Seymour offered a loan of £2000 in advance – no doubt somewhat less than she would ultimately fetch – and £500 down immediately with no security required 'but only to have the lord marquis's daughter as a gage [guarantee]'.[22] The admiral was 'so earnest in persuasion' that Henry Grey weakened. At the same time, taking advantage of the opening hinted at in Frances's letter and clearly aware that she would have the decisive voice, Seymour sent Sir William Sharington to persuade her, and her acceptance cut whatever ground remained under Dorset's feet. With his wife agreeing, 'then', as he said, 'he could not but consent'.[23] Harington was sent to collect Jane at Bradgate and on the journey they passed through Leicester and were entertained with beer, cold meat and ale'.[24]

Whether Seymour had worked out a specific plan to exploit Jane Grey in his campaign against his brother seems unlikely. Rumour had it that his plan was to marry Jane himself, but this he treated as a joke.[25] Just controlling her was an asset in itself. It meant that no-one else could exploit the third in line to the throne, least of all the protector who could not but see Jane as the desirable bride for his son and heir, Lord Hertford.[26] Over and beyond that Thomas appears to have regarded the girl as a speculative investment. His object, as he told Dorset, was 'to get the king at liberty', i.e. out of the protector's control and into his own, and if that could be achieved, it would certainly do him no harm to have waiting in his household a high-born girl of the king's age who shared Edward's bookish interests and passion for Protestant reform.[27] 'If I might have any in my house whom the king might fantasy, I were much to blame if I would be against it'.[28] Jane was promising lure. And, as always, the deal with Dorset would frustrate the protector. Soon after Jane's return he was talking to his crony, the marquis of Northampton, in the gallery of Seymour Place and remarked:

> there would be much ado for the Lady Jane, the lord marquis's daughter and that my lord protector and my Lady Somerset would do what they could to obtain her of my lord marquis for my lord of Hertford, but he said they should not prevail therein for my lord marquis had given her wholly to him upon certain covenants that were between them. And then I [Northampton] asked him what he could do if my lord protector handling the marquis gently, should obtain his good will and so the matter to lie wholly in his own neck. He answered that he would never consent thereunto.[29]

Having the deal also helped to keep Jane's father in line. The marquis admitted subsequently that he was 'so seduced and inveigled' that he promised to spend his blood in support of Seymour against all men except the king 'personally' – hence the support he gave in parliament to the attempt to block the ratification of the protectorate.[30]

Jane Grey had been back in Seymour's household for barely two months before the patience of his brother and the rest of the council ran out and Thomas was arrested. Four frantic weeks of interrogation followed, with Seymour's noble supporters – including Jane's father – rushing to put as much distance as possible between themselves and the prisoner. Dorset was particularly exposed. He had been closer to Seymour than most, visiting and riding with him in the Midlands and, indeed, the marquis and his brother Thomas were living at Seymour Place when the arrest took place.[31] Frances Grey referred to Seymour as 'my good brother' and Jane as 'your dearest niece'.[32] After his fourth interrogation her husband decided it would be wise to cash in the value of this daughter by offering Jane to the protector as a bride for his son. The details we do not know, only that Grey ended his fifth and final deposition with this direct appeal to Somerset: 'For the marriage of your Grace's son to be with my daughter Jane, I think it not meet to be written, but I shall at all times avouch my saying'.[33] Perhaps the bribe was enough. Parliament passed a bill attainting only Seymour and he was executed on 19 March. The charges were the usual farrago of half-truths and imaginative construction which characterize so many Tudor treason cases.[34] It was hardly news that Seymour had tried to put himself in Edward's good books, nor was his intention to trim the protector's authority if he could, while his search for support became the accusation that he had 'laboured and gone about to combine and confederate with himself with some persons to have a party and a faction in readiness' for a coup. Other charges included an intention to swindle the mint and abuse of his office of lord admiral while his efforts to match Jane and Edward became 'traitorous intent and purpose as he spared not to promise your most excellent person in marriage to a nobleman's daughter of your realm'. What supported these charges was little more than Seymour's own loose tongue and wild talk, and according to memories in Elizabeth's reign, the royal lawyers were not wholly persuaded that the charges amounted to treason.[35] Thomas Goodrich, a privy councillor and future lord chancellor, and John Gosnold the solicitor-general insisted that the most the evidence would support was the lesser charge of 'misprision [concealment] of treason'.[36] The response to this from Sir Edward Montagu CJCP is revealing: 'Well, if you were fleshed as we be, you would not stick at this matter.' Clearly the intention was to get rid of Seymour at all costs. That also explains the decision to use a bill of attainder which denied the accused a hearing. Goodrich challenged Montagu:

> 'If you take this matter to be treason, let him be indicted and tried by the order of the common law'. 'No, not so,' quoth Montague, 'it shall be better done by the parliament, for if he be condemned by order of the common law, the fault might hereafter, the king coming to his age, be imputed to us. If it be done by parliament, we be discharged.'

Clearly Dorset had got out just in time. Not that the Commons were easily persuaded. The bill was 'very much debated and argued', and the peers had to send the lawyers down to make sure the measure passed.[37]

The relevance of all this to Jane Grey is the personality and character of the man under whose protection and influence she lived for the best part of two years. Seymour inspired very diverse reactions during his lifetime and has done so ever since, in particular his relations with Elizabeth. To modern eyes these qualify as child abuse but his accusers were less concerned over horseplay with the princess which had taken place during his wife's lifetime, than with his subsequent interest in her. Contemplating marrying an heir to the throne in defiance of the privy council appeared the final challenge in a long record of attempts to destabilize government. Thomas Seymour's reputation also suffered posthumously from being damned in the sermons of Hugh Latimer, the future Protestant hero and martyr.

> He was, I heard say, a covetous man, a covetous man indeed. I would there were no more in England. He was, I heard say, an ambitious man: I would there were no more in England. He was, I heard say, a seditious man, a contemner of common prayer: I would there were no more in England. Well he is gone. I would he had left none behind him.[38]
>
> As touching the kind of his death, whether he be saved or no, I refer that to God only. ... but this I will say if they ask me what I think of his death, that he died very dangerously, irksomely horribly ... He was a man the farthest from the fear of God that I knew or heard of in England ....[39]

Even as Seymour went to the scaffold his mind was on secret messages he had left urging Mary and Elizabeth to 'conspire' against the protector.[40]

That Seymour was a thorn in the side of the government is evident, but there can be little doubt that he was got rid of because of who he was and what he might do, rather than anything he had actually done. As he had said himself, 'I am sure I can have no hurt if they do me right; they cannot kill me unless they do me wrong'.[41] Not that this confidence helped him.

Quite the reverse. Bragging about the widespread support he enjoyed simply made him appear more dangerous than he really was and his denial that he had done anything wrong led him to refuse to defend himself. Effectively he defied the privy council to do their worst. Seymour went to the scaffold rationalizing his death as a final act of devotion offered by the only loyal servant of an abused king.[42] On the other hand he did enjoy some popular sympathy, and it was widely believed that he was condemned by attainder because there were no grounds for a proper trial at common law. So strong was the feeling that Latimer devoted a substantial section of a further sermon a fortnight after the execution to rebutting criticism of Seymour's condemnation by parliament.[43] Moreover not everyone shared the bishop's scepticism about Seymour's religious sincerity. Peter Martyr, writing within days of his arrest, described him as 'a great friend of religion'.[44] Thomas inspired real loyalty amongst servants and well-wishers from different levels of society. Three decades after his death 'the memory of his service was such a band among them all of kindness as the best of them disdained not the poorest, and the meaner had recourse to the greatest for their countenance and aid in their honest causes'.[45] Edward clearly liked him and the privy chamber staff were won over by his affability. There was very little guile in Thomas Seymour. The story was told that having once complained to Henry VIII that Cranmer was a miser who did not live up to his income, when he discovered that this was far from the case, Seymour went back to the king to apologize.[46] The epitaph Elizabeth offered was: 'This day died a man of much wit and very little judgement'.[47] Women were very taken by him. Katherine Parr was clearly in love. Elizabeth, whatever one makes of the horseplay, certainly flirted with him and may have cautiously toyed with the idea of marriage. Her attendants drooled over his qualities. There is no evidence that Jane was treated as familiarly as Elizabeth was, but it is quite clear that he wrote her flattering letters and that she too was very much attracted. The letter she sent to him when she learned that she might return to him in the autumn of 1548 is revealing.

> My duty to your Lordship in most humble wise remembered, with no less thanks for the gentle letters which I received from you. Thinking myself so much bound to your Lordship, for your great goodness towards me from time to time, that I cannot by any means be able to recompense the least part thereof, I purposed to write a few rude lines unto your Lordship, rather as a token to show how much worthier I think your Lordship's goodness than to give worthy thanks for the same; and these my letters shall be to testify unto you that, like as you have become towards me a loving and kind father,

so I shall be always most ready to obey your godly monitions and good instructions, as becometh one upon whom you have heaped so many benefits. And thus fearing lest I should trouble your Lordship too much, I most humbly take my leave of your good Lordship.

Your humble servant during my life,

Jane Graye[48] [plate 23]

Tudor young people were constricted by conventions and there were exempla to follow when writing to an important adult. Yet underneath the formality, Jane was clearly excited at the prospect of returning to Seymour's household – and possibly more. 'Like as you have become towards me a loving and kind father' surely says something.

The suspicion that Jane had blossomed under the care of Katherine and Thomas is certainly strengthened by the letter Henry Grey wrote in September 1548 insisting that Jane should come back home.[49] True, the reason he gave was prosaically credible. Jane needed to return to the care of her mother; and he was clearly doubtful about the promised alternative of Thomas's mother who was in her sixties and possibly more.[50] It was reasonable too, that he should reassure Seymour that their deal over Jane's marriage was in place: 'My meaning herein is not to withdraw any part of my promise to you for her bestowing, for I assure your lordship [that] I intend, God willing, to use your discreet advice and consent in that behalf, and no less than mine own.' But beyond politeness and assurances, it is clear that Henry Grey believed that Jane's upbringing had reached a critical stage: 'I seek in these her young years wherein she now stands, either to make or mar (as the common saying is) the addressing of her mind to humility, soberness and obedience.' The tactful references to the efforts of Katherine Parr and Seymour, and to his interest in Jane's progress, pale beside the rest:

> Considering the state of my daughter and her tender years, wherein she shall hardly rule herself as yet without a guide, lest she should for lack of a bridle take too much the head and conceive such opinion of her self that all such good behaviour as she heretofore hath learned by the queen's and your most wholesome instruction should either be quenched in her or at least diminished, I shall, in most hearty wise, require your lordship to commit her to the governance of her mother, by whom for the fear and duty she owes her she shall most easily be ruled and framed towards virtue which I wish above all things to be most plentiful in her. ... weighing that you be destitute of such one as should correct her as a mistress and nourish her as a mother, I persuade myself that you will think the eye and oversight of my wife shall be in this respect most necessary.

Grey had paid at least one visit to Katherine and Thomas at Sudeley and so observed his daughter's progress at first hand; a firmer hand was now called for.[51]

It is true that Seymour's importunity overcame the fears of Dorset and his wife on that occasion, but concern to oversee Jane's development might explain why, after the arrest of Thomas Seymour, she was not 'placed out' again but remained with her parents. There may, of course, be other explanations. Jane was both quick and clever. Was it felt that she had already made sufficient progress? Perhaps Frances Grey, as a member of the royal family, considered that since there was no longer a queen to train her daughter, trusting Jane to anyone less would be infra dig.[52] Alternatively, had Seymour so convinced Jane's parents of her value that they were henceforth determined to keep such an asset under their eye? After all, she would soon be twelve and qualified for marriage. But evidence from eighteen months later does suggest that Jane was being subjected to a much stricter regime. It comes from the recollection of the humanist scholar and educationalist Roger Ascham, who in August 1550 was on his way abroad and broke his journey to visit Bradgate and his friend John Aylmer, Jane Grey's tutor. Ascham already knew Jane. The two probably first met when early in 1548 he took up a post in the Parr/Seymour household at Chelsea.[53] His primary duty there had been to tutor Elizabeth, but as he also taught calligraphy to both Edward and Jane's Brandon cousins, it seems likely that, until Elizabeth left in May, he taught Jane as well. Thereafter, according to a letter he wrote from a diplomatic posting at the court of Charles V, 'at court I was very friendly with her, and she wrote learned letters to me'.[54] On arrival at Bradgate he had found the household out hunting, but Jane was alone in her room, reading Plato in the original Greek. Twenty years later, he retailed the story in his most famous work, *The Scholemaster*.

Before I went to Germany, I came to Broadgate in Leicestershire, to take my leave of that noble lady Jane Grey, to whom I was exceeding much beholding. Her parents, the duke and duchess, with all the household, gentlemen and gentlewomen, were hunting in the park. I found her in her chamber, reading *Phaedo Platonis* in Greek, and that with as much delight as some gentlemen would read a merry tale in Boccaccio. After salutation and duty done, with some other talk, I asked her why she would lose such pastime in the park? Smiling, she answered me: 'I wist all their sport in the park is but a shadow to that pleasure that I find in Plato. Alas, good folk, they never felt what true pleasure meant.'[55]

This certainly looks like teenage rebellion. Refusing to go hunting and staying in to read Plato was a very public repudiation of the person who 'never felt what true pleasure meant' – undoubtedly her mother. Frances's sights were on making a great match for Jane and might well have little sympathy for a bluestocking daughter, even if her father encouraged her. Jane, for her part, could well have despised a mother who had no time for higher things. Perhaps, too, there was an element of showing off. Jane clearly intended to flatter her tutor and, perhaps, to confirm to her famous humanist visitor that even in Leicestershire she remained one of the elite. The words Ascham attributed to Jane may not, after such an interval, be verbatim, but the event itself is well attested. In the January following his visit, he wrote to Jane that:

> Nothing has caused in me so much wonder as my having fallen upon you last summer, a maiden of noble birth, and that too in the absence of your tutor, in the hall of your most noble family, and at a time when others, both men and women, give themselves up to hunting and pleasures, you, a divine maiden, reading carefully in Greek the Phaedo of the divine Plato, and happier in being so occupied than because you derive your birth, both on your father's side and on your mother's from kings and queens.[56]

Having been told that she preferred Plato to hunting, Ascham pressed Jane on how she had discovered a truth so profound that 'not many women, but very few men, have attainted thereunto'. Her reply has since figured in almost every study of Tudor childhood:

> I will tell you, and tell you a truth which perchance ye will marvel at. One of the greatest benefits that God ever gave me is, that he sent me so sharp and severe parents, and so gentle a schoolmaster [John Aylmer]. For when I am in presence either of father or mother, whether I speak, keep silence, sit, stand or go, eat, drink, be merry or sad, be sewing, playing, dancing, or doing anything else, I must do it, as it were, in such weight, measure, and number, even so perfectly, as God made the world, or else I am so sharply taunted, so cruelly threatened, yea, presently sometimes with pinches, nips and bobs and other ways (which I will not name for the honour I bear them) so without measure disordered, that I think myself in hell, till time come that I must go to Mr. Elmer, who teacheth me so gently, so pleasantly, with such fair allurements to learning, that I think all the time nothing whilest I am with him. And when I am called from him, I fall to weeping, because whatsoever I do else but learning is full of grief, trouble, fear and whole misliking unto me. And thus my book hath so much pleasure and more, that in respect of it, all other pleasures, in very deed, be but trifles and troubles unto me.

This twenty-year-old memory must be approached with caution. Unlike the recollection of Jane reading Plato, this part of the conversation is not documented near to the event. True, Ascham said that he particularly remembered the discussion because it was 'the last time that ever I saw that noble and worthy lady', but he produced the story to prove an educational moral: children respond better to a kind than an unkind teacher.[57] But allowing that Ascham had a good memory and did not distort Jane's alleged remarks, what they suggest is not just a recent confrontation over Jane's refusal to hunt that day, but a deeper dissatisfaction with her treatment. Even if Seymour did not turn her head with his gallantries, life at Bradgate was a harsh contrast to the 'loving and kind' atmosphere she had enjoyed at Seymour Place and Sudeley.

Looking back from the twenty-first century West, sympathies go very much to Jane, but Henry Grey's letter to Thomas Seymour puts it beyond question that what motivated the marquis and his wife was duty, duty to Jane. The priority was to produce a 'gracious' daughter to live up to her proper station and be groomed to make a splendid marriage, and for that, discipline was vital. Good parents were strict parents, especially when it came to bringing up daughters. Katherine of Aragon commissioned the renowned humanist Juan Luis Vives to write a treatise on the avant-garde topic of the education of women, and he had no doubts:

> Specially the daughters should be handled without any cherishing. For cherishing mars the sons but utterly destroy the daughters. And men be made worse with over much liberty, but women be made ungracious for they be so set upon pleasures and fantasies, that except they be well bridled and kept under, they run headlong into a thousand mischiefs.[58]

It is in this light that we must gloss the phrases in Grey's letter: 'for lack of a bridle', 'for the fear and duty she owes to her [mother] she shall most easily be ruled and framed', someone 'to correct and admonish her as a mistress and a mother', 'the eye and oversight of my wife', her mother's 'waking eye in respecting her demeanour'. Such was the essence of good parenting.

Jane herself must have known this and that prompts a question about her own attitude. If strictness was to be expected from a responsible mother and father, why complain? Does the fact that she expressed her resentment so forcefully mean that she was being expected to reach exceptional standards – possibly to justify marriage with Edward? Was it just teenage exaggeration? Or had she begun to kick against parental discipline? A number of scholars have taken the latter view, seeing her as 'a stubborn, unusually bright, articulate and opinionated adolescent', 'a stubborn, acerbic, even arrogant young woman'.[59] These are twenty-first-century values, but Henry and Frances Grey were not alone in worrying as their daughter spread her wings. John Aylmer, the very tutor Jane so admired, was also becoming concerned about her vulnerability to what he saw as 'moral' temptation. In May 1551, Aylmer wrote to Henry Bullinger of Zurich – as we shall see, the father-confessor to most English reformers – asking him to write advising Jane on what 'may assist her towards living well and happily'.[60] At just fourteen, she was of an age when 'all people are inclined to follow their own ways, and by the attractiveness of the objects and corruption of nature are more easily carried headlong into pleasure ... than induced to follow those studies which are attended with the praise of virtue'. Nine months before, Ascham had found Jane totally absorbed in Plato, so could it be that she had begun to find other things more interesting than Greek? Nor, as the letter shows, was this the first time Aylmer had called on the Bullinger fire-power. What this new interest was is made clear in a further letter, dated 23 December, in which Aylmer asked Bullinger to 'prescribe to her [Jane] the length of time she may properly devote to the study of music, for in this respect people err beyond measure in this country'.[61] Greek was more important than the lute or the virginals. The tutor, moreover, added that when the English studied music 'their whole labour is undertaken and exertions made for the sake of ostentation', so was Jane becoming a bit of a show-off? Before she was ten Princess Mary had given her a 'lace for the neck of gold smith work containing small pearls xxxij' and in that same December letter Aylmer wrote 'It now remains for me to request that ... you will instruct my pupil in your next letter as to what embellishment and adornment of person is becoming in young women professing godliness.'[62] Clearly Jane was becoming increasingly interested in clothes. Interestingly he suggested that Bullinger might

> bring forward the example of our king's sister, the princess Elizabeth, who goes clad in every respect as becomes a young maiden; and yet no one is induced by the example of so illustrious a lady, and in so much gospel light, to lay aside, much less look down upon, gold, jewels and braidings of the hair. They hear preachers declaim against these things, but yet no one amends her life.[63]

Evidently he felt that Jane might regard Elizabeth, four years her senior, as something of a pattern with 'her maiden apparel which ... made the noblemen's daughters and wives to be ashamed to be dressed and painted like peacocks'.[64] The contrast had been particularly obvious a month or so earlier when, as Aylmer observed later, the princess's 'maidenly shamefastness' stood out on the occasion of the visit of the queen dowager of Scotland.[65] Jane had been present, presumably one of the peacocks, but she seems to have taken heed. She was clearly the person Aylmer had in mind when he reminisced:

> This I know that a great man's daughter receiving from the lady Mary before she was queen goodly apparel of tinsel, cloth of gold, and velvet, laid on with parchment lace of gold, when she saw it, said 'What shall I do with it?' 'Marry,' said a gentlewoman, 'wear it'. 'Nay,' quoth she, 'that were a shame to follow my lady Mary against God's word and leave my lady Elizabeth which followeth God's word.'[66]

6

FAMILY PRIORITIES

AFTERSHOCKS from the attack on Thomas Seymour were confined to council and parliament, but in a matter of months the whole country was racked with change, change which drew in the Greys too. In the spring rumbles of popular unrest began to be heard – driven by a variety of discontents, religious, economic and social, and by June 1549 the populous counties in the southern half of the country were all involved – agitation, strikes, protest rallies and in some areas serious violence. Tudor England had no standing army and no police force – power in the localities rested with those whose wealth and influence gave them social and economic authority – so the marquis of Dorset and the earl of Huntingdon, as the dominant landowners, were ordered to maintain stability in Leicestershire and Rutland. They were successful and prevented trouble from becoming really serious, in contrast to East Anglia and the south-west.[1] In those areas normal law and order broke down and pitched battles had to be fought to re-establish authority. Both the initial protests and the incompetence shown in handling them in certain counties were blamed (with some justice) on the protector, and the political fall-out saw Somerset stripped of office by a council coup in early October.[2] As Grey was not a privy counsellor he was not directly involved, but he was drawn in when a dispute broke out among the victors, with the earls of Southampton and Arundel and their allies – many of them religiously conservative – vying for power with a group led by John Dudley, the earl of Warwick. This time, in contrast to his commitment to Thomas Seymour, Dorset was fortunate. He sided with Warwick and on 29 November he was appointed a privy counsellor in order to help tip the council balance in the earl's favour. The benefits were immediate. He was cut in on a profitable currency swindle and granted new offices.[3] Even more significant, he was promoted in February to be one of the six lords personally responsible for Edward.[4] Such attendance suited him, and as a result the family, including Jane, began to be more seen in London and the court.[5]

The evidence of Jane's growing experience is too patchy to be certain of either the frequency or the length of her various visits. Having moved the household to the court in February 1550, by May at least the family was back at Bradgate; in July Jane was again in London but in August she was once more at Bradgate in time for the famous interview with Ascham.[6] We can assume that such continued travelling set the rhythm of her life from then on. Thus she was in London over Christmas and New Year 1551–2, and must either have attended the court festivities at Greenwich or, at least, watched the descent on the city of the Lord of Misrule and his entourage.[7] Shortly afterwards she became seriously ill.[8] Jane's presence can be assumed, even when she is not mentioned by name. For example, it seems pretty certain that she was alongside her mother when Princess Mary was given a lavish welcome at court in February 1553.[9] The most splendid occasion in which Jane was involved was the reception of the regent of Scotland, Mary of Guise, which drew Aylmer's strictures about 'peacocks'.[10] Returning from France in October 1551 after visiting her daughter, Mary Queen of Scots, the regent had been forced by bad weather to land at Portsmouth, and requested permission to complete the journey by road and also to meet Edward. She was then escorted to London by increasingly honorific reception parties. At Hampton Court, which was 'very finely dressed' for the occasion, Mary was welcomed by sixty ladies and gentlewomen, accommodated in the queen's apartments and entertained to two days 'in dancing and pastime'. But Frances Grey and Jane were held back until the regent had arrived by water at Paul's Wharf and been settled in the bishop of London's palace next to the cathedral. There, on the afternoon of Tuesday 3 November, the regent's sister-in-law, Lady Margaret Douglas, and Frances Grey led the elite of England's womenfolk to greet her; with Jane ranking as number five. The next day, Jane's father and mother with over a hundred lords, ladies, gentlemen and gentlewomen, again including Jane, escorted the regent to Westminster to meet the king and enjoy a state banquet. Edward and the regent dined in the presence chamber with Margaret Douglas, Frances Grey and the French ambassador, eating off gold plate. Jane and the other ladies in attendance, English and Scottish, dined in the great chamber, 'off silver'. Two days later the regent left, accompanied to Shoreditch church by 'divers noble men and women' and a mounted escort numbering three hundred.

Jane's appearances in public were possibly less than they might have been because, despite having reached the centre of power, her father soon began to show signs of being disillusioned. At first he attended the privy council assiduously, but very soon his appearances became spasmodic.[11] The suspicion must be that he had little stamina for public business or, perhaps, no aptitude. Despite this, in February 1551 Grey was given the major appointment of warden general of the Scottish Marches and left soon after Lady Day with a sheaf of instructions to promote a settlement with Scotland and press forward the fortifications at Berwick.[12] Once in post he differed with Westminster over the amount of support he needed and for months felt the council left him completely in the dark. On one occasion he wrote to William Cecil, 'I long to hear from you as they that inhabit hell would gladly hear how they do that be in heaven.'[13] By September Grey was back, handing in his resignation and telling the king that he was 'grieved much with the disorder of the marches toward Scotland'.[14] The feeling that the job was too big for him may not, however, have been the only motive which brought Dorset back to court. His wife's father, Charles Brandon, duke of Suffolk, had remarried after her mother's death, and when he died in 1545 had left two sons to continue the dukedom. In the summer of 1551 the title suddenly became void as both boys caught the dreaded sweating sickness at Cambridge and died within hours of each other. Not only did that leave Frances as the senior co-heir to Brandon wealth, it was the convention that if a title died out in the male line, it might be revived for the husband of the eldest daughter. So once Henry Grey got back from Scotland, not only was the family able to abandon its London base, Dorset House, and move into Suffolk Place – the great house which Charles Brandon had built in Southwark – Henry was able 'as well for his service sake as for that by way of marriage to have claim to the title of duke of Suffolk'.[15] He was duly invested on 11 October 1551, and so became one of only three dukes, along with the duke of Somerset, the erstwhile protector, and another new creation of 11 October, John Dudley, duke of Northumberland.[16] Three months later Edward Seymour was beheaded on Tower Hill which made Henry Grey the premier ranking noble in the land.

Henry Grey's increased status might be expected to be followed, if not by a return to the Borders at least by an increase in responsibility elsewhere. But no. That there were doubts about his public competence or at least his commitment is implicit in the most intimate near-contemporary assessment we have of the duke. This is the comment on his execution which appears in Raphael Holinshed's *Chronicle*, and reads as if based on personal knowledge. The passage begins:

> Such was the end of this duke of Suffolk, a man of high nobility by birth, and of nature to his friend gentle and courteous, more easy in deed to be led than was thought expedient, of stomach nevertheless stout and hardy, hasty and soon kindled, but pacified straight again, and sorry if in his heat [anger] ought had passed him otherwise than reason might seem to bear, upright and plain in his private dealings, no dissembler, nor well able to bear injuries, but yet forgiving and forgetting the same, if the party would seem but to acknowledge his fault and seek reconcilement.[17]

This was written in the light of the fiasco of Grey's treason in January 1554 and is hardly an encomium. Despite the praise, it presents Grey as obstinate, short-tempered, somewhat naive, touchy and malleable. His mother certainly believed that he was easily led. Early in his court career she wrote to Thomas Cromwell, the king's chief minister:

> When you shall happen to see my son Marquis either at large playing [gambling] or great usual swearing or any other demeanour unmeet for him to use, which I fear me shall be very often, that it may then please you, good Master Cromwell, for my late lord his good father's sake, whose soul God pardon, in some friendly fashion to rebuke him thereof, whereby you shall bind him at his further years of knowledge and discretion, if he then have any virtue or grace, to consider, and remember your goodness now showed unto him.[18]

Mother and son did not have good relations, and the degree of her anxiety for the seventeen-year-old is obvious in the double gift which accompanied the letter, £10 and a small silver gilt pot which the king had given the dowager marchioness some months earlier. If Cromwell tried, he certainly did not nip in the bud Grey's love of gambling. To the end of his days Henry thought a game of cards insipid if nothing hung on it.[19] Also he was certainly touchy. In 1546 he was accused of poaching deer, evidently with justification, but John Beaumont, the lawyer for the complainant, had been Grey's mother's steward and took the opportunity also to accuse the marquis of theft.[20] The court fined Beaumont £50, to which he replied by complaining to the privy council, evidently in colourful terms. The result was that Beaumont found himself condemned for lack of respect to the marquis, while Dorset was ordered to keep the peace towards the lawyer.[21] Despite this, the feud continued. In December 1550 Beaumont became master of the rolls and he used his position to devise with Charles Brandon's daughter a way of swindling Dorset out of property. The scheme backfired and other offences by Beaumont led to the lawyer being ruined, almost certainly with the marquis's encouragement.[22]

That was Henry Grey, duke and public figure, but the Holinshed comment goes on to reveal a more private side of the man, and this is very much more positive and particularly relevant to his adolescent daughter:

> Bountiful he was and very liberal, somewhat learned himself, and a great favourer of those that were learned, so that to many he showed himself a very Mæcenas, no less free of covetousness than void of pride and disdainful haughtiness of mind, more regarding plain meaning men than claw-back flatterers: and this virtue he had, he could patiently bear his faults told him by those whom he had in credit for their wisdom and faithful meanings towards himself, though sometimes he had not that hap to reform himself thereafter.

A patron of the classical learning of the Renaissance, and not without pretensions in that direction himself, someone who enjoyed the society of scholars and moralists, even though he did not always apply what they told him – if Holinshed is right, the ambience which produced Jane Grey can be traced to her father.

Evidence of this is to be found in the many letters written by foreign scholars in England to Henry Bullinger in Zurich. The earliest reference to Jane's father is in a letter sent from Oxford, dated 2 March 1549, by Johannes ab Ulmis, a student recently arrived from Ulm in Württemberg, as his name suggests.[23] Ulm had called on the marquis of Dorset (as Grey then was), 'a most courteous and discreet personage', and the results had been highly satisfactory. 'Immediately on my first waiting upon him, [he] ordered eight crowns to be given to me on that instant, and faithfully promised me the same or a larger sum every year.'[24] All Renaissance scholars had to be beggars, and two Oxford academics, Ralph Skinner and John Wullock, immediately realized that this new arrival, boasting of his influence with the great Bullinger, was someone to be exploited.[25] They therefore proposed that Bullinger should be asked to honour Grey by dedicating one of his forthcoming books to him, something which John assured them he could arrange. However, he did nothing and continued to cultivate Dorset directly. Indeed, having attended the national disputation on the eucharist which took place at Oxford in the summer of 1549, he made a fair copy of his notes for Grey and stayed at his 'palace' for several days. Meanwhile, and without telling Ulm, Skinner and

Wullock approached the marquis direct and found him highly flattered by the suggestion of a Bullinger dedication. This put the recent arrival on the spot and in August Ulm had to write a somewhat apologetic letter to Zurich, the more so since (encouraged by a letter of commendation to Grey from Bullinger) the marquis had upped the promised pension to 20 crowns and had paid him twelve of that in hand. And, so Ulm tempted Bullinger, there could be more: 'I dare assure you that this nobleman, so greatly distinguished by all liberal learning, will afford such manifestations of his good feeling and gratitude as shall be most worthy of himself, and most honourable to you and all your friends.' In October Ulm was pressing for a reply and citing more of Dorset's favours: 'Woe betide me, if the marquis of Dorset has not this very day treated me with the greatest kindness, upon hearing that I had been commended by you to [Richard] Cox.'[26] By the following March, Bullinger had agreed to the dedication and was waiting for Ulm to spell out what the wording should be. Dorset provided this at first hand:

'To the Lord Henry Grey, marquis of Dorset, Baron Ferrers of Groby, Harrington, Bonville and Astly, one of his majesty's most honourable privy council, his right courteous master etc.'

However, somewhat confusingly Grey went on to tell Ulm

that he had the rank of prince, but that he did not wish so to be styled by you; so that you may judge for yourself whether to keep it back or not. For my own part, I always use this title, and shall henceforth do so with much greater freedom, now that I perceive him at this time raised to the highest and most illustrious dignity. For this honour is given by the English to one who is descended from the royal family, and is one of the king's council and also a lord of parliament.[27]

'The highest and most illustrious dignity' is clearly a reference to Dorset's appointment as one of the six lords waiting on the king, but the expression 'the rank of prince' has presented scholars with something of a puzzle, even being interpreted as the marquis bragging about his royal connections.

Grey, however, was only royal by marriage and it is more likely that he was explaining English courtesy usage to this foreigner. Dukes were addressed face to face as 'prince' and the inference is that a marquis with a royal wife could be similarly addressed. It is, of course, essential to take this letter with the pinch of salt necessary to this day in reading applications by academics for research grants. A month later Ulm told Bullinger to be careful to flatter Grey and his leading servants with 'warmest acknowledgements for his kindness in honouring me with his friendship and patronage for your sake'.[28] Not that he feared that Bullinger needed telling: 'why am I teaching a dolphin to swim?'[29] The reformer took the point, decided on maximum flattery and dedicated the book to 'The most illustrious prince and lord, Henry Grey . . . '.[30]

The letters written by Ulm show that Holinshed's praise for Henry Grey's interest in scholarship was well justified. Evidently it was in marked contrast to his approach to public life. In April 1550 Ulm wrote to Bullinger giving further information about Dorset and introducing Jane Grey for the first time. The marquis, he wrote,

> is descended from the royal family, with which he is very nearly connected; and is the most honourable of the king's privy council . . . He is very much looked up to by the king. He is learned and speaks Latin with elegance. He is the protector of all students, and the refuge of foreigners. He maintains at his own house the most learned men: he has a daughter, about fourteen years of age, who is pious and accomplished beyond what can be expressed.[31]

The marquis certainly was 'the protector of all students, and the refuge of foreigners'. As well as funds for John Ulm himself, which appear to have flowed like water, Grey also supported a young Swiss student, Alexander Schmutz.[32] Michelangelo Florio too remembered that 'If I had been of his own blood, one of his nearest and dearest relatives, he could not have shown me greater kindness nor have honoured me more with the sincere and truly divine charity which he had towards all those who found themselves persecuted for Christ's sake by Antichrist.'[33] It is equally true that Grey maintained 'at his own house the most learned men'.[34] Of his four chaplains, the most formidably learned was Thomas Harding, the second holder of the Regius Chair in Hebrew at Oxford. Another was James Haddon, a founding fellow of Trinity College, Cambridge. The third, John Willock or Wullock, we have already met. A former Dominican friar, he had studied at Cologne. The last of the quartet was Jane's tutor, John Aylmer. He had been supported by Grey through university, and after Jane's death made a long tour through European universities which ended in the offer of the lectureship in Hebrew at Jena. Also under Dorset's patronage was the Ralph Skinner who worked with Willock over the Bullinger dedication. He was first a fellow of New College, Oxford and then its pro-warden.[35] John Parkhurst, who knew the five men well, celebrated them in a much admired epigram. Dedicated to

Dorset, 'the noblest of men', it declared that far more meritorious than lineage, personal piety and 'manifold merit' was Grey's commitment to

> Support the ideas and projects of learned men
> And to strengthen the growth of [liberal] studies among the young.
> Why should I mention the lustre which Willock, Skinner, Haddon
> And Aylmer have shed upon your family?
> O God, what young men were these! What master was worthy of them?
> Ennobled with such lights as these, your house shines out and the
> Whole of England is the more ablaze with the fire of your light[36]

Although Ulm does not mention Dorset's daughter until April 1550, by then he knew Jane sufficiently well to be translating Bullinger's book on marriage for her, from German into Latin.[37] Exactly when in the previous twelve months they had met is not clear. Ulm first met her father late in 1548 or early 1549 and he had stayed at the London house in the following August, but at that time the family was at Bradgate.[38] The translation was finished by July 1550, although when he came to present it Jane was again away from home.[39] Bullinger's *Decade* with its dedication to her father arrived in the spring of 1551, by which time Dorset had gone north on his brief foray as lord warden of the Scottish Marches.[40] Bullinger, however, had asked for the book to be presented as soon as possible, so Ulm was able to justify a journey north to see Scotland under the excuse of presenting a 'long and anxiously expected' book.[41] The *Decade* made a very satisfactory impact on the assembled company at Berwick, and 'every night when we were employed on the Scottish borders' Grey insisted on having large sections of the *Decade* read and explained to him.[42] Ulm found the common people of Scotland 'exceedingly well disposed' to reform but 'in the chiefs of that nation one can see little else than cruelty and ignorance, for they resist and oppose the truth in every possible way'.[43] In late May he was back, stopping off at Bradgate 'where I have been spending these last two days very agreeably with Jane, my lord's daughter, and those excellent and holy persons [John] Aylmer and [James] Haddon'.[44] Dorset, he explained, had been unable to respond in person to Bullinger's gift, being 'entirely occupied by very important business of the king's majesty and by public affairs', but sent his apologies by Ulm and by Jane. No doubt it was on this occasion that Ulm presented Jane with her copy of the *Decade*. Bullinger also seems to have sent a copy of his *Treatise on Christian Perfection*, very probably an occasion for the 'most weighty and eloquent epistle' which she later

acknowledged. The letter which Ulm sent to accompany the acknowl-
edgement is eloquent in praise of Jane.

> [Y]ou will easily perceive the veneration and esteem which the marquis's
> daughter entertains towards you from the very learned letter which she has
> written to you. For my own part I do not think there ever lived any one more
> deserving of respect than this young lady, if you regard her family; more
> learned if you consider her age; or more happy, if you consider both. A report
> has prevailed and has begun to be talked of by persons of consequence, that
> this most noble virgin is to be betrothed and given in marriage to the king's
> majesty. Oh, if that event should take place, how happy would be the union
> and how beneficial to the church. But the supremely great and good God
> will preside in this matter.[45]

What is difficult to evaluate, after more than four centuries, is how good
a scholar Jane really was. Three of her Latin letters survive at Zurich and
any thirteen-year-old today would be challenged to produce, for instance,
the seven or eight hundred words of elegant prose which Jane sent to
Bullinger in the spring of 1551.[46] But since classics in her day was the
jewel in education, we can expect standards to have been higher, and there
is also the unknown extent to which she was helped or at least vetted by
her tutor. Equally we may wish to discount the widespread flattery of Jane
such as John Parkhurst's widely copied epigrams: 'None has ever sung
better or speaks Greek more attractively or talks more eloquently in Latin';
'Are you surprised that Jane is fluent in the Greek tongue? From the
moment she was born she was "Greek"' – a pun on 'Grey' and 'Greek'
(*Graia*).[47] Similarly we may want to suspect self-interest in the praise from
Aylmer her tutor and John of Ulm her father's pensioner.[48] On the other
hand both knew Jane well and her gift to her father at New Year 1551 was
a translation into Greek from the translation which Ulm had made for her
of Bullinger's German treatise on marriage, or rather 'a good part' of one,
as she had had his manuscript only since the summer.[49] There is judicious
praise too from those who ought to have known. Six months after he had
met Jane in August 1550, Ascham had told his friend, the famous Strasbourg educator Johann Sturm, that he would bracket her with Mildred,
the wife of William Cecil, as joint leaders of the country's prominent
female scholars. 'She speaks and writes in Greek so that you would scarcely
believe me if I gave you a true account.'[50] Significantly he did not include
his protégée Princess Elizabeth, and if Jane was better than the future
queen who could speak Latin at length and extempore, that is a very
positive indicator. Lady Cecil clearly agreed for in 1552, if not before,

she presented Jane with a Greek text of the discourses of Basil the Great, 'an author most suitable for you, who are of noblest origin, illustrious for learning and piety'.[51] Jane was also being seen abroad as an up-and-coming patron. Ulm encouraged Bullinger to send her a copy of his next theological work: 'besides other things you will elicit a letter from her, and that a very learned one'.[52] Roger Ascham wrote to Sturm urging him to dedicate

> something to that most excellent maiden, Jane Grey, who I know has always been most devoted to you and yours, whose mind is more cultivated in the teaching of Plato and the eloquence of Demosthenes than distinguished by mere fortune; ... To what purpose do I mention this? Not in the least, my dear Sturm because I wish to trouble you in this or any other matter, but to show how long I have been devoted to you both, and how anxious I am now also for you to join together in mutual friendship.[53]

What we know about Jane Grey's linguistic ability applies principally to the languages which Renaissance scholars valued most highly, Greek, Latin and Hebrew. There can be no doubt that she knew French – it was an essential part of polite education – but we have no particulars about her being taught it. If she was like her cousin Edward, she started the language when she was about nine.[54] His teacher was Jean Belmain, a French Calvinist exile who was well enough accepted in English reformed circles to have married John Cheke's niece. He also taught Henry Hastings who would marry Guildford Dudley's sister, and he helped Princess Elizabeth with the language.[55] Given those connections he very possibly taught Jane too. Michelangelo Florio, who taught Italian to Jane, was a Franciscan friar who had embraced Protestantism and been imprisoned by the inquisition for preaching in Naples, Padua and Venice. He managed to escape and reach London where he served as the first pastor of the Italian congregation which met in the church of Austin Friars.[56] Jane became a pupil after Florio had parted with the church under a cloud and, encouraged by William Cecil, had switched to teaching Italian. Another of his pupils was Henry Herbert, the son of the earl of Pembroke who would marry Jane's sister Katherine, and Florio dedicated to each of them a copy of his Italian grammar, *Regole de la lingua thoscana*. The *Regole* shows that Florio's teaching concentrated on fidelity to 'the "living" early modern Italian vernacular', but Jane and Henry Herbert were obviously chosen as dedicatees because they were his most prestigious pupils, not because of whatever progress they actually made in the language in the short time between Florio leaving the church in 1551 and the crisis of June 1553.[57]

Both presentation copies of the grammar have survived. Herbert's is at Cambridge and Jane's is in the British Library, still in the original binding, saluting Jane as 'illustrious and learned lady' and praising 'the indulgence, kindness and courtesy' of her father.[58] [plate 25]

The most remarkable tribute to Jane's linguistic skill is found in the elegy written by Sir Thomas Chaloner. He asserted that

> She had joined Chaldean words to the language of the Arabs, with a skilful grasp of the idiom of the Hebrews, for to mention her on speaking in Greek or Latin would be of small account; other women speak these languages in civilized places. Likewise Gallic and Etruscan speech had added their number to this English lady. If you were to number her languages, this one lady spoke eight.[59]

This total was still being marvelled at in 1810.[60] Chaloner is certainly right that Jane knew Greek and Latin as well as English and Gallic (i.e. French), plus the Etruscan (i.e. Italian) she studied with Florio. The start of her Hebrew studies can be followed in the Bullinger letters. In May 1551 Ulm told the eminent Hebraist, Conrad Pellican, that 'the daughter of the most noble marquis of Dorset, a lady who is well versed both in Greek and Latin ... is now especially desirous of studying Hebrew'. She had already consulted Bullinger but if Pellican would take her on 'she will be more easily kept in her distinguished course of learning', and it would be even better if he dedicated to her the Latin translation of the Talmud which he was preparing.[61] But what of Chaloner's languages seven and eight? The temptation is to write off his assertion that 'she had joined Chaldean words to the language of the Arabs' as blatant hyperbole.[62] And where, for that matter, did Jane go for Hebrew texts? In fact one answer resolves both doubts – the king's library. There she could find a set of the six-volume *Complutensian Polyglot Bible* (1514–17) which printed parallel texts not only in Hebrew, Greek and Latin but in Chaldaic, along with Aramaic, which provides a very plausible explanation for Chaloner's 'Arabic'.[63]

How far Jane got with the more esoteric languages again we do not know, but after eighteen months under his guidance, Conrad Pellican reported that 'she was well prepared and making a steady progress' in Hebrew and that he had received 'a Latin letter written with admirable elegance and learning from the noble virgin, Jane Grey, of the illustrious house of Suffolk'.[64] Well before then her Latin correspondence with Bullinger had become frequent, written in the latest humanist style, replete with all the elaborate conceits of rhetoric and appropriate quotations in Greek and Hebrew.

No better fortune can await me than to be thought worthy of the correspondence and the most wholesome admonitions of men so renowned,
whose virtues cannot be sufficiently eulogised; and to experience the same
happiness as was enjoyed by Besilla, Paula and Eustochium, to whom, as is
recorded, Saint Jerome imparted instruction, and brought them by his
discourses to the knowledge of divine truths; or to the happiness of that
venerable matron, to whom St. John addressed an exhortatory and evangelical epistle; or that, lastly, of the mother of Severus, who profited by the
counsels of Origen, and was obedient to his precepts.[65] [plate 24]

And this was a girl not yet fourteen. Bullinger's letters to the duke seem
not to have been answered in person. On one occasion Aylmer was his
amanuensis, on others his daughter replied for him.[66] In February 1552,
despite recovering from 'a severe and dangerous illness' she seems to have
been busy on something to dedicate to Bullinger, very probably the
translation from Greek into Latin of a work by one of the early fathers,
certainly 'some extraordinary production, which will very soon be brought
to light'.[67] By then Jane felt that she was on less formal terms with the
Zurich scholar and had sent a pair of gloves for Bullinger's wife – a very
fashionable memento. She also wanted to send a gold ring, but that had
not been forthcoming.[68] Despite her youth, Jane Grey really had been
accepted as a recruit to the fellowship of European reformist scholars. 'It is
incredible how far she has advanced already and to what perfection she will
advance in a few years.'[69]

7

A Godly Upbringing

THE England Jane Grey was brought up in was a country in turmoil – religious turmoil. In 1533 Henry VIII had rejected the authority of the pope and made himself head of the church in England, so breaking a thousand-year link with the rest of Western Christianity. Then material and institutional change took over and by the end of his reign monasteries, shrines and pilgrimages were no more and the massive industry of praying for the dead was in terminal decline. There had been doctrinal and liturgical reform too – most significantly licensing an English Bible and having it placed in each parish church. As an inscription in Whitehall palace proclaimed:

> the presumptuousness of popes has yielded to unerring virtue and with Henry VIII bearing the sceptre in his hand, religion has been restored, and with him on the throne the truths of God have begun to be held in due reverence.[1]

'Religion restored' could, however, mean different things to different people. On the continent the urge to recover a more personal religion had led to an anarchy of ideas, ranging from those who wanted reform within the existing church to reformers like Luther who held that the new wine of faith could not be contained in the rigid bottle of tradition, and beyond him to radicals who rejected the whole idea of ecclesiastical structures. However, by assuming the headship of the church of England, Henry had seized control of reform and allowed only what agreed with his idiosyncratic understanding of Christianity. Thus he had fatally weakened one central pillar of the late medieval church – praying for the souls of the dead in purgatory – while at the same time adamantly defending that other pillar, transubstantiation – the miracle in the mass, by which bread and wine, on being consecrated, became physically the body and blood of Christ (though retaining their outward appearance). Such an individual mix could not be sustained when a nine-year-old boy succeeded as head of the church. Not only could England no longer be insulated from what was happening abroad, the leaders of the council which Henry had appointed to run the country during his son's minority were reform-minded, a price which the old king evidently saw as worth paying in order to prevent a papal restoration. The outcome was major doctrinal change, especially in the successive Prayer Books of 1549 and 1552, and official English religion lined up with Protestant reform on the continent. Now, instead of teaching transubstantiation, the English church taught that the significance of the consecrated bread and wine was spiritual.

Through all this Jane Grey was growing up, but although she lived half her life under the rule of Henry VIII there is no evidence that she ever learned anything but a reformed Christianity. How that came about it is difficult to say. Denying the truth of transubstantiation was a capital offence – Anne Askew and three others were burned at the stake in July 1546 – and that remained the law until the end of the first year of the next reign.[2] But since a similar problem arises in accounting for Edward VI's stoutly evangelical views, we can only assume that within the immediate royal family Henry had been willing to turn a blind eye to tutors engaged as experts in humanism, the latest intellectual fashion, even though they might be incubating dangerous reformist ideas. Also the tutors were almost certainly circumspect, and it can be as effective to ignore disputed truths as to attack them. The king may also have been less concerned because the reformed teaching which Jane and Edward were given was no longer the teaching of Martin Luther, whom he abhorred. Religious reform had by the middle decades of the century become fragmented, and in the 1540s and 1550s reformers in England had much their closest links with the reformed Christians of the Rhineland and Switzerland.

One early religious influence which we can document is the eighteen months in 1547 and 1548 which Jane spent with Katherine Parr, Henry VIII's widow.[3] She had long been of the evangelical persuasion, stressing above all the importance of the Bible. Thus she translated the Latin of John Fisher's *Psalms or Prayers taken out of Holy Scripture*, which was published anonymously in 1544 and then included in the *King's Primer* (1545) alongside Cranmer's *Litany*. In that year *Prayers or Meditations* appeared under Katherine's own name, part paraphrasing Thomas à Kempis and part original. She promoted the major venture to produce English *Paraphrases upon the New Testament* (1548), based on the Latin of

Erasmus, and was probably personally responsible for paraphrasing the
Gospel of St Matthew and possibly parts of *The Acts.* Katherine's increasing
commitment to reform got her into considerable trouble in the last
months of Henry VIII's life when the king's irritability boiled over as he
found himself bested by her in theological argument, and he would not
have approved of *The Lamentation of a Sinner*, published in November
1547, in which she moved from the promotion of scripture to what has
been described as 'a markedly Lutheran work with Calvinist flourishes'.[4]
In Katherine's household Jane would have attended the daily prayers held
morning and evening – unlike, perhaps, Thomas Seymour, whom Latimer
claimed 'gets him[self] out of the way like a mole digging in the earth'.[5]
The services were undoubtedly in English and fully reformist in tone – as
Katherine's burial service at Sudeley would be.[6] Among the residents in
the queen dowager's household were her chaplain, John Parkhurst, a
friend of John Aylmer whose epigrams we have met. Also a close friend
of Aylmer was Katherine Parr's almoner, Miles Coverdale, who would
later publish some of Jane's writings. Another reformer she would
have met there was Nicholas Throckmorton, who would be one of her
supporters.[7]

The death of Katherine Parr removed Jane from this circle of reformers,
but from that point it is possible to follow her subsequent religious upbringing, thanks to the correspondence of Henry Bullinger in Switzerland.
On the evidence of letters written to him from England, the Bradgate
household clearly took over as the principal aristocratic nursery of reform
in England. The humanists whom we have seen Jane's father patronizing
can just as properly be categorized as religious reformers; indeed they
would have made no such distinction.[8] At Convocation in October 1553,
James Haddon took a major part in the scholarly defence of reform against
resurgent Catholicism.[9] John Willock, the close ally of John Knox in the
Scottish Reformation, had a major role in preparing the first Presbyterian
Book of Discipline and the *Confession of Faith*.[10] The layman Ralph Skinner
opposed Mary's religious legislation in three of her five parliaments, was
ordained at Elizabeth's accession and then appointed dean of Durham.[11]
As for John Aylmer, he did not take the Hebrew post at Jena but returned
to publish his infamous and only work, *An Harborowe for faithfull and
trewe subjects* (1559) – infamous because what purported to be a counter
to John Knox's *First Blast of the Trumpet against the Monstrous Regiment
of Women* (1558) defended Elizabeth's right to rule so half-heartedly that
it took Aylmer years to recover her favour. Subsequently he did become
her third and longest-serving bishop of London and for a number of years

effectively substitute archbishop of Canterbury, roles in which he exhibited none of the emollient virtues Jane had so much admired.[12] Thomas Harding was, as we have seen, a turncoat. Apparently a committed Edwardian reformer, on Mary's accession he abandoned his beliefs – to Jane Grey's horror and disgust – and in Elizabeth's reign emerge as the principal Catholic protagonist in 'the Great Controversy' with John Jewel, the Anglican bishop of Salisbury, a clash of erudition which contemporaries described as a meeting of 'two thundering and lightning orators in divinity'.[13]

John of Ulm was as much impressed with Henry Grey the reformer as with Henry Grey the patron of scholars. The marquis, he wrote, 'has exerted himself up to the present with the greatest zeal and labour courageously to propagate the gospel of Christ. He is the thunderbolt and terror of the papists, that is a fierce and terrible adversary. He spoke most nobly in defence of the eucharist in the last parliament.'[14] For Ulm to claim that Jane's father was 'a thunderbolt and terror of the papists' is in marked contrast to his political profile, but he was undoubtedly prominent in the national religious debate. Lawrence Humphrey, Elizabeth's dean of Winchester, saw the king, Cranmer and Grey as a Protestant triumvirate.[15] The parliament of November 1548–February 1549 witnessed a dour struggle to force through a reformed English Prayer Book in place of the traditional Catholic liturgy. During the session which approved this replacement, Grey attended the Lords far more regularly than any other senior lay reformer. He was present at 92% of the sessions, whereas Warwick recorded 82% and the protector Somerset only 66%.[16] Apart from an evident personal commitment, a probable reason for this high profile is the hint in Ulm that he was an eloquent speaker. Indeed, one of the reasons Thomas Seymour had tried to attach Dorset to his cause was that he was on the lookout for effective parliamentary performers.[17] No details are known of the speech which Ulm says Dorset made 'in defence of the eucharist'. The imperial ambassador stated that Grey had 'publicly declared in parliament' that he was a sacramentarian, that is someone who denied the miracle of transubstantiation, but the occasion was probably the wider four-day national debate organized in the House of Lords in December 1549; the young king noted it as 'a notable disputation of the sacrament'.[18] Ulm's praise of Dorset's antipapal stance may also indicate that he knew of the support Grey had been in securing control of the council for John Dudley and his supporters, a struggle which was widely interpreted in religious terms. The reform-minded Richard Scudamore wrote that the appointment of the marquis to the council put 'all honest hearts in good comfort for the good hope that they have of the perseverance of God's word'.[19] From the opposite camp came the lament of the imperial ambassador that

> no mention has yet been made of restoring religion and those who desired to see the step taken have been displeased to see that the marquis of Dorset and the bishop of Ely, both of them entirely won over to the new sect, have recently been admitted to the Council which may well have been done by the earl of Warwick in order to strengthen his party.[20]

Dorset figures very rarely in accounts of the Edwardian reformation. At most he appears to support the claim that 'the chief point of noble virtue in Protestant eyes was the nobility's support of the reformation'.[21] But he was far more than that. As a member of the privy council, Dorset continued to serve religious reform. In the autumn of 1550 he and Archbishop Cranmer actively canvassed a peaceful solution of the problem posed when the future martyr, John Hooper, refused to wear the prescribed clerical vestments for his ordination as bishop of Gloucester.[22] Grey served as the senior layman on the commission to reform ordination and later to regulate church benefices and he led on the successful bill to suppress trade in church offices. Yet despite this activity in parliament and on the council, it can be argued that Dorset's priority was in advancing reform on the ground.[23] When, in 1550, John Bankes dedicated to Grey his translation of *A Treatise against the Folishnesse of Men in Differinge the Reformation of their Living* by Erasmus's pupil Johannes Rivius, he singled out 'the order taken in your lordship's house, concerning the true worshipping and due serving of God' and noted that men 'have conceived a singular opinion of the zeal of your lordship hath to set forth the pure word of God and to root out false and feigned superstition'.[24] This also included advancing the cause of reform at parish level by the appointments he made to parish livings in his gift, particularly in the Midlands.[25] One such appointee was Henry Bull, an Oxford theologian who became notorious when mass was restored at Magdalen College for snatching the censer from the hands of the officiating priest – which got him expelled.[26] He survived Mary's persecution, became a prominent author and played a major part in preserving the writings of the martyrs. Another of Dorset's presentees was John Webbe, and he was burned at the stake.[27] A second future martyr well known at Bradgate was Robert Glover of Coventry, and when Mary came to the throne Bradgate provided a refuge for the prominent reformer Thomas Lever before he escaped to Zurich.[28]

That Leicestershire was a Protestant heartland under Elizabeth was seen as a legacy of the marquis.[29]

A reformer whom Jane Grey herself acknowledged as an early spiritual mentor was Martin Bucer of Strasbourg (1491–1551). An ecclesiastical statesman and organizer of importance, the leading theological mediator of the day, Bucer had long been among Cranmer's scholarly correspondents, and when political developments forced him to leave Strasbourg in 1549 he accepted the archbishop's invitation and was appointed to the regius chair of divinity in the university of Cambridge. How quickly he came to know the Greys is not clear but a possible link was via Grey's chaplain, James Haddon, whose brother William was a close colleague of Bucer.[30] Be this as it may, in the eighteen months before his death, Jane Grey came to depend on this leading European Christian. Soon after, she wrote of being

> bereaved of the pious Bucer, that most learned man and holy father, who unweariedly did not cease, day and night, and to the utmost of his ability, to supply me with all the necessary instructions and directions for my conduct in life; and who by his excellent advice promoted and encouraged my progress and advancement in all virtue, godliness and learning.[31]

The language has to be taken with the pinch of salt appropriate to all Renaissance rhetoric, but even so this looks a good deal more than receiving an occasional letter of advice. It is hard to believe that the two did not meet on occasions when the Grey family was in London and Bucer was staying with Cranmer at Lambeth.[32] The reformer's influence can certainly be traced in the pieces Jane wrote in the Tower, which echo his two emphases on the doctrine of election and the abomination of the Roman Catholic mass.[33] Jane's Italian teacher Florio was, of course, a further link with reform on the continent, though in a lower league than Bucer. Nevertheless, and despite teaching being his principal task, it is clear that he did have a religious input.[34] Thus the example he may have used in teaching Jane the relationship between the subjunctive and the conditional moods was: 'If I were to obey the Pope, I would be obeying the Anti-Christ.' Contrariety was illustrated by the sentence 'The Pope claims to be the Vicar of Christ, but contrarily the Holy Spirit shows us that he is Anti-Christ.' He also fed Jane Catholic atrocity stories:

> One day when I was recounting to her the outrages, the insults, the torments which I had endured for the space of 27 months in Rome under Paul and

Julius III for having there and in Naples, Padua and Venice preached Christ
without disguise, I myself saw her weep with such deeply felt compassion
that it could well be seen how much she had true religion at heart. And
raising her eyes to heaven she said 'Oh God, if I displease thee not with this
my petition, do not suffer it any longer that the world should abuse thy
servants thus.'[35]

Does all this mean that Jane Grey grew up in an atmosphere of unre-
lieved piety? We have seen how her tutors were at times concerned for her,
and it is also clear that the chaplains were less than entirely successful in
imposing 24/7 godliness on the Grey household. Our knowledge of this
comes, again, from the Bullinger letters. This time the correspondent was
the chaplain, James Haddon. In the first one extant, Haddon urges the
case of Jane:

> You can confer no greater obligation upon his grace [the duke] than by
> continuing (as you have done once already) to impart godly instruction to
> his daughter. For already she is so brought up that there is great hope of her
> advancement in godliness, yet your exhortations afford her encouragement
> and at the same time have their due weight with her either as proceeding
> from a stranger, or from so eminent a person as yourself.[36]

Some months later he wrote again, this time to seek Bullinger's views on a
pastoral problem. In what he termed 'the houses of our men of rank' the
amusements included not only the 'moderate and godly' but also 'such as
occasion sloth and beget idleness and ungodliness'. What he had in mind
were games of cards and dice, played for money. The duke had already
banned his servants from gambling. However, 'He himself and his most
honourable lady with their friends, not only claim permission to play in
their private apartment, but also to play for money.' The argument put
forward was

> that game loses all its interest without a stake, so that its sleepy character, as it
> were, must be awakened; that no one feels any excitement unless there is a
> stake laid down; that in many other things there are superfluous and unne-
> cessary expenses, as in diet and clothes &c. Wherefore in this respect also, we
> must yield somewhat to fashion, and not act with so much strictness or bring
> every thing to the test of conscience and of duty, since no man can live
> entirely without faults of some kind.

Limited stakes were, therefore, quite permissible.[37]

Haddon then set out at very great length the arguments he had used and on more than one occasion 'in private or in conversation with a few'. But he admitted that he had 'publicly denounce[d] it from the pulpit last Christmas' with the (understandable) consequence that Grey and his wife decided that he was aiming at them and took it 'in bad part'. Since then he had 'put up with and allow[ed] the practice' but his employers, having decided that he was unreasonably strict on the gambling issue, had begun to say of other issues, 'in this or that point Haddon cannot agree with us, though they are just as much matters of indifference as the play which hardly anyone finds fault with but himself.' Clearly his authority was at stake. Did Bullinger think he was right? When the reply came Haddon found, no doubt to his relief and satisfaction, that the great man did agree with him and, moreover, had supplied a statement of 'good practice' – a description of 'the order' in place at Zurich.[38] But, perhaps to the duke's relief, the chaplain was also about to leave his post in the Grey household to take up an appointment as dean of Exeter. The one tantalizing question is where Jane Grey stood in this. Since she found fault with the enthusiasm of her parents for hunting, is it hard to guess? And what of her father's licensed theatricals and tamed bear?[39]

Mary Tudor

8

FATHER AND DAUGHTER

IN the summer of 1553 Jane Grey was just sixteen years of age. Her cousin Mary was past thirty-seven, but the twenty years between them might as well have been fifty. Religion was the dominant factor in the life of each, but Mary had been reared in the richness of late medieval Catholicism while Jane had known nothing but reform. Her contacts were with reformist chaplains and tutors at home, and Protestant leaders abroad. Mary had seen her spiritual mentors executed one after another and her ties with the Western Church stigmatized as treason. A story, possibly apocryphal, points the contrast. In one of the visits which, as we have seen, Jane's mother made to Mary, Jane was passing through the chapel with Anne Wharton, one of Mary's ladies. Over the altar was the reserved sacrament, the consecrated wafer which was Christ's body, and Anne dropped a devout curtsey. 'Why do you so?' asked Jane. 'Is the Lady Mary in the chapel?' 'No, Madam,' came the answer, 'I make my curtsy to him that made us all'. 'Why?', responded Jane, 'How can he be there that made us all, and the baker made him?'[1] The modern reader is left to decide whether Jane spoke innocently or was being disingenuous or, as Foxe clearly prefers, taking the opportunity to witness to the truth.

The cousin who challenged Jane Grey in the summer of 1553 was short, skinny, myopic – she could only read by holding the page close to her face – old for her age, wrinkled with anxiety and with a piercing voice which was loud and rough.[2] She loved finery and fabrics, had no dress sense and no sexual magnetism.[3] One of Prince Philip's courtiers wrote in 1554 that although his master was not marrying her for 'fleshly' reasons 'It will take a great God to drink this cup'.[4] Impressions varied from 'not at all beautiful', 'small and rather flabby than fat' to 'were not her age in decline, she might be called handsome'.[5] Her manner was that of a saint and something of a martyr.[6] Mary had not always been thus. When young she was thought to have 'beauty exceeding mediocrity'.[7] Educated for a brilliant future as the wife of a major European sovereign, Mary at fifteen was described as 'not very tall but has a pretty face and is well proportioned, with a very beautiful complexion'.[8] Even at the end of her reign a neutral observer could still call her 'a seemly woman and never to be loathed for ugliness, even at her present age'.[9] Throughout her life she inspired great affection among those close to her. At the height of rejection by her father, even Anne Boleyn's cousin, who was acting as her guardian, defended Mary by saying that even if 'she was the bastard daughter of a poor gentleman, her kindness, her modesty and her virtues called forth all respect and honour'.[10] Judged as a private person, Mary was probably the most attractive member of the Tudor family.

It is one of history's ironies that such a woman should have earned the name 'Bloody Mary'. None of the thousands who rallied to her support in July 1553 had any inkling that her five-year reign would arguably be the most inglorious in English history. Admittedly, in recent years some scholars have made strenuous efforts to rescue her reputation, stressing the good sense which justified many of her policies (even when they failed), noting her run of bad luck and her limited freedom of action (for neither of which was she responsible). The more extravagant allegations about incompetent government have been shown to be groundless. Her reign was not the total disaster which extreme Protestant propaganda portrayed and it at least ensured that the Tudor dynasty survived. Nevertheless the need for such special pleading tells its own tale. Making a bitterly unpopular marriage which dragged England into a disastrous foreign war, losing possession of Calais by negligence and instigating the only true religious pogrom in English history is a record hard to live down. The absence of popular mourning at her death in November 1558 said it all. Yet while a full rehabilitation is unrealistic, after five centuries the verdict should perhaps be mitigated by sympathy. In one of the ironies of history, Mary Tudor, like Jane Grey, was a victim of her family. True, she was not, as far as we know, physically abused but a messenger from her father went so far as to tell her that if she was his daughter 'he would beat her to death or strike her head against the wall until he made it as soft as a boiled apple'.[11]

Even Mary's birth at Greenwich on 18 February 1516 was not greeted with unmixed joy. Her parents had been married for nearly seven years and this was the first of several pregnancies to produce a child which survived more than a few weeks. Evidently, despite rumours, the Spanish princess Katherine of Aragon was able to produce a healthy child. But a girl? What the country and Henry had desperately wanted was a son. His own parents, in seven years of marriage and despite disappointments, had produced two sons and one daughter.[12] In a similar period, his grandfather Edward whom Henry so much resembled had fathered one boy and three girls, all healthy. On one hand, therefore, Henry treated Mary as any excited father would, carrying her about and extolling her good temper: 'By God, this girl never cries.'[13] On the other he had to pretend that she was an earnest of better things. 'The queen and I are both young, and if it is a girl this time, by God's grace the boys will follow.' [14] But by contemporary standards the queen was not young. Henry might be only twenty-five, but his wife Katherine was thirty-one, and her best chances of child-bearing were receding rapidly. Henry's sexual preference was for mature women, but that was not the best route to parenthood.[15] As it was, although Katherine did conceive two years later, that was for the last time; again the baby was a daughter, and this time did not survive. Like it or not, Mary was Henry's sole legitimate offspring.

In a century when gender equality is taken for granted, it is hard to imagine the unease which the prospect of a woman ascending the throne caused in Tudor England, and, not least, in Henry personally. It was only thirty years since his father had seized the crown, and continued stability demanded a strong succession. Yet for a woman to rule would be against all precedent. Four hundred years before, Henry I's daughter Matilda had transmitted the claim to the crown to her son, but despite a lengthy armed struggle had never worn it herself. More recently Henry's grandmother, the Lady Margaret Beaufort, had openly devoted her life to promoting first his father and then Henry himself to the English throne, ignoring the fact that if their claim was legitimate, her own title had priority. Foreigners – including Queen Katherine and her Habsburg nephew the emperor Charles V – found this suspicion of female inheritance hard to understand. A crown was a piece of property; and property passed by accidents of birth. But that was precisely the problem. Property went in the male line so that when a female ruler married, her dominions simply passed to her husband, just as any other piece of real estate. Habsburgs, of course, would think that way. The family's vast empire had been built over the previous seventy years on the principle 'Let others fight, you, oh happy Austria marry'. In consequence, as well as being Holy Roman Emperor, Charles V ruled directly not only his ancestral Austrian lands but the formerly separate kingdoms of Aragon and Castile, plus the dynastic complex which the dukes of Burgundy had built up in the rich Low Countries. In a similar way dynastic marriage had enabled France to absorb Brittany, and within twenty years Scotland would be facing a similar fate. Nobody, however, could absorb France. Its so-called Salic Law provided that the nearest male heir would always succeed on the death of the king. The recently crowned Francis I, Henry VIII's rival, would otherwise not have inherited, and the kingdom of France might have been added to the possessions of a non-French dynasty. England had nothing equivalent, but the continuous history of inheritance in the male line 'time without mind' certainly created a parallel expectation on this side of the Channel.[16] Indeed, after Mary eventually reached the English throne, she would find it necessary to silence the 'error and folly' of 'malicious and ignorant persons' by securing a statute declaring that 'the kingly or regal office of the realm and all dignities ... being invested either in male or female are and be and ought to be taken the one as in the other'.[17] And that was not the end of the risks. A female sovereign was expected to marry and so bring in a new king to rule for her – in Mary's case, the emperor's heir Philip. Hence her reign became the reign of Philip and Mary. Moreover, if Mary had had a child by him, it would not only have inherited England but the Low Countries and in certain circumstances Spain also. Indeed, the interest of Philip and his father was precisely to get their hands on England; as the latter wrote, 'I trust [the marriage] will prove a factor of weight in our endeavours to serve God and guard and increase our dominions'.[18]

The baby girl, of course, had no awareness that she was a mixed blessing. She was given her own well-funded household almost immediately and by the time she was four was under the charge of her godmother, Margaret Pole, countess of Salisbury, Edward IV's niece. However, it seems that in the early days she may have been more often with her parents than the average royal princess. On one Sunday when she was two, the Venetian ambassador was presented to her and solemnly kissed her hand. But Mary caught sight of the king's chaplain and choir master and called out 'Priest, Priest' until he came over to play for her while her father picked her up so she could watch.[19] It also seems that her mother taught her to read and write.[20] Outside the family circle her importance was that of every royal princess, as a diplomatic asset and ultimately a diplomatic bride. At two-and-a-half Mary was betrothed to the dauphin of France who was two years younger. When she was six, that engagement was broken in favour of her cousin the 22-year-old Charles V. He visited England in 1522 and actually met Mary who danced for him. However, at the same time abortive discussions were opened for an alternative match with her cousin the king of Scots. When in 1526 Charles jilted Mary to marry a Portuguese princess, Henry's response was to dangle his daughter before Francis I, a man only two years younger than he was himself. The result was the Treaty of Amiens of April 1527 but with Francis's second son, Henry, as a possible (and more realistic) alternative to his father.

Mary was then eleven, only a year below the minimum age for marriage, and her education went on apace. She was taught to write in the new italic style and careful attention was given to courtly behaviour and accomplishments. Her father's personal contribution was to encourage her musical talents – spinet and lute – and she became good enough to teach her maids of honour, though Mary appears to have let her own playing slip somewhat in later life.[21] From an early age, despite Henry's masculine assumptions and those of the nation, Katherine of Aragon saw Mary as potentially queen of England. Her own mother, Queen Isabella of Castile, had made sure that she and her sisters were given a sound humanist education – her Habsburg cousins too had a record of producing competent female rulers – and Katherine now ensured the same for her daughter. She commissioned educational books for women and more specific guidance for the daughter she believed was Henry VIII's heir.[22] One scholar she commissioned was the Spanish educationalist Juan Luis Vives who in 1523 produced *De Institutione Foeminae Christianae* [*The Instruction of a Christian Woman*], and followed that up with more specific advice for Mary, *De Ratione Studii Puerilis* [*On the Education of Children*]. This recommended Thomas More's *Utopia*, Erasmus's *Institutio Christiani Principis* [*Handbook for Christian Princes*], his most important work on government which he wrote for her cousin the future Charles V, and his handbook on practical Christian living, the *Enchiridion Militis Christiani* [*The Weapon of the Christian Soldier*] along with a number of Latin authors. At the age of twelve Mary 'could not only perfectly read, write and construe Latin, but furthermore translate any hard thing of the Latin into our English tongue'.[23] Erasmus commented when she was some months older that 'We have in the Queen of England a woman distinguished by her learning, whose daughter Mary composes fine Latin epistles'.[24] True, she was not a bluestocking like Jane and seems not to have tackled Greek, but Katherine Parr did recruit her to translate Erasmus's Latin paraphrase of the Gospel of John. In the event ill health meant that this had to be finished by her chaplain, but Mary's contribution drew considerable praise.[25] Her modern languages were also notable: fluent French and Spanish and the ability to understand Italian, though not speak it. However, unlike Jane, she did not prefer books to people, and her greatest love was dancing. In May 1546 the nine-year-old Prince Edward wrote to his stepmother asking her to preserve 'my dear sister

Mary from all the wiles and enchantments of the evil one, and beseech her to attend no longer to foreign dances and merriments, which do not become a most Christian princess'.[26]

Love of dancing notwithstanding, the dominant theme of Mary's training was the service of God. Humanism in northern Europe was anything but irreligious – witness Thomas More – but Katherine of Aragon brought Mary up in the fervent Catholicism she had herself imbibed in Spain from her mother Isabella. It was Isabella who, with her husband Ferdinand, secured permission in 1478 to establish a state-controlled Inquisition, principally to deal with Jewish converts to Christianity who had relapsed. Two years later, with Isabella much in evidence, the crusade against the Moslem emirates in southern Spain was triumphantly revived and Granada captured (when Katherine was six). Weeks later Isabella achieved a long-cherished ambition and expelled all practising Jews from Spain. Then the Moslems of southern Spain were pressed to convert and, six months after the sixteen-year-old Katherine sailed for England, her parents expelled all adult Moors who refused baptism. During these formative years Katherine must also have known her mother's confessor and ally, Cardinal Ximénes, whose substantial efforts at church reform married humanism and rigid orthodoxy. Nor is there much to suggest that England softened this Hispanic Catholicism. Richard Fetherstone, the only one of Mary's teachers we know of, was warmly commended by the queen and would die a martyr for tradition.

Preparing Mary to serve God and to govern might satisfy Katherine but not Henry. By the mid-1520s it was clear that he had no hope for a son by her – indeed he gave up marital relations. However, he did have a bastard son, and in 1525 Henry Fitzroy was brought out of obscurity and created earl of Nottingham and duke of Richmond, the title which Henry VII had enjoyed. The implication infuriated Katherine and some of her servants were dismissed as a warning. However, in the following year when Richmond was sent north as the king's nominal lieutenant, Mary was sent to Ludlow to head the Council of the Marches of Wales, a role which under Henry VII had been fulfilled by the prince of Wales. Henry VIII did not go so far as to create her princess of Wales but the move seemed to suggest that he wanted to keep her in play as well as his son. If so that intention did not last. The dangers of being succeeded by a bastard or a woman were simply too great. By the spring of 1527 Henry had decided to have his marriage with Katherine annulled and to seek a new wife who would give him a son. Of itself that would not have been unusual. Annulments for reasons of state raised few eyebrows; Henry would only be following the example of other contemporary rulers who exploited loopholes in canon law when faced with succession problems. Nor would Mary have been threatened. According to the law of the church, the offspring of a marriage entered in good faith [*bona fide*] remained legitimate, even if its validity was subsequently impugned. Thus while the ending of her parents' marriage would undoubtedly have hurt Mary, if handled properly it would hardly have affected her status or her diplomatic value. But the route Henry chose was different. Katherine had previously been married to his brother, Arthur Prince of Wales, and Henry claimed that because of this his subsequent marriage to the widow was not just invalid but an affront to God; it had not been an error in canon law which the pope could put right; it had been contrary to immutable divine law as laid down in scripture. And the proof that it had been sinful was that none of his sons had lived, and he believed he had a Bible text which threatened exactly that. At this Katherine – who might have responded positively to quiet reason – became totally intransigent. Live in fornication for twenty years? Her babies die because of her sin? Mary a bastard?

As well as the personal affront, Henry's determination to challenge the head of Western Christendom went directly against Mary's devout upbringing and her mother's influence. And if that was not offence enough to Mary, a second decision made by Henry in the summer of 1527 was an even more intimate blow. To replace Katherine, he chose Anne Boleyn. That had not been his original intention. Anne was exciting but not immediate queen material and for more than a year he had sought her as his mistress. In the summer of 1527 she refused him clearly and finally, and, with his emotions deeply engaged, Henry saw a way to resolve both of his needs. Anne Boleyn, not a foreign princess, was the wife to make him happy and give him a son; he would marry for love. We do not know when it was Mary discovered her father's intention, but its impact was all too predictable. Not only was her father determined to reject her mother, but also to demean the established practice of princes by wedding beneath him. Katherine and Mary might well have tolerated Anne as his mistress – the queen had, as far as is known, already tolerated an earlier affair with Anne's sister – but if Henry did succeed in marrying Anne, the daughter of a newly ennobled courtier and sister of an ex-mistress would become Mary's stepmother.

How long it took for parental difficulties to affect Mary is difficult to tell. Her mother continued to reside at court in a curious *ménage à trois* and Mary spent a month with her in March 1531. Almost immediately, however, the princess fell ill with some menstrual problem so it is not improbable that the implications of what was going on had hit her at last. In June the king paid her a visit, but in July he split with his first wife. Henry did allow mother and daughter to stay together for some weeks, but the two were then separated for good. Eighteen months later Henry married his new wife and proceeded to assert that he, not the pope, was head of the church in England, and in May 1533 the English Church declared that his union with Katherine of Aragon was void. This reduced her to the status of dowager princess of Wales and left Mary in limbo waiting for the result of Anne's pregnancy. In September Princess Elizabeth was born and declared to be the king's heir. Mary's household was reduced, her servants instructed now to wear the king's livery, not her own, and she was no longer to be addressed as 'Princess'. When Mary insisted on her title and status, Henry cut her off from her friends by dissolving her separate establishment and sending her to live in the household set up for the infant Elizabeth. Mary responded with intransigence made worse by her offensive treatment of Anne Boleyn's attempts to make peace. On one occasion Queen Anne mistook Mary's bow to the altar as a personal courtesy and sent a message that 'she desires that this may be an entrance of friendly correspondence which your grace shall find completely to be embraced on her part'. Mary declared that the queen could not possibly have sent the message because she was 'so far from the place'; the messenger should have said 'the Lady Anne Boleyn for I can acknowledge no other queen but my mother, nor esteem them my friends who are not hers'.[27] Pressure on Mary continued and in the autumn of 1534 she again collapsed. Even when her mother became terminally ill in November 1535 Mary was kept from her and Katherine's death on 7 January meant that she was now on her own.

Then, out of the darkness, the sky seemed to brighten. On May Day 1536 Anne Boleyn was suddenly rejected and in three weeks she was dead. Mary at once assumed that her sufferings were over and at the end of the month she wrote to Henry begging his forgiveness and promising to obey him in all things 'next to God'. But it was a false dawn. Henry had no intention of backing down. The reservation in Mary's letter showed that she was as intransigent as ever on the key points of the validity of her mother's marriage and the king's headship of the church. Henry responded with a document which left no doubt that he would only accept her if she gave way unequivocally on both issues, and at the same time legislation was prepared declaring both her and Elizabeth illegitimate. On 15 June Mary was faced with a blunt demand to accept the supremacy and the nullity of her mother's marriage and, in a stormy scene, refused. That was an act of treason. There was talk of condemning her and she found her sympathizers were being interrogated and arrested. After a week of agony, Mary broke, and wrote to her father surrendering unconditionally. Kind messages immediately came from Henry and his new wife, Jane Seymour, and early in July they visited her and stayed for two days. Mary had saved her friends and recovered her royal status, but at the expense of her integrity. She begged the imperial ambassador to secure absolution from the pope, but all she received from Rome was vague reassurance. Securing anything like a formal papal exoneration would have alienated Henry beyond all recovery. Instead Mary had to bury her conscience and meticulously endorse her father's position.

When her father decided to divorce her mother, Mary was eleven years old. When she finally admitted that she was illegitimate she was twenty, and those teenage years scarred her for life. They ruined her self-confidence. She had broken under pressure, accepted a lie, and dishonoured her mother and all Katherine had stood for and suffered for. Worst than everything, she had betrayed her God. Nor had her humiliation brought anything except worldly comfort and status. True, after her surrender, her father had asserted his right to nominate her to succeed, despite being a bastard, and had assured the French king of that, but his eyes were on his pregnant third wife, Jane Seymour, and from the birth of their son Edward in October 1537 he had little thought for anyone else. Although reinstated as a princess, Mary was not employed in government as she had been in the 1520s, even when in 1544 an act of parliament confirmed that she was illegitimate but nevertheless able to succeed if her brother died. She received none of the instruction which, as Isabella of Castile's granddaughter, she might have expected. Nor had she been found a husband, despite being used as a counter in diplomacy.[28] Instead she had had to watch the normal prospects for a princess steadily recede. In 1542 she was reported as being convinced that she would never be allowed to marry while Henry was alive, saying that 'she would be, while her father lived, only Lady Mary, the most unhappy lady in Christendom'.[29] When Henry died in January 1547, Mary was coming up to her thirty-first birthday; her mother had been married a month short of her sixteenth.

9

SISTER AND BROTHER

GIVEN the abuse she had suffered from her father, it is hardly surprising that Princess Mary frequently displayed a naivety in affairs and a chronic lack of self-confidence. Nor would it be surprising if some of the illnesses she suffered had a psychosomatic explanation. Even after her successful coup against Jane Grey, the Venetian ambassador could contrast her 'strong constitution' with the fact that she had suffered 'of late from headache and serious psychological stress'.[1] True, her father's final marriage to Katherine Parr in 1543 did bring a blessing. The new queen showed Mary kindness and affection and she spent several years in Katherine's household. Indeed she remained with her for about ten weeks after Henry's death until her father's bequest of a net income of £3,000 had come through and she was free to set up her own household in two former royal residences, Hunsdon in Hertfordshire and Newhall (Beaulieu) in Essex, and in the recently forfeited palace of Kenninghall in Norfolk, lately built by a duke of Norfolk to rival Hampton Court.[2] But what made that move urgent was Katherine's blossoming relationship with Thomas Seymour and it is not clear how close Mary was to the queen dowager subsequently. Seymour tried to enlist the support of the princess for the marriage and Mary's reply suggests that she felt it all too soon. She described the proposal as 'strange news' and suggested that 'if the remembrance of the King's majesty my father (whose soul God pardon) will not suffer her to grant your suit, I am nothing able to persuade her to forget the loss of him who is as yet very ripe in my own remembrance.'[3] In any case by the autumn of 1548 Katherine was dead and Mary was left looking exclusively to her mother's family. Katherine of Aragon had taught her to see herself as half a Habsburg and her cousin Charles V became her sheet anchor; even while her father was alive she had relied on his then ambassador, Eustace Chapuys. Mary's links with the emperor often show a pathetic need for someone else to make up her mind for her. One key example of this occurred in 1550. By late April in that year Mary had convinced herself that her only hope was to flee the country; as she said to the imperial ambassador: 'I am like a little ignorant girl, and I care neither for my goods nor for the world but only for God's service and my conscience.'[4] When, however, the imperial rescue party arrived in disguise and with a ship waiting, they found the princess in confusion over what she was to pack and insisting on delay, and she was able to contribute little more to the frantic discussions which ensued than 'What shall I do, what will become of me?' In the end Mary heeded the warning of her comptroller, Robert Rochester, that if she left England she would lose all chance of the succession. Two years later, at the end of May 1553, Mary was reported to be 'in great trouble and perplexity', and even in mid-June, by which time she must have had a pretty clear idea of the contents of Edward's 'deuise', she was reported to be 'in great perplexity' and desperate for advice from Charles V.[5]

There was, however, another side to Mary Tudor's character. When armoured by an absolute conviction about her duty to God, Mary possessed remarkable courage. In the isolation of house arrest in 1536, it was only fear of what the king would do to her friends and the corrosive worldly wisdom of her advisers which forced her to yield to psychological abuse and admit she was a bastard. When Edward's advisers began to introduce religious reform, Mary, a decade older and with her less intimidating brother on the throne, refused to yield an inch to the demand that she abandon the old ways. She would not violate her conscience a second time. The first clash came within nine months of her father's death when the country was nudged in an unmistakably reformed direction by the first set of religious injunctions issued in Edward's name. Mary wrote to the protector in protest, and although her letter is only known by his reply, its apparent thrust was that the headship of the church was personal to the king and so the council had no authority to make changes while the king was under age. One injunction she would have undoubtedly objected to was the prohibition of the rosary, and probably too the banning of parish processions and the substitution of the ringing of a bell before the sermon for the sanctus bell, traditionally rung in the mass at the moment of consecration.[6] When on Whitsunday 1549 a new reformed English liturgy became law, Mary held a magnificent Latin mass in her household chapel. The council called on her to conform and were roundly told that 'I have offended no law unless it be a late law of your own making for altering of matters of religion, which in my conscience is not worthy to have the name of a law'.[7] She had already alerted Charles V to the coming changes and he demanded that she be formally excused from the new require-ments. This was not conceded, but eventually she was allowed to have mass said in her private apartments for herself and not more than twenty ladies and gentlemen whose names had to be notified to the council.[8] This adamantine insistence on the veracity of traditional faith and the obser-vance of traditional liturgy was the more significant because Mary's cir-cumstances had altered following her father's death. She was now recognized as the next in line to the throne and the estates she received in fulfilment of Henry VIII's will had transformed her from the king's acknowledged but illegitimate daughter to an autonomous noblewoman. This independence she used quite consciously to endorse resistance to Protestant reform and set herself up as the acknowledged focus of Catholic resistance. Her personal exemption from the new services was flagrantly abused; persons with only a minimum connection to her court and rank outsiders were welcome, and mass was even celebrated in her absence. Mary, heir presumptive to the crown, was deliberately encouraging defi-ance of the law. No government could tolerate that, particularly one committed to further religious reform, and the privy council waged guer-rilla warfare with Mary for the remainder of the reign. In April 1550, now led by John Dudley, earl of Warwick, it resolved to end Mary's flagrant abuse of the private toleration she had been allowed. The princess protested – backed up by the imperial ambassador – and it was then that flight from England was planned. Nothing came of that except to increase council suspicion of Mary, and orders were issued to her chaplains to cease saying mass. Mary protested again and once more invoked the emperor's support. Taking drastic action against an heir presumptive supported by the might of the Habsburgs was a very serious step and the council allowed the temperature to drop.[9] But at the end of 1550 a new player joined the drama. Edward VI was now a precocious thirteen-year-old, deeply committed to reformed religion and by no means averse to impos-ing his Tudor will on a half-sister.[10]

Edward had questioned Mary earlier in the year over her insistence on hearing mass, but the emotional encounter had ended with each of them in tears and Mary left confident that 'my poor priests' were safe.[11] There-after she avoided coming to court for fear of being forced to endure the new service. By the end of the year, however, the king was finding his feet and on 2 December the council ordered Mary to cease obstructing the arrest of her chaplains. She responded in the usual way – her personal privilege covered them too – but the council now replied specifically denying that interpretation.[12] Correspondence continued into January and on the 24th the king wrote to his sister personally:

> The whole matter we perceive rest in this, that you being our next sister in whom above all other our subjects, nature should put the most estimation, of us would wittingly and purposely, not only break our laws your self, but also have others maintained to do the same. . . . In our state it shall miscontent us to permit you, so great a subject, not to keep our laws. Your nearness to us in blood, your greatness in estate and the condition of this time maketh your fault the greater.[13]

And in case Mary thought that the Council was using the king's name for its own purposes, Edward wrote the closing passages in his own hand:

> I will not say more and worse things because my duty would compel me to use harsher and angrier words. But this I will say with certain intention, that I will see my laws strictly obeyed and those that break them shall be watched and denounced.[14]

Inevitably the imperial ambassador appeared to remind the council of its earlier promise to allow Mary to use the liturgy as under Henry VIII 'in her house, for herself and her family', a wording as elastic as it was insulting to claim that this concession was to last 'till the King's Majesty that now is should come to years of more perfection'.[15] In March 1551 the princess was summoned to court and used the occasion for a public demonstration, riding into London behind fifty knights and gentlemen in velvet coats and chains of gold with eighty gentlemen and ladies at her back, 'every one having a pair of beads of black' – i.e. prohibited rosaries – 'to make', as Strype says, 'an open profession of their devotion for the mass'.[16] But facing Edward in person was a different matter. The ultimate test of sixteenth-century loyalty was the challenge to obey 'on your allegiance' and Mary had no doubt of the enormity of openly defying the king.

For many of the confrontations between Mary and the council we are dependent on the vehemently, even virulently partisan evidence of the imperial ambassador. But when Edward enters in person we have the account in his own journal. He tells how on Wednesday 18 March his sister appeared before him and the council and she was reminded

> how long I had suffered her mass in hope of reconciliation, and how now, being no hope, which I perceived by her letters, except I saw some short amendment, I could not bear it. She answered that her soul was God's, and

her faith she would not change, nor dissemble her opinion with contrary doings. It was said I constrained not her faith, but willed her not as [though she were] a king to rule but as a subject to obey. And that her example might breed too much inconvenience.

The debate clearly became heated. When Mary repeated her line that time would teach the king more, Edward replied 'that she might still have something to learn for no one was too old for that'. In the aftermath of the confrontation, each side seems to have concluded that things had gone too far. Two days later Mary assured Edward of her readiness to obey his commands as far as her conscience would allow and she would always remain his 'humble, obedient and unworthy sister'. In reply the king and Council assured her of 'the most cordial affection' and the Council promised her that it would always be ready to render her service, 'for she was the second person in the kingdom and her virtues deserved no other treatment'.[17] Part of this milder tone was down to an appearance by the imperial ambassador making menacing noises; Edward thought that he actually threatened war. This is unlikely. Charles V's entanglements in Germany would hardly allow him to risk open hostilities, but banning England's trade with Flanders was a very real option. As Edward clearly understood, such economic sanctions could be fatal: 'Seeing my subjects lacking their vent [cloth sales] in Flanders might put the whole realm in danger [seeing that] the Flemings had cloth [for their finishing industry] enough for a year in hand.' Moreover an embargo would hit England militarily. There were seventy-five tons of gunpowder in the Low Countries and a significant purchase of armour awaiting collection. So king and council agreed that the important thing was to buy time by withdrawing Richard Morison, the ambassador (his aggressive Protestantism had offended the emperor), and instructing his replacement 'to deny the matter wholly'.[18]

But what then of Edward's religious duty to compel his sister to conform? His journal says that before making the decision to send a new ambassador, the archbishop and the bishops of London and Rochester appeared and gave a ruling on Mary's offences. The explanation of this strange episcopal involvement is supplied in a 'discourse' (again not wholly objective), written after Edward's death by the ousted ambassador, possibly writing in voluntary exile following Mary's accession.[19] According to Sir Richard, the reason the bishops were brought in was that, although Edward agreed to replace Morison, he had refused outright to sanction the 'idolatry' of Mary's masses. Sent in to persuade the young king, the clerics pointed out that the Old Testament continued to describe rulers as 'good', even though they had not completely stamped out pagan worship. Edward's counter-argument was that wrong things done by good kings were no example to follow. He pointed out that the psalm read at morning prayer only two days previously (Psalm 78) was a condemnation by God of his people precisely for disobedience, and he reminded the bishops that national disaster had followed.[20] A king was responsible to God.

> I know God is able to defend me against as many emperors as ever the world had, if they came all at once with as many men as they had in all their whole times. I must do as God gives me in commandment, and then I shall not want to lay for myself [be inconsistent] in reason, nor want an aid able to overturn the force of the whole world, in case it come wholly against me. The emperor is no warrant to you to stir me to that you ought not, nor no discharge to [excuse for] me, if at your desires I would be led to do that after we might all repent.

According to Morison the bishops were routed but Edward's journal suggests that they persuaded him to a compromise. They fully endorsed that 'to give licence to sin' – i.e. permit the idolatry – was itself sinful, but suggested that 'to suffer and wink at it for a time might be borne', provided 'all haste possible might be used'. In the light of this and the economic arguments, Edward accepted that the right decision was to temporize, and Mary left convincing herself that he had made her a 'gentle answer'.[21] The attack, instead, was turned on well-born individuals who were attending the masses at Mary's houses. Several gentlemen thereupon found themselves in the Fleet Prison, the most prominent being the royal standard bearer, Sir Anthony Browne, 'for setting a notable ill example', and Richard Morgan, the serjeant-at-law whom Mary would make chief justice of the court of common pleas.[22] Shortly afterwards Mary's comptroller, Rochester, was interrogated to discover particulars of Mary's chaplains, one of whom, a Dr Francis Mallett, was subsequently sent to the Tower.[23] Browne and Morgan were released after six weeks, but Mallett was held for a good deal longer.[24]

Matters hotted up again in the summer. On 9 August the council held a special meeting to consider the problem of the Princess, and a unanimous decision was taken to end Mary's licence to hear mass privately. The meeting was special because two religiously conservative peers – the earls of Arundel and Derby – were called in and exceptionally made councillors for that one occasion only; Mary was to be left in no illusion that sympathizers would be free to support her against the king.[25] Rochester and his senior colleagues, the chamberlain Sir Francis Englefield and the steward Edward Waldegrave, were summoned and ordered to convey the prohibition to Mary – Rochester refusing to do so until commanded on his allegiance – and they were told that if Mary carried out her threat to dismiss them, as they had warned, they were to ignore her and enforce the order nevertheless.[26] Nine days later they returned to confess defeat and present Mary's reply.[27] Edward, she agreed, was gifted beyond his years, 'yet it is not possible that your Highness can at these years be a judge in matters of religion. And therefore I take it that the matter in your letters proceeds from such as do wish those things to take place which be most agreeable to themselves by whose doings, your Majesty not offended, I intend not to rule my conscience.' And she issued a direct challenge. If she was not to be excused as hitherto 'till your Majesty may be a judge herein yourself and right understand their proceedings … otherwise, rather than to offend God and my conscience, I offer my body at your will and death shall be more welcome than life with a troubled conscience.' Once more her officers were called in. Each refused to execute the orders and was sent to the Fleet Prison.[28]

The morning of Friday 28 August saw the climax. The time was over for letters and working through Mary's officers. Two senior privy councillors, the chancellor, Richard Rich, and the comptroller of the king's household, Anthony Wingfield, arrived at Copthall, another of Mary's houses in Essex, together with William Petre, one of the secretaries of state. Confronted by the highest representatives of council and the royal court, Mary defied them directly.[29] She declared that the 'matter' did not come from the king 'but you of the council' and she would 'lay her head on a block' rather than use any other liturgies than those sanctioned by her father. 'None of your new services shall be used in my house and if any be said in it, I will not tarry in the house.' A horrid prospect opened of pursuing a recalcitrant Mary from place to place. The meeting which Rich and his colleagues had with her chaplains was superficially more successful; they at least did promise to obey the order.[30] The price of Mary's intransigence was, however, once again paid by her officers. They were moved from the Fleet to the Tower and put in effective isolation.[31] Kept there for over six months, they were allowed back to their homes in March 1552 only because of ill health.[32]

Why this attempt to bring Mary to heel was made less than six months after the decision to 'wink' at her disobedience is difficult to decide. Was it that Edward thought that delay could no longer qualify as 'all haste possible'? Was Mary, by her continuing resistance, giving Charles V a pretext to intervene and establish a base in England to assist in his renewed war with France?[33] That option was actively discussed in Brussels in the autumn.[34] Alternatively, did the council feel that unless she conformed, the princess would inevitably become a magnet for domestic opposition to further religious change?[35] A more immediate factor is that Mary had become a football in a political crisis which was brewing in England. The duke of Somerset was seeking to undermine John Dudley and recover the primacy he had lost in the autumn of 1549. As part of his campaign he espoused toleration for Mary which forced Dudley and a majority on the council to be more rigorous. Once Somerset had been arrested there were no more attempts to force the princess herself to use the new services.[36] Her chaplains were still harassed and the probability is that mass was no longer said for her household and visitors, but it was celebrated for the princess and two or three of her ladies in the privacy of her own chamber, as the council had initially intended.[37]

Perhaps in consequence of the calmer atmosphere, Mary visited Edward at Greenwich in June 1552. She did not stay overnight and there is no evidence of any discussion about her mass.[38] A further sign of a modus vivendi was a significant augmentation of her estates later in the year.[39] The lands initially granted to Mary had included the Essex manor of St Osyth and three other manors between Colchester and the sea. However, in April 1551 the reversion (i.e. next possession) of these properties had been granted to Thomas Darcy, the lord chamberlain, when he was ennobled as Lord Darcy of Chiche (i.e. St Osyth). Reversioners were always anxious to see the backs of existing occupants and by the autumn of 1552 Darcy was getting impatient. As lord chamberlain he was in regular attendance on Edward and in late November the king intervened. He wrote to the princess suggesting that if she would allow the crown to recover the manors, he would grant her more lucrative property in lieu. What is more, the council reimbursed her for the £570 she had had to spend on 'lands decayed by the rage of the sea last year'.[40] Mary accepted with some surprise. A simpler way to improve her financial position would be to resume other manors less 'commodious or profitable' – a comment which suggests that she knew nothing of Darcy's involvement. The compensation was certainly advantageous – major properties in Norfolk, in Suffolk (including the castle of Framlingham), in Essex and in Hertfordshire including Hertford castle where she had lived in her twenties.[41] A further gesture towards reconciliation was apparent when Mary came for what would be her final visit to Edward.[42] She travelled with a retinue of two hundred, but on Monday 6 February 1553, as she approached

London, she was met and escorted by the earl of Warwick, John Dudley's eldest son, Henry Sidney, his son-in-law, and a hundred other notables and members of Edward's household. The cavalcade entered the city, proceeded along London's main street, the Cheap, and continued out through Newgate to St John's Clerkenwell, the princess's town residence in the north-western suburbs.[43] Because the king was unwell there was then a three-day hiatus but on Friday an even more magnificent procession was organized.

> The 10th day of [February] rode my lady Mary's grace from St John's and through Fleet Street unto the king at Westminster, with a great number of lords and knights, and all the great women ladies, the duchesses of Suffolk and Northumberland, my lady marquess of Northampton and the lady marquess of Winchester and the countess of Shrewsbury, and the countess of Arundel, my lady Clinton, my lady Browne and many more ladies and gentlewomen [no doubt including Jane Grey].

The reception at Whitehall was equally grand. She was met at the outer gate by 'my lord of Suffolk [i.e. the duke] and my lord of Northumberland, my lord of Winchester, my lord of Bedford and the earl of Shrewsbury, the earl of Arundel, my lord chamberlain [Darcy of Chiche], my lord admiral [Clinton] and a great number of knights and gentlemen', who, as the imperial ambassador put it, 'did duty and obeisance to her as if she had been queen of England'. Edward too, added his endorsement, by receiving Mary in the presence chamber.[44] And to seal this public recognition of Mary as 'the second person in the kingdom', Northumberland restored to Mary her 'full arms as princess of England, as she used to bear them in her father's, the late king's lifetime'.[45]

JOHN DUDLEY

10

JOHN DUDLEY: THE CAREER

IN any discussion of the events of 1553, John Dudley, duke of North-umberland, looms large. Indeed, decoding the duke's character, actions and motives is central to understanding the mystery of 1553 and the fate of Jane Grey. Welcoming Mary to Whitehall in February 1553 'as if she had been the queen of England' was the last time John Dudley saw the princess. On Friday 18 August, 1553 he stood in Westminster Hall on trial for his part in the attempt to exclude her from the throne and establish Queen Jane Grey. Beside him stood William Parr, marquis of Northampton, and Dudley's eldest son, John earl of Warwick.[1] The great hall had seen many a treason trial and would see many more, but none would so reek of hypocrisy. The dais was crowded with a jury of peers supported by a phalanx of judges. They had come not to try, but to condemn, not because the prisoners were guilty, but because the jury was. A month before, almost all of them had, like the prisoners, sworn allegiance to Jane Grey as queen of England.[2] Only the prisoners had kept their oaths, and all must be condemned to prove the loyalty of the rest to the victorious Queen Mary. Among the few honest men in the court was Thomas Howard, duke of Norfolk, the high steward presiding. He had been in the Tower when the events took place and had been there for six years. Still, despite his eighty years he needed little briefing for the job. He had pronounced sentence on many illustrious people before – including a queen – and only some of them had been guilty.[3]

One only of the prisoners was of real consequence. Six weeks before, Northumberland had been the most powerful man in England; now he was the worst-hated man in the country. It had been a major feat of crowd control even to get the duke into the Tower after his arrest.[4] The trial was brief – almost a formality. The duke pleaded not guilty and offered his defence.[5] He posed it in two questions. First: 'Whether a man doing an act by the authority of the prince and council, and by a warrant of the great seal of England, and doing nothing without the same, may be charged for treason for any thing which he might do by warrant thereof?' The implication was unanswerable. Everything Dudley had done had been fully sanctioned by proper authority, most of which made up the jury. The court responded that he could not hide behind the great seal of Jane since she was a usurper. This was almost certainly a blatant and calculated misrepresentation; Dudley was trying to cite the final version of Edward's 'deuise' which was given the great seal on 21 June. If so, he was to learn that obedience to a living monarch was no protection when he was dead, a lesson exemplified in his father's fate, forty-three years earlier to the day.[6] By an irony he could not have known about, it was Edward's seal which hung from the commission appointing the duke of Norfolk as his judge.[7]

The duke's follow-up question challenged the right of his judges to try him and was morally just as unanswerable: 'Whether any such persons as were equally culpable of that crime and those by whose letters and commandments he was directed in all his doings, might be his judges or pass upon his trial at his death?' But whether others were equally guilty was not the issue. The court replied that 'as long as no attainder were on record against them, they were nevertheless persons able in the law to pass upon any trial and not to be challenged therefore, but [to be selected] at the prince's pleasure'. The weasel answers cannot have been unexpected – indeed, according to Simon Renard the duke had protested before the trial that the council was as guilty as he.[8] But having made the point which even the imperial ambassadors thought just, Northumberland surrendered to the inevitable and sentence was pronounced.[9] He asked consideration that he might have the death of 'a nobleman and not the other' – simple beheading instead of the ghastliness of drawing, hanging and quartering – that sympathy be given to his children, and for opportunities to confess 'to a learned divine' and to meet four of the council to convey state secrets. The marquis of Northampton was tried next – more emotional and arguing at length. 'His position had been impossible. He had received orders issued under the great seal and disobeying them would have meant being charged with treason by Jane's council.'[10] The court remained deaf, so the final defendant, the young earl of Warwick, simply pleaded guilty. And it was over.

The John Dudley who stood in Westminster Hall that day hardly seemed the same as the earlier John Dudley, who to that point had been one of the most able, principled and successful figures of the Tudor period.

If it had not been for the final debacle, his name would now be remembered alongside Cardinal Wolsey, Thomas Cromwell and William Cecil.[11] In almost fifty years of life, John Dudley, successively Viscount Lisle, earl of Warwick and duke of Northumberland, was many things, but traitor he was not. First and foremost Dudley was a military man and a courtier, one of the breed that Henry VIII had enjoyed having round him and liked to encourage. He was knighted as a teenager in the 1523 invasion of France – possibly when he was not more than sixteen. Since he and Robert Oughtred were dubbed together in the field – 'at the passage of the Somme' – we can suppose some exploit.[12] What this was is not precisely known, probably a response to a French attempt to break down the river bridge and so impede the withdrawal of the invading English army under the command of the duke of Suffolk. From this precocious beginning, John Dudley went on to become England's premier commander, with a reputation which persisted even after the debacle and disgrace of 1553.[13]

Achieving fame as a teenager in one of the largest invasions of France for fifty years is not what one might expect given Dudley's sad start to life. His father Edmund Dudley had been one of the lawyers who had dominated the counsels of Henry VII and a principal enforcer of the king's policy 'to keep all Englishmen in obedience through fear'.[14] When an intense reaction seized the court immediately on the king's death, Dudley's loyalty became the mark of Cain and he was in the Tower within hours.[15] There he lingered for fifteen months until the new king, Henry VIII, decided that there was some popularity to be gained by executing him for high treason, along with his father's other loyal servant, Richard Empson. A conviction for treason not only condemned the traitor to a horrific and disgusting death, but his estates were confiscated and his family 'corrupted in blood', that is stripped of its titles and debarred from inheriting property. In practice, however, the permanent legal oblivion which the law promised was reserved only for the most intransigent. More usually a prominent family could expect that following the death of the individual traitor, the heir would be brought up as befitted his or her birth. In a few years the corruption would be removed and the heir married to someone in the king's favour, recovering, in due course, much of the property which had been lost. Not that the process was quite so simple in the case of John Dudley because his now widowed mother Elizabeth was, in her own right, heiress presumptive to the Lisle barony, and this was not affected by her husband's attainder. Edmund's death, therefore, had left her a prize of some value, so although guardianship of the young John

Dudley – he was probably about seven years old – was granted to the king's friend Sir Edward Guildford, Elizabeth Dudley was married off to Edward IV's illegitimate son Arthur Plantagenet, whom Henry VIII wanted to rehabilitate. This brought to Arthur the Lisle lands in right of his now wife and the forfeited Dudley lands were split by the king between Plantagenet and Guildford. In 1519 Dudley's mother succeeded as Lady Lisle, which meant that when John went on the 1523 campaign he was already next heir to the Lisle family property with a claim to the title of viscount.

Dudley owed his place in Suffolk's army to the man who had become his guardian. Edward Guildford was marshal of Calais and took John as his lieutenant.[16] The relationship also stood him in good stead after the 1523 invasion when twenty years of peace with Europe gave English gentlemen no opportunity for martial exploits abroad. Sir Edward was master of the royal armoury and a key figure in that war-substitute, the tournament, at which the king excelled. Dudley became Guildford's assistant and a major performer in the lists as well. According to a French report of about 1546 he was 'the most skilful of his generation, both on foot and on horseback', as well as in wrestling and archery.[17] One notable exploit he took part in was perhaps the most drawn-out and violent of the chivalric performances which graced the first two decades of Henry's court – the defence of the *Chasteau Blanche*.[18] This was a timber fort, twenty foot square and fifty foot high, specially constructed in the Greenwich tiltyard. The spectacle began with a challenge issued on St Thomas's Day (21 December) 1524 by fourteen courtiers, including Dudley, to fight in the lists against all comers and to defend the castle against assault. Henry himself led the response and the encounter lasted (with intervals) until 8 February. We know the names of twenty-five of those involved and the list includes everyone with the least pretension to military skill. It was also one of the last entertainments of 'the happy time' before the king's matrimonial problems would come to dominate everything and send a quarter of those involved in the *Chasteau Blanche* to die by the axe or worse. Dudley, however, was able to retain royal favour throughout, making the most of the king's interest in the joust, and on the death of Guildford in 1534 he succeeded to the post of master of the armoury, which meant immediate personal responsibility for the king's own equipment. He attended Henry and Anne Boleyn to Calais in 1532, served at her coronation, was present at the christenings first of Princess Elizabeth and then of her brother Edward, and finally and briefly became master of the horse to Anne of Cleves. It was in front of Anne that Dudley had the most embarrassing experience of his jousting career. He had taken the lead with five other courtiers in promoting a week of jousting and feasting to celebrate May Day 1540, but fell off his horse in full view of everybody.[19] However, to be fair to Dudley, he seems to have found it difficult to get horses of sufficient quality for the tournament.[20]

Some opportunity for active military service did arise at home. In 1536 the northern third of the country rose to protest at royal interference in what is known as the Pilgrimage of Grace. Dudley was ordered to take two hundred men to reinforce the king's commander, the same duke of Norfolk who would one day condemn him, first picking up instructions from the king for the conduct of the campaign.[21] He clearly did well because the next year he was sent afloat as vice-admiral of a fleet of four vessels ordered to suppress Flemish piracy.[22] The two ships under Dudley's immediate command had particular responsibility for the coastline between Poole and the Downs and fortune favoured him as good intelligence and a decent wind allowed him to catch one of the leading corsairs at anchor in the Downs and to capture him and his vessel.[23] It was the start of an association with the sea which would last for more than a decade and bring him promotion to lord high admiral in 1543. By then his stepfather Arthur Plantagenet had died, so allowing John to claim his ancestral peerage as Viscount Lisle on 12 March 1542.[24]

The problem of piracy soon gave way to a growing probability of war with France. Immediately after his viscounty, he was sent to investigate the slow progress with the refortifying of Berwick, a key defence to prevent the Scots invading in support of the French, and in November 1542 he was on his way back to the Marches to act as warden when English forces routed their old enemies at Solway Moss. This was closely followed by the death of the Scottish king and the accession of his week-old daughter, Mary, which meant that Lisle found himself involved in 'jaw-jaw' rather than the 'war war' he had expected. However, he was not in the north for long. By early June 1543, just before war was formally declared on France, he was in London busily getting a fleet to sea. The main military effort came in the following year. Following Solway Moss, Henry had attempted secure the infant queen of Scots as a bride for Prince Edward, but when that failed he had to find another way to neutralize 'the auld alliance'. Dudley, therefore, was sent in late March with ten warships to rendezvous with an army and transports at Newcastle upon Tyne under the overall command of Edward Seymour, earl of Hertford. Headwinds delayed matters but by 1 May Dudley had embarked the troops and supplies and left the Tyne for what would be a faultless combined operation. Forty-eight hours later he was in the Forth, landing a raiding party to burn St Monans in Fife and anchoring near Leith. There the army was landed, leaving the seamen to destroy or commandeer as much shipping as possible and raid both banks of the Forth as far as Stirling. Dudley, however, left that to underlings and came ashore with the land force to take command of the vanward. His men failed to force Edinburgh's main gate – it was made of iron – and a fierce fire fight ensued until he called up a culverin and blew the gate open.[25] The troops poured in and fired the city including Holyrood and the royal palace. Everything for seven miles around met the same fate. The English then loaded the artillery and the booty on the ships and, in a three-day march, cut a swath of further destruction all the way back to Berwick. Seymour warmly commended Dudley's work and the king responded with a grant of land.

Barely back from the Scottish raid, Dudley was at sea protecting the English build-up in Calais. In June the actual invasion of France began, with Henry in personal command, and on 14 September Boulogne surrendered. Dudley was thereupon called ashore to become governor of the town with the urgent duty to fortify it. He had to survive a night-time *coup de main* by the French and there were the usual tensions between the field commander and the home government about supplies and slow progress on the new fortifications, to say nothing of the king's own ideas on defensive design. Clearly, however, enough was done for Boulogne to resist all the attempts of the French to recapture it in the next campaigning season. By then, however, Dudley was back at sea, preparing to face a French fleet intent on preventing the English reinforcing Boulogne. In what followed the lord admiral was to experience very mixed fortunes.[26] A pre-emptive strike in June against the French fleet in the Seine estuary using fire-ships came to nothing, but when, in turn, the French arrived in the Solent the first day's fighting went well. Not so the second, which was marred by the loss of the *Mary Rose*, though a French force which landed on the Isle of Wight was wiped out. The invaders then withdrew, raiding ineffectually along the coast as they went but when Dudley caught up with them, weather conditions allowed the French to escape. The counter-raid which he then mounted on Normandy was a good deal more successful but it was too small to be a real riposte to the Solent and, it was vowed, 'next year would be different'. However, Tudor wars did not last long and as impetus and resources began to run out, minds turned to peace. The planned fleet of forty-five ships was stood down in favour of a routine of protecting supply routes and minor

skirmishes with the admiral of France in order to exert pressure in what
were (eventually) successful peace negotiations.

The biggest military action in which Dudley took part occurred in the
year after the peace with France under the new young king. English
attempts to force through the marriage of Edward to Mary Queen of
Scots had still made no progress and, with the new reign, a change of
policy was decided on: an invasion to set up a series of English bases in the
Lowlands. Dudley, no longer lord admiral but now earl of Warwick, served
as second in command to Edward Seymour, now protector and duke of
Somerset.[27] In contrast to the 1544 campaign, 1547 was principally a land
assault. Warwick's task was to muster the army of 18,000 and bring it
forward to Berwick and thereafter to command the van. The account of
the expedition suggests that the earl's style in the field was to lead by
example and be 'one of the foremost in danger'. On one occasion when
the rearguard was lost in a local haar, Dudley himself set out with a small
escort to regain contact, only to be ambushed and plunged into hand-to-
hand fighting.[28] The casualties, one dead Englishman and two wounded
(one seriously) against three Scots prisoners, one of them injured, suggests
that the affair was too close for comfort.

> It is certainly thought that if my Lord Lieutenant had not thus valiantly
> encountered them ere they could have warned their ambush how weakly as
> he was warded, he had been beset round about by them, ere ever he could
> have been aware of them or rescued of us; where now hereby his Lordship
> showed his wonted worthiness, saved his company, and discomfited the
> enemy.

When the full Scottish army blocked further advance at Musselburgh,
Warwick commanded the left of the English line, steadied it after an initial
Scottish attack and went on to secure a hill which was the key to the
battlefield, from which the English superiority in artillery battered the
Scottish pikemen to defeat.[29]

Compared with the battle of Pinkie, John Dudley's next military
responsibility was an anticlimax. In the summer of 1549, bad handling
of the protests in Norfolk transformed complaint into a full-scale rising
which occupied Norwich and forcibly resisted attempts by the less than
competent marquis of Northampton to re-impose order. The earl of
Warwick was due to go to the West Country to assist in repressing
rebellion there, but the loss of the country's second city diverted him to
East Anglia with an army of 7,500, largely foreign mercenaries. When his
initial offers of pardon were rejected, he cleared Norwich, offered pardon

again and then loosed his cavalry and German mercenaries on what was a larger but ill-armed force of amateurs, and overwhelmingly enough to achieve a quick victory. However, it was not without cost. Thomas Drury, one of Dudley's captains, lost a third of his men.[30]

Dudley's experience in civil affairs was for many years much less extensive than in matters military. He succeeded Guildford as member of parliament for the county of Kent from 1534–6, served as sheriff of Staffordshire in the aftermath of the Pilgrimage, as MP for an unknown constituency in 1539 and in 1542 for Staffordshire itself. Overlapping with these responsibilities in England were a short stint as second in command of the Calais garrison (where his stepfather, Viscount Lisle, was lord deputy) and an embassy to Spain in the company of Sir Thomas Wyatt. Not that this meant that he lost ground at court. Quite the reverse. He entered the privy council in March 1543, following his promotion to lord high admiral, was elected KG the following April, and was, if not then, within a matter of months on the staff of the privy chamber, that group of royal intimates who enjoyed the closest contact with the king. What, however, is clear is that it took Dudley some time to become confident in civil affairs. When in 1543 Dudley realized that Solway Moss had made his job as warden of the Marches more political than civil he expressed open concern: 'Your lordships doth know my bringing up, I have never been practised nor experimented in no matters of council before this time. At my first coming hither it was open war; it was then more easier to conduce those affairs than these which be presently in hand.'[31] A similar distaste for civilian finesse underlies his sparring with the admiral of France during the negotiations for peace in 1546. On one occasion he seized on a French negotiating ploy as an excuse to get back to the fleet in the Downs, and if contrary winds had not kept him there to receive letters of recall, the war might well have burst into life.[32] However, once diplomatic wrangling was over, Dudley was again in his element, leading a grand delegation to Fontainebleau to secure the French king's formal ratification of the treaty. It was a triumphal procession and in the French court Dudley was again at home, though possibly less comfortable during Francis I's discussion with Bishop Tunstal on translating Greek into French than when assisting the Dauphin in the tiltyard later the same day.[33]

As for administrative experience, this too was never extensive. Dudley's military efficiency demonstrates that he was a competent director and he has been credited with a hand in the creation of a 'Council for Marine Causes' to administer the navy – but he was no *apparatchik*. Under Henry VIII he had held no major civilian office outside the court – and his promotion on Edward's succession from lord admiral to lord great chamberlain brought greater status but no new portfolio in place of the chores of the Admiralty. Dudley's council experience, too, was hardly impressive. During the six and a half years since being sworn a counsellor in April 1543 he was away on service for lengthy periods, so although he does seem to have attended when available, the attendance lists show, for example, that during the last twelve months of Henry's reign he was absent on two occasions in three. Henry nevertheless valued him and named him as one of the Council of Regency which he appointed to govern England during the minority of his son. He left Lisle a legacy of £500 and the promise to make him earl of Leicester (later changed to Coventry) with a land grant worth £300 a year.[34]

To start as the son of a traitor and achieve an earldom when barely forty was an achievement unique in Tudor England and self-evidently demanded personality, character and ability. The witness to John Dudley's intelligence is uniform. Richard Morrison famously said that the duke had 'such a head that he seldom went about any thing but he first conceived three or four purposes before hand'.[35] A French diplomat described him as 'always thinking', and as

> an intelligent man who could explain his ideas and who displayed an impressive dignity. Others, who did not know him, would have considered him worthy of ruling a kingdom. [He was] bold and haughty in carrying out his business. In council there was no wiser advice than his as he could foresee from afar the outcome of war. In bad times and in good he always showed himself fearless, valiant and bold ... His father was beheaded and as soon as he was of an age to make a reputation [of his own], he acquired through his generosity, courage and other qualities, the goodwill of everyone and he showed he had some excellent and rare qualities surpassing others.[36]

That John Dudley had a powerful presence is beyond question. While Henry VIII was alive he is reported as having struck the bishop of Winchester in open council.[37] In the skirmish before the battle of Pinkie he is supposed to have said, 'Why and will these knaves never be ruled? Give me my spear', and then to have chased the Scottish captain 250 yards in an attempt to impale him.[38] In the parliament of 1553 Cranmer met the full force of John Dudley when he attempted to recover something of the church's lost independence.[39] Yet the impressive individual transmutes into the bully of tradition only after the collapse of support for Jane Grey and the move to make him a general scapegoat. It was when Cecil's servant Richard Troughton was trying to clear himself that he averred that the bruit in Lincolnshire was that no man loved Northumberland 'but for fear'.[40] Chief Justice Montagu wrote a graphic description of the bully Dudley in action but only in order to bolster the story that in June 1553 he and his fellow lawyers had attempted to block the elevation of Jane Grey:

> The duke of Northumberland ... cometh into the Council Chamber before all the Council there, being in a great rage and fury, trembling for anger, and amongst his rageous talk called the said Sir Edward, 'Traitor', and further said that he would fight in his shirt with any man in that quarrel ... whereby the said Sir Edward, with the rest, were in great fear and dread, in special Mr [Justice] Bromley and the said Sir Edward; for Mr Bromley told the said Sir Edward after, that he dreaded then the duke would have stricken one of them.[41]

It was after he blamed the duke for the catastrophe of 1553 that Knox referred to Northumberland ruling 'the roost in the court all this time by stout courage and proudness of stomach'.[42] Robert Wingfield's account of the crisis attributed the involvement of Jane Grey's father to 'fear of the fierce nature of the man more than he ought to have done'.[43] Yet those who claimed after the event that John Dudley was a bruiser were still left with incongruities. The pen picture produced by the French diplomat is in the end of a Jekyll and Hyde character.

> Never did a man govern in England with such great authority as he. He made himself formidable to all because he carried out his acts of hostility and vengeance so violently that while he was in power no-one was assured of his life or possessions if they were not favoured by him. He promoted those that he loved so dearly that he made himself adored by them all & they felt favoured on greeting him as it seemed that he looked kindly on them ....
> He kept both great and small in fear and obedience so that all were anxious to please him. On the contrary, no-one dared undertake to support anything which displeased him. Nevertheless he spoke affably, giving the impression of being gracious and warm but inwardly he was a proud *felon* and as vindictive as one ever was. He was magnificently generous at home and in all his actions, demonstrating at all times during his lifetime a liberal nature and he gave large presents. But those who knew him could well see that this did not proceed from a generous nature nor goodwill but from artifice, to obtain the favour of those who could be useful to him or harm him, and they were the only people he gave to.

One factor which the diplomat omitted – or most probably was unaware of – was the importance to Dudley of his family. This was personal, to a degree which was not always the case among his contemporaries.

As a fatherless seven-year-old he had been bought by Edward Guildford in order to marry his two-year-old daughter Jane, but despite this the marriage was solid and genuinely affectionate.[44] Together they had thirteen children. In the summer of 1546 when Dudley was on the peace embassy in France Jane wrote asking for some goldsmith's work 'from Parys', and he ducked the request by asking William Paget to explain to her that he had barely enough cash to get himself home – if that.[45] When he passed the news to his son-in-law Henry Sidney in July 1552 that business would keep him in the north, he added the warning, 'I pray you keep this from my wife'.[46] In the desperate time which followed the collapse of Jane's government, the countess exploited every contact she had to save her husband. In a letter pleading for the help of Lady Paget, a postscript stressed the need also of her sons 'though not so much care for them as for their father, the most best gentleman that ever living woman was matched withal.'[47] When writing her will with her own hand in December 1554, her thoughts were still for 'my lord, my dear husband'.[48] Dudley's relations with his children were warm. When his son and heir got into financial difficulties he wrote with remarkable sympathy:

> Well enough you must understand that I know you cannot live under [the burden of] great charges. And therefore you should not hide from me your debts, whatsoever they be, for I would be loathe but you should keep your credit still with all men. And therefore send me word in any wise of the whole sum of your debts, for I and your mother will forthwith see them paid.[49]

Earlier in life he had taken responsibility for at least one of his younger half-sisters, Elizabeth Plantagenet. She lived with the Dudleys and in 1538 he took up the cudgels when it seemed that his stepfather might be about to treat her unfairly: 'for my part I have and will do as becomes a brother to do to his sister'.[50] Eventually she married Francis Jobson who became one of his closest allies.[51] He was concerned to marry his own children well and accepted their spouses into the family circle; the death of the young wife of his second son Ambrose affected him deeply.[52] Undoubtedly it was with future generations in mind as well as himself that he petitioned to become 'earl of Warwick' rather than 'Coventry'.[53] It secured for the Dudley family a senior title rather than a parvenu dignity at the bottom of the order of precedence.

In 1553 John Dudley was approaching fifty – old age in Tudor times. As Jane Grey put it, his 'fatal course could not have long continued'.[54] But nothing either public and private had suggested it would be determined in Westminster Hall on Friday 18 August.

11

John Dudley: The Black Legend

From a twenty-first-century perspective, the earlier career of John Dudley makes him appear a most unlikely adventurer. His contemporaries showed no such caution. Once the Grey monarchy had collapsed, there was an explosion of speculation and gossip. At a popular level the duke was believed actually to have caused the king's illness. Antonio de Guaras depicted a Northumberland saddled with guilt. Bearing responsibility, so he alleged, for a whole series of violent events – the arrest in December 1546 of the duke of Norfolk and his son the earl of Surrey, Surrey's subsequent execution, the execution of the protector's brother Thomas Seymour, the execution of the protector himself, and the deprivation and imprisonment of Catholic opponents of 'the schism' – the duke was desperate 'to provide how he might deliver himself from the many troubles which it was to be foreseen might overtake him on these accounts as soon as the king should be of an age to govern.'[1] His answer, de Guaras reported, was to get control of all the country's wealth and military force, and then to poison the king. 'The poor innocent languished for seven months.' The poison story spread Europe-wide but is evident nonsense. Nothing could have been less to Northumberland's advantage than Edward dead. According to some reports, medication of a very extreme kind was administered to the boy in the desperation of his final days and that may have accentuated his decline – as it certainly did his misery.[2] Yet nothing was administered other than in a vain attempt to prolong life.

Robert Wingfield, author of the earliest English account, had a more sober explanation of the duke's motivation.[3] Dudley had 'with excessive impudence' controlled 'the king and the kingdom' and committed numerous 'execrable, not to say intolerable crimes' in the three and a half years since 1549 and the ousting of Somerset. Consequently he was fully aware that the accession of a new sovereign could result in his being called to account for 'the misgovernment of the kingdom during his administration'. This coincides with the conclusions of an impressive galaxy of modern scholars. A. F. Pollard set the tone: '[Dudley] had committed so many crimes and made so many enemies that he was only safe so long as he misdirected the government and prevented the administration of justice. His power depended upon his control of Edward VI and Edward was slowly dying before his eyes.'[4] S. T. Bindoff echoed Pollard: 'Northumberland knew that his days of power, if not of life, were numbered if the king were to die and be succeeded by his half-sister Mary.'[5] Mary's biographer, David Loades, agreed: 'His whole position and that of his faction depended upon the life of the king.'[6] For G. R. Elton there was an element of personal contest between the duke and the princess: 'Northumberland had climbed to power by treading Mary down; the duke knew well that his ascendancy depended on the king's life.'[7] Even B. L. Beer, who believed that the duke could have escaped merely with loss of office, recognized the danger he was in: 'Dealing with Mary involved risk, and Northumberland could not ignore the possibility of being selected as the scapegoat for Edward's reign.'[8] On this reading, Northumberland's actions in the summer of 1553 were a despairing leap for safety.[9]

The alternative and more malevolent explanation of Northumberland's behaviour was breach of the tenth commandment – 'Thou shalt not covet'. Wingfield, a Catholic, described him as 'an ambitious man descended from an ambitious father', while a Protestant critic, John Ponet, called him 'the ambitious and subtle Alcibiades of England'.[10] According to one witness of what John Dudley said at his execution, he 'wished every man not to be covetous, for that was a great part of his destruction'.[11] What therefore would be more likely than that he would seize on the impending death of Edward without direct heirs as an opportunity to put the Dudley family on the throne? As Giovanni Commendone wrote, 'events … have clearly proved that the ambition and greed of reigning prevailed over his duty of loyalty'.[12] Jane Grey certainly thought as much; she said of her father-in-law, 'he hath brought me and our stock [family] in most miserable calamity by his exceeding ambition'.[13] And once self-aggrandizement was seen to be the explanation of 1553, it was easy to interpret the whole of Dudley's behaviour since the death of Henry VIII as a subtle and successful pursuit of supreme power. When, in Mary's reign, the Catholic writer George Cavendish included the duke in his Metrical Visions, he had his ghost say:

> The ground (quoth he) and beginning of my destruction
> I shall to you rehearse shortly in sentence;
> It was covetous pride and high presumption,
> Disdaining all men of royal excellence,
> Coveting by ravin [force] to have the pre-eminence;
> And whom I suspected that stood in my way,
> I shortly by falsehood intended their decay.[14]

That view was echoed by some commentators early in the reign of Elizabeth.[15] Like de Guaras they see Dudley's hand in all the political crises of Edward's reign.

Conspiracy theories and Machiavellian plots make good copy, but the detachment of four centuries should make us pause before we completely swallow the black tale of Dudley's ambition. It is incredible that he or anyone in 1547 could have had the foresight to envisage the long-term strategy which the black legend demands – to say nothing of the role which accident played throughout.[16] At the start of Edward's reign the imperial ambassador did think he might compete with the protector Somerset, being 'most splendid and haughty by nature and in higher favour both with the people and with the nobles than the earl of Hertford, owing to his liberality and splendour. The Protector ... is looked down upon by everybody as a dry sour-opinionated man.'[17] However, by July 1547 he had changed his mind: 'I think now that contenting himself with the pre-eminence he at present enjoys before all others except the Protector, he will not persevere in the management of affairs nor is he, indeed, so able to support the work, which appears unable to tire the Protector.'[18] Dudley's military exploits secured him a good press and as late as the middle of 1552 he was reported as being on the best of terms with the people of the north.[19]

Why, then, did the earl become, from 1549, a popular hate figure in London and parts of the south of England? First there was his role in suppressing that summer's rebellion in East Anglia. As we shall see, peasants from the area deliberately rallied to Princess Mary in 1553 in order to have their revenge.[20] The second nail in the coffin of Dudley's reputation was his supposed ousting of the popular duke of Somerset from power in the following October in order to seize supreme power for himself. The unpopular policies of the ensuing government were laid at his door and the final seal on the black legend was the arrest and execution of Protector Somerset on trumped-up charges in January 1552. Evidence, however, tells a somewhat different story.

The first sign that Dudley was becoming dissatisfied with the protector was in the summer of 1549. In the context of widespread disorder, and serious uprisings in East Anglia and the West Country, he joined three other counsellors – the earl of Southampton (Thomas Wriothesley), the earl of Arundel, and William Paulet, Lord St John – to sound out Princess Mary on a possible move against 'the protector and his new council', that is the private advisers Somerset was believed to be increasingly relying on in place of the privy councillors.[21] Mary made a neutral response but made it clear that she would welcome a return to the religious settlement left by her father in 1547. Arundel would have applauded that and Wriothesley and Paulet were willing fellow travellers, but not Dudley, and nothing further transpired. Indeed, when the marquis of Northampton failed to pacify unrest in Norfolk and Somerset called for Warwick to take a force and establish order, he went willingly enough. It was when the risings there and in the west had been repressed that at the start of October the earl allied with other counsellors in an attempt to remove Somerset from office. The final straw seems to have been the protector's behaviour when Dudley returned from victory at Norwich with troops to pay and captains to reward. Somerset was anything but generous.[22] According to the stories the mercenary soldiers told, Warwick and a delegation of captains even had a meeting with Somerset which ended in the earl losing his temper. Be that as it may, he certainly asked Cecil to press the protector on behalf of at least one captain whose men had not been paid for two months.[23] He was also insulted personally – or so he felt – when two offices he petitioned for, to reward the bravery of his son, were granted to a man he disliked but who was one of the protector's servants.

Although the dissident lords held their first meeting at Dudley's house in Holborn, nothing at this stage marked him out as the leader.[24] John Ponet was a partisan of the duke of Somerset and espoused the black legend, but even he had to admit that

> When Wriothesley, [Sir Thomas] Arundel and Southwell conspired with ....
> the earl of Warwick, after[wards] duke of Northumberland to pull the good
> duke of Somerset ... out of his authority and ... brought to pass Warwick's
> purpose, who then for a while but they three? Wriothesley ... is lodged with
> his wife and son next the king: every man repaireth to Wriothesley, honour-
> eth Wriothesley, saith unto Wriothesley as the Assyrians did to Haaman, and
> all things be done by his advice, and who but Wriothesley? Arundel is
> promised to be next to the King, groom of his stool or comptroller of his
> house at the least. Southwell, for his whisking and double diligence, must be
> a great counsellor in any wise.[25]

Dudley's concern was not power but Somerset's refusal to take advice and the need to bring listening back into government. As he wrote to Lord Clinton, the deputy at Boulogne, four days after the protector's surrender, 'The man that ruled all by wilfulness is restrained, and now things are like to pass otherwise than of long time they have done, more for the king's honour and wealth and [the] surety of his realm and subjects.'[26] Bringing the protector to heel was, however, not the end of the crisis. Agreement on what to get rid of rarely implies agreement on what to put in its place, and Wriothesley opened a second act by setting out with conservative support to recover the precedence he had lost in 1547 when the protector had sacked him as lord chancellor. Dudley appears to have had no inkling of this. Indeed, if we are to trust Elizabethan accounts, only when he was shown that he too was to be dragged down as an erstwhile supporter of Somerset did he act in self-defence.[27] In early November he secured the appointment to the privy council of two allies – Jane Grey's father and the bishop of Ely – and with numbers now on his side Somerset was saved and Wriothesley and his allies expelled. That, in consequence, Warwick himself became the dominant political figure in the country seems almost an accident, certainly not the achievement of an aggressive careerist in search of supreme power.

There is even less reason to believe that the final destruction of the duke of Somerset was the next item on Dudley's agenda. Once he was securely in control of the privy council, Dudley rehabilitated the duke. He was freed, fully pardoned, restored to the council board on 10 April, and to his place in the privy chamber a month later.[28] Relations thereafter began well, with Dudley agreeing to act as a go-between for a marriage between the young duke of Suffolk and one of Somerset's daughters.[29] Nothing came of that, but on Tuesday 3 June there 'was a great marriage at Sheen between the Lord Lisle, son and heir to the earl of Warwick, and the duke of Somerset's eldest daughter [Anne], the king's majesty being there present, where was made a great feast, with masking and divers other pastimes.'[30] Edward clearly enjoyed himself, noting in his journal the 'fair dinner made', the two chambers 'made of boughs' where he went with the ladies and the elaborate combats which they watched.[31] However, in reinstating Seymour so completely Warwick was taking a risk. Somerset outranked everyone socially – he was the only adult English duke – and whether or not he wanted to be, the former protector was the obvious magnet for critics of the government.[32]

The danger of a split between the two was increased by the need for policy changes. Following the ill-judged leniency of Somerset's rule, the

council led by Dudley imposed a strict law and order policy, and while this
was warmly supported in parliament and by the gentry in the localities,
commoners saw it as revenge for the unrest of the previous year:

> the gentlemen watch now very fast, and they have not so much need to
> watch now, but to watch all the days of their lives as well as now. For they
> have not had so good a scourge of late among them, but it is not unlike they
> shall have as great a plague as they had before, and except God be merciful
> unto them, they shall have such a plague as they had not had before;
> although it be not this year, the time will come it shall so fall.[33]

There was a parallel reaction to Dudley's commitment to financial
retrenchment. Fiscal deflation created very real hardship and deep resentment, particularly as it was believed (with some justification) that favoured
nobles and their minions were making a killing out of it.[34] Yet Dudley and
his fellow counsellors had no choice. Devaluation, refusing to pay bills and
the frantic search to bring in money from every possible source were crisis
policies imposed on them by the desperate financial plight of the crown.

The increasing unpopularity of an administration which progressively
reversed policies that the general public, far from recognizing the ex-
protector's incompetence, still saw as the achievements of 'the good
duke' gave Somerset little encouragement to give his wholehearted support.[35] And it continued to rankle that he, the king's blood relative and
England's premier nobleman, was no better than number two politically, if
that. Dudley, however, did his best to keep the duke on board. At mid-
summer he warned Somerset through intermediaries about

> his proceedings in the council, wherein his grace – for lack of good con-
> sideration in the order of his proceedings therein – hath brought the whole
> of the council in suspicion that he takes and aspires to have the self and same
> overdue an authority to the despatch and direction of the proceedings as his
> grace had, being protector.

He continued:

> Alas, what means my lord in this wise to discredit himself, and why will he
> not see his own decay herein? Thinks he to rule and direct the whole council
> as he will, considering how his late governance is yet misliked? Neither is he
> in that credit and best opinion with the king's majesty, as he believeth, and is
> by some fondly persuaded.[36]

Matters, however, did not improve. Somerset flirted with Dudley's conservative critics and in the spring of 1551 planned a *coup d'état*. This came

to nothing, but with the policies of his administration becoming even more unpopular and with signs of further Seymour scheming, Warwick struck back in October. On the 11th he was raised to the dukedom of Northumberland and on the 16th came the arrest of Somerset and some three dozen supporters. Edward Seymour had no-one to blame but himself, even though, as Northumberland later admitted, the charges on the indictment had to be massaged – hardly a novelty in Tudor politics.[37] But because Somerset had never ceased to be popular among the general populace, his execution in January 1552 went down as cold-blooded judicial murder by a newly elevated rival who was determined to secure unfettered power. As a result, the black legend spread. Everything Dudley did thereafter was interpreted in the worst possible light. There was even the ludicrous rumour that the happily married duke was himself planning to marry Princess Elizabeth![38]

12

John Dudley: Motives

To reject the black legend as caricature is, of course, to be challenged to find another explanation for the behaviour of the duke of Northumberland in 1553. If not naked ambition, what was it motivated a man with his record to act as he did? A possibility which is rarely considered is religion. Mary's behaviour since her father's death left no doubt that her accession would turn the clock back and Dudley's commitment to religious reform is well attested. In 1552 the duke claimed that he had 'for twenty years stood to one kind of religion, in the same which I do now profess', and the writings of Nicholas Bourbon, a French reformer and classical scholar who took refuge in England for some months in 1535, show that Dudley and his wife were then firmly in the evangelical camp.[1] In February 1543, at a time when a bill was going to parliament to restrict access to the Bible, Lisle advocated the distribution of vernacular Bibles and New Testaments on the Scottish border, and offered to secure copies from England.[2] In the last conservative purge of Henry's reign, he and William Parr the future marquis of Northampton tried to get the martyr Anne Askew to compromise, and were roundly told that 'it was a great shame for them to counsel contrary to their knowledge'.[3] Imperial observers had no hesitation in describing him as 'a stirrer up of heresy', and within months of Edward's accession the Dudley household had ceased to celebrate mass.[4] He intervened twice on the reformist side in the debate on the eucharist held by the Lords in December 1548 and the following month voted for the Act of Uniformity and the first Prayer Book.[5] When struggling with Wriothesley and his conservative allies in 1549, the appointment of two reformers, Jane's father and the bishop of Ely, gave him control of the council, and even before that, the board had announced its determination to maintain religious changes made to date and 'do in all things, as time and opportunity may serve, whatsoever may lend to the glory of God and the advancement of his most holy word'.[6]

Events soon justified the promise. In March 1550 a revised procedure was published for ordaining clergy [the Ordinal], and this made clear that, in the reformed English church, priests were 'to preach the word of God and to minister the holy sacraments' in contrast to their predecessors who had received 'authority to offer sacrifice and celebrate mass both for the living and the dead'.[7] Stephen Gardiner, bishop of Winchester, was imprisoned, with Warwick one of those giving evidence against him.[8] Other conservative bishops were also weeded out, so allowing reforms to be introduced diocese by diocese. Church valuables were seized for the state. The earl was reported as having commissioned the translation of Bullinger's complete works into English at his own expense and he even took time personally to browbeat peasants unhappy with religious changes.[9] As for Princess Mary, Dudley is reported as having been very angry when the protector had agreed to limited toleration.

> The mass is either of God or of the devil: if of God, it is but right that all our people should be allowed to go to it; but if it is not of God, as we are all taught out of the scriptures, why then should not the voice of this fury be equally proscribed to all?[10]

Once he had taken over as president of the council, pressure on Mary was stepped up, as we have already seen.[11] Dudley clashed directly with the princess during her argument with her brother in March 1551; irritated at her insistence that it was the council, not the king, which was pushing reform, he burst out, 'How now my Lady? It seems that your Grace is trying to show us in a hateful light to the king our master without any cause whatever.'[12]

History, however, has refused to believe that John Dudley's religious commitment could be genuine. Calling him an 'unscrupulous cynic', S. T. Bindoff claimed that 'behind his championship of the godly cause there was less of conviction than of calculation'.[13] David Loades suggested that 'he seems to have drifted into reform, and from reform into Protestantism, on the tide of political opportunism: saying the right things, but perhaps hardly knowing himself what he believed', and so took 'a calculated political risk in promoting protestant evangelism'.[14] It can also be argued that speaking 'the language of Zion' was a calculated way to curry favour with an Edward who was growing up to be a Protestant zealot. Such scepticism may seem entirely justified given the split which developed from the start of 1552 between the duke and the reformist clergy, previously his allies.[15] Cranmer opposed the execution of Somerset and two months later voted against a government attempt to condemn the conservative Bishop Tunstall for misprision [concealment] of treason. By April archbishop and duke were at loggerheads.[16] Cranmer's second Prayer Book, authorized by parliament in April, was held up for six months and at the last minute the Scots reformer John Knox raised objections to the requirement to take communion kneeling. Knox was Dudley's protégé, brought in, as the duke put it, to 'be a whetstone to quicken and sharp the Bishop of Canterbury, whereof he hath need', in other words to force Cranmer to accept more radical reform which would allow the crown to confiscate surplus church assets.[17] Knox, however, did not take to being manipulated and retorted that he was not certain whether or not the duke was 'a dissembler in religion'.[18] Indeed the Scot joined reformers of various hues to make the pulpits ring that winter with denunciations of the secular leaders of society for 'covetousness' – pursuing personal advantage rather than social responsibility.[19] This massive campaign touched Northumberland on the raw – hence his public confrontation with Cranmer – and he deliberately sabotaged the archbishop's plan to reform canon law, something which had been on the agenda ever since Henry VIII broke with the church of Rome.[20]

Yet is this episode really evidence of John Dudley as a wolf in sheep's clothing? Arguably it only demonstrates that he did not understand the church in the way Cranmer and the reformist clerics did. They wanted a revised canon law to confirm and strengthen the independent authority of the church without which there was little hope of the moral regeneration of the English people, a cause as important to them as rooting out Catholic superstition and planting true doctrine. Northumberland's view was diametrically opposite – the church must be subservient to the state. The recent preaching campaign was 'scandalous behaviour, tending to foster disorders and sedition'; in particular, 'certain agitators had dwelt recently on the incorporation of church property and lands and on the dividing up of bishoprics contemplated by the king, proclaiming that those who sought to diminish and restrict the rightful perquisites of the church were heretics, breaking God's law.'[21] The church was forgetting its proper place. 'Let [the bishops] forbear calling into question in their sermons the acts of the prince and his ministers, else they should suffer.' Let them target vice. He opposed canon law reform because it would mean a church which had powers independent of the state. And Dudley was adamant that confiscating 'surplus' ecclesiastical wealth was justified; the financial pretensions of senior ecclesiastics deserved to be cut back:

rather a stout honest man that knoweth his duty to God and to his sovereign lord than one of these new obstinate doctors without humanity or honest conditions. These men, for the most part, that the king's majesty hath of late preferred be so sotted of their wives and children that they forget both their poor neighbours and all other things which to their calling appertains; and so will they so long as his Majesty shall suffer them to have so great possessions to maintain their idle lives.[22]

Of course the bishops hated this, but it does not follow that Dudley was insincere. And, whatever rumour said, his wish to prune church assets was not motivated by personal gain. The major allegation – that he set out to break up the prince-bishopric of Durham in order to establish a northern power base for himself – is simply not borne out by the facts.[23] The crown stood to gain, not Dudley.

Despite this evidence to the contrary, for many at the time and since, the clinching proof that Northumberland was calculating and cynical towards religion came after Jane's cause collapsed. As David Loades put it, 'the defection of those who had adhered to the reformation out of ambition or greed was symbolised by the behaviour of Northumberland himself'.[24] His execution was announced for 8 a.m. on 21 August 1553, on Tower Hill. Ten thousand people were there to watch, but then, without warning, the execution was called off – either cancelled or merely postponed, it was not clear.[25] Instead, the lord mayor and fifty of London's leading citizens had assembled in the chapel in the Tower to see Northumberland and others hear mass 'even as they were wont, forty years ago', 'both with the elevation [of the host] over the head, the pax giving, blessing and crossing on the crown, breathing, turning about and all other rites and accidents of old time appertaining.' Then, before receiving the sacrament 'in form of bread' Northumberland addressed the gathering:

My masters, I let you all to understand that I do most faithfully believe this is the very right and true way, out of the which true religion you and I have been seduced these sixteen years past, by the false and erroneous preaching of the new preachers, the which is the only cause of the great plagues and vengeance which have light[ed] upon the whole realm of England, and now likewise worthily fallen upon me and others here present for our unfaithfulness. And I do believe the holy sacrament here most assuredly to be our Saviour and Redeemer Jesus Christ; and this I pray you all to testify and pray for me.[26]

When next day the execution did go ahead, his speech from the scaffold was equally contrite. There are several accounts of this, some of which may have been 'improved' in the reporting, but there is some agreement that he quoted from the creed, 'I believe in the holy catholic church', and then declared that the country's recent disasters had resulted from separation from the Catholic church. 'Good people, there is and hath been ever since Christ one catholic church ... and yet doth [continue] throughout all Christendom only us excepted; for we are quite gone out of that church'.[27]

Jane Grey and other reformers saw the duke's conversion as blatant hypocrisy: 'like as his life was wicked and full of dissimulation, so was his end thereafter'.[28] Yet twentieth-century experience suggests that confessions and show trials are rarely to be taken at face value.[29] Did the duke see defeat as evidence of God's judgement?[30] Had twenty years experience of being told that the monarch possessed a divine right to determine religion conditioned him to obey Mary? Although suggesting that questions respecting Northumberland's apostasy 'are in fact unanswerable', W. K. Jordan and M. R. Gleason conjectured that he 'was at the bottom of his nature an Henrician politique who really thought in none other than political and military terms' and who 'found comfort in the end in the ancient church whose mercy embraced him'.[31] Another possibility is that Dudley hoped that compliance would take pressure off his family; it is noticeable that his eldest son and his brother followed his example and both survived.[32] Alternatively, did his request on being sentenced to see 'some learned man for the instruction and quieting of my conscience' mean that he had already decided to try to trade conversion for a reprieve? A. F. Pollard suggested it was 'one more expedient' and the popular explanation at the time was that the duke had looked for a pardon.[33] That certainly was the hope he expressed to Edwin Sandys when together they proclaimed Mary at Cambridge.[34] Contemporary French sources say that the duke specifically expressed regret to Bishop Stephen Gardiner 'that he had entered the Protestant sect and abandoned the ancient observances of the church [and] that if God gave him the grace of longer life he would endeavour to amend these past faults, requiring the bishop to intercede with the queen to grant him life in some low and vile condition'.[35] The story which circulated in the English Catholic community of Elizabeth's reign was that Northumberland, who knew 'the gentle nature' of Bishop Stephen Gardiner, had pleaded with him to secure a reprieve. Gardiner promised to do what he could while warning the duke that plenty of people wanted him dead. Mary did begin to yield but the duke's enemies then called up the imperial ambassadors to stiffen her nerve.[36]

On the other hand the scene in St Peter ad Vincula was a stage-managed propaganda coup for the crown, so had the crown allowed Dudley to think that his offer of recantation in exchange for his life had been accepted?[37] It is clear that it was a total surprise for the duke to learn that same evening that he was to die the next morning.[38] He had no notion that he would have no time to seek a pardon. The suddenness of the warning is itself suspicious; the Tower custom was to give the condemned person a full twenty-four hours to compose the soul.[39] On hearing the news the duke wrote to Gardiner and the earl of Arundel beseeching them to intercede for him. The bishop's letter has not survived but the appeal to the earl makes anguished reading and includes the plea: 'how great and glorious an honour it will be in all posterity when the report shall be that so gracious and mighty a queen had granted life to so miserable and penitent an object'.[40] 'Penitence' must surely include the disavowal of Protestantism he had made earlier in the day. Three years later the crown played a similar cat and mouse game with Thomas Cranmer. Corroborative evidence certainly points to the possibility of deceit. Preparations for the duke's execution had all been in place for 8 a.m. on Monday 21 August, with the guard on parade and the executioner waiting, but the mass in the chapel was timed for 9 a.m., and the lord mayor had been summoned to it 'by a letter from the queen'. Clearly there was a degree of notice and as the mayor was instructed to bring with him fifty 'of the head commoners and common council of the city', he must have been warned sometime on the day before.[41] Why then go ahead with the scaffold preparations? Administrative muddle could be the reason, but so could the determination of the crown to reap maximum publicity from Dudley's recantation. Sending 10,000 spectators away knowing that the duke was making his peace with the church was a very definite coup.[42] As the imperial ambassador said, it 'will assist religious affairs here … and not merely in England, but in Germany, Italy and wherever it may become known'.[43] Charles V certainly thought so and ensured a wide distribution of the confession in his territories, both in Latin and in vernacular translations; one was published in Vienna within months of the execution.[44]

The extent to which John Dudley was motivated by reforming opinions will probably always be debatable. But even a deeper religious commitment than most commentators would allow could only account for part of his behaviour. We need something more, and to find it we have to delve into the conventions of Tudor letter writing. Courtiers habitually ended letters to the king with some expression of devotion. Not surprisingly, frequent correspondents (or their secretaries) tended to use the same phrase in letter after letter. Thus the diplomat Nicholas Wotton regularly concludes with: 'Jesu preserve your Majesty long in health and all felicity'; Edward Seymour, the future protector, uses 'Almighty God ever preserve your Majesty in your royal estate, most felicitously to endure'.[45] There are, however, occasions when what is written is personal and much more revealing, and these are notably frequent in the case of John Dudley.[46] In one of his earliest letters to the king after being appointed to the north (towards the end of 1542) he went out of his way to laud the king's offensive policy and the desirability of occupying the Borders: 'O what a Godly act should it be to your excellent Highness to bring such a sort of people to the quiet knowledge of God's laws, the country so necessary to your dominions, by reason whereof so many souls should also live in quietness.'[47] When letters from Henry endorsed his actions he became lyrical:

> And where I have of late received your most gracious letters those same being to me more comfortable than ever my poor wretched life can deserve in the like of that which by the poor carcase cannot be performed to the which good will shall never fail. I shall pray to the eternal God for the long and prosperous felicity of your most royal person with the continual desire of your most kingly heart.[48]

Writing to Henry in January 1544 acknowledging receipt of another royal letter he burst once more into a credo of loyalty: 'my only desire unto the Lord [is] to give me grace to do all your Highness's commandments to your most gracious contentation, with my earnest prayer that I may never live the day to do any thing that may be contrary to the same.'[49]

The possibility of royal displeasure obsessed him. In a letter written to the council early on in his Border appointment, Dudley confessed:

> Therefore knowing mine own infirmity and the fear that it puts me in day and night, lest anything should pass through my negligence contrary to the king's majesty's pleasure, I can no less of my bounden duty and for mine own discharge, but still to trouble your lordships herewith. I have already written my insufficiency to the king's majesty, trusting his highness will pardon me therein for the very zeal that I have to the due proceeding of his grace's affairs enforceth me thus to do. As touching my own travail, I take God to record I mean nothing less than the sparing my poor body in anything wherein I may do his majesty service to his honour and pleasure.[50]

When he had to ask Henry for advice, he grovelled.

These things weighing with myself to this effect hath enforced me to trouble your excellent majesty with my rude letters at this present, being most sorry that I cannot do your highness such service in this your majesty's great affairs as my hearty desire is to do, as knoweth the everlasting Lord who knoweth the hearts of all creatures and to whom I pray and during my life shall do for the prosperous estate of your most royal majesty long to endure to his pleasure and the continual desire of your most kingly heart.[51]

Caution coloured the whole of Dudley's naval career. In writing from the *Great Harry* in July 1545 to put forward a plan to attack the French, he assured Henry that

[neither in it nor] in no other enterprises to be done upon them being never so feasible I will not attempt, your Majesty being so near, without first making your highness privy thereunto and not without your grace's assent to the same; albe[it] that I would of my own part little pass to shed the best blood in my body to remove them out of your sight, but have your grace no doubt in any hasty or unadvised or presumptuous enterprise that I shall make (having the charge of so weighty a matter under your majesty) without being first well instructed from your highness. For if I have any knowledge how to serve you in any kind of thing, I have received the same from yourself; and being so near the fountain[head] and would die for thirst it were little joy of my life. And thus I wish all joy and continual felicity unto your most excellent majesty's person.[52]

Fear of inadequacy recurs again and again. He felt inferior to the captains of the ships he commanded: 'I shall endeavour my self as far as my poor wit and discretion will serve to give them the best advice that I can, albeit that I know it right well I had more need to be instructed in such like case by some of them than they by me.' And he, the lord admiral who had been commanding ships for eight years![53] On occasion fear of making a mistake paralysed him. In August 1545, William Paulet the lord chamberlain asked Dudley whether supplies for the army besieging Boulogne should be routed via Dover or Portsmouth. Prevailing winds made Portsmouth the only realistic option, but Dudley felt unable to act without royal approval, even though the king was away in France: 'I can make him none answer, until such time as your Majesty hath determined your pleasure in that behalf.'[54] The most remarkable example of Dudley's insecurity comes in a letter he wrote to Henry in the following July, detailing progress in the embassy to Francis I.[55] Accidents had reduced the team of envoys to himself and Wotton so he was careful to explain to Henry that when

Francis had invited them to join in a deer hunt 'of force', he had declined saying that 'if we should break our legs or arms' there would be no-one left to do business.[56] Francis 'laughed very heartily' – as well he might – and agreed to excuse Wotton, just in case. The letter ends with even more sycophancy. Lisle told Henry that he had received a personal invitation to join Francis on a boar hunt, but had refused this signal honour: 'I could not attend it, for [preparing] this despatch, for I had rather forbear such pastimes than neglect my duty to your Highness.'

Since Dudley's letters display this almost morbid fear of royal displeasure, we have an essential key to understanding him. Obedience to the king was his absolute; it gave him his identity. The root of this fixation is not hard to seek. As a child he had lived the consequences of his father's disgrace. Indeed that had effectively determined the whole of his life and John Dudley never forgot the injustice. Six months before his own arrest he articulated his neurosis:

> the living God, that knoweth the hearts of all men, shall be my judge at the last day with what zeal, faith, and truth I serve my master. And though my poor father who, after his master was gone, suffered death for doing his master's commandments, who was the wisest prince of the world living in those days, and yet could not his commandment be my father's [dis]charge after he was departed this life. So for my part, with all earnestness and duty I will serve without fear, seeking nothing but the true glory of God and his highness' surety: so shall I most please God and have my conscience upright, and then not fear what man doth to me. They can kill but the body; he that seeks to save that with impure conscience kills the soul.[57]

Even when he had become the most powerful man in England he could describe himself as someone

> who neither hath understanding nor wit meet for the Association nor Body apt to render his Duty any ways as the will and heart desireth. And as yet is a most great grief to me to think it, so I cannot but lament it, that it is my chance to occupy a room in this common weal meet for a man of much wit and gravity. But as Christ in the Gospel did allow the mite or farthing of the poor woman wherein she showed the good zeal and will that was in her, so I trust the same Christ, through the work of his grace will put in the heart of His Majesty to accept the earnest will and good heart that remaineth in me, though there be no other thing, as indeed I of force am driven to confess.'[58]

Obsessive loyalty to the king at all times and in all circumstances declared that Dudley and his family were not traitors; indeed, effectively it rehabilitated his father. And here, perhaps, we have a partial clue to the duke's commitment to Jane Grey in 1553. Suppose that it was not the duke but Edward who initiated the attempt to place Jane Grey on the throne, everything in Dudley's psychology and record would have compelled him to back the king to the hilt. How could a man who found his identity in loyalty deny that identity?

The notion of a duke of Northumberland who was fundamentally insecure flies in the face of contemporary – but pre-Freudian – opinion. It is, however, all of a piece with other evidence of psychological vulnerability. John Dudley needed constant reaffirmation. Tudor courtiers always had an eye out for lucrative opportunities, but Dudley is notable in his passion for status.[59] When following the death of Charles Brandon duke of Suffolk in August 1545 there were offices to be redistributed, William Paulet, Lord St John, was proposed for the senior vacancy, that of lord great master of the household. But Paulet was thought to be seriously ill and Lisle and the king's secretary William Paget immediately began to discuss whether, if he died, it would be worth Dudley trying to secure the office and give up one of the appointments he then held.[60] A month later Dudley wrote to say that simply because the post had been held by a man of Brandon's stature, it was worth having: 'Albeit the thing is no higher than what I have, its being occupied by such a personage would give it more estimation to the world. Take not this for ambition for were it not my duty to offer continual service I had rather seek no promotion.'[61] Concern with 'estimation' is even clearer in another letter to Paget earlier in the same month: 'I would the king had appointed me to serve in the meanest room under some nobleman of reputation for all the world knows that I am not of estimation for so weighty a charge. I should do better service as directed than director; for directions in great affairs appertain to such as have great credit and are feared.'[62] As he wrote to Paget in January 1546 in connection with another possible appointment, 'The more estimation the better credit. The better credit, the more obeyed of those under his charge. This is not ambition, for the King's pleasure will always be acceptable to him.'[63] When he was appointed to Boulogne Dudley was very worried that this might mean being replaced as lord admiral. A memo for the council asked to be allowed to hold on to the post and employ a deputy: 'My trust is that I shall have the king's majesty's favour to enjoy the office of High Admiralty of England, for it is an office of honour of estimation and profit, and within the realm; and having his Gracious favour thereunto I may occupy it with a deputy and serve in this notwithstanding, which I beseech your lordships to consider'.[64] He then set out a

formidable list of the privileges and perquisites needed to sustain his
dignity in the Boulogne appointment.

When a person thinks like this, it is not hard to believe that he might be
morbidly sensitive to perceived disparagement.[65] As we have seen, it was
being undervalued which explains Dudley's decision to join the move
against Somerset in October 1549.[66] According to a later account, a
bitterly offended Warwick called Somerset 'a coward, a breaker of promises, a niggard, covetous and ambitious, and such a one as never none of
service could hope to have any good by'.[67] It is significant, too, that in the
fall of the protector, Dudley recovered the Admiralty, that 'office of
honour of estimation and profit' he had reluctantly surrendered to Thomas Seymour 'for [his] brother's sake'.[68] He was also given full value in
the new provisions which were set up for 'governing the king'. He was
himself appointed one of the six lords in attendance, and his brother
became one of the three chief gentlemen of the privy chamber.[69]

Human motivation is, of course, a minefield. Individuals are always
ready to hide behind cosmetic self-perceptions and, indeed, rarely fully
understand what drives them. When the person lived four hundred and
fifty years ago, analysis is made even more speculative because of the
patchy survival of evidence and the difficulty in fully appreciating the
mentality of such a distant period. But if we accept the evidence that he
was obsessed with status, we have a second clue to his behaviour in 1553.
If loyalty was what drove Northumberland, in logic – once Edward was
dead – he should have transferred obedience to Mary. But if he felt that by
then he was so committed to Jane Grey that he could not withdraw
without extreme loss of face, he might have felt obliged to hold his course.
Indeed one might speculate that what finally made the price of withdrawal
too high was that his son was married to Jane Grey. Where tradition has
seen the Dudley–Grey marriage as Northumberland grasping for the
throne, perhaps we should see that marriage as the fatal consideration
which boxed the duke in.

It is of course possible to reject the whole of this analysis and refuse to
take John Dudley's letters at face value.[70] He would not be the first
prominent person with a distorted self-image. But that he had psychological problems is certainly indicated by his notably poor health record. He
was a hypochondriac. For example, early in October 1552 he was bed-
ridden for at least a month: 'I must seek remedy. I am told it is good to
keep the house warm', 'I am forced to keep my chamber', 'Scribbled in my
bed, as ill at ease as I have been much in all my life', 'I was so ill that I could
not promise to come'.[71] He admitted himself that he talked of nothing

but 'cure and medicine'.[72] In December 1552, 'my health daily worsens, neither close keeping, furs nor clothing can bring any natural heat to my head and I have no hope of recovery'.[73] In January: 'I fear to be sick, as I burn as hot as fire; so did I yesterday, but thought it to proceed of an accident, having great pain in the nether part of my belly. But feeling no such grief now, the heat is nevertheless fervently upon me.'[74]

Admittedly he did have physical problems, specifically a damaged arm which might be traceable to tilting or hunting injuries, and trouble with his leg over the winter of 1547–8 which could have been the result of the hand-to-hand fighting during the invasion of Scotland in September.[75] But there is the strange comment of the imperial ambassador in 1547 that he was not strong enough to handle a great weight of business.[76] The frequent mention of stomach trouble suggests a chronic gastric condition or even an ulcer.[77] In May 1548 he was said to be continually ill and he was confined to his house in September. A long illness is reported in early 1549, stomach trouble in July and at the end of the year a 'rheum'; ill health kept him away from court in April 1552 and again in December 1552 and the New Year.[78] So frequently was the earl confined to bed that on 19 December 1549, at the climax of the struggle following the fall of the protector, the imperial ambassador hinted that he used ill health as a device.[79] Yet on that occasion the earl was certainly not wholly malingering, if at all. A Richard Scudamore called on 19 November and found that Warwick 'hath been and yet is troubled with a rheum in the head that it cause his lordship to keep his chamber'. He had to talk to the earl in bed and Dudley was still housebound a fortnight later.[80] Either it was the most severe sort of cold or Dudley was mollycoddling himself. All in all one must guess at a psychosomatic element in his endless problems – real symptoms caused by mental pressure.

In a modern consulting room, psychological diagnosis can be fraught with difficulty. After an interval of four hundred and fifty years it can never be better than speculative. But in the case of John Dudley there is enough evidence to suggest that contemporaries who were impressed by his confident persona and authoritative manner and who took his recurrent ill health as routine were seeing a carapace he had grown to protect his life-long neuroses.

EDWARD

13

THE YOUNG KING

EDWARD VI was born at Hampton Court amid great rejoicing on Friday 12 October 1537. Every town and village was called upon to celebrate, and the garrison of the Tower fired off a 2,000-gun salute. After more than a quarter of a century, England again had a male heir to the throne. The darkness and foreboding of uncertainty had ended. As the evangelical bishop Hugh Latimer wrote to the king's chief minister, his friend Thomas Cromwell, 'Sir, here is no less joying and rejoicing in these parts for the birth of our prince whom we hungered for so long than there was, I trow, at the birth of John the Baptist.'[1]

Fifteen years and eight months later Edward lay dying in Greenwich Palace. His last words were 'I am faint; Lord have mercy upon me and take my spirit'.[2] It was Thursday 6 July 1553, about 9 p.m. His successor was his sister Mary, and her five years' rule left a legacy of burnings, domestic division and foreign humiliation. It is small wonder that Edward's subjects grieved for their lost king as one of the great might-have-beens, the promise of a spring cruelly nipped in the bud. By and large, later generations have followed the lead of contemporaries. Of the details of Edward's life we know a great deal. By eleven months he could stand, had three teeth and another coming through; soon after this he was weaned on to solid food.[3] We even have a portrait of Edward at twenty-seven months – a favourite in Henry VIII's 'family' album.[4] A great deal is known about his education. We have many of his school exercises and, most remarkable of all, the Chronicle which he began at twelve and a half and kept up until November 1552. But consequent on Edward's untimely demise, all of this, which would have been so illuminating of an adult sovereign, is reduced to ephemera. He becomes the victim of men intent on exploiting his naivety to their own advantage. Or so we are told.

Given that Edward died surrounded by nobles old enough to be his father, it is no surprise that his role in the promotion of his cousin Jane concerns the traditional accounts not at all. They take for granted that he played no independent role in the crisis; he was a cipher. Jane Grey was advanced on the authority of a settlement drawn up in his name, but the duke of Northumberland, not Edward, was the mind behind the proposed changes. When Edward Montagu, the chief justice of the common pleas, was excusing his own part in the episode he ended his petition by saying:

> Who put the king in mind to make the said articles, or who wrote them, or any of them, or by whose procurement or counsel they were made, or by what means he and others were called unto this matter, he knows not; but he thinks in his conscience the king never invented this matter of himself, but by some wonderful false compass.[5]

Robert Wingfield, who was not having to save his skin, was less coy:

> The unhappy king – born to disaster, and subject to abuse and plunder from both his guardians, first by his dearest uncle, the duke of Somerset, then as if from the frying-pan into the fire, by Northumberland – dared not make any protest, but fell in with the duke's wishes; he soon ordered the most skilled lawyers to be called to note his will, or rather that of Northumberland, and to write it with all the ancient legal elaboration.[6]

The voice of later generations is represented by the Victorian historian, J. A. Froude:

> Northumberland had made important progress: he had persuaded Edward. Edward had consented by a strained imitation of the precedent of Henry VIII to name his successor by letters patent or by will; and the council and the lords could thus be forced into an appearance of acquiescence which they would find it difficult to refuse to the entreaties of a dying prince.[7]

Entrenched historical myths are almost impossible to dislodge – and the myth of Northumberland the manipulator of the child Edward has been entrenched for four hundred and fifty years. Questioning is particularly difficult when, as in the case of the 1553 crisis, anyone who wishes to see conspiracy within the surviving evidence will certainly find it. There is, nevertheless, good reason to question more closely. Take the notion of the passive victim. This is certainly a canard needing to be shot; it flies in the face of the political realities of Tudor England.[8] In the mid-sixteenth century, government was a highly personal business, with the king taking all the significant executive decisions directly, so that his word – or more precisely his signature – was of paramount importance, in matters of appointment and patronage no less than policy. Even decisions agreed by his privy council required the king's personal imprimatur. But the daily life of a Tudor king was located (official engagements and public appearances apart) in a private suite of royal apartments known as the privy chamber. There he was attended by gentlemen servants and other congenial companions and there he made his society. In consequence, when making decisions he could find himself the target of advice, persuasion and manipulation by his immediate attendants; office-holders too were well aware that if they were to succeed as politicians and counsellors they must be courtiers first. Hence the privy chamber becomes the true focus of government. It is there royal policy is finally determined, there the king makes executive decisions, there he acts as a patron and there the royal signature is actually obtained. In 1547 Henry VIII even decided that, for his son's reign, the heads of the privy chamber, the two 'chief gentlemen', should sit on the royal council.

None of the dynamic inherent in this was fundamentally altered by the accession of Edward. The king was a child, but he still possessed intrinsic authority and that was still located in the privy chamber. Thus, when the duke of Somerset took up the task of governing in his nephew's name, he set out to isolate the king and his attendants. The object of Thomas Seymour was, as we have seen, to defeat this and access the king's power by making himself persona grata with Edward and building up support among the privy chamber staff. He was successful in getting Edward to approve his marriage to Katherine Parr, but not in persuading him to write in support of his policies in the winter parliament of 1547.[9] This was probably because the protector, before he left for the invasion of Scotland in August 1547, had taken the precaution of having his brother-in-law, Sir Michael Stanhope, appointed to the most senior post in the privy chamber, that of chief gentleman and groom of the stool.[10] On Somerset's fall in October 1549, Stanhope too was dismissed and, as we have seen, three 'principal gentlemen' took over responsibility for the king, but once Warwick had come out on top in the subsequent struggle, the other members of the privy chamber staff, such as the vice-chamberlain Thomas Darcy and John Gates, one of the gentlemen, threw in their lot with the earl.[11] When Darcy was subsequently promoted to the post of lord chamberlain, Gates replaced him and so became the principal channel of information from Dudley to Edward. Between them Darcy and Gates also managed the royal signature – Gates through holding the 'dry stamp', a pro-forma signature which allowed the king's approval to be indicated 'administratively', and Darcy when it was necessary to get the king to sign personally. Dudley sympathizers such as Jane Grey's father were also placed in the privy chamber and so too Warwick's son-in-law, Henry Sidney, who had been brought up with Edward while he was prince of Wales.[12] Thus, from 1550, the king's authority was no longer managed by keeping him in purdah, but by mobilizing the potential of the privy chamber.

Was this manipulation? It can easily seem so. The anonymous French diplomat not only stresses Dudley's personal dominance over Edward but emphasizes the calculation in the system:

> [Northumberland] had placed [at court] a chamberlain, Master Gaz [Gates], who was his intimate friend and [the] principal agent he employed to induce the king to something when he did not want it known that it had proceeded from himself. [Gates] was to report back to him everything said to the king, for this Gates was continually in the [privy] chamber ... All of the others who were in the [privy] chamber ... were creatures of the duke. Sidney was his son-in-law and it can be said that he had acquired so great an influence near the king that he was able to make all of [Edward's] notions conform to those of the duke.[13]

It is, on the other hand, not easy to see how any of this differed fundamentally from the situation under Henry VIII or the situation as it would be under Mary or in Elizabeth's early years. The monarch did not live like Jupiter, sagely dispensing policy, favour and justice from on high. Far from it. The ruler was the focus for intense pressure, and any minister, be he Henry VIII's Wolsey and Cromwell, Elizabeth's Cecil or Edward VI's John Dudley, had to recognize this pressure, attempt to bring it under some control and direct it if possible to the ends he wanted or believed the country required. The reality is not that the continuity of monarchical authority was interrupted between 1549 and 1553 by the venal and ruthless exploitation of a helpless youth. It was the mixture as before. Political action was the consequence of interaction between ruler, ministers and attendants, whichever ruler we are talking about.

Yet surely it made a difference that Edward was a minor? Fundamentally no. The balance between a king and his servants was always determined by accidents of age and personality. Edward's youth necessarily meant that the scales were tilted in his ministers' favour. But that had been the case when his father came to the throne at seventeen and to some extent it was also the case when Henry VIII was in the last weeks of his life. There was not some monarchical 'age of consent' which had to be respected, nor protection for a ruler slipping into his dotage. The functioning of English government and society presupposed an adult sovereign; Edward's minority was an aberration. Hence as he matured, there was a progressive awareness of the impending return to full adult male rule and an automatic and progressive adjustment by individuals and systems. Edward did not have to assert his right to rule, it was expected of him. When only ten, Edward had been told by Thomas Seymour 'that I was too bashful in my own matters and asked me why I did not speak to bear rule as other kings do'.[14] This alone would make one take with a sizeable pinch of salt the story of the cowed victim, or even of the besotted adolescent who 'revered [Dudley] as if he were himself one of his subjects – so much so that the things which he knew to be desired by Northumberland, he himself decreed in order to please the duke'.[15] From John Dudley's point of view, too, the role of Svengali offered nothing. Investing in control of a boy was investing in a wasting asset. The long-term interest of the duke, his family and associates was far better served by encouraging the king in the way he did, bringing Edward more and more into the political arena, letting him 'own' government policy, making him a partner with a progressively larger and larger say, and incidentally demonstrating to him that the Dudleys were the most loyal and able of his servants. This is where Northumberland proved himself to be an effective politician as well as an effective leading minister, and this was where Somerset had proved himself no more competent as one than the other. By an irony of history, Dudley's attention to Edward has been taken as evidence of evil intent and Edward Seymour's far more dangerous attempt to act as a surrogate monarch has largely escaped censure, although the perils were explicitly recognized at the time and should be glaringly obvious in hindsight. And we must not be naive. The age differential was a fact of life, and given that, how else could John Dudley have behaved? What do critics who condemn him for 'exploiting' the king expect? That Dudley should have replaced John Gates with a hostile critic so that the young king could 'hear all sides' of each issue? That Edward should have been 'free to find his own identity'? That the minister should have refrained from pressing policies which he thought ought to be pursued? Moreover the situation cannot be reduced to Edward and John Dudley. With government being essentially government in the court Edward had many contacts, and the surprising ease of access to the royal household meant that he met a diversity of other important people. Total control of a monarch, even one who was an adolescent, was simply impossible to achieve. To be successful, someone like Dudley had not just to influence the king but to carry the court with him – not everyone, but sufficient to present something like a consensus. That was precisely the case with the regime that replaced the protectorate. Analysis shows that 'close connections of career and family bound together the men around the king', and, one might add, the cement was in large measure a commitment to religious reform.[16] This was true not just of Edward's longer-term attendants but also of associates brought in by Dudley, such as Nicholas Throckmorton and most of all William Cecil, who successfully made the transfer from serving Somerset. It is this cohesion which allowed John Dudley to act as *primus inter pares.* His lieutenants such as William Cecil were loyal and reliable, and he was able to leave matters to his fellow counsellors with complete confidence. This was particularly the case with finance. His declared priority was 'to have his majesty out of debt' but, admitting that he was no financial expert, he was happy to leave matters to those with expertise.[17] Rivals did not emerge to take advantage of the duke's frequent bouts of illness; more commonly there were complaints that he was missing when he was wanted.[18] In modern parlance, the duke headed a pretty united team, united because he was loyal to Edward.

Unlike the legend, therefore, Northumberland and the rest of the political elite expected Edward to be increasingly prominent in public life, indeed, welcomed it. The boy was bright, he was precocious and he had been brought up to command. A teenager, his horizons and his independence were expanding month by month. In October 1552 Edward entered his sixteenth year; his father and great-grandfather were each fully independent at the age of seventeen. He had, in fact, shown signs of independence as early as thirteen when in July 1550, on his own initiative, he altered the wording of the oath of supremacy.[19] In the following March he told his sister Mary that he had taken a share in affairs 'during the last year' which was in line with the provision he drafted if a minor were to succeed him: 'after he be 14 years, all great matters of importance [are to] be opened to him'.[20] Edward kept a careful eye on what was going on. His Chronicle records every one of the eleven proclamations issued between 30 April and October 1551, frequently on the day it was authorized by the council or shortly afterwards.[21] In April 1551 a plan was made to debase the coinage and the account of it which Edward wrote has been described by a modern historian as 'proof of his penetrating grasp of the intricate policies with which his government wrestled'; he was then still not fourteen.[22] We have also seen how over the following months he intervened personally to make Mary toe the reformist line. The young king's gradual emergence as a figure in his own right was also noticed by contemporaries. Jehan Scheyfve, the imperial ambassador, remarked on it in January 1552 and again eleven weeks later:

> [January] He seems to be a likely lad of quick, ready and well-developed mind; remarkably so for his age ... Northumberland whom he seems to love and fear is beginning to grant him a great deal of freedom in order to dispel the hostility felt for him. [March] The king is usually present at council meetings now, especially when state business is being transacted in order to lend his personal authority to the council's decisions. He began attending a little before the duke of Somerset was arrested.[23]

That January comment was made in the light of the invitation the ambassador had accepted to dine with Edward on the first Sunday of the New Year. In the relaxed atmosphere the ambassador had taken the opportunity to raise directly with the king the problem of Mary's freedom to hear mass. Edward described what followed as 'no little reasoning' and Scheyfve's account of what was a lengthy discussion makes it clear that the king stoutly defended the line the council had agreed earlier.[24] The ambassador noticed that, all the while, Edward was being watched by Northumberland, and when the debate had gone on long enough he signalled him to end it. Clearly, in a situation re-enacted with countless other young people over the centuries, the duke was allowing a well-briefed Edward to go solo, while keeping a friendly eye on him.[25]

Another sign of Edward's increasing independence was a brush he had with Richard Rich, the lord chancellor, at the end of September. Rich sent back a letter authenticated by Edward and counsellors with him at Hampton Court because the chancellor and his colleagues in London thought that it needed more signatures. Edward replied: 'we think your lordship not ignorant hereof that the number of our counsellors or any part of them maketh not our authority, although indeed their advice and good counsel necessarily becometh the same'.[26] In November there was a further indication of approaching adulthood. To that point documents which needed the king's signature or, more generally, the dry stamp were supposed to be endorsed by six or more counsellors. This was to prevent individuals attempting to bypass the proper checks. However, on 10 November the council announced that the signatures implied 'some derogation to his Majesty's honour and royal authority' and that his instructions ought to 'appear to the world to be, as they are in deed, of such force as needs not to be either authorized or directed by any other'. It was, therefore, decided to resurrect for Edward the procedure set up in 1545 to regulate the management of his father's dry stamp.[27]

Thus an Edward increasingly involved in policy, but an Edward who made policy? Edward responsible for what happened to Jane Grey? That is a quantum leap, and whether the king had taken it or how ready he was to take it is crucial to determining his part in the 1553 crisis. It is also contentious. In August 1551, according to his Chronicle, '[it was] appointed that I should come to, and sit at council when great matters were in debating or when [ever] I would', and in the autumn the imperial ambassador noted that he was doing this.[28] Edward also wrote what can be called 'political' papers, a dozen or so items which include the fatal document transferring the crown to Jane Grey, and others concerned with privy council matters. From these, some scholars – notably W. K. Jordan – have concluded that Edward 'was clearly now beginning to rule'.[29] The opposite argument is that the meetings Edward attended were not executive sessions of the council but special training exercises, and that, though he was bright, his schemes for council business effectively endorsed the status quo.[30]

To resolve the matter we need to put Edward's papers in context as the writings of a thirteen- then a fourteen- and then a fifteen-year-old, and assess how far his grasp of affairs had developed. The first point which is clear is that Edward's political papers hark back to the way he had been educated. From the age of, at the latest, eleven, his tutors had set him to write substantial essays on moral themes. Over one hundred survive, half in Latin, half in Greek, on occasion 2,500 words long.[31] He also wrote exercises in French; his essay attacking papal supremacy runs to 7,500 words.[32] Thanks to this intensive training Edward's instinctive response to any issue was to reach for a pen and work out his thoughts on paper. Thus in April 1550 he handed the Statute Book of the Order of the Garter to the knights to be 'corrected and reformed' by removing traditional religious language.[33] Nothing was done, so next year the order was repeated, but thereafter Edward set out to see what he himself could do. Three attempts to revise the Garter statutes followed, although none was the text finally adopted in March 1553. At least eighteen of Edward's papers on political issues have survived.[34] The earliest – a list of nine points 'to be immediately concluded on by my council' – was presented by the fourteen-year-old in person to sixteen privy counsellors specially assembled at Greenwich on 18 January 1552.[35] At least seven of the topics had been raised in council in the previous three months. Thus it would seem that the object was to allow Edward to play the king, but by proposing what his counsellors already had in hand. About the same time Edward made a schedule of eight 'acts for this [1552] parliament', but again that almost certainly recorded what was already in the pipeline.[36] It was probably with the same session in mind that he sketched an outline for a statute to hold back the tide of fashion and prevent individuals dressing above their station in life.[37] On 3 March 1552 Edward noted in his Chronicle that it had been decided 'for the better despatch of things' to set up groups of counsellors and others to handle issues such as law enforcement, and, predictably, one of his papers sets down the membership and duties of the various 'commissions and charges'.[38] A number of scholars have seen that piece as highly significant and have written of the king 'composing' the lists, even of 'Edward's reorganization of the work and structure of the council'.[39] Yet it is likely that again the paper was only a personal exercise.[40] All the king was doing was to take commissions which had been agreed and explore implementation. Very probably the paper went no further than his desk. Taken together these examples suggest that Edward wrote his papers not to influence policy but to clarify his own thinking.

All of the papers discussed above were produced before Edward was fourteen and a half, but a significant difference appears in the documents from the last year or so of his life. There are five of them, and they show that Edward was again working out his thoughts but now with an evident eye to implementation.[41] The first belongs to September 1552 and followed what his Chronicle called 'a long reasoning', presumably in council, on the question of giving military aid to the emperor. William Cecil, the junior secretary of state, produced a summary of this for the king. Edward then added a conclusion of his own and, as the Chronicle notes, filed the opinion in his desk for future reference.[42] The second document is annotated by Cecil 'the king's majesty's memorial 13 October 1552', a day on which the council met at Whitehall. The opening section picks up and amplifies expert discussions which had taken place earlier in the month, listing twenty-six steps to relieve the desperate financial crisis which the government faced. Next Edward specified ten points to be dealt with 'For Religion' and followed these with fifteen more headed 'For the strength and wealth of the realm'.[43] Probably linked to this is a third and briefer paper in which Edward put down ideas on the best way to realize and use crown assets.[44] In the fourth paper, Edward worked with William Petre, the senior secretary of state. It is headed 'Certain articles devised and delivered by the king's majesty for the quicker, better and more orderly despatch of causes by his majesty's council' and was endorsed by Petre 'for the council, 15 January 155[3]'; the meeting that day was at Greenwich.[45] Characteristically the paper is only in draft, but it is detailed and practical, with sixteen sections plus three more paragraphs added later. Petre then took the draft and reduced Edward's somewhat discursive text to bureaucratic conciseness, with the evident intent that it be actioned.[46] Precisely why Edward drew up the memorandum in the first place is unclear; in a number of ways it endorsed standard practice.[47] There is also no subsequent record of implementation, in all probability because, within days, Edward became seriously ill. But the important point is that Edward now clearly thought (and Petre concurred) that he was entitled to initiate, probably not without help or advice, but sufficiently to put in hand 'orders' for the council. Edward had arrived at the point where his will had to be taken seriously. And the last of these five later papers? Entitled by the king 'my deuise for the succession', it eventually led to Jane Grey being proclaimed queen.

These indications that by 1552–3 Edward was beginning to have a mind of his own can be confirmed by events elsewhere. As we have seen, the parliament of March 1553 saw Northumberland block the revision of the canon law, Cranmer's favourite project.[48] This was in direct contradiction of Edward's memorial which the council had discussed on 13 October 1552, where the 'matters to be concluded' had specifically included 'The abrogating of the old canon law and establishment of new'.[49] [plate 20] A youth under the duke's thumb would have retreated. Not so Edward Tudor. In the notes prepared for his will he charged his executors to 'diligently travail to cause godly ecclesiastical laws to be made and set forth, such as may be agreeable with the reformation of religion now received within our realm, and that done shall cause the canon laws to be abolished.'[50] Clearly, when he wished, the king was able to part company with his mentor.

Reflecting on the evidence about Edward and factoring in his own writings, it is hard not to conclude that, as he entered his sixteenth year, he was becoming a person of some independence and some authority. The habit he had learned of communicating with himself on paper was being extended to communicating with others, and simple reflection was being augmented by action. If he had lived, this development might have given us a better understanding of the mind of a Tudor monarch than anything we have for the rest of his family. It was not to be, but as 1553 dawned, Edward was ready to play a distinctive role in the crisis which was about to break.

14

'MY DEUISE FOR
THE SUCCESSION'

O F Edward VI's political papers, the one central to the crisis of 1553
is a single sheet headed 'My Deuise for the Succession', 314 words
which launched the attempt to make Jane Grey queen.[1] [plate 27] Written
by Edward himself, it is, like his other 'political papers', a working draft
with numerous corrections and alterations which clearly represent
thoughts at the time of drafting and allow us to follow something of his
thinking. Plainly he had yet to show it to an adviser. Originally his plans for
the royal succession had six clauses, setting out who should succeed and at
what age, who was to rule in a minority and what the role of the privy
council would then be. At some point, however, a single, small, but
crucially significant alteration was made in line 3 of the first clause, and
it was this which named Jane Grey as the next sovereign. This change
differs from the other corrections because it contradicted the rest of the
clause and required deletions later in the 'deuise'. Thus it cannot be
the king's original thinking. We have, therefore, to distinguish between a
VERSION ONE which did not single out Jane and a VERSION TWO which did.
A fair copy of VERSION TWO is known to have been made and submitted to
the lawyers, but this VERSION THREE does not survive, although something
can be reconstructed from other material. Finally there is VERSION FOUR – a
formal document that came back from the lawyers – and this Edward
signed on 21 June, two weeks before he died. The great seal was applied
and leaders of the country added their signatures 'to witness, record and
testify the same'.[2] Eventually 102 individuals signed.

VERSION ONE gives no indication of date, and when it was that Edward
began to speculate on paper about the succession has been a matter of debate.
VERSION THREE certainly existed by 11 June 1553, the date of a letter
summoning the lawyers to receive instructions about putting it into legal
form, but the earliest possible date (*terminus a quo*) is more problematic.[3]

S. T. Bindoff believed that the essential object of the document was to facilitate the transfer of the crown to the Dudley family, and so dated VERSION ONE to approximately the time of Jane Grey's marriage to Guildford Dudley – say mid-May – when it was still possible to hope that Edward might survive until the couple had a son.[4] On the other hand, the 'deuise' is in Edward's own italic calligraphy and shows no sign of any advanced weakness. Indeed, nothing in the document suggests that Edward's capacity was impaired or that he thought his death imminent. This, and the fact that VERSION ONE left open the possibility of Edward having children of his own and of an heir who might be over eighteen, inclined W. K. Jordan to date it as early as January or February 1553.[5] In fact a *terminus a quo* for the 'deuise' can be established. It refers to councillors 'to be appointed by my last will' and some notes for that will survive in another of Edward's papers.[6] They cite a statute which received the royal assent on 31 March 1553, which means that the will and hence the associated VERSION ONE of Edward's 'deuise' are unlikely to be earlier than April 1553.[7] An April date is also suggested by preparations beginning in that month for the marriages of Edward's two Grey cousins. Edward needed these in prospect because otherwise, as we shall see, his VERSION ONE would have been even more unrealistic than it is. It is also the case that the public endorsement of Mary during her visit in February and his own recent illness must have made the point that, unless the succession was changed, she would succeed.

Establishing a latest possible date for VERSION ONE (*terminus ad quem*) is more difficult and depends on the view taken of the progress of Edward's illness. He was confined to his bedchamber from 6 February to at least 17 February but was up and, although convalescent, able to appear in public from at least 21 February to 4 March and again on 31 March when he prorogued parliament.[8] By 10 April the boy was allowed to take walks in the palace gardens and on 11 April he went to Greenwich.[9] The next news is contradictory. On 28 April Spanish ambassador reported that Edward had been allowed out only once, and on 5 May that additional doctors had been called.[10] On 7 May the French ambassadors were not able to be received by the king in person.[11] On the other hand, that very day Sir William Petre wrote from Greenwich to William Cecil saying that:

> the King's Majesty, thanks be to Almighty God is very well amended and that so apparently as continuing to keep himself close, as his Majesty has done, a few days longer, there is no doubt his Majesty shall be well able to take the air in a better case than he hath been a good while. And this, being both true and a most comfortable news I send you'.[12]

Northumberland wrote similarly.[13] On 12 May Edward was expecting the annual feast for the Order of the Garter to go forward on 21 May and he also sent encouraging news to Mary which she acknowledged on 16 May as 'not a little to my comfort'.[14] Against this, the imperial ambassador, with his mole among the medical staff, had reported on 12 May that the doctors had finally diagnosed an *apostéme* (suppurating tumour) on the lung and that the story of Edward's recovery was propaganda.[15] On 15 May the Garter feast Edward had been looking forward to was deferred because 'they [presumably the physicians] think it not expedient the King's Majesty should yet come to the open air and remain so long abroad as this ceremony requires', and although when the French ambassadors saw Edward on 17 May they reported that he was 'thought to be out of danger though worn out and bothered by a continual cough', they were clearly not at all convinced.[16] Given this case history, Edward seems most likely to have put his mind to the problem of the succession during the remission he seems to have enjoyed before and immediately after he moved to Greenwich, i.e. not later than the first part of May.

Dating the original of the king's 'deuise' just after the first phase of his illness suggests that what we have is another instance of Edward's habit of working out on paper the implications of a problem which had occurred to him – or, in this case, been forced on his attention by the recent dip in his health. If so, a crucial fact becomes clear. The idea of changing the succession arose *before* he realized that his illness was terminal, and this is borne out by the provisions of VERSION ONE. Its first clause limited the succession to the descendants of his aunt Mary, Henry VIII's younger sister, in other words of his cousins Frances Grey and Eleanor Clifford (now deceased). His half-sisters Mary and Elizabeth were each ignored along with the descendants of his father's elder sister, Margaret Queen of Scotland. In VERSION ONE the king's initial wording reads:

> For lack of issue of my body: to the Lady Frances's heirs male; for lack of such issue to the Lady Jane's heirs male; to the Lady Katherine's heirs male; to the Lady Mary's heirs male; to the heirs male of the daughters which she [Frances] shall have hereafter; then to the Lady Margaret [Clifford]'s heirs male; for lack of such issue, to the heirs male of the Lady Jane's daughters and so forth till you come to the Lady Margaret's daughter's heirs male.

Thus the clause envisaged that if Edward were to die without children of his own, the crown would go to a son of the duchess of Suffolk ('the Lady Frances'), and failing that (in order) to the sons of her three daughters – Jane, Katherine and Mary Grey – then to the sons of any more daughters Frances might have, after which came the sons of Margaret the daughter of Eleanor Clifford. In the event of there being no sons among that generation, the crown was to go to the grandsons, in the same order of seniority. Edward then tried a number of improvements but in the end he kept only one change of substance – this was to add 'to the Lady Frances's heirs male' the proviso '*if she have any such issue before my death*'.

The first comment to make is that Edward's 'deuise' had no relevance to a king in declining health or a country faced with an imminent change of ruler. Indeed, the alteration requiring Frances Grey, the only married woman in the list to produce a son while Edward was alive, made his best bet depend on surviving. Edward's plans were only realistic on the assumption that he would live. If he were to die the 'deuise' would become a device for disaster.

To generations familiar with the subsequent story of the Tudor dynasty, the obvious question to ask of the 'deuise' is why Edward's two sisters, Mary and Elizabeth, were omitted. Each would in turn claim the throne by right of inheritance, but their brother simply ignored them.[17] In the past this has raised some discussion, for although it is obvious that Edward might wish to omit Mary on religious grounds, why the Protestant Elizabeth? One possibility is that it was simply unrealistic to treat the sisters differently. Another – suggested by those who see the 'deuise' as prompted by Northumberland – is that the duke recognized that he had no hope of dominating the younger woman. But the simplest and most convincing explanation is that Edward never even thought of his half-sisters. Fifteen months before he was born, each of them had been declared illegitimate and illegitimate they had remained ever since. He never recognized that they had any claim on the throne.[18]

Personalia apart, what is most striking about this original version of the 'deuise' is that its clear intention was to make female rule impossible. Far from being a move towards putting Lady Jane on the English throne, neither she nor any other woman was ever to be queen in her own right. In effect, Edward was attempting an English equivalent of the Salic law of France which ensured that the monarch was always male.[19] In wanting to confine the succession to men Edward was not exhibiting a personal quirk. His father had rocked Europe in his efforts to avoid being succeeded by Princess Mary. Ruling England and the English was the job for a man. Unfortunately in 1553 there was no suitable man. Other than Edward himself, only one male descendant of his grandfather, Henry VII, was alive. This was Henry Stuart, Lord Darnley, grandson of Henry's eldest daughter Margaret Tudor, but Darnley was only eight years old, was the son of a recently naturalized Scottish refugee and his pedigree passed through two dubious marriages. Going back a generation to the children of their great-grandfather Edward IV netted only one possibility – Edward Courtenay, son of the executed Marquis of Exeter – but for the last fourteen years he had been imprisoned in the Tower of London. As for Edward IV's siblings, their descendants were now only represented by Cardinal Reginald Pole and his brother Sir Geoffrey, both traitors and in exile.

Edward's 'deuise' set out to square the expectation of masculine rule with the parlous genetic position of the English royal house. He resolved the problem by deciding that the women of the Tudor family could transmit a claim to the throne but not themselves inherit, that is they must follow the example of his great-grandmother Lady Margaret Beaufort who instead of promoting her own claim to the throne advanced her son, Henry VII. Initially Edward applied his sexist logic with complete rigour. Having opened with the phrase 'for lack of issue of my body', he remembered that he might only have a daughter, and so altered this to 'lack of issue male of my body'. That, of course, would have given precedence to a male non-Tudor at the expense of his own immediate child, so on further thought he weakened, and crossed the change out; a woman was admissible, but only if his daughter – which, of course, made nonsense of his masculine agenda. Having determined who was to follow him, Edward went on to deal with the way the succession should operate. If the heir was already eighteen years old he was to have immediate authority. Failing that his mother was to be 'governess' [of the realm] but she was to follow the directions of any six of the twenty councillors Edward would appoint by his will. In the event of the mother dying before the heir was eighteen, the council was to rule. But what if at the time of the king's death there was no male heir? In that case the duchess of Suffolk was to be governess – Edward had originally written 'regent' – and failing her the other women in sequence until a son was born, at which point the mother of the boy would take over as governess.

Edward's scheme is very much what could be expected of a teenager, ingenious but wholly unrealistic. What Edward had designed was a gigantic lottery, a race to the maternity ward. Suppose the first male was born to one of the junior women and the second to one who was more senior; can a more certain recipe for conflict be imagined? What is more, in no way did 'my deuise' recognize reality. Frances Grey was still of childbearing age, but her sons only qualified if born while the king was alive. Jane Grey and her sister Katherine were about to be married, but that was no guarantee that or when Jane might have a child nor when Katherine might come to childbearing age. And what if the child was a girl? The 'deuise' envisages England having to wait for its next king until possibly the eighth woman in line or even later. Equally unrealistic was Edward's prescription for government if he should die before a male heir was born. Since Frances Grey would give way as governess of the realm to whichever woman was the first to have a son, she and everyone else would know that her authority was only temporary. Were Frances dead, her daughters would serve in order of seniority but with a similar likelihood of being replaced. But should the mother of the first son to arrive herself die when the boy was again under age, not the next relative but the privy council would take over. This was the uncertainty principle with a vengeance.

Why then did Edward draw up the 'deuise'? Surely the order of succession to the English crown had been settled by a statute of 1544 and then by his father's will?[20] Was he just amusing himself? The answer is 'no'; what he was doing was deliberately attempting to follow in his father's footsteps.[21] Henry VIII had determined the succession 'for lack of heirs of his body'. Edward followed suit. The 'deuise' and the notes for his will together add up to a blueprint for a will which directly mimics Henry VIII's own. In 1547 Henry provided for the country to be governed by a group acting as both executors and privy councillors. In 1553 Edward did the same. In 1547 Henry ordered that gifts and grants which he had promised but not actioned were to be completed – a notoriously risky invitation. Edward made a parallel provision. In 1547 Henry placed the descendants of his younger sister Mary in the line of succession but made no mention of the Stuart offspring of his elder sister Margaret. Edward did the same. In 1547, as we have seen, Henry gratuitously excluded Frances Grey from the succession, while allowing her offspring to succeed. Edward did likewise. Henry used statute to register his decision; when Edward instructed the lawyers to put the 'deuise' in legal form he assured them that it too would be put through parliament.[22] Son was copying father.

Yet recognizing that simply redefines the question. Why did Edward believe that he was entitled to set aside his father's settlement? The answer to that takes us back to the time of his parents' marriage in the summer of 1536.[23] One month after the wedding, a bill was, as we have seen, submitted to parliament to recognize Jane Seymour as the lawful queen and to declare that Henry's two previous marriages were void and both his daughters illegitimate.[24] But Henry had more on his mind than shrugging off progeny from his earlier attempts at matrimony. He believed that God had specifically and incontrovertibly revealed that his first marriages had defied an immutable sacred edict. Mary and Elizabeth were therefore not simply illegitimate according to man-made law, but illegitimate by divine decree. Hence they had to be 'taken, deemed and accepted illegitimate to all intents and purposes, and shall be utterly foreclosed, excluded and barred to claim, challenge or demand any inheritance as lawful heir to your Highness by lineal descent'. Henry, however, had learned by the ill success of his earlier hopes of having children, so the bill went on to state that if he had no legitimate heirs 'of his body', he had 'full and plenary power' to assign the crown to whoever he wished either by issuing letters patent or by the terms of his last will.[25] This was revolutionary; Henry did have heirs – the children of his two sisters. But in specifying legitimate heirs 'of his body' Henry was asserting the right to disinherit his heirs at common law in favour of his own nominee. The act does not identify the nominee, but the king undoubtedly had in mind his bastard son, the duke of Richmond. Unhappily the young duke died four days after the parliamentary session ended, but the legislation meant that if Jane Seymour did not have a son, the king now had a fall-back mechanism to put his daughters in line to the throne while at the same time honouring God's verdict on their illegitimacy. A further point of great importance is that nowhere does the legislation say that parliament had given Henry the power to determine the succession. How could it? Kings called parliaments, not the reverse. What parliament had done was to accept that Henry had this power ex officio; he had it because he was the king. In 1544 a follow-up statute publicized Henry's intentions by naming Mary and Elizabeth to succeed Edward, despite being bastards, not by right of inheritance but by virtue of their father's nomination and on whatever conditions he laid down.

Henry VIII no doubt died believing that he had been faithful both to his God and to the unique worth of his own blood line. But in reality, the way he had manipulated the law had called the royal succession and the monarchy itself into question. In the first place the legislation was too clever by half. In one clause parliament had declared that Mary and Elizabeth were each illegitimate and so barred from inheriting. In a second clause in the same statute, parliament had declared that the nation would if necessary accept first a Queen Mary and then a Queen Elizabeth. The subtle difference between daughters inheriting the crown and daughters succeeding to the crown would be over the heads of most people. For that reason the draftsman of the 1536 act built several unique defences into the statute itself, most notably its ending:

> every clause, article and sentence comprised in the same shall be taken and accepted according to the plain words and sentences therein contained; and shall not be interpreted nor expounded by colour of any pretence or cause or by any subtle arguments, inventions or reasons to the hindrance, disturbance or derogation of this Act or any part thereof; any thing or ... acts of parliament heretofore made or hereafter to be had, done or made to the contrary thereof notwithstanding; and that every act ... heretofore had or made or hereafter to be had, done or made contrary to the effect of this statute shall be void and of no value nor force.[26]

The second weakness was that, despite this final proviso, the act could not survive Henry's own death. After all, if he *as king* possessed the power to determine the succession, then in due course his successor would possess that power and be entitled to make his own choice of the next monarch. This explains why at the start of Edward's reign a statute had to be passed to confirm Henry's provisions on the authority of the new monarch.[27] But that statute would not bar Edward if he subsequently wanted to settle the succession as he wished. In 1553, as we shall see, the lawyers were fully aware of the problem. Above all so was Edward. Faced with the internal contradictions of his father's settlement, he decided to use the prerogative which he now possessed to make a new disposition of the crown. And although his attempt failed, the accession of Mary (and later Elizabeth) simply meant that the fundamental incongruities created by their father's meddling saddled the English monarchy with a contentious succession which was not stabilized until the accession of James VI and I in 1603.

Some weeks after Edward had experimented with stepping into his father's shoes, his medical condition began to deteriorate alarmingly. We know this because the mole in Edward's medical team, a medical student named John Banister, was keeping the imperial ambassador as well informed as Northumberland was:

> In what concerns our king's health be assured of this that he is steadily pining away. He does not sleep except he be stuffed with drugs which doctors call opiates ... first one thing and then another are given him but the doctors do not exceed 12 grains at a time, for these drugs are never given by doctors (so they say) unless the patient is in great pain or tormented by constant sleeplessness or racked by violent coughing ... The sputum which he brings up is

livid, black, fetid and full of carbon; it smells beyond measure. If it is put in a basin full of water it sinks to the bottom. His feet are swollen all over. To the doctors all these things portend death and that within three months except God of his great mercy spare him.

According to Banister the crunch came on Sunday 28 May. The duke confronted the doctors and they were unanimous. Edward was past saving; by the autumn he would be dead.[28]

The fortnight between that case conference and the summons to the lawyers on 11 June was crucial for Jane Grey. Edward's 'deuise' underwent two changes. The first and most important was the amendment which produced VERSION TWO. Edward's original had read: 'For lack of issue of my body: to the Lady Frances's heirs male if she have any such issue before my death; to the Lady Jane's heirs male; to the Lady Katherine's heirs male; to the Lady Mary's heirs male'. Now 'Jane's' was altered to 'Jane' and the words 'and her' inserted above the line, so reading 'to the Lady Jane and her heirs male'.[29] Dropping the 's and adding two three-letter words transformed Jane from the potential mother of a king into the heir presumptive.[30] The next step was to put this amended text into a shape which lawyers could work on – VERSION THREE. How this was done was described a few days afterwards:

> his majesty's own device touching the succession, first wholly written with his most gracious hand [i.e. VERSION TWO] [was] after copied out in his majesty's presence by his most high commandment and confirmed with the subscription of his majesty's own hand, and by his highness delivered to certain judges and other learned men to be written in full order.[31]

Dying he might be, but Edward clearly still had sufficient energy and determination to ensure that VERSION THREE and the changes to Jane were just as he wanted. Indeed, he signed the paper 'in six several places'.[32]

Making this change to his original ideas was the only realistic way in which Edward's long-term aim of an all-male succession could be achieved, but it was suggested at the time – and has been since – that another and possibly more important reason was his wish to protect religious reform. Edward Montagu claimed that one reason Edward gave him for excluding Mary was fear that his 'proceedings in religion might be changed'.[33] The great historian A. F. Pollard argued that 'to the dying king religion was the main consideration'.[34] It has even been suggested that Edward drafted VERSION ONE 'because of his fanatical determination to bar the Roman Catholic Mary'.[35] Yet the women he nominated to produce the next heir faced no religious test, and despite what Montagu said, the same was true of VERSION FOUR the 'declaration and limitation' which he and his fellow lawyers drew up in June. This stressed that if Mary took a foreign husband it would threaten 'the laws, statutes and customs here of long time used' on which 'the title of inheritance of all and singular our loving subjects do depend, which would then tend to the utter subversion of the common wealth of this our realm'.[36] If a bastard could inherit, and inherit the very crown, no property was safe. Of course Edward must have been aware of what would ensue if Mary succeeded, and after his death Jane's supporters, as we shall see, made much of the need to prevent a Catholic *revanche*.[37] Yet Montagu is the only source for the suggestion that the king was driven by concern for religion and Montagu was certainly not objective.[38] What concerned him was saving his property and possibly his own skin, and it was wiser to suggest that religion motivated Edward, not a conviction that Mary was illegitimate.

The task which Edward gave the lawyers was not as simple as the phrase 'to be written in full order' might imply. What was VERSION FOUR supposed to be? Eventually they settled on calling it a 'declaration and limitation concerning the succession of the crown', but such a thing was entirely unknown. Some contemporaries referred to it as Edward's will; others saw it as letters patent, that is a document which announces a grant or an appointment.[39] In fact VERSION FOUR is a hybrid, part patent, part proclamation, part will – an instrument as unique as was the situation. It opens as a patent: 'to all our nobles and other our good loving faithful and obedient subjects, greeting'. It then effectively becomes a proclamation, explaining the problem which needed to be dealt with: 'Forasmuch as it has pleased the goodness of Almighty God to visit us with a long and weary sickness ...'. That done the declaration becomes a will, not in form but in content, stating who is to inherit 'the imperial crown of this our realms of England and Ireland'.[40] Finally it reverts to the style of a proclamation and commands obedience:

> We will that this our declaration ... be truly observed ... and further, we will and charge all our [subjects] upon their allegiance, that they and every one of them do perform and execute this our present declaration and limitation concerning the succession of the crown ... [and see] the same established ... and to repress all other things that shall ... be ... to the contrary ... as they will answer afore God, tender the common wealth of these our realms and avoid our indignation and displeasure; and in witness that this is our very true mind and intent touching the succession of our said imperial crown, we have hereunto set our sign manual [signature] and our great seal.[41]

All this underscores the novelty of the whole procedure. Henry VIII could use his will and testament to settle the line of succession long term because he knew that Edward was the immediate heir. To Edward a normal will was useless. If he was to assert the same prerogative as his father, public expectations had to be changed while he was alive, and that called for something unique.[42]

The puzzle in all this is to decide who it was put everything in motion by making the initial alteration to VERSION ONE, and to that riddle there is no clear answer. The change to 'the Lady Jane and her heirs male' is so slight that it is impossible to be certain, although the probability is that, like the rest of the document, the alteration is in Edward's own hand. But even if it is not, the fact that he personally monitored the copying out of VERSION THREE demonstrates that the change had his full endorsement. What is more, although that version, in the interests of sibling logic, named not only Jane but her sisters as heirs to 'the estate of the crown', the remainder of the text preserved the king's original plan for an all-male succession.[43] Any further daughters Frances might have could only be mothers of a king, and likewise her niece Margaret Clifford. Nor did the exception that Jane and her sisters might become queens regnant pass to any daughters they might have. As in the original, only sons could succeed. In other words, the changes from VERSION ONE to VERSION THREE were fully in line with Edward's original thinking and were watched over by him to sanction the bare minimum of change necessary to deal with the immediate vacancy. After that unavoidable breach of principle, male succession was to apply in perpetuity.

If VERSION THREE of the 'deuise' shows how deeply Edward was involved, the young king's role is also made much of in Edward Montagu's plea to Mary to pardon his own involvement.[44] This tells how on Sunday 11 June he received a letter signed by eleven councillors instructing him to be at the court at 1 p.m. the following day, with Sir John Baker, a former attorney general and now chancellor of the court of first fruits and tenths, Thomas Bromley, justice of the king's bench, and the two law officers – Edward Griffin the attorney and John Gosnold the solicitor. Technically Montagu, Baker and Bromley were all privy councillors, but they were clearly not in the information loop. When they arrived they were taken directly to Edward (where only William Paulet, the lord treasurer, William Parr, the marquis of Northampton, John Gates and a couple of other unmemorable councillors were present). The king stated that 'now in his sickness he had considered the state of this his realm'. He was concerned that Mary was unmarried and might well bring in a foreign husband as king 'whereby the laws of this realm might be altered and changed and his highness's proceedings in religion might be changed'. He had therefore decided that the crown should go as in VERSION THREE, which was read out to the lawyers, and they were told to put it into due form. At this point, according to what Montagu told Queen Mary, the lawyers found 'divers faults not only for the uncertainty of the articles, but also declaring unto the king that it was directly against the act of succession [of 1544] which was an act of parliament which would not be taken away by no such device'.[45] Nevertheless the king insisted and the only concession the lawyers secured was 'a reasonable time' to do the work and to consider 'the law and statutes'. The next day they decided, so Montagu claimed, that they could not obey and would insist that what they had been ordered to do was treason. When they appeared before the council the chief justice noticed that Northumberland was absent, but once their view had been explained either the earl of Huntingdon or the lord admiral (Montagu did not know which) slipped out to warn the duke. Then it was that Dudley came in, and 'in a great rage and fury, trembling for anger' threatened to fight Sir Edward.[46] Attending once more at 1 p.m. on 15 June the lawyers were first given the cold shoulder and then called into the royal presence. Edward 'with sharp words and angry countenance' bore down their objections, insisting that the document be prepared and that he would ratify it in parliament later. At this, Montagu surrendered, 'seeing the king so earnest and sharp and the said duke so angry the day before, who ruled the whole council as it pleased him, and were all afraid of him (the more the pity) so that such cowardliness and fear was there never seen amongst honourable men'.[47] All he asked was that he should be given a valid commission to do the work and a general pardon afterwards. Then Edward switched the force of his authority on to the others. The commission, Montagu added, was duly sealed 'and is to be showed', but Northumberland refused to have the pardon sealed 'because he would have no man in better case than himself'.[48]

By the time Montagu wrote, Northumberland was dead and the obvious fall guy for him to choose, but even so he was unable entirely to disguise the extent of Edward's responsibility. There is also good reason to be unimpressed by the judge's tale of 'an old weak man and without comfort' bullied to do what was illegal. If the judges were as sure as he claimed that the 1544 statute stood in the way of Edward's 'deuise', how is it that VERSION FOUR – which they drafted – includes what is a virtual quotation from that statute to the effect that 'the said Lady Mary and Lady Elizabeth to all intents and purposes are and be clearly disabled to ask, claim or challenge the said imperial crown'. Evidently the experts could, after all, find grounds in law to justify Edward's action. One wonders too about Montagu's claim that it was only on 15 June that Edward mentioned calling a parliament. The example of his father would have suggested this from the start and the imperial ambassador reported that the writs calling for an election were already complete and signed by 19 June; the session was to open on 18 September.[49]

Quite clearly Montagu's account has been edited and embroidered to minimize his own commitment and that of his colleagues. This is not to say that they may not have objected at first. That would have been their instinctive reaction – the judges had a very strong tradition of evading political exposure. But when pressed, as always, they did what they were paid for and moulded the law to give the crown what it wanted.[50] Their subsequent behaviour says everything. On 22 June Montagu and all but one of the men who were 'bullied' returned and signed 'the declaracion and limitation', and so did at least ten more of the country's senior lawyers. Only one is known actually to have refused.[51] This level of professional support for Edward's plan is much nearer Robert Wingfield's understanding, recorded soon afterwards and from a Marian perspective. He claimed that all the lawyers, except Hales JCP and Gosnold SG, supported the plan 'up to the hilt', with Montagu the leading culprit.[52] Thomas Cranmer implies something similar. He was unhappy about the scheme but was assured by the privy council that the king was fully entitled to override his father's settlement, and Edward in person told him that 'the judges and his learned council said, that the act of entailing the crown, made by his father, could not be prejudicial to him, but that he, being in possession of the crown, might make his will thereof.' Even so he asked Edward if he might approach the judges and the attorney general, and when he did they confirmed that 'he might lawfully subscribe to the king's will by the laws of the realm'.[53] All in all this confirms that Edward had strong legal support for the exclusion of Mary and that the lawyers did a good deal more than put Edward's revised 'deuise' into due form.[54] Right was on the side of Jane Grey. Mary Tudor was the rebel.

15

KING AND MINISTER

ACCEPTING that Edward thought up the first version of the 'deuise' and drove it through in its final form of course tells us nothing of any part played by the duke of Northumberland. Marrying his son Guildford to Jane Grey inserted the name Dudley into the original cast list of Edward's 'deuise' and the change to 'the Lady Jane and her heirs male' gave that son a star role. But was Northumberland the impresario? When did he become aware of VERSION ONE of the 'deuise'? Did he persuade Edward to make the amendments in VERSION TWO or was his role limited to implementing what Edward wanted? Jane Grey blamed him entirely for bringing 'me and our stock in most miserable calamity and misery', but, understandable though her conviction is, was she being fair? Direct evidence there is none. On the scaffold the duke said that he had 'done wickedly ... against the Queen's Highness ... but not I alone the original doer thereof, I assure you, for there were some other which procured the same: but I will not name them, for I will hurt now no man'.[1] The French diplomat who claimed that Northumberland controlled Edward through Sir John Gates adds that Gates was 'l'un des principaux' who induced Edward to make a 'testament' prejudicial to Mary, and Jane Grey told Mary that Gates had confessed that he was the first to persuade Edward to make her his successor.[2] When the duke met Sir John immediately before the executions, he said to him 'you and your counsel was a great occasion hereof'.[3] Gates, however, may have been responsible for nothing more than pointing out to an Edward worried that time would frustrate VERSION ONE of his 'deuise' that the answer was 'make Jane your heir'. His counter to the duke was: 'you and your authority was the only original cause of all together', but again this need not refer to anything more than Northumberland's determination to see Edward's will carried through. In effect Dudley said 'it was your idea' and Gates responded 'Nothing would have happened if you hadn't backed it.'

Northumberland's behaviour had aroused suspicion long before Jane came on the scene, even before the execution of the duke of Somerset in January 1552 which was so widely interpreted as a cynical power play by Dudley. In the previous autumn rumours had circulated that Dudley was actually issuing his own coinage and, although this was a vulgar misreading of mint marks on recently issued debased coin, the Council was forced to issue a denial on 14 December; the rumour was still current in January 1552.[4] Some of this gossip came from partisans of the former protector, but not all.[5] In November 1551 the imperial ambassador had reported that the current programme of financial reform and the recovery of assets led some to 'harbour the suspicion and fear that the duke.of Northumberland's object is to gather into his own hands all the resources of the realm, besides his own faction, amounting it is said to 300,000 angels (£150,000) and being master of the strongholds in the kingdom and holding as he does the chief offices either himself or through his friends, make himself king'.[6] Fifteen months later and Scheyfve continued to express doubts, despite the reception of Mary at court in February 1553 'as if she had been queen of England', and despite the fact that the duke was keeping Mary informed about Edward's condition and had sent her 'her full arms as princess of England, as she used to bear them in her father, the late king's lifetime'.[7] 'This all seems to point to his desire to conciliate the said lady and earn her favour, and to show that he does not aspire to the crown as I said in my preceding letters. Nevertheless his conduct is open to suspicion.' What particularly concerned him at that point was the betrothal of Guildford Dudley to Jane Grey, 'whose mother is the third heiress to the crown by the testamentary dispositions of the late king and has no heirs male', and commentators later in the year were convinced that the Dudley–Grey marriage had raised the curtain on a planned coup. Writing from London in September 1553, Antonio de Guaras has Dudley 'causing' the king to bequeath the crown to the Grey family while at the same time poisoning Edward. As soon as he was sure 'of the death of the king' he engineered the marriage with Lady Jane 'in order that in right of his wife' Guildford 'might come to be king'.[8] Commendone's understanding was that the decisive meeting with the doctors took place not in May but in February, after which Northumberland decided 'to possess himself of the realm'. He thereupon arranged the marriage to Jane 'with a very precise purpose', but only when the king was much worse did he prevail on Edward to make a will in her favour.[9] But accounts like these are suspect; they are all post-hoc attempts to reorder the story to fit an assumption about the duke's malevolent intent.

Yet even dismissing retrospective interpretations, the fact remains that Guildford Dudley did marry Jane Grey, and thus we still have the possibility that a Machiavellian duke did engineer the match as step one in a plan to get control of the English throne. Indeed, this can be said to be the dominant interpretation of the centuries since and it is probably the majority opinion today. Some would even have it that Northumberland directed Edward's attention to the succession in the first place. Yet if the duke did prompt the king he was singularly unsuccessful. VERSION ONE of the 'deuise' gave him almost nothing. It only allowed him to hope that Jane Grey would quickly become a mother, which, at the earliest, would be in the spring of 1554, and suppose the grandchild was a girl! Until his grandson arrived Frances Grey would be governess of the realm, leaving the duke to exploit whatever leverage he could through her husband Henry, and that might be very little. Henry Grey was certainly a Dudley supporter but, as we have seen, he also lived in mortal terror of his wife.[10] There was no advantage either in Edward's requirement that, as governess, Frances would have had to have the approval of six councillors for what she did. That was a bare quorum of the board and Edward did not specify that it must include Dudley and his more important colleagues. Nor were Edward's contingent proposals helpful to the duke. The first of Frances' daughters to bear a son would replace her and rule during the ensuing minority, and although once the Grey–Dudley marriage was arranged the odds were in favour of his daughter-in-law being that governess, that was hardly a firm basis for power. The tradition which sees Edward as Trilby requires us to accept a Svengali whose manipulation was decidedly speculative.

However, if Northumberland seems unlikely to have prompted the 'deuise', might he not have taken advantage of it? On that construction, the marriage was step one and, once that was safely achieved, John Dudley persuaded Edward to make the changes which put Jane and Guildford on the way to a throne.[11] Yet what evidence is there of an ulterior purpose? Suspicion is no proof. Even the most innocuous marriage into the royal family invited gossip. When the previous September Northumberland had proposed a marriage between Guildford and Jane Grey's cousin Margaret Clifford, daughter of the earl of Cumberland, the reaction had been 'Have at the crown with your leave', and this despite the intended bride being no better than seventh in the line of succession.[12]

The first indication of an impending marriage between Jane Grey and Guildford Dudley dates from the last week of April 1553.[13] Clearly the agreement to marry must have been reached somewhat earlier and thus would have coincided with or been a little before the time that Edward produced VERSION ONE of his 'deuise'. But three weddings, not Jane's alone, were celebrated at Whitsuntide 1553. Her sister Katherine married Henry Herbert, the son of the earl of Pembroke, and Northumberland's daughter Katherine married the heir of the earl of Huntingdon.[14] Did all three relate to Edward's 'deuise', at this point still in its VERSION ONE state? The Huntingdon match clearly did not, but the Grey/Herbert match put Katherine Grey alongside her sister Jane in the line-up to produce the male heir Edward looked for. Thus if Northumberland's object in marrying Guildford to Jane was to give him a stake in the succession, the marriage of Pembroke's heir to her sister gave an equivalent stake to the earl. Why would a Northumberland, intent on laying his hand on the crown, have sanctioned the marriage of a second Grey sister if this meant that the race to be the first to give birth to the next king would be between his daughter-in-law and the daughter-in-law of as powerful a peer as the earl of Pembroke? Still less would Dudley have personally brokered the negotiations between Pembroke and the bride's father, the duke of Suffolk, which was what the information reaching Jehan Scheyfve indicated, to say nothing of the rumours (which even reached Edward) that the two nobles had an uneasy relationship.[15] Moreover that consideration also applies even if Northumberland had all along intended to engineer the changes which produced VERSION TWO.[16] These did mean that Jane would become queen, but they also made Katherine the heir presumptive, and one has only to look at the threat Katherine would pose to Queen Elizabeth in the 1560s to realize the danger she would have posed to Jane and Guildford.[17]

Taken all in all, it is hard to see that the Whitsun weddings of 1553 were other than routine aristocratic alliances. If there was an ulterior motive, it was to bind the political elite more closely together – which explains the inclusion of Huntingdon and steps which were begun to see Northumberland's brother marry Margaret Clifford.[18] Indeed, the evidence is that the initiative for Jane's marriage did not come from Northumberland at all. William Cecil said that the match had been promoted by Lady Northampton.[19] When interrogated after Mary's victory, Northumberland said that the marriage was promoted by Pembroke, along with the marriage of the earl's son to Jane's sister; later he added the marquis of Northampton (not the marchioness), the duke of Suffolk and 'others', which implies a general welcome for these marriages among the elite group.[20] The imperial ambassador himself came round to the view that the Grey–Dudley marriage was in itself unexceptional. He remained convinced that 'the duke has formed some mighty plot against the princess and feels confidant that he will prevail', but concluded that the weddings of May 1553 were part of a broad strategy to muster the support which would allow Dudley to seek the crown in person.[21] None of his speculations included Jane Grey.[22] Of course with the attempt to put Jane on the throne, what had seemed ordinary did become suspect, so when the imperial ambassadors tried to follow up the clue of 'others' they were denied the names because 'it was thought best not to inquire too closely into what had happened, so as to make no discoveries that might prejudice those [who tried the duke]'.[23] Their chief suspect seems to have been the earl of Pembroke.[24]

If Jane Grey's marriage was not a planned first step towards a crown matrimonial for Guildford Dudley, we are thrown back on the evidence that Edward was determined to ensure a male successor and discounted any possible claim from his half-sisters. At that point, conspiracy theory could suggest that an ambitious Northumberland seized the opportunity and pointed out to Edward the weakness in his draft. Neither he nor his cousins had sons as yet, so the scheme for a succession restricted to men could only come about if the king would tolerate the single anomaly of being himself succeeded by a queen regnant. Once Edward was persuaded, the duke could have promoted the option of Jane and encouraged Edward to make the alterations which produced VERSION TWO. In other words, Edward's concern about the succession coupled with Jane's impending marriage to Guildford created a temptation which, for a man as ambitious as John Dudley, was irresistible. Yet that construction too must be rejected.[25] On 7 May 1553, the French ambassadors in London, René de Laval de Boisdauphin and Antoine de Noailles, wrote a letter to Henry II which proves that Northumberland was already seriously concerned about the succession, and this was a fortnight before the wedding and three weeks before the case conference of 28 May, which we have seen is the most plausible trigger for the alterations in VERSION TWO of the 'deuise' that brought in the Dudley interest.

De Noailles had arrived in London on 30 April to take over from de Boisdauphin who had been in post since July 1551 and whose staff we have already noticed. Having recovered from his journey, on 4 May he and de Boisdauphin asked for an audience with Edward to go through the formalities of accreditation but the king, as we have seen, was too unwell to receive them. The diplomats therefore suggested to Northumberland that the appearance of a private audience should be engineered on 7 May.

Once this fake audience was over, the duke came to the ambassadors and asked them point blank what they would do were they in his place.[26] What did he mean? He is unlikely to have asked the question naively. When seeking the audience the ambassadors had suggested that 'those who were waiting to acquire the succession are not asleep', so was Northumberland simply asking what he should do if Mary and her supporters looked like coming to power?[27] Yet back in February he had greeted the princess as the heir, and on the very day he posed his question to the ambassadors he wrote to William Cecil: 'I will recomfort you with the joyful comfort which our physicians have these two or three mornings revived my spirits withal, which is that our sovereign lord doth begin very joyfully to increase and amend, they having no doubt of the thorough recovery of his highness.'[28]

So if he was not fazed by the prospect of Mary succeeding, and, anyway, now had reason to expect that Edward would recover, what made Dudley ask the question he did? Clearly something had happened since he restored to Mary her full armorial bearings.[29] The most likely something in early May 1553 was a first sight of VERSION ONE of the 'deuise'. It would have struck down the assumption that Mary would succeed, and faced the duke with a huge political challenge – how to secure legislation to exclude the half-sisters. Even when victorious, Mary blenched at asking parliament to exclude Elizabeth.[30] De Noailles and de Boisdauphin put the worry on the faces of John Dudley and the rest down to Edward's condition. Worried the counsellors well might be if they had also learned that Edward was determined to reconfigure the succession to exclude Mary. There would be international repercussions. Where would France stand? Northumberland needed to know.

French interest arose from the alternating cold war and hot war which the Valois monarchs had been waging for fifty years with the expanding Habsburg empire – Austria, the Low Countries, Spain, Germany, Italy and the New World. Each power was interested in England for much the same reasons. Negatively, the concern was that the English would favour the enemy, and worse still give active assistance. Positively, the objective was to build up as advantageous a relationship as possible with an island whose Channel coast was of enormous strategic importance. A king of France could no more contemplate with equanimity an imperial acolyte in power across the Straits of Dover than a Habsburg emperor could be happy if regimes hostile to him were in control of each coast of the seaway through which ran the strategic and economic lifeline of his empire.[31] To these long-term considerations, events towards the middle of the century had added specific dangers and opportunities. Following the death of Henry VIII, the place his will had allocated to Mary in the line of succession had given her cousin, the emperor Charles V, a significant interest in her immediate fortunes and at least an outside gamble that she could become queen. As for France, eighteen months after Edward's accession, Mary Stuart, Queen of Scots, the bride the English had intended for him, had been spirited to France and betrothed to the Dauphin. Not only did that promise a future in which Scotland would be ruled from Paris (so putting England in a vice), but Mary Stuart was Edward's senior legitimate cousin, so that the future wife of the dauphin now had the strongest dynastic claim to the English crown after Edward and his sisters, or immediately, if Mary and Elizabeth could be disqualified. And in the back of Henry II's mind, as always, there was the target of a Calais occupied by the English since 1347.

Recognizing Dudley's gambit, immediately after the fake audience, de Noailles and de Boisdauphin informed Henry II of the quandary the duke was in. The French king responded by rushing over his confidential diplomatic secretary, Claude de l'Aubespine. The visit was disguised as a gesture of sympathy to Edward, and the English ambassadors at the French court were assured that he would be travelling by easy stages and would happily convey a letter from them.[32] But so urgent was the secret agenda that either a trick was played on the ambassadors or de l'Aubespine could not wait. As Sir Thomas Chaloner complained in a letter to Cecil written on the evening of the 16th when the envoy left, 'We marvel not a little at the sending of de l'Aubespine, we never having been made privy to the same. And specially that they should tell us of his readiness to depart in the afternoon when he was already departed in the morning.'[33] De l'Aubespine travelled express, in a coach and four, and was in London in about five days, in time to join in the second day of the wedding festivities.[34] Unfortunately no instructions for de l'Aubespine are extant nor any report on the visit. Indeed, in all probability everything was done by word of mouth to ensure maximum security. The imperial ambassador reported that the envoy went with de Boisdauphin to Greenwich on May 28 to a very full meeting of the council; Dudley, who he said had been away, had come back specially.[35] The meeting was in secret (there is no record of it in the council register) and for extra cover de l'Aubespine had brought a request that Princess Elizabeth would stand godmother to Henry II's newborn daughter. Nevertheless Scheyfve got hold of a story that France had offered help to Northumberland in the event of the king's death and that the price for this might be ceding possession of Ireland.

The first part of this could well be near the truth, perhaps a guarantee by France to counter possible imperial interference in the succession, something which the English would see as worth having. And the French certainly thought that England had jumped at the offer of united action against Charles. Of course, given Henry's private agenda, the English had to be cautious, but it would be in the French interest to neutralize whatever Charles V might do. Subsequent French diplomatic correspondence reveals very little more of what passed at the meeting, only the most cagey of references to the visit. In a letter to the king, de Noailles called it 'no less necessary for the present than presumably it will be useful and profitable to you in the future', and Henry expressed satisfaction 'that the union there, is such as you write me'.[36] But whatever the detail of de l'Aubespine's offer of assistance, the council now knew that if it obeyed the king's wish to implement VERSION ONE of the 'deuise', France would hold the ring and prevent the emperor interfering. Significantly, the courier who conveyed de l'Aubespine's despatch to France was provided by the council.[37]

Northumberland and possibly other councillors had a second and, as it proved, even more momentous meeting on that Friday in May – the case conference with Edward's doctors. The revised opinion of the profession, that Edward had weeks not months to live, created an immediate crisis. Within days the decision would have to be taken whether or not to implement the king's wishes. So between the conference on 28 May and the summons to the lawyers on 11 June, Jane Grey's future teetered in the balance as Northumberland, and the 'some other' he would not name, wrestled among themselves and with the king. If Edward was to be obeyed, then the only practical course was to modify VERSION ONE and nominate a stopgap female ruler. There were only two possible names, Jane Grey and her mother, and both Henry VIII's will and VERSION ONE of the deuise had ruled out Frances Grey. So Edward altered his original draft to produce VERSION TWO of his deuise and on 12 July the assembled lawyers were ordered to produce the documents making Jane Grey heir to the throne. Two days later Frances visited Edward, no doubt to have matters explained to her.[38] John Dudley cannot have failed to recognize the huge prize all this promised to his family – but equally the danger. Perhaps he did jump at the opportunity, but his past record suggests he would have preferred caution. Yet in reality he had no choice. The alternative was to defy the king, and that he could not do.

Making Jane Grey heir to the throne was not the climax of a long-maturing plan, it was a decision cobbled up in a fortnight and possibly made easier because of the guarantee of French support. Putting that conclusion in the context of what we know of the progress of Edward's illness, and making due allowance for conjecture, the sequence which emerges from this discussion is as follows:

End of January 1553	Edward falls ill
February	Mary visits the court and is effectively endorsed as heir apparent by Northumberland and the council.
March	Edward improves sufficiently to handle parliamentary duties. Northumberland keeps Mary informed.
April	Plans for the Grey–Dudley wedding.
April	Edward drafts VERSION ONE of the 'deuise'.
before 28 April	Northumberland restores Mary's heraldic achievement.
late April	Edward shows VERSION ONE to Northumberland.
7 May	Northumberland approaches de Boisdauphin and de Noailles.
25 May	Jane marries Guildford.
28 May	d'Aubespine brings the council a message from Henry II.
28 May	Case conference indicates Edward's condition is terminal.
28 May–11 June	Edward alters the 'deuise', so producing VERSION TWO. Edward supervises the writing of VERSION THREE.
11 June	Lawyers summoned to turn VERSION THREE into VERSION FOUR.

If this construction is sound, Edward's wish to change the succession faced Northumberland with a choice not unlike the one his father had faced – does the duty of a minister to obey the king that now is mean that he has to ignore the risk of future repercussions? To add to this dilemma, the marriage of his son Guildford to Jane Grey meant that Edward's scheme would draw in his own family. At first the duke could hope that the boy would recover and so remove the need to choose, but the report at the case conference made decision inescapable.[39]

16

THE WILL OF A KING

IN the meeting with the French ambassadors on 7 May and the follow-up on 28 May the diplomats were received by Edward's privy council, not by Dudley alone. This prompts the question, 'How do these other privy councillors fit into the story?' The duke claimed that he had acted 'by the instigation of many whom he would not name', but was he telling the truth, or had his colleagues, as they claimed afterwards, been browbeaten into subservience?[1] Was their story, like that of the lawyers, a desperate attempt to row back from the extent of their commitment to Jane?[2] John Ponet, the reformist bishop of Winchester, was no admirer of Northumberland, but as he looked back from exile on the events of 1553–4 he had no doubt that the duke was not acting alone.

> They that were sworn chief of council with the Lady Jane, and caused the queen [Mary] to be proclaimed a bastard throughout all England and Ireland; and they that were sorest forcers of men (yea, under the threatened pains of treason) to swear and subscribe unto their doings ... afterward became counsellors (I will not say procurers) of the innocent Lady Jane's death; and at this present are in the highest authority in the queen's house, and the chiefest officers and doers in the common wealth.[3]

Council attendances certainly indicate that the leading lay members of the privy council were at least complicit.[4] During the first four months of Edward's illness a council meeting was, on average, attended by five or six senior councillors. From the conference with the doctors on 28 May to 16 June when the council register ceases, the average attendance of seniors was ten.[5] Individual attendances jumped likewise, from a senior councillor being present on average at 53% of the meetings to attendances of 92%. Even more striking, there were no absentees at all in the crucial period between 11 and 16 June, that is between the lawyers first being called and the day after work began on drafting VERSION FOUR.[6] To this numerical evidence can be added faces and hands. Montagu named every senior councillor except for Jane's father as active in supporting Edward's demands. All of them signed the king's final 'declaracion'.[7]

Every signature on the 'declaration' does, of course, represent a unique personal decision, and in most cases we have no way of knowing what lay behind it. Northumberland's psychology suggests that for him the overwhelming motivation would have been obedience to the king. Edward Montagu's account strongly suggests that others felt the same and that the line-up of the privy council behind Edward's 'declaracion' was a conditioned deferring to royal commands. Montagu claimed that what ended his personal resistance was being charged to obey 'on his allegiance' with 'divers of the lords that stood behind' muttering that 'if they refused to do that, they were traitors'.[8] Yet Edward was dying. Surely in the five days it took the lawyers to produce VERSION FOUR, some councillors must have asked what they had let themselves in for. Was loyalty to the current king enough to carry forward so momentous a commitment?[9] Would VERSION FOUR stick? If not, they could be horribly exposed once Edward was gone. Whether or not they had second thoughts, Edward certainly feared that councillors might repudiate his 'deuise' as soon as he was dead. He therefore ordered them to covenant together to implement 'his majesty's own devise … by his highness delivered to certain judges … to be written out in full order'.[10] The resulting agreement can conveniently be called 'an engagement', and is a single sheet signed by sixteen counsellors, the three secretaries of state, the law officers and the lawyers who most probably were those closely involved in drafting the deuise.[11]

> We whose names are underwritten … do … agree and by this present [document] signed with our hands and sealed with our seals, promise by our oaths and honours to observe, fully perform and keep all and every article [of VERSION THREE].
>
> And we do further promise by his said majesty's commandment never to vary or swerve, during our lives, from the said limitation of the succession but the same shall to the uttermost of our powers defend and maintain. And if any of us or any other, shall at any time hereafter (which God forbid) vary from this agreement or any part thereof, we and every of us do assent to take, use and repute him for a breaker of the common concord, peace and unity of this realm, and to do our uttermost to see him or them so varying or swerving, punished with most sharp punishments according to their deserts.

The 'engagement' does not, in fact, carry the seals of each participant, but the signatures were witnessed by Edward in person. Such a document was, of course, hardly worth the paper it was written on, but it is a final indication that Edward was determined to be obeyed, even beyond the grave. It carries no date but very probably it had been agreed by Sunday 18 June when the French ambassador detected a relaxed mood at court, which suggested to him that some decision had been reached.[12]

Despite the fact that the 'engagement' was 'just a scrap of paper', getting people to commit to it seems not to have been plain sailing. Despite the security at council meetings, the imperial ambassador picked up a story that some councillors were in favour of Mary being allowed to succeed provided she bound herself to make no religious changes; others said, 'on no account'.[13] Be that as it may, Scheyfve and de Noailles each identified opponents – the marquis of Winchester, the earls of Shrewsbury and Bedford and Sir Thomas Cheyne, the treasurer of the household.[14] As Mary made clear after her victory, the only one she believed had been truly reluctant was Cheyne. Within four days she put him in charge of the Tower of London, whereas the rest were only grudgingly admitted to grace.[15] And Mary's suspicions may well have been justified, since there is a whiff of something less than high principle about those thought to have opposed the 'engagement'. After signing, Bedford and Shrewsbury each received a significant grant of land, so any reluctance could have been standing out for the right price.[16] Pembroke's support might have been thought guaranteed by the potential dividend from his son's marriage to Katherine Grey, but he received a land grant too.[17] Winchester too must have had some private motive to explain what, according to John Knox, was his vociferous support for Jane:

> Who was most bold to cry, 'Bastard, bastard, incestuous bastard Mary shall never reign over us?' And who, I pray you, was most busy to say 'Fear not to subscribe with my lords of the king's majesty's honourable privy council. Agree to his grace's last will and testament, and never let that obstinate woman come to authority. She is an arrant papist; she will subvert the true religion and will bring in strangers, to the destruction of this common wealth'; which of the council I say had these and greater persuasions against Mary, to whom he now crouches and kneels? Shebna the treasurer [i.e. Winchester].[18]

Self-interest also brought the earl of Arundel on board. He had been dismissed from the council and heavily fined for complicity with the duke of Somerset, but, although he would later reject his niece Jane Grey, being restored to the council on 21 June and having his fines cancelled seem to have been inducement enough to secure his signature not to the 'engagement' (rehabilitation came too late for that), but to the 'declaration' which came back that day from the lawyers.[19]

As well as persuasion, threats may have helped to secure compliance, hence Edward Montagu's hint that the solicitor general was leaned on – he signed both the 'engagement' and the 'declaracion'.[20] Hence too, John Ponet's reference to the 'forcers of men (yea, under the threatened pains of treason) to swear and subscribe unto their doings'.[21] Not threats, perhaps, but certainly pressure was put on Archbishop Cranmer who, as we have noted, had serious reservations about the advice being given by the royal lawyers.[22] According to a memoir used by John Foxe, Cranmer was not approached until 'the whole council and chief judges had set their hands' to the 'engagement'.[23] Evidently he was expected to be difficult; indeed, as the archbishop assured Mary, Northumberland had seen him as a lost cause, and 'never opened his mouth to me to move me any such matter, nor I him; nor his heart was not such toward me (seeking long time my destruction) that he would either trust me in such matter, or think that I would be persuaded by him'. Cranmer's initial ground was that to subscribe would be to break the oath he had sworn to uphold Henry VIII's will, and on being told that the council 'had consciences as well as he' the archbishop responded that 'I am not the judge over any man's conscience but mine own only'. Next he insisted on speaking to Edward but he could get no opportunity to dissuade the boy since he was never allowed to speak with him alone; the marquis of Northampton and Darcy the lord chamberlain saw to that. It must have been after he had, with Edward's permission, approached the judges and the attorney general that the archbishop had his one confrontation with Dudley 'openly at the council table [where] the duke said unto me that it became not me to say to the king as I did, when I went about to dissuade him from the said will'. Even though the lawyers confirmed that 'he might lawfully subscribe to the king's will by the laws of the realm', the archbishop still thought the opinion 'very strange' and only signed after a personal appeal from Edward 'that he trusted that I alone would not be more repugnant to his will than the rest of the council were'.[24] Cranmer may even have tried to gather a protest group in council since his subsequent plea to Mary was on the ground that 'so many' had already been pardoned 'which travailed not so much to dissuade both the king and his council as I did', and he subsequently challenged erstwhile colleagues, now on Mary's council, to speak up for him: 'Some of you know by what means I was brought and trained unto the will of our late sovereign lord King Edward VI and what I spake against the same, wherein I refer me to the report of your honours'.[25]

The other person who claimed that he had tried to avoid signing was William Cecil. Immediately after the collapse of Jane's government he prepared a submission to Mary ending 'God of justice, who saves the righteous in heart, be my advocate'.[26] Much of it concerns events after Edward's death, but it does assert that, when he first heard of the project, Cecil decided to go into exile, only for John Cheke, recently appointed as a third secretary of state, to dissuade him by recommending that he read the Plato dialogue which explains why Socrates refused to flee Athens and a sentence of death. The submission also says that he told both Cheke and William Petre, the senior secretary, that he was going to 'stand against the matter', and it asks that he be distinguished 'from them who I served'. Mary believed, or was prepared to believe this – Cecil's sister-in-law was one of her favourites – but a guilty conscience troubled him for at least the next twenty years. We know about this because a curious letter survives from one of his oldest servants, Roger Alford.[27] Dated 4 October 1573, it was a response to a Cecil enquiry for some particular detail of 1553. We cannot tell what Cecil was concerned about or why, nor whether this was a private worry or the result of being challenged, because rather than answering a specific question Alford decided to respond 'from the begin-ning, choosing rather to write you more than you desire, than less than you would be remembered [reminded] of '.[28] This decision makes one suspect that Alford had realized (or gathered from the covering letter from Cecil's secretary, now missing) that the real wish was to have his detailed recollection of events put on record. It was not as if Cecil did not have a copy of his 1553 submission; in a postscript to his letter, Alford told him where to find it.[29] Moreover, Cecil himself endorsed the letter 'Roger Alford, concerning his knowledge of the times, 1553', so it is hard to believe that Cecil simply wanted to remedy a lapse in memory.

According to Alford's 1573 account, Cecil told him a few days after the Grey–Dudley marriage that information had been leaked to him of 'a device of King Edward's, whereby the succession should be settled', and further leaks revealed that the plan was to make Jane queen. 'And', Alford wrote, 'you thought, when the matter was more riper, it is like you should be called to it; but whatever became of you, said you, you would never partake of that device'. The letter goes on to say that Cecil began to show signs of fear, went 'weaponed' and did his best to insure his assets against confiscation, but all the while hoping to avoid being called and relying on the judges to hold out. Once their resistance crumbled Cecil was summoned to the council: 'When the duke of Northumberland was present, where after others had ordinarily set their hands, you were called on (as after you told [me] by the old earl of Shrewsbury, and after by others, the said duke present saying nothing) to put yours.' When Cecil would not sign, his refusal was put on hold, but once the judges and everyone else had signed, he was called before the king.

> Upon [Edward's] commandment that you should subscribe his instrument, you answered it, that allowing it, as a counsellor you could not, for causes you showed him. Whereupon as I remember also, he said, he willed you to subscribe as a witness, that it was his pleasure to have it so to pass: which you have no reason to deny. And so as the last man you subscribed.

William Cecil had as much as any man to gain from a Grey monarchy. He was Northumberland's right-hand man and related by marriage to the Greys; Jane's father called him 'cousin'.[30] But he was also an astute politician and may well have expressed doubts to close friends whom he could then call on if things turned sour and he needed an alibi. That said, the excuses offered in 1553 and 1573 are less than convincing. The appeal to Mary claims that while Jane was on the throne he carefully avoided writing anything offensive – sacrificing others in the process – but his signature appears on both the first council letter repudiating Mary's claim and the letter to the Kent JPs which described her as 'the Lady Mary, bastard daughter of the late king ... Henry VIII'.[31] The appeal also has 'I did refuse to subscribe the book, when none of the council did refuse'. Alford, however, admits that Cecil did sign 'the instrument', but last and only as a witness. The terms used – 'the book' and 'the instrument' – plainly refer to the 'declaracion' when it came back from the judges, and thus conveniently blur the fact that before Cecil was faced with that, he had already signed the engagement. So do we have an accidental or a deliberate confusion? Sir William's agreement to 'subscribe as a witness' only makes sense if it refers to the 'engagement', not 'the book'. There his signature is out of the order of seniority – after rather than before that of John Cheke – and that has been construed as 'the last man'.[32] Yet even if Cecil was the last of the lay counsellors to sign the engagement, that hardly rescues his honesty.[33] The engagement is a compact between the signatories, and the person who witnessed it was the king. Whatever he said later, Cecil's signature made him party to the agreement 'to fully perform ... all and every article [of VERSION THREE]'.

There are other reasons too for suspecting that Cecil's stories are as self-exculpatory as Edward Montagu's. He told Alford that he deliberately avoided attending the council except when 'sent for', but, specially summoned or not, Cecil was present on 11 June when the letter went out summoning the lawyers; indeed he signed it.[34] No formal council meeting was held on 12 June when Montagu and his colleagues received their instructions and Cecil did not sign the letter of 14 June which summoned them to meet with the king on 15 June, but the privy council register shows he was present at that crucial final confrontation.[35] The plea 'I didn't know, I wasn't there' clearly will not wash. Cecil's 1553 submission also stresses the risk he ran in refusing to sign – 'in what peril I refer it to be considered by them who know the duke'. However, Alford said that on the one occasion when Cecil expected to be arrested, he came back from council saying that nothing had been 'done in that matter', and when eventually he was asked to sign, Northumberland stood aloof and the urging came from the earl of Shrewsbury and the other councillors. The most charitable view of Cecil's excuses is that, to save his skin, he was decidedly 'economical with the truth'.

While the lawyers were drafting and engrossing VERSION FOUR ready for the great seal and Edward's signature, messages went out summoning prominent figures to court so that as soon as the 'declaracion' was back from Chancery on 21 July and the king had signed, countersigning by 'our counsellors and other our nobles' could begin.[36] The archbishop of Canterbury and the chancellor, the bishop of Ely, head the list, followed by twelve of the eighteen adult dukes, earls and viscounts. Most of these had previously signed the engagement but the new names included the earl of Westmorland, a councillor hitherto absent, and also the earls of Oxford and Worcester. Among the absentees, the earl of Rutland and the privy councillor Viscount Hereford can probably be accounted for by distance; each became a committed Jane supporter. Three of the earls who were missing are represented by their sons, although it could be significant that Derby was later reported as raising troops for Mary, and John Bourchier, earl of Bath did rally to the Princess; the earl of Sussex, Thomas Radcliffe, did so too, but reluctantly.[37] The junior peers are much less well represented, a mere twelve out of a possible thirty.[38] The remainder of the hundred and two signatories were lawyers, courtiers, the lord mayor of London and six aldermen, and miscellaneous notables. Collecting that number took several days. The judges 'and many others' signed on the 22nd and the Londoners as late as 8 July. It is quite clear, too, that those signing knew they were endorsing the king's decision. Jane Grey's accession proclamation specifically says so, and before the Londoners signed Winchester explained the document and drew their attention to the 'engagement', stating 'that all the … councillors, together with nearly all of the chief nobility of the realm had faithfully promised and bound themselves by oath and manual subscription to a writing … that they would accomplish and perfect this arrangement conceived by the king's majesty during his illness'.[39] As with the 'engagement', gathering as many signatures as possible to the 'declaracion' was a deliberate attempt to bind men to her cause. The promotion of Jane Grey to the crown was not a maverick adventure of Northumberland and a few cronies.

Reaching this conclusion brings with it a problem. Why did all the senior members of the privy council and so many of the political elite commit themselves to rejecting Mary's right to succeed Edward, a right which had been formally in place for ten years and anticipated for even longer? The risk is obvious even today, and at the time must have been blatant. The explanation that an assemblage of such distinction were simply frightened of the duke of Northumberland can be dismissed out of hand. For a more substantial answer we must look to the way Henry VIII had interfered with the common law of inheritance. As S. T. Bindoff wrote on the four-hundredth anniversary of the 1553 crisis, the changes Henry attempted 'encouraged the idea that the succession to the throne was not something settled and unalterable but that it could, and perhaps should, be regulated by the reigning sovereign in what he considered the national interest.'[40] So far Henry's schemes had been untested; now members of the elite had to make up their minds. Accepting Mary meant setting aside the inheritance rights of legitimate heirs in favour of a bastard. Accepting Jane meant a return to common law. That was the choice. True, Edward was asserting royal prerogative, but in doing so he was restoring the legitimate line of inheritance and that was what mattered. The hoi polloi, of course, could not be expected to appreciate the casuistry in Henry's legislation; his distinction between illegitimate children who were unable to succeed to the crown as heirs but were able to succeed as nominees made no sense to most people. How could anyone who was in line to become the monarch not be in the line of succession? When, in a Paul's Cross sermon on Sunday 16 July, Nicholas Ridley, the bishop of London, pointed out that neither princess could inherit because each was 'illegitimate and not lawfully begotten in the estate of true matrimony according to God's law. And so found both by the clergy and acts of parliament made in this realm in King Henry the VIII's days', 'all the people was sore annoyed with his words, so uncharitably spoken by him in so open an audience'.[41] The nobility and gentry and those with education might be expected to understand, and perhaps when the legislation was passed in 1536, the thrust of Henry VIII's thinking had been made clear to peers and MPs. But that was twenty years earlier and some, perhaps many, of the political nation took the naming of Mary in the 1544 act as effectively legitimizing her. John Harington of Exton in Rutland had been an MP in both 1536 and 1544, yet when he learned that Mary had been proclaimed queen at Bury St Edmunds, he called for a toast, 'brought forth a Statute book, and laid open upon the board that every man might read it; And [he] had noted [marked] the substance of the Statute for the "declaracion" of the Queen's Majesty's right to the Crown of England, after the death of King Edward. And so, pointing to it with his finger said never a word.'[42]

A 'heavy man for her grace', Harington was not in the least concerned to scrutinize Mary's statutory right. The act said that she should be the next ruler and that was that. Yet for anyone unimpressed by or ignorant of Henry's original 'subtle arguments', it was simply illegal for a king to nominate a successor who was not his heir. Robert Aske, leader of the 1536 Pilgrimage of Grace, had said of the offending statute, 'since the Conqueror, never king declared his will of the crown of this realm, nor never was there known in this realm no such law'.[43] Moreover, if it was unacceptable for a king to pluck a successor out of the blue, it was utterly unthinkable that illegitimate children should inherit. That basic tenet of the common law had been challenged and confirmed by statute as long ago as 1236.[44] Even foreign observers were clear on this. The Venetian ambassador reported that what persuaded Edward was Northumberland's argument that Henry had acted illegally in making bastards his heirs, and that the statutes were null and void since parliament could not deprive the legal heir.[45]

The need to persuade prospective signatories of the justification for Edward's decision explains why, in its final form (VERSION FOUR), the 'declaracion' was given a long opening apologia.[46] It recites in detail the provision in the 1544 Succession Act that Mary should succeed Edward and, failing her, Elizabeth. Then it rehearses that 'Mary our said father's daughter' and Elizabeth 'our said late father's second daughter' are illegitimate because the Aragon and Boleyn marriages were each 'clearly and lawfully undone ... by sentence of divorce according to the ecclesiastical laws' which had been ratified by 'divers acts of parliament remaining in full force'.[47] Finally the conclusion: 'the said Lady Mary and Lady Elizabeth to all intents and purposes are and be clearly disabled to ask, claim or challenge the said imperial crown ... as heir or heirs to us or to any other person.' Whatever the common people felt, any informed person reading the 'declaracion' could have no doubt that Edward had good grounds for his action. If bastards could succeed to the crown, what security was there for the heirs of ordinary men? What is more, Edward's 'declaracion' is careful to point out that although the king had 'no issue of our body lawfully begotten', the Grey sisters and Margaret Clifford were 'very nigh of our whole blood, of the part of our father's side, and being natural born here within the realm' – this last a way of dismissing the Stuarts.[48] He was not, like his father, assigning the crown 'to such person ... as shall please your highness'. His half-sisters were illegitimate, so the true heirs were Jane and his other cousins. It was a persuasive case and the numbers willing to endorse the provisions speak for themselves.

Yet in this need for careful justifying argument lay a weakness. The 'declaracion' might convince the hundred or so persons who were shown it, but what of the nation at large? Nothing seems to have been circulated outside London. Despite being partially in the form of a proclamation, the 'declaracion' was not distributed as a proclamation. The provinces never heard the case for Jane. Why Edward's justification was not circulated while he was alive can hardly have been because of pressure of time; there would be a fortnight between the engrossed document becoming available for signature and Edward's death on the evening of 6 July. Was the calculation that issuing it risked unrest? Or was it simply assumed that once government, the leaders of society and the capital were known to be obeying Edward, the rest of the country would acquiesce? The French, indeed, were specifically assured that Northumberland could safely rely on 'the council and the aldermen of London'.[49] There was much in past history to warrant that confidence, but on this one occasion it would prove to be a horrible misjudgement.

PART III

THIRTEEN DAYS

17

PREPARATIONS

WHEREVER the responsibility for Edward VI's 'deuise' lies, by the beginning of June 1553, Northumberland and the principal councillors knew very well that the king had only weeks to live. What preparations did they or could they make to bring in Queen Jane? To modern eyes what stands out is the obvious step they did not take – getting hold of Mary Tudor. For power to be transferred from Edward VI to Jane I unchallenged, the princess had to acquiesce or else be neutralized. In the week of Edward's death she was at one of her favourite houses, Hunsdon near Ware, and highly vulnerable – a mere twenty miles from London and with only about fifty or sixty servants.[1] Yet not until the morning after the king's death would Robert Dudley be sent to Hunsdon with three hundred men, by which time the bird had flown.[2] Among the puzzles surrounding the attempt to enforce Edward's will, this is the most unexpected. Detaining Mary seems such an obvious move that a child would make it.

One possibility is that despite the long duration of Edward's illness, death took his ministers by surprise.[3] In one sense it should not have done. On 4 July Scheyfve wrote to Charles V to say that the previous day friends had warned Mary that 'the king is very ill today and cannot last for long; he will die suddenly and no one can foretell whether he will live an hour longer'.[4] On the other hand, the doctors had at one stage talked about the king lasting until the autumn and it was important not to move prematurely. In mid-June the boy's condition had led to the call for public prayers, and the imperialist spy in the sick room had said he would not last three days, only for Edward then to rally.[5] So one explanation might simply be that caution was carried too far. Northumberland, however, was not Mr Micawber. On 26 June at a private meeting, he assured De Noailles 'that they had provided so well against the Lady Mary's ever attaining the succession' that the French need have no anxiety about a pro-Habsburg government coming to power in England.[6] The starting point of the plan seems to have been a reading of Mary's character. Everything Northumberland knew about her was that, except where the Catholic mass was concerned, she would crumble in a crisis. He had been around the court when she had been whipped into line by her father. He had seen her take refuge in tears when under pressure and was well aware of the escape attempt in the summer of 1550.[7] Positive action by Mary must have seemed the last thing to expect; the only risk to be concerned about was a panic-stricken flight to Charles V. The first essential, therefore, was to do nothing to panic the princess. Despite Edward's revelation of the 'deuise' the duke continued to woo Mary.[8] On the day the lawyers were summoned to hear the king's orders, the ambassador reported that the duke had 'shown the princess kind treatment' and even when the 'deuise' became common knowledge Northumberland was 'still behaving courteously towards the princess as if nothing were about to happen'.[9] Of course after Mary's triumph, her partisans told a different tale. Wingfield hints that she was at Hunsdon in order to monitor events.[10] Antonio de Guaras says that while the duke had been confident that he could pick Mary up at any time, she, in fact, was deceiving him:

> He almost daily wrote to her Highness letters full of respect, informing her of the grievous sickness of the King, but that if God ordered other than well with him, he himself would manifest by his deeds the attachment and fidelity which he protested he entertained towards her Highness. But the Queen's Majesty. temporizing with him, and replying that she held him for the most faithful, did what was meet for the time.[11]

An Italian in the imperial embassy reported the same: 'she succeeded in lulling the duke to such good effect that he really believed her to be so good and simple that he would be able to seize her person whenever he might care to do so'.[12] A modern twist to this is a suggestion that highly advantageous land grants made to Mary early in 1553 were the price Northumberland and the council paid to buy out her claim to the throne. There was, thus, no reason to move against Mary until she double-crossed them, by which time it was too late.[13] The ground for the suggestion is that the patent for Mary's new lands was completed in May, a key month in the evolution of the king's 'deuise'. However, there is no supporting evidence for any link and the reception for Mary at Whitehall in February 1553 (after the land exchanges were in hand) indicates that she had every reason to be confident that her status as heir presumptive was unquestioned.

Far from any double-cross, in the opinion of the Venetian Giacomo Soranzo –
the most objective of the foreign ambassadors – it was Mary who was taken
in.[14] In believing that the princess was a soft touch, the duke would not
have been alone. The informed opinion in London was that Mary was mad
to think of challenging the Tudor state. The imperial ambassadors in
London described her decision as 'strange, full of difficulties and danger
... All the forces of the country are in the duke's hands and my Lady
[Mary] has no hope of raising enough men to face him nor means of
assisting those who may espouse her cause.' With suitably diplomatic
meiosis they suggested that Mary should have given her move more
thought.[15]

According to the earliest biography of Edward VI, Northumberland's
first step was to summon Mary to her brother's bedside 'as well to be a
comfort to him in his sickness as to see all matters well ordered about
him'.[16] Only in the nick of time was she warned that she was walking into
a trap. John Hayward's *Life and Raigne of King Edward the Sixth* was
written more than sixty years after the event and it gives no source for the
story.[17] Deceiving Mary would, however, have been pointless without
neutralizing Elizabeth, and William Camden's *History of Elizabeth.* states
that the princess was indeed put under pressure, in her case 'to resign her
title to the crown for a sum of money and certain lands'.[18] This support
from Camden is particularly significant because, while his *History* also
appeared in James's reign, he had been a protégé of William Cecil, under-
took the *History* at Cecil's request and had access to his papers. From the
summer of 1553 there is further evidence congruent with Hayward's
story. The duke's manoeuvre meant waiting and John Throckmorton,
the young lawyer who went on to draft Jane Grey's accession proclamation, overheard John Gates remonstrating with Northumberland: 'But,
sir, will you suffer the Lady Mary escape, and not secure her person'?[19]
There is also a manuscript among Cecil's papers at Hatfield endorsed 'The
letters of the sudden removing of Queen Mary'.[20] It was written for those
lords lieutenants not then in London to put them in the picture, and it
shows that during much of Edward's illness Mary had not been living at
Hunsdon. The council wrote:

so it is that the Lady Mary not many days past removed from Newhall in
Essex to her house of Hunsdon in Hertfordshire; the cause whereof although
we know not, yet did we rather think it likely that her grace would have come
to have seen his majesty, but now upon Tuesday last [4 July] she hath
suddenly without knowledge given either to us here or to the country

there, and without any cause in the world by us to her given, taken her journey from Hunsdon toward Norfolk.[21]

Newhall was the grander of Mary's two Home Counties houses but it was ten miles further from London than Hunsdon.[22] The letter therefore establishes that as Edward weakened, Mary deliberately moved to be nearer the court. What is more, the council went on to say that she had caused 'great provision to be made in the country about Hunsdon for keeping of her household there a long time'. That hardly suggests a sick visit to Edward. It indicates, rather, that Mary moved to Hunsdon to be ready for a call to London and the crown. Five years later when Mary's own death was expected, Elizabeth waited at Brocket Hall, twelve miles west of Hunsdon and a similar distance from London. Evidently, Mary either took her accession for granted – ignoring the warnings which Charles V's ambassador had been feeding her – or something or somebody told her that she needed to be at Hunsdon, on call. That obvious some-body would be the council led by Northumberland, and to the critical eye, the letter to the lords lieutenants is very suspicious. 'The cause whereof we knew not', she fled 'without any cause in the world by us to her given', 'provision for keeping her household there a long time' – the unnecessary elaboration protests too much. Protocol would not have allowed Mary simply to turn up at court to see Edward, so why 'yet did we rather think it likely that her grace would have come to have seen his majesty' unless to cover up an invitation by the council? On this construction, Northumber-land attempted what the imperial ambassador had feared. Scheyfve had written at the end of May:

> the Duke may dissemble with the Princess until the King dies or is very near his end. ... He may then send a body of horse, secretly and by night, to the Princess, inform her of the King's death and summon her to come to London for the Crown ... conduct her to the Tower for the safety of her person [and incarcerate her there].[23]

If we accept that Northumberland's plan was to lure Mary by false promises, did he simply leave it too late? The probable answer is that arresting Mary was more difficult than historians in their twenty-first century armchairs have supposed. Imperial diplomats certainly always assumed that the duke would not move until the last minute.[24] It was not enough just to take out Mary. Potential supporters had to be neutra-lized as well and such a widely scattered group of individuals could not be rounded up quickly, and could not be moved against in advance for fear of stirring up open protest.[25] Was, then, the alternative to bring Mary to court? A summons in Edward's name would certainly have brought her, and she could then have been kept there, respected but effectively under house arrest. Leaving Mary at Hunsdon unmonitored handed her the initiative. But again problems suggest themselves. The 'deuise' was not in place until 21 June and given the king's known condition at that point, a summons would surely have aroused suspicion.[26] Moreover, Mary would undoubtedly have come with at least some retinue. Not only would a further major demonstration of conservative opinion have been just what was not wanted, separating the princess from her escort would invite confrontation and very probably violence. And if that could somehow be avoided, Mary at court might be an even greater problem than Mary at liberty. Even if confined to her rooms, on past experience she was perfectly capable of screaming from a window in order to make her point.[27] Then might Mary have been isolated at Hunsdon? If put under house arrest quietly and with speed, her retinue would not be to hand and she would be well out of the way of any sympathizers at court. However, this was only sustainable in the very short term and no-one knew how long Edward would live. The news would inevitably leak and set in motion a tide of local and then wider unrest. Irrespective of any plan to dupe Mary, the course adopted was probably the only realistic option: leave seizing Mary until the last moment and face the nation with a fait accompli.

One preparation which Northumberland did make – or so the imperial ambassador believed – was to create a war chest. On 28 April Scheyfve informed Charles V that

> money has been collected carefully in great quantities from every source; and this might well have something to do with the fact of [the betrothal of Jane Grey and Guildford Dudley]. The money is in the hands of those who are devoted to Northumberland, to the exclusion of the old officers and ministers who once had the control of it.[28]

To Scheyfve as to us, the importance of money in a potential crisis was self-evident. But did his information really bear the sinister construction he put on it? In 1553 Northumberland and the other councillors were grappling with the more fundamental of the two financial problems they had inherited in 1549. The first – the consequences of ten years of military adventuring by Henry VIII and the duke of Somerset – had largely been solved. The £3.5 million which the two had spent on war and military matters over the previous decade had pushed the country into debt to financiers both in England and Antwerp and the currency had been

debased to the point where coins contained barely a third of the silver they
had done in 1543.[29] The debt had peaked in 1552 at perhaps £250,000
and forced Northumberland to put a temporary stop on the payment of
government bills. However, by the summer of 1553, the priority he had
given 'to have his majesty out of debt' had turned the situation round,
eliminating debt to foreign bankers and stabilizing the coinage. But still
to be addressed was the daunting and fundamental second problem –
insufficient income and inadequate liquidity, the chronic structural weak-
nesses of the English fiscal system. Major plans for reform were under
consideration but they needed time to implement and significant results
would take years. In the meantime all that could be done to manage the
current account deficit was massive land sales and a stringent policy of
making every economy possible and collecting every debt imaginable – the
frantic search for cash which the ambassador reported. The consequence
of this was that the regular resources of the crown were incapable of
supporting any major additional expenditure. So how was the implementation of Edward's 'deuise' to be funded? Strangely to modern eyes,
surviving documents display no hint of anxiety on that score, such as
trying to siphon off income to create an emergency fund. After a detailed
study of Exchequer records Dr Sybil Jack concluded that 'There is no
evidence of a planned plot in the financial records before the matter
became a matter of council policy (21 June) and little evidence thereafter
of anything which might be identified as improper behaviour.'[30] True, the
search for money had been successful enough for Northumberland to
establish in the privy chamber a cash fund for 'all events'. This, however,
was not a reserve but was regularly drawn on by the Council for the king's
current 'special service and affairs' and then replenished. Since January
1552 £39,948 had passed through the fund, but all that was left in hand in
May 1553 was £1,647 19s. 2d.[31]

So was personal wealth available to support the attempt to maintain the
legitimate line? By 1553 John Dudley had himself accumulated considerable assets and so too the leading political and social figures associated
with him. But wealth in land and possessions is one thing, cash in hand is
another, and the likelihood of significant immediate support from private
financial sources seems pretty remote. It would be wholly exceptional for
Tudor aristocrats to be in a position to lend money; usually the boot was
on the other foot. Dudley was carrying unpaid debts in the 1530s and
1540s.[32] Twelve months before the 1553 crisis he admitted to being
'strained of necessity' and in June 1553 he was only able to pay off the
instalment due on the purchase of the marriage of his son's wife by raising

a loan of 2000 marks.[33] Thus Northumberland was in no position to pay significant sums from his own pocket, still less recruit foreign mercenaries. Might, then, the duke's closest financial allies, Sir Francis Jobson and Sir John Yorke, have come forward with funds of which we know nothing? Each was to be a primary target of Mary's supporters during their coup.[34] Jobson was a court of augmentations officer and had become master of the jewel house early in 1553. He had been Dudley's secretary, had married his half-sister and was one of the fourteen actually indicted with the duke.[35] Sir John Yorke was a former sheriff of London and under-treasurer of the mint and he was nearly lynched when he tried to rebuff the proclamation of Mary in London on 19 July.[36] He was not in the end indicted, but his goods were confiscated in preparation and he was also clearly suspected of making the most of his involvement with the coinage.[37] After the collapse of Jane's government Jobson did claim that the duke had 'borrowed a good part of my money', but when and in what context is not clear, and there is no evidence that this was in 1553.[38] Nor is there evidence that Yorke came forward with funds. It would, of course, have been in both their interests to fund the Grey cause: each had the connections to do so and there may be a hint of something of the kind in the report of the imperial ambassador on 24 June that London merchants were being pressed to lend the crown £40,000 repayable in October, and on 27 June that a loan had actually been concluded and for £50,000 or more.[39]

Setting aside suspicions about compliant Londoners, the failure to make substantive financial preparations in the summer of 1553 might seem further confirmation that Mary's intransigence took the council by complete surprise. But are we right to assume the duke would need to have substantial funds to hand? In pre-industrial England, much of the economy ran on credit, including the military establishment. No modern government, for example, would allow the pay of a key military unit to fall twenty-one months in arrears as the pay of Edward VI's gentlemen pensioners had by July 1553.[40] It is also important to remember that whether military provision is adequate or not must be judged against the danger that can realistically be expected. Being prepared is not an absolute condition. What, then, could Northumberland reasonably expect to need if he was called on to enforce the rule of Queen Jane? Ask that question and the picture begins to looks significantly different. A major campaign of the kind Lord Russell waged against the rebels in the south-west in 1549 was never on the cards, still less a requirement for a large fully articulated army. The most the duke was likely to face was what in fact he would face, a scratch force of a few thousands, and one battle would settle it. Obviously the expense involved in diverting the crown to Jane (over and above the necessary cost of a change of monarch) could not be accurately predicted, but a rational assessment must have suggested that it would be limited.[41] Any need to purchase support in advance or give favours to tie in committed allies could be covered by grants of crown land or warrants for future payment. Some military expenses would be covered by routine assignments.[42] Others could be left to the future. The costs of the fleet which was sent to guard the East Anglian coast appear to have been defrayed in arrears – in September 1553 Benjamin Gonson, the treasurer of the navy, received two council warrants to a value of nearly £2,000.[43] Antony Antony of the Ordnance Office received a warrant on 2 September for the payment of £1,000, so some of the military supplies and equipment may have been covered similarly.[44]

The immediate need of cash would be for the campaign chest required by an army in the field. Here it is only possible to make an indicative calculation of the amount needed. In Edward's reign the normal wage for a foot soldier was 6d. a day and for a horseman 8d. Soldiers were expected to buy their own food, and if the crown had to issue supplies, the cost was debited against pay.[45] If we allow wages of this kind, for Northumberland to take the field with, say, 2000 cavalry and 1000 infantry, the bill would have been of the order of £90 *per diem*.[46] Even if we credit the stories which circulated in London of the duke recruiting infantry at as much as 10d. a day, the requirement only rises to about £110.[47] A fortnight's campaign for a force of the size posited would, thus, have cost in the order of £1,260 to £1,550 plus the expense of transport and the wages of any expert gunners specially engaged. In fact the daily expenditure would have been lower. The expenses of the royal guard and the gentlemen pensioners were already covered, and so too the wages of any gunners already in crown employment. Moreover, much of the force was made up of the retinues of the councillors and their noble supporters, and they would undoubtedly have served on credit.

If these figures are at all of the right magnitude then we are wrong to presume the requirement for the duke to have a large amount in cash ready to hand. He needed a few hundreds or thousands of pounds, not a five-figure sum. And when we start to look for that kind of money we find that Northumberland did have funds of that order to hand in 1553. In the first place the £1,647 19s. 2d. in the 'special service and affairs' account was paid over to his brother, Sir Andrew Dudley, on 15 May.[48] The next month Northumberland himself took up a loan for £1,500 from three

London merchants (and benefactors), two of them, John Gresham and Andrew Judd, former lord mayors and close associates of Yorke, and the third, Stephen Kyrton, an alderman and prominent merchant tailor.[49] We are unable to calculate if any of this total of almost £3,150 had been spent by the date of Edward's death, but as the £1,500 loan was to be repaid as early as 1 August, it looks very like a facility which was set up in the expectation that it would probably not be required.[50]

There is, thus, little evidence in the final months of Edward's reign to suggest preparatory financial moves. Much the same can be said about military readiness. The despatches of the imperial ambassador are full of tales about military and naval preparations and the gossip he picked up about the movement of individual peers was regularly presented as suspicious. However, he had to admit on 15 June that 'no one is able to find out what Northumberland is planning to do'.[51] The reality is that except for the tightened security normal at a change of monarch, the council made no military preparations. Indeed, quite the reverse. The thousand-strong permanent militia which had been set up in the winter of 1550–1 had been discharged at Michaelmas 1552 in order to save money.[52] If that had been on standby in July 1553, the outcome could have been very different. There were no moves, either, to bring in mercenaries, a frequent recourse in recent years. Political preparation was equally lacking. Tudor England had neither a standing army nor a police force, so power in the localities rested with those whose wealth and influence gave them social and economic authority. The crown sought to legitimize this by appointing such men as justices of the peace, but in the last resort, law and order depended on the readiness of these men and their rich neighbours to mobilize their servants and tenants as vigilantes. Many tenancies included a requirement to serve – what was called manred – while the manred of royal tenants went with the grant of a crown lease or local office. In some cases the government would even license individuals to recruit a group of retainers wearing the licensee's badge. An additional layer of authority was introduced following the extensive uprisings and general unrest of 1549 which had proved too much for these local 'men of power' to handle unsupported. This was a system of royal lieutenants – privy councillors and other notables – who were commissioned annually to take overall responsibility for law and order in named shires or groups of shires, 'for the summer' – the season of risk. The commissions for 1553 were issued on 24 May and as Edward's death came closer there is no sign that the council saw the need for any further exceptional measures.[53] Indeed, far from being out in their districts anticipating unrest, the majority of the lieutenants waited at court for the change of ruler.[54] The expectation was that the system would cope.

Given that sentiment, the response of the council to the news of Mary's flight was prompt but not jumpy. Lieutenants not in London were informed of Mary's move, which was put down to the 'malicious rancour of such as provoke her thus to breed and stir up as much as in her and them lies, occasion of disorder and unquiet in the realm'.[55] Officers were to silence rumours and guard against outbreaks 'as of late years'. Where there was anxiety was at the possibility of foreign invasion and the need as 'true and mere Englishmen [to] keep our country to be English without putting our heads under Spaniards' or Flemings' girdles as their slaves and vassals'. Lieutenants were, therefore, to have the coasts watched both 'for the arrival of any strangers into the land or the going out of the lady or any of hers' and to have the beacon system ready. Letters sent out on 8 July to the deputy lieutenants and justices of the peace went into less detail but also assumed that Mary intended to escape abroad or, at the worst, to wait for imperial troops to assist her.[56] The instruction was to 'put yourselves in a readiness after your best power and manner for the defence of our natural country against all such attempts' and to be ready 'upon an hour's warning with your said power to repair unto us', but this alert was only precautionary:

> in the mean time we require and pray you to take such good orders for the maintenance of the continual watch in every place within that shire as no stir nor uproar be attempted but that the doers thereof be by your industries and policies stayed and the stirrers apprehended and advertisement sent to us by you from time to time as occasion shall serve.

As Edward's condition deteriorated, Northumberland and his colleagues also had to keep their eyes on the international position. We have seen how at the end of May some offer had come from France – probably to take action if Charles V actively intervened on the side of Mary. Whether in the actual crisis anything followed from this, and if so what, is hard to tell. After the event, the attempts of both Mary and the emperor to find out the facts came to nothing.[57] In consequence we are almost entirely dependent on the correspondence of the imperial ambassadors and of the French ambassador – material from diametrically opposed positions. Jehan Scheyfve had for months been warning Charles V that Northumberland was preparing a dastardly plot against Mary, and from de l'Aubespine's visit onward, he increasingly saw France as the real villain. When in August Charles V's representatives looked back on events, it was France's 'strange and intolerable behaviour' which preoccupied them.[58] In this they were only reflecting the anxieties of their master. On 23 June the emperor had sent a high-powered delegation to reinforce Scheyfve with the bluntest of instructions.[59]

[In the event of Edward's death] you will take such steps as you shall consider necessary to defeat the machinations of the French and keep them out of England, and endeavour to safeguard the friendly relations that it is important to preserve between that country and our dominions of the Low Countries and Spain. Commercial interests render this desirable; and your chief care will be to prevent the French from getting a footing in England or entering into a close understanding with the governors of that country for our dominions and the peace of Christendom might otherwise suffer.

There was no mention of armed intervention; Charles already had his hands full with his war against Henry II.

We see no better course for the present than to reassure the English by dwelling on the affection we have always borne the king and his country ... In this our friendship has been seen to be different from the affection professed by the French who have taken advantage of the king's minority to drive him out of his dominions and subject him to their tyranny. Let the English be warned that the French will do all that in them lies to achieve this object, and let them remember that the French are England's ancient enemies; whilst from us they shall always experience favour and aid.

Even before the new men arrived – the most important of them the lawyer and diplomat Simon Renard – reports from Scheyfve had stoked these fears. He informed the emperor that after dark on 22 June Northumberland and Suffolk went, with a single servant, to visit De Noailles, only to be stopped by the watch, and that four days later Northumberland paid another clandestine visit, at 9 p.m. and escorted by only three servants.[60] On 4 July a report followed with the substance of the 'deuise' and the conclusion that the duke was 'negotiating a great deal with the French ambassador and shows him great friendship in order to make sure of his support and strike terror into the adversaries'.[61] This was not the way that the French saw matters. They saw the claim of Charles V's special envoys that they had only come to express sympathy with Edward as a front for an attempt to engineer a conspiracy in favour of Mary. The English thought so too. Nevertheless, although the French ambassador was let into the secret of 'deuise' on the day it was signed, Northumberland was careful never to get too close to France. He knew as well as anyone that Henry II had his own agenda. De Noailles's instructions had been to build on the understanding which had been reached with de L'Aubespine and he was sent a personal letter from Henry to deliver to the duke, but Northumberland refused him permission to visit Greenwich.[62] Only when the duke came up by boat for a private visit on 26 June was the letter handed over. The meeting lasted two hours and de Noailles again urged the offer made by L'Aubespine, but despite his eloquence and the gracious letter from the king, Dudley was not responsive. He had come alone (possibly in secret) for reassurance that France would still be an ultimate guarantor against Charles and he did confirm that he would call for help if the imperialists were to intervene. But against Mary the council would, he said, not need help. Beyond that 'because he [himself] could and would do nothing alone', the duke would only agree to an early opportunity for the ambassador to address the whole council. The French, however, were much less sanguine, still feeling that the dire warnings which Charles was receiving about Northumberland had caused the emperor 'to commit himself immediately to pushing on with the intrigue he had already begun with the Lady Mary to ensure that the [English] succession did not slip through his hands'.[63] As Edward's life ebbed away, the great powers of Europe sensed the looming danger of a 'War of the English Succession'.

18

JANE THE QUEEN

IN the early spring of 1553, while foreign governments, foreign diplo-mats and the English privy council were becoming aware of a impending crisis, Jane Grey remained in total ignorance. Life continued as before – household, scholarship, religion. Like the overwhelming majority of girls of her class, she came to attention only when it was announced that she was to marry. The chosen bridegroom was Guildford Dudley, Northumberland's only unmarried son. Much imagination has been exercised over Jane's reaction to that prospect. Agnes and Elizabeth Strickland popularized the notion that her consent was forced by 'the urgency of her mother and the violence of her father who compelled her to accede to his commands by blows' – an episode graphically depicted in at least two major films.[1] The sisters were, however, effectively translating the 1558 pirated edition of Girolamo Raviglio Rosso's *History of Events in England*, and when Rosso's own text came out in 1560, it was more guarded: 'Although she resisted the marriage for some time ... she was obliged to consent, urged by her mother and threatened by her father.'[2] Of itself such treatment is not impossible. In Tudor times parental choice was the dominant factor in aristocratic marriage, and we have seen how Jane's was 'bought' by Thomas Seymour and how her mother was involved in the transaction. The church did insist that marriage should be entered into voluntarily, but willingness could range from positive attraction through tolerance to putting the best face on it or even surrendering to pressure, physical as well as psychological. Marriage cannot have come as a surprise to Jane; she could not but be aware that she was reaching an age when her father and mother would soon realize her cash value by finding a husband for her. Notwithstanding, given her robust attitude towards her parents it is easy to imagine that she was capable of objecting to a marriage she did not want.

Commendone was the first to have the story – 'Jane strongly deprecated the marriage' – but gave no explanation.[3] Rosso put it down to prescience – 'as if she had a premonition of the ills that would happen to her'.[4] Queen Mary certainly knew, or had been told, that Jane's marriage was open to challenge. In August 1553 she said to Simon Renard that 'it had been found that there could be no marriage between [Jane] and Guildford, the son of the duke [of Northumberland] as she was previously betrothed by a binding promise that entailed marriage to a servitor of the bishop of Winchester.[5] 'Betrothed by a binding promise' means more than simply engaged. It indicates a formal commitment to marry which would need a judicial decision to cancel. Who this 'servitor' of Stephen Gardiner, bishop of Winchester was is a matter of conjecture. Since we have seen that Jane's father was in discussion with the protector in February 1549 'for the marriage of your Grace's son to be with my daughter Jane', Somerset's son Edward, earl of Hertford, is an obvious possibility.[6] On the other hand, although Somerset was not entirely unsympathetic to Gardiner, the bishop does seem an unlikely mentor for the young earl.[7] From the start of the reign Winchester had been a trial to the privy council and from June 1548 he was in prison. One possible explanation of Mary's remark is that she did not say 'bishop of Winchester' but 'marquis of Winchester' and the identification became garbled in transmission. Alternatively she could have used the ambiguous term 'my lord of Winchester' and been misunderstood.[8] William Paulet, marquis of Winchester, would certainly seem a more likely mentor for the young earl. He was a long-time senior member of the political elite and was related to the Seymour family. He owned a country estate some twenty-five miles from theirs, and it could be significant that after the duke's death he helped Edward Seymour to recover family property.[9] Taken together, the promise Suffolk made to the protector and the conjecture that Mary meant Paulet make it likely that Jane had good reason to consider that she was already committed to the young earl, at the least morally. But by 1553, whatever had gone on before was over. While Somerset lived, the advantages in marrying Jane to his heir were obvious. With the duke executed, the dukedom forfeit and the family property confiscated by a statute of 1552, the match lost all attraction. Jane might not see that, but her parents most certainly could. Guildford Dudley was now the very best bet, a marriage which would tie the Greys to the most powerful man in the country. For his part, what attracted Northumberland was that his son could expect to secure a second Dudley dukedom when Henry Grey died.

The earliest evidence of Jane's betrothal to Guildford is a warrant dated 24 April 1553 to deliver 'wedding apparel' to the bride and groom, their respective mothers and also the lady marquis of Northampton, thus confirming that she was indeed the original matchmaker.[10] The apparel comprised 'parcels of tissue and cloths of gold and silver', forfeited by the duke and duchess of Somerset, and Jane's sister Katherine was similarly helped, along with Guildford's sister (another Katherine), and also their respective bridegrooms, Henry Herbert and Francis Hastings, the sons of the earls of Pembroke and Huntingdon.[11] Edward may also have sent jewels, specially for Jane to wear.[12] Jousts and games were laid on and Northumberland booked two teams of masquers, one male, one female, 'to perform before the noble company'. The costumes were to be 'rich' and 'seldom used'.[13] Thanks to this mobilization of splendour, the wedding festivities which took place at Whitsun dazzled foreigners. The imperial ambassador wrote of the weddings being 'celebrated with great magnificence and feasting at the duke of Northumberland's house in town' and extending over two whole days.[14] The outgoing French ambassador was a guest on both days and the fact that de l'Aubespine and the Venetian ambassador also attended on the second made the failure to invite an imperial representative distinctly pointed.[15] However, any hurt Charles's envoy felt would have been quickly salved – the bridegroom and several guests fell ill from food poisoning.[16] The ostentation may also have been aimed at Mary, reminding her of the power of Northumberland and his associates. Commendone certainly wrote of 'the attendance of large numbers of the common people' – presumably the various family retainers – 'and of the most principal of the realm'.[17] On the other hand, English observers do not mention the celebrations, so it is possible that foreigners were simply impressed by English wedding extravagance.[18]

How Jane reacted to being married to Guildford is hard to tell. He was described as 'a comely, virtuous and goodly gentleman' and the message he wrote in Jane's prayer book for the duke of Suffolk was very dutiful: 'Your loving and obedient son wishes unto your grace long life in this world with as much joy and comfort as ever I wish to myself, and in the world to come joy everlasting. Your humble son to his death, G. Dudley'.[19] Other than this we really know very little about Guildford.[20] At the time, the imperial ambassador reported that the marriage was not to be consummated yet 'because of their tender age', and for much of June, Jane and Guildford do appear to have lived apart, visiting and building up a relationship.[21] However, by the time she was proclaimed queen, the couple were living at Durham House and sleeping together.[22]

That Jane, at least, saw this as a symbol of commitment is certainly suggested by the complaint in the letter of explanation which she subsequently wrote to Mary that the duchess of Northumberland 'induced her son not to sleep with me any more'.[23] Moreover, in the letter she described herself not just as a 'wife' but 'a wife who loves her husband'.[24] On the other hand Jane also revealed some disappointment with Guildford who remained very much under his mother's thumb, and she made it very clear that she did not see eye to eye with her mother-in-law.[25] But whatever the quality, Jane's married life lasted less than nine weeks. From 19 July Jane and Guildford were prisoners, and by at least 22 July they had been separated.[26]

For the story of how the newly married Jane Dudley learned that she was to become Queen Jane, we again depend on the letter which she wrote to Mary in August 1553.[27] It has all the disadvantages inherent in pleas in mitigation – can Jane really have been so naive? Or was it that her blue-stocking focus had distorted her perception of the real world? Moreover we have the letter only at third hand – in a variety of Italian texts which are themselves translations from the English original – possibly via Latin intermediaries – and the resultant obscurities do not allow very close reading. Something, nevertheless, can be attempted.[28] When Jane's account begins, she was still living with her parents, as agreed with the duchess of Northumberland, her mother-in-law. Her first inkling of change came when, apparently during one visit to the Dudleys, she was told by the duchess that she had to stay. Jane says that this was about the time it became generally known that Edward would not live, which places the warning around 19 June when the call went out for public prayers for the king.[29] The reason the duchess gave was that when the king died Jane had to be ready to go immediately to the Tower since Edward had made her heir to the crown. She says she was puzzled and disturbed by this but took little account of it and returned to her mother. That is somewhat hard to believe but what follows suggests that Jane thought it was a ploy by the duchess to get her to cohabit with Guildford, not merely visit. The consequence was that 'the duchess got angry at [my mother] and at me, saying that if she [the duchess of Suffolk] wanted to keep me, she [the duchess of Northumberland] would also keep my husband by herself, thinking that anyway I would go to him'.[30] In fact Jane did go and stayed two or three nights, but then became ill – stress perhaps – and was allowed to go to Chelsea. She put the sickness down to poison but conjecture would suggest either reluctance to consummate or a consequence of it. Clearly she saw Chelsea as a refuge. A fairly small royal house, on the river and noted for its knot gardens and orchards, it held good memories from her time there with Katherine Parr.[31] But on Sunday 9 July, while she was still not well, her sister-in-law Mary Sidney arrived with a solemn and mysterious summons from the privy council to go that very night to the former protector's mansion at Syon 'to receive that which had been ordered by the king'.

The two women were rowed up river, but when they arrived no-one was there to meet them. Eventually Northumberland, Northampton, Arundel, Huntingdon and Pembroke appeared and stilted conversation ensued. Jane implies that she had no idea what was afoot and the nobles were confused about how to behave. Very probably they had assumed that Jane would have grasped the duchess of Northumberland's warning. Huntingdon and Pembroke knelt to Jane and honoured her, but this only made her more embarrassed. In the end, in typical male fashion, the men called in her mother, along with the duchess of Northumberland and the marchioness of Northampton. The duke then reported that the king was dead, offered something of a tribute and announced that Edward had nominated Jane to succeed him. The councillors all knelt to Jane as the heir 'of straight descent' and said that they were bound by their oaths to Edward even to lay down their lives. At this Jane collapsed in a torrent of weeping, grieving for her young cousin. Thus far Jane, but one of the councillors present told de Noailles that when the girl got her voice under control she protested. 'The crown is not my right and pleases me not. The Lady Mary is the rightful heir.'[32] Northumberland replied: 'Your Grace does wrong to yourself and to your house.' It was Edward's command that she succeed him. By then her father had arrived (with Guildford) and with her mother insisted it was her religious duty to obey them. Next Guildford tried a softer line – 'prayers and caresses'. Battered this way and that, eventually Jane gave way. As she told Mary,

> Declaring to them my insufficiency, I greatly bewailed myself for the death of so noble a prince, and at the same time, turned myself to God, humbly praying and beseeching him, that if what was given to me was rightly and lawfully mine, his divine Majesty would grant me such grace and spirit that I might govern it to his glory and service and to the advantage of this realm.[33]

After this, though Jane does not say so, the group appears to have relaxed at 'a great banquet', though whether she herself was in a mood to eat much is to be doubted.[34]

The following day, the heralds publicized Edward's 'patents' and proclaimed the new queen 'in four parts of the City of London', while a procession of barges took Jane to the Tower, along with her husband, her parents, the duchess of Northumberland and 'other ladies attended by a great following'.[35] They landed at the royal stairs which gave access by a bridge over the moat to the Byward Tower, but since she was 'received as queen' and there were spectators, it is more likely that Jane processed along the wharf and into the Tower by the main entrance, the Lion Gate.[36] [plate 22] Her dress was green velvet embroidered in gold, with fashionably large sleeves and a very long train which was borne by her mother – a reversal of the natural order which attracted several comments.[37] Her headdress was white, close-fitting and heavily jewelled, and a ceremonial canopy was held over her as she walked. Beside her was Guildford, tall, blond, dressed in white and gold, paying Jane a great deal of attention. As precedent demanded, she was conducted to the royal lodgings where she was immediately surrounded by protocol and the ceremony of monarchy. A cloth of estate was set up over the royal chair and trappings of a court were rustled up. The lists we have are partial – the regular paraphernalia of monarchy was no doubt still with the deceased Edward at Greenwich – but the magnificence into which Jane had been pitched is very clear. Pendants, buttons, precious stones, bracelets.[38] There was a cap of black velvet with a square table ruby as a brooch 'and divers pictures enamelled with red, black, and green, with 18 buttons, with small rock rubies and 18 buttons also of gold with three small pearls' each.[39] This sounds like a man's cap whose jewels could be recycled for Jane's use. There were a number of clocks including a

> sable skin with a head of gold, containing in it a clock, with a collar of gold, enamelled black, set with four diamonds, and four rubies, and two pearls hanging by the ears, and two rubies in the ears, the same skin also having feet of gold, the claws thereof being sapphires, two of them being broken, and with a diamond upon the clock.[40]

Clothing is represented by three mufflers or 'chinclouts', which covered the lower part of the face and the neck, as worn until recent times by certain orders of nuns.[41] In England, only ladies from the higher aristocracy were supposed to wear any which extended above the chin and they could be lavishly decorated.[42] One of those brought out for Jane was 'of black velvet, striped with small chains of gold, garnished with small pearls, small rubies and small diamonds ... furred with sables and having thereat a chain of gold enamelled green, garnished with certain pearls'. What Jane, with the advice from the likes of Aylmer and Ascham ringing in her ears, made of all this we can only guess.[43]

We know that one item produced from the Jewel House did worry Jane. The marquis of Winchester, the lord high treasurer, brought the royal crown and urged her 'to put it on my head to try whether it really became me or no'.[44] Jane refused. She had not asked for it nor had anyone on her behalf and her discomfort increased when Paulet said she 'could take it without fear and that another also should be made, to crown my husband. Which thing I, for my part, heard truly with a troubled mind, and with ill will, even with infinite grief and displeasure of heart.'[45]

Hard though it is to credit, only then had the penny dropped. If Queen Jane then King Guildford. In nominating Jane, Edward had nominated the Dudleys. What ensued was an exchange between Jane and her husband. She described it as 'reasoning of many things with my husband [who] assented that if he were to be made king, he would be so by me, by act of parliament', but probably it was Jane insisting on having her own way.[46] Later she called for Arundel and Pembroke and said that she was content to make Guildford a duke but would never consent to make him king. The title she had in mind was duke of Clarence.[47] Whether she was simply informing them that she would make Guildford a duke immediately, but that anything more would have to wait for parliament, or whether she had hardened her views since the debate with her husband is not clear, but when the decision reached the duchess of Northumberland, she was furious. She made Guildford say that he would not sleep with Jane and that he wanted to be king, not a duke. She also told the boy to go home to Syon, and so he would have done next morning had not Jane flexed her royal muscles and sent Arundel and Pembroke to tell Guildford to remain at court. Jane's eyes were now open, and she was understandably upset. As she told Mary, she had been deceived by the duke, by the council and by her husband, and ill-treated by his mother. The mention of Guildford suggests she was particularly wounded by his deception. He had taken for granted that he would be king so must clearly been in the secret of the 'deuise', but Jane he had left in the dark. Once again stomach trouble got the better of her.

Guildford, no doubt encouraged by his mother, did as much as he could to ape the royal status Jane refused to endorse. He dined in state, alone, and attempted to preside at council meetings – or so the imperial ambassador alleged. Perhaps that story should be dismissed as spite, but certainly the Habsburg court at Brussels was convinced that Guildford was king.[48] For Jane it was otherwise. The gates of the Tower had opened for her ceremonial entry, but court protocol now shut her off from the life and values she had been used to. Her order to stop Guildford suggests that she slipped easily into the habit of command, but the signs are that she was never fully persuaded of her right to rule. On his election, Leo X is alleged to have said: 'Since God has given us the papacy, let us enjoy it'.[49] When told that she was queen, Jane Grey's prayer was 'if what was given to me was rightly and lawfully mine ... that I might govern to his glory and service'.[50] The crown was a burden laid on her by God and one she would lay down with relief.

19

THE COUNCIL IN LONDON

WHEN asked what his biggest problem was, a famous British prime minister (supposedly) replied, 'Events, dear boy, events'.[1] Northumberland and the privy council must have felt much the same in the days following Edward VI's death. Within hours Mary's house at Hunsdon had been found empty. Immediate steps had to be taken to publicize Edward's wishes, with a letter to local magistrates on 8 July promising to circulate 'with as convenient speed as we may' 'such ordinances as be prescribed unto us by his Majesty signed with his own hand and sealed with the great seal of England', but with Edward's death supposedly a secret, the letter had to be written as though he was still alive.[2] To cap this, Lady Jane had needed persuading to take the crown, and then, after the council had put in hand precautionary moves against an imperial invasion, the scene changed again. Thomas Hungate, an elderly servant of Princess Mary, presented himself on Monday 10 July, with a letter from Kenninghall, dated the day before, demanding that the council accept her as queen.[3] Far from planning to flee the country or hang on for imperial troops, the princess was determined to assert her claim immediately.

According to the imperial ambassadors, Hungate arrived when the council was actually in session and his appearance produced great consternation; the duchesses of Suffolk and Northumberland burst into tears.[4] That wives would be at a council meeting seems improbable, but not so the report that the council immediately threw Hungate into a dungeon. Northumberland told him that at his age he should have had more sense.[5] However, uncompromising though the letter was, Mary's tone was moderate and conciliatory. The princess said that she was 'not ignorant of your consultations, to undo the provisions made for our preferment [i.e. by Henry VIII], nor of the great bands, and provisions forcible, wherewith ye be assembled and prepared – by whom and to what end, God and you know, and nature cannot but fear some evil.' Nevertheless she would take these actions 'in gracious part' and pardon them. The response of the council was prompt and confidently robust. They replied to Mary that Jane was 'invested and possessed with the just and right title of the imperial crown', both by 'good order of old ancient laws' [i.e. the common law of inheritance] and Edward's patent. Mary was disqualified because of the divorce between her parents. She must, therefore, cease her vexation and show herself 'quiet and obedient'.[6] The whole weight of the Tudor establishment signed the letter, twenty-three privy councilors headed by the archbishop of Canterbury and all the great officers of state.[7] Mary's letter does nevertheless seem to have stung the council into action. Not only did the proclamation of Queen Jane and her formal entry into the Tower go ahead as planned, but by the end of the day, an accession proclamation was ready for Jane to sign, so fulfilling the council's promise of the previous Saturday. Richard Grafton, the royal printer, was sent the text and must have worked his press late into the night, because the next day London was being plastered with copies.[8] The proclamation was backed up by a circular to local authorities, drafted by the duke himself and signed by the queen personally.[9] The letter announced that Jane had entered into the rightful possession of the kingdom according to Edward's last will. This had been subscribed by 'the nobles of this realm for the most part and all our council and judges, with the mayor and aldermen of our city of London and divers other grave personages' and with their consent she had made her 'entry into our Tower of London as rightful queen of this realm'.[10] Local officers were then called on to support her 'just title' and 'to disturb, repel and resist the feigned and untrue claim of the Lady Mary, bastard daughter to our great uncle Henry the eighth of famous memory'. Finally the letters renewed, as appropriate, the commissions issued by Edward VI to the lieutenants and local officials. On 12 July a follow-up council letter launched a full-scale assault on Mary for doing all she could to

> stir and provoke the common people of this realm to rebellion but also [for seeking] means to bring in great forces of papists, Spaniards and other strangers for the aid of her unjust and unnatural pretence, to the great peril and danger of the utter subversion of God's holy word and of the whole state of this realm.

This was an appeal to the visceral responses of the English gentry. The need to preserve 'the true religion and ancient liberty of your natural country against foreign powers' and the danger which 'the baser sort' represented 'to men of worship and good degree and wealth', meant that magistrates had not only to preserve order locally but also

> to put your selves in order, with such numbers of horsemen and footmen as you shall be able to make of your servants, tenants and others under your rules and offices, so as you may upon sending for or other knowledge given you repair to … the duke of Northumberland, who having with him [Northampton, Huntingdon and] other personages of estate is presently in the field with our said sovereign power for the repression of the said rebellions, or otherwise be employed for the defence of the realm as the case shall require.[11]

What the response was to these council instructions is very hard to tell. Once Jane's regime collapsed, individuals had every reason to distance themselves and censor the degree to which she had initially enjoyed support or at least acquiescence. Thanks to this 'pruning', very few of her official letters survive. However, the dozens of non-councillors we have seen obeying the call to commit to Edward's 'declaracion' indicate that to that point there was little open objection. To assess whether that support continued after the king was dead we have the evidence of those who were interrogated or arrested for actively supporting Jane, either in the field or elsewhere. In all over 150 names are known, and that ignores the anonymous rank and file who were not worth chasing for a fine.[12] The marquis of Northampton and three other senior peers – the earls of Rutland, Huntingdon and Westmorland – marched with Northumberland. So did two Irish nobles (Thomas Butler, earl of Ormonde and Garret Lord Fitzgerald), and Huntingdon's son Lord Hastings.[13] Bedford's son, Lord Russell, held Windsor for Queen Jane, and Viscount Hereford was active enough for him to be arrested soon after Jane's defeat, though what he had done is unknown.[14] Lord Bray and Lord Willoughby were suspects, so too the earl of Bath's son.[15] Others attracting attention included the veteran diplomat Sir Ralph Sadler.[16] Outside the council and the peerage, two dozen of those interrogated were or had been members of parliament. Over twenty were knights. For a measure of a wider reaction, there is revealing data covering the JPs of Norfolk, Suffolk, Cambridgeshire and Essex, the focus of Mary's support. Fifty-seven local magistrates lost their places on her accession, perhaps one in three. Of course not all of these went because of their support for Jane, but perhaps eighty per cent of them had been compromised.[17] Then there is the evidence from London. All sources indicate that Jane's accession came as a surprise to the citizens but there was apparently only one protestor – Gilbert Potter, whose temerity cost him his ears.[18] Three days later an open letter praising

Potter claimed that 'there were thousands more than thyself, yet durst they not once move their lips', but silent streets could have been as much because Jane was unexpected as because she was opposed. Civic authority was fully behind her.[19] No opposition was voiced in the hours between Saturday 8 July, when the mayor and thirty-one of the City notables signed Edward's 'deuise', and Jane being proclaimed on Monday afternoon, although the absence of some signatures could suggest reluctance or silent protest.[20] Companies began using the new regnal date, and contributions were collected for the loyal gift always given to a new sovereign.[21] It is no surprise that on the 13th Northumberland could assure the French that 'the council and the aldermen of the city of London' were all the support he needed.[22] Not until Sunday 16 July do we hear of any action to promote Mary – a letter left in St Paul's – and on the 18th a poster at Queenhithe which alleged that the rest of the country had proclaimed Mary and London should follow suit.[23] At Westminster the routine of government swung into action in Jane's name. Council communications were distributed as usual and Chancery took up the new regnal dating.[24] Some light on the situation at the grass roots of society is thrown by a petition submitted to Mary's council by a Richard Troughton, one of Cecil's servants, possibly in 1554.[25] Accused of disloyalty, he set out in furious and wordy detail how he had exploited his position as bailiff of a royal estate to act as a one-man publicity agent for Mary in the area around Stamford. But reading between the angry lines we can see that the justices of the peace were fully behind Jane – organizing musters, binding rumour-mongers to appear at quarter sessions, concerned to shut Troughton up – while the lowest tier of officials, the village constables, energetically obeyed orders to conscript men for Northumberland and, indeed, had troops already on the march. As for the ordinary folk Troughton met, although some felt that self-preservation argued for obedience, the overwhelming desire was to keep heads down. It is also clear that responses differed according to locality. Across the border in west Norfolk there is evidence of popular resistance to Mary's claims.[26]

To reinforce the justices, the council decided that the lords lieutenants must go down to their counties. The evidence for this is an undated letter among William Cecil's papers, written in a clerk's hand but signed by the secretary of state.[27] The particular addressees were the Lincolnshire gentry, but on the back is a rough list of fourteen counties with the names of their lieutenants, so the text was quite clearly the master for a series of similar communications.[28] The letter announces that Edward Clinton, the lord admiral (the county's lieutenant), 'is purposed to come down to those parts by order from hence [i.e. the council] for the good order of that country and other service there, [but] for the more expedition of the same is sending down Mr Carr and Mr Irby before him with speed'.[29] Justices were, nevertheless, not to wait for the messengers: 'shew yourselves diligent and ready in the service of your country to the best of your powers and to the furtherance of the queen's service'. In Cecil's papers there is also a sheet which lists a number of English counties plus Wales, along with the names of prominent local gentlemen. A later hand has endorsed it 'Names of the gentlemen etc. who transacted affairs for the establishment of Queen Jane', but, as we shall see, it should more correctly have read 'who were expected to transact affairs for the establishment of Queen Jane'.[30] Everywhere in these early days the assumption was that the existing system could be relied on to stand the strain. Nowhere is there any suggestion of the council needing forces other than those going to East Anglia with the duke.

One issue which the council continued to monitor was the possible diplomatic repercussion from Mary's challenge. Initially Charles V's ambassadors had been in baulk. Well aware of the emperor's adamant refusal to become involved militarily, they were also convinced that the scales were so loaded against Mary that her cause was hopeless.[31] De Noailles, on the other hand, was quick off the mark.[32] For some days Northumberland had fobbed off requests for another interview, and although the ambassador was eventually promised a meeting over dinner on the 7th, on that morning de Noailles first received a message putting back the time and then a second which cancelled the arrangement entirely. A rumour of the king's death soon told him why and the next day the ambassador hurried to the Council, determined to get his message in ahead of the imperialists: Mary was nothing but a stalking horse for Charles V; it was France which offered security. De Noailles even read extracts from one of Henry II's letters which he had copied out specially.[33] The council then went into private session, emerging, as he thought, to accept the offer of French military help 'when the occasion presents itself'.[34] In fact the council seems to have done little more than repeat its thanks for the offer while having no expectation of ever needing to invoke it.[35] Councillors nevertheless did recognize that imperial intervention would change everything and so on 11 July they decided to send Lord Cobham and Sir John Mason, the French Secretary, to warn Charles's representatives not to 'intermeddle as it is very likely they will and do dispose themselves'.[36] The visit took place the next day but the outcome was not what the English expected – or so Charles V was subsequently told. His ambassadors reported that they had seized on the opportunity to put the case for Mary and emphasize that France was only interested in seeing the Queen of Scots on the English throne, and so persuasively had they argued that Cobham and Mason were 'astonished and confused' and asked them not to leave the country. Ambassadors always tried to talk up their own effectiveness, but the probable reason which gave the two councillors pause was not eloquence but being told that some English correspondence with Henry II had fallen into imperial hands, so that Charles was 'most amply informed of the intrigues carried on by the duke and the council with the French'. The story of the intercepted letters had in fact been concocted by the ambassadors 'to check' de Noailles, but it cannot be a coincidence that Northumberland's cousin, Sir Henry Dudley, was immediately ordered to France and set off the next day.[37]

The imperialists were certain that Sir Henry was being sent to trigger planned French intervention, and there was talk of six thousand men embarking at Boulogne and Dieppe, but although Northumberland was interviewed on three occasions after his arrest, he seems to have said nothing of any communication with France.[38] We do, however, know something of the interrogation of Henry Dudley after he too had been arrested while attempting to return to England via Calais. Dudley reported that he had had an interview with Henry II on, it seems, 18 or 19 July.[39] The message he brought was that Northumberland did not think that he needed French help; relying on the council and the London elite would be enough to deal with Mary. But the duke was anxious to confirm yet again that France would help if Charles V intervened. The French king replied that then he would come in person with an army and the fleet, and Dudley was convinced that he meant what he said. Confession evidence must always be treated with caution because an individual intent on self-protection may say what he thinks his interrogators want to hear. But in this case, not only did Dudley not provide the hoped-for evidence of French treachery, a letter of congratulations which he had been carrying from Henry II to 'Queen' Jane, bore out his story.[40] There was no 'smoking gun'. It is true that when Simon Renard reported events to the emperor's son, Prince Philip, he did allege that 'it has also been discovered' that Northumberland had promised to hand over Calais and the attached English territories to France, along with Ireland.[41] However, he does not say this was learned through the interrogation, and since he and his colleagues had been spreading the story well before Henry Dudley had been arrested, the probability here is Renard wish-fulfilment. The allegation is too far-fetched to be believed.[42] All that any such surrender could have achieved was to unite England behind Mary. The rational conclusion must again be that only suspicion of the emperor led Northumberland to toy with France, and that in sending over Henry Dudley the council was doing no more than doubly checking on its insurance policy.[43]

Although Dudley told his interrogators that he was convinced by the French king's assurances, a further letter which he carried suggests that Henry II was no more anxious to intervene in England than the emperor was. It was from Henry's chief minister, Anne de Montmorency, constable of France, to Lord William Howard, the governor of Calais, and offered to protect England from foreign (i.e. imperial) scheming, in particular by assisting with the defence of Calais.[44] In reality Calais was already effectively protected by a French army whose position would allow it to attack an invading imperialist force from the rear.[45] The French offer was, thus, pure opportunism – offering what would have been a seaborne force to 'reinforce' Calais and its environs, with the unstated intention of staying there. Events, however, overtook the constable. Howard replied that he needed no help; Northumberland was a traitor and if de Montmorency attempted anything he would get a hot reception.[46] In the end, therefore, the 'intrigues' which Charles had so feared came to nothing. French guarantees had been no help to Jane, the French had got nothing out of the English crisis and not a single imperial bullet had needed to be fired. There would be no European 'War of the English Succession'.

The concern of the English councillors about possible imperial intervention did not mean that they were blind to the future need for Jane to have the best possible relations with Charles V. He would remain a potential counterweight to France and there was also the vital economic tie with the Low Countries.[47] The meeting on the 12th had left Cobham and Mason in no doubt how offended Charles would be at Mary being 'proclaimed a bastard', in defiance of the 1544 statute and Henry VIII's will.[48] The ambassadors, therefore, were invited to a further meeting the following day (Thursday 13 July) at the house of the earl of Pembroke, this time with a number of council members. Those attending were the earls of Bedford, Arundel, Shrewsbury and Pembroke, along with Cobham and Mason and William Petre, the senior of the secretaries of state. The object of the English seems to have been to prevent imperialist envoys leaving before the Council could send its own envoy to Charles.[49] Sir Richard Shelley did leave for Brussels on July 15 and, according to the ambassadors, their own messenger was turned back by the council 'in order to be able to get in a first word with your Majesty'. So sure were the imperial ambassadors that the plan was to soft-soap Charles that they sent a special warning to alert him.[50]

While council letters warned the counties to be on the look-out for trouble, and while diplomacy took its course, the primary concern of the councillors was what to do about Mary. Once more the evidence is confused. Various sources date the decision to send a force into East Anglia to Monday (10th), Tuesday (11th), Wednesday (12th) or even Thursday (13th). Some of the contradiction may be between when it was decided that force was unavoidable and when the council agreed who was to command. That decision was settled in time for letters to go out on Wednesday 12 July announcing that Northumberland, Northampton, Huntingdon 'and other personages of estate is presently in the field with our said sovereign's power for the repression of rebellions'.[51] But reaching that decision may not have been plain sailing. For the second time in her reign, Jane is said to have asserted herself. She had vetoed a crown for Guildford; now the issue was the choice of the commander 'to go and bring in the Lady Mary'. Unfortunately, sources once more tell different stories. Robert Wingfield has it that the council picked the duke of Suffolk to command and that the queen 'strongly urged him to embark on this expedition, saying with great boldness that she could have no safer defence for her majesty than her most loving father'.[52] Suffolk refused, pleading ill health, but really under the influence of his wife, who was, as we have seen, close to Mary.[53] The chronicler present in the Tower (unlike Wingfield, miles away in Suffolk), reported the exact opposite. Suffolk's appointment

> was clean dissolved by the special means of the lady Jane, his daughter, who taking the matter heavily, with weeping tears, made the request to the whole council that her father might tarry home in her company; whereupon the council persuaded with the duke of Northumberland to take that voyage upon him.[54]

As Stow tells the story, it was not tears but Jane's determination which settled the question: 'this is the short and long, the queen will in no wise grant that her father shall take it upon him'.[55] Yet whether it was royal weeping or royal firmness, how much did either really determine the outcome?[56] So important a decision must surely have involved Northumberland. He faced a classic dilemma. Does an overall commander stay at headquarters to provide stability and be ready for the unexpected, or does he lead from the front? The answer depends entirely upon the quality of possible subordinates, and in a Tudor army these had to be ranking noblemen. Suffolk's less than energetic showing on the Scottish border in 1551 hardly encouraged confidence and the marquis of Northampton was ruled out by a disastrous performance during Ket's Rebellion.[57] Northumberland may thus have felt obliged to take command of the expedition for fear that Jane's father would, as Wingfield put it, 'fail to meet the imminent danger in time, through temporizing'.[58] With hindsight there can be little doubt that leading from the front was the wrong decision. There is no evidence that Mary ever intended to move from the defensive position she took up at Framlingham, so a force with orders to 'temporize' – that is, watch but not engage – would have been perfectly adequate.[59] Jane would then have had time to build up her army and Northumberland would have remained at the centre to meet any threats which appeared nearer London. In fact, news of local protest did arrive just as he was leaving, but by then the decision had been taken and the duke had to trust the council to take the necessary action.[60]

The size of the force which the council managed to assemble is hard to measure. The imperial ambassadors gave six or seven hundred as the number being thought of on 11 July, but they reported that recruitment was continuing and on the 16th as well.[61] Northumberland himself left London with some 600 men, made up of the 200 retainers he had with him after sending 300 with Robert Dudley on the morning after Edward's death, plus the 400 licensed to supporters in May and June. Other contingents followed, no doubt including some of the 300 retainers Suffolk was reported to have at hand on 4 July.[62] Additional men were recruited en route, but the general promise by the councillors to send their 'powers' to rendezvous at Newmarket was never honoured.[63] Later estimates of numbers reach as high as 2,500 horse and 8,000 foot, but the indictments for high treason give the total as only 3,000 – and, notoriously, such indictments rarely understate.[64] That 3,000 may be not far from the reality is suggested by the fact that the imperial ambassadors in London, although convinced that Northumberland's forces spelled doom for Mary, gave the Cambridge figure as only 1,000 horse and 3,000 foot with twelve pieces of artillery, while de Guaras, who certainly wanted to emphasize the seriousness of the danger Mary had faced, still felt unable to go beyond a figure of 'more than' 3,000 horse.[65] Where the ambassadors were certainly wrong was about the balance of the army.[66] Infantry was in short supply, which is hardly surprising given the rapid development of the emergency. We have seen that a precautionary instruction had been given to county leaders on 8 July to have their 'powers' at an hour's readiness, but more specific orders to mobilize servants, tenants and 'manred' were only circulated on 12 July.[67] Thomas Cranmer did manage to send twenty men to Cambridge that same day, and it was probably in response to the circular that the Lincolnshire JPs had some foot soldiers on the move by the 15th.[68] Nevertheless, recruiting overall seems to have been slow. Despite the JPs being 'very busy' to respond, some Lincolnshire musters had still not been held on the 18th.[69]

The council's difficulty in raising a significant force in short order emphasizes how little Mary had been seen as a problem. As it was, the need to put the fire out quickly made it impossible to call on that final resource of the ruler, the royal household in arms. All royal servants were under an ultimate obligation to appear on due warning, armed and ready to fight with whatever men they could raise, and the resulting force was by no means negligible. It very nearly carried Richard III to victory at Bosworth and it had formed the kernel for Henry VIII's armies; in 1554 it would play a useful part in resisting the rebellion led by Thomas Wyatt. However, mobilizing the household required time – weapons and horses for a campaign were not ready to hand – and time was precisely what Northumberland did not have. What is not likely is that royal servants were left behind because of doubts about their loyalty. The guard took the oath to Jane and there is no evidence that other staff refused to serve the Queen.[70] Failure to do so would immediately have cost them at least their jobs, and since if Mary were to win some of them would lose their places anyway, self-interest argued the same way as fear. Mary's challenge also meant that safety precautions for the new queen had to be increased. The duke could not afford to leave behind him a council stripped of resources. Guns were mounted on the Tower to overawe London and the garrison was increased, increased sufficiently, indeed, to require special tented accommodation.[71]

Stories circulated that in order to get any sort of force together Northumberland was forced to offer grossly inflated wages. A Londoner noted that on Tuesday 11 July men were called to assemble on Tothill Fields and promised 10d. a day instead of the standard 6d.[72] When Cardinal Commendone arrived he was told that eight crowns a month had been offered, with no deductions, equivalent to 20d. per day, clear.[73] The imperial ambassadors reported the inducement of a month's pay in advance.[74] If this information is correct – and we have no way of knowing – the high wages were probably not to bribe men to serve but because they were in effect being asked to drop everything and march off with virtually no notice. Various sources have Northumberland leave London on different dates from July 12 to July 14, but even the last only allowed three days to enlist and equip recruits.

One aspect of the force could not be faulted: leadership. Northumberland was the most experienced and finest soldier in the country and he had with him William Lord Grey who was renowned for courage and impetuosity (though less for caution) while Edward Clinton completed what was the trio of England's leading commanders.[75] Grey's presence was also significant for another reason – he had been an ally of the duke of Somerset, but still he marched against Mary. Organization was not overlooked. Thomas Mildmay, the country's premier auditor, was present to act as the army's treasurer, assisted by a professional colleague (and MP), Edward Fortescue.[76] Sir Peter Mewtas, governor of Guernsey, and a long-time soldier, courtier and secret agent to Henry VIII, provided four hundred men.[77] The earl of Westmorland had considerable experience in Border skirmishes. He appears to have brought with him a number of the leading gentlemen of the Scottish border such as Fergus Graham, Sir Thomas Dacre, deputy warden of the West March, and the captains of Bowcastle and Carlisle Castle.[78] Without question, the leadership and organization of Jane's forces outranked and outclassed anything Mary would ever be able to muster.

20

THE MARCH ON
FRAMLINGHAM

THE first move in the campaign to defend the new monarch had been the despatch of Robert Dudley on the day after Edward's death, to secure Mary.[1] The attempt failed and Robert had to report back to the Council that 'the Lady Mary being at Hunsdon is suddenly departed with her train and family toward the sea coast of Norfolk'.[2] He must, however, have had alternative orders, for instead of returning he followed the princess and began patrolling to prevent supporters reaching her at Kenninghall. At one stage he was at Attleborough, only ten miles away, where he managed to convince Henry Ratcliffe, earl of Sussex and the only competent soldier in the region, that Edward was still alive.[3] Then fresh orders must have arrived from London, because although Mary at this stage was still at her great house at Kenninghall in Norfolk with at most five or six hundred men and barely five or six 'persons of rank', Robert moved fifty miles away via King's Lynn to raise the country south of the Wash for Jane, reaching Wisbech on the 11th.[4] The following day Mary also moved, to the more defensible castle of Framlingham, twenty-five miles away in Suffolk.[5]

Jane's main force left London in stages and sources give a variety of dates but the observer present in the Tower is quite specific that Northumberland himself left the fortress after dinner on Thursday 13th, mustered his force that night at Durham Place and Whitehall and marched off the following morning.[6] From Durham House on the Strand the troops rode into and through the crowded streets of the City and out of Bishopsgate, and it was in Shoreditch that the duke made one of the famous remarks of the whole rebellion. 'The people press to see us, but not one saith "God speed us".'[7] Later that day Sir John Gates set out, with the household troops. The artillery and supply train followed the next day, that is Saturday 15 July.[8]

The progress of the army can be followed in some detail because, after the event, treason charges were promoted by the individual counties it had passed through.[9] Both the duke and Gates reached Ware on the Friday, an easy march of twenty-five miles. There he was joined by his sons and additional troops, almost certainly more of the Dudley 'manred' from the Midlands. The next morning he set off to Cambridge, sanctioned a detour to sack the house of John Huddleston at Sawston where Mary had sheltered, and reached the town in time for supper. The Cambridge indictment places the duke in the town until Tuesday 18 July when he left for Framlingham 'with the intention of depriving [Mary] of her royal estate and killing her'.[10] At some point along the route he was joined by the lord admiral with further reinforcements which are described as 'large [in number] and excellently equipped', but since Clinton escaped indictment we cannot be sure where or when.[11] The jury return for the county of Suffolk shows that the duke was in Bury on 18 and 19 July, but late that evening he abandoned the town – according to Robert Wingfield 'when the lamps had been lit' – and retreated to Cambridge where he spent the night at the house of Sir John Cheke, the provost of King's College.[12] It is clear that his troops went with him because, according to Robert Wingfield who was at Framlingham, the first fugitives from the army did not arrive to make their peace with the new queen until late on the following day, Thursday 20th.[13] At some point, possibly in the small hours, news reached Cambridge that during Wednesday 19 July the council in London had done a U-turn, ousted Jane and proclaimed Mary. Northumberland responded next day by himself proclaiming Mary in the market place.[14] Only then did his force disperse, and possibly not until letters were received from the council saying that everyone was free to go home.[15] The campaign had lasted a week.

This account contrasts sharply with the traditional story that Northumberland's campaign was in difficulties from the very beginning. Desertions began as soon as he had left London or, alternatively, his ranks were riddled with Mary's sympathizers waiting the time to desert.[16] According to Foxe, the Council had prescribed the stages of the duke's march 'to the intent he might not seem to do anything but upon warrant', but this concern for the legalities simply gave Mary more time to build up her forces; Holinshed adds the gloss that this was precisely what 'some in favour of the Lady Mary' had intended all along.[17] The story of unwise delay is certainly not true. If he started in the morning of Friday 14 July and reached Cambridge in the late afternoon of Saturday, Northumberland covered fifty-five miles in a maximum of thirty-six hours of daylight.[18] Actual travelling time was less, given the wait for his sons at Ware and the time spent on a detour to sack Sawston. For comparison, the figure for the distance which a horse could be expected to cover in a day was forty miles. Messengers could move significantly more quickly, but their mounts would not be used day on day, let alone be ready for operations.[19]

Whatever infantry Northumberland had with him must have taken longer, and the guns could have been even further behind.[20] In the *Vita Mariae Reginae* Wingfield wants to emphasize the duke's unpopularity and at the same time make the most of the danger Mary faced, so he reports that the desertions only started at Cambridge. Until then the duke had carefully kept up momentum in order to maintain morale, but delaying at Cambridge for longer than was militarily necessary allowed morale to collapse with men abandoning him every day.[21] Again one is sceptical. From arriving at Cambridge late on Saturday 15th to leaving on the morning of Tuesday 18th was a significant sixty hours, but could Northumberland have marched earlier? In the first place, he appears to have expected additional forces to join him at the small market town of Newmarket and it clearly made sense not to move the main army from the facilities Cambridge offered until he could expect the reinforcements to be nearing the rendezvous.[22] In the second place and more fundamental, it was essential, given the weakness of the royal army in infantry, not to allow the cavalry to get too far ahead of the guns. Ten miles a day was a fair rate for Civil War armies a century later and even then the artillery could straggle. It is hard to imagine that in 1553 Northumberland's artillery train could have arrived much before the muster which he held on Monday 17 July. The imperial ambassadors certainly expected the duke would move at much the pace he did.[23]

The stories of desertion are also suspect because based on rumour. In reality Northumberland succeeded in bringing a larger number of troops to Cambridge than had left London with him – and troops which had already demonstrated some commitment by attacking Sawston.[24] Despite this, on Tuesday 18 July it was being said in London that dissension in the army over the attack on Sawston had resulted in four hundred casualties, including one of the duke's sons and his son-in-law Henry Sidney dead, and Lord Grey, the earl of Warwick and Lord Hastings injured, leaving Northumberland free to go forward on a scorched-earth mission.[25] Rumour similarly reported that Lord Rich had deserted to Mary, something which did not happen until the following day, Wednesday 19 July.[26] And once the army had indeed broken up, it was easy for commentators writing at a distance and after the event to project disintegration backwards – especially in a desire to underplay the degree of support the duke had enjoyed. Also against the assumption of a daily haemorrhage by desertion is the significant proportion of the force made up of the retinues of various nobles.[27] Desertions there were much less likely than among troops enlisted for the occasion; individuals had so much more to lose. No doubt retainers would run if their masters ran, but until the end at Cambridge the leadership of the army remained solid. The one group about whom some data has survived is the gentlemen pensioners, the troop of gentle and noble birth which Henry VIII had set up in 1539 as an aristocratic guard around the sovereign.[28] After the crisis of 1553, careful checks by Mary's government revealed that twenty-nine of the forty-nine pensioners then in post 'went not with the duke of Northumberland'. Taken at face value this could suggest that a majority of the band deliberately refused to support Jane Grey. What is more, if the individual background of the pensioners is investigated it can be argued that there was a difference between the two groups, those who marched with the duke being the more recently appointed members of the 'band' and especially those who were more akin to professional soldiers than to courtiers. There is, however, a fatal objection to reading the data as an index of the duke's support. The band of pensioners served as a unit only when there was a general muster. Otherwise a shift system was operated with half of the number at court at any one time. There is no evidence that there was any general summons in July 1553 and anyway there was not time for one to be effective. The conclusion must, therefore, be that the twenty pensioners who went with Northumberland were those who happened to be on duty and thus took the oath to Jane after Edward's death, and that at most only five of the shift refused to take the field against Mary. Nor is this conclusion challenged by pensioners turning up among those who rallied to Mary. Any member of the band not on duty or refusing duty in July 1553 and who was prepared to assert the princess's title would have been guaranteed a warm welcome at Framlingham. None seems to have made the journey.[29] Clearly even those who were unenthusiastic about Jane were unwilling to do anything about it. A similar conclusion probably applies to the less prestigious 'men-at-arms' (a group of veterans from the Boulogne garrison); 'a great number' of these are noted as having marched with the duke.[30] What makes that more indicative is that it was possible for them to avoid going. Edward Underhill recalled that 'I went not forth against her majesty, notwithstanding that I was commanded, nor liked those doings' – and Underhill was a Protestant zealot.[31]

We may, thus, suspect that there were fewer desertions from the army Northumberland commanded than tradition has supposed. Can anything be discovered of what the duke intended? Here the make-up of the force has something to say. There was the large and 'fearsome' artillery train of the 'great army toward Cambridge' which impressed Henry Machin mightily: 'great guns and small ... [and] gunstones a great number'.[32] De Guaras speaks of thirty pieces of cannon, while the report of Robert Wingfield that, as well as field pieces, the duke even took the 'bombards' from the Tower is supported by a reference by Charles V's envoys to the duke having cannons and demi-cannons with him.[33] The horse was equally impressive. Comprising the gentlemen pensioners, the 'men at arms' and the personal retinues of the duke and the nobles with him, it clearly justified its description as 'a splendid force of cavalry'.[34] This emphasis on an elite force of mounted troops and artillery suggests that Northumberland calculated that if he had to fight it would be against a mob of peasants whom he could terrify by a display of firepower before using the cavalry to disperse them with minimum casualties; he went, as de Guaras put it, 'weening to disburse the peasants with his horse for they were ill-armed'.[35] It was the tactic he had used successfully against Ket and his rebels at Dussindale four years before.

When, on the other hand, we consider the route Northumberland chose, the question arises whether he really expected to have to fight at all. From London via Ware to Cambridge and then east to Bury St Edmunds and Framlingham is a distance of 115 miles. The direct route through Colchester and Ipswich is twenty-five miles shorter – effectively a day's march saved and Mary facing his guns a day weaker. By the same token, reinforcements would be quicker into action. Why then the Cambridge route? That would have been the normal way to take if Norfolk was the objective but by the date Northumberland left, London knew that Mary had moved south to Framlingham.[36] Logistics cannot have determined the issue either. Colchester would have been a better forward base than Cambridge, because it could readily be supplied by sea and the duke's supporters there were strong.[37] Perhaps the additional troops he linked up with at Ware had necessitated taking the Cambridge route, but it seems more reasonable for reinforcements to find the main body than vice versa. A more probable consideration is suggested by Robert Dudley ceasing to monitor Mary and moving instead to the area south and west of King's Lynn. With his father based at Cambridge, control of the area southwards from the Wash would be complete, so preventing Mary from either breaking out into the Midlands or receiving reinforcements herself from the west. An added advantage was that Northumberland was himself expecting extra troops from Lincolnshire, and these would pass through Robert's command to link up with the duke and not have to work round Mary's position as would be the case with the main royal army coming from the south.[38]

However, what could have been the decisive consideration in choosing the route was the assessment which the London council initially made of the princess's options: 'either to fly the realm or to abide there some foreign power'.[39] If Mary's intention was flight, to send an army via Colchester risked driving her to embark at any one of the ports in a hundred miles of coastline from Orford Ness to the Wash. On the other hand, to be in command in King's Lynn and to approach from Cambridge via Bury would effectively limit Mary's escape routes to a handful of ports in the thirty-five miles or so between Lowestoft and the Orwell, and they could be readily blockaded. The same disposition would apply if Mary was waiting for Charles V; pinning her down between Bury and the coast would compel the imperial forces to target a restricted area and break through the same blockade. An imperial invasion elsewhere could be discounted since it would merely have demonstrated the truth of Jane's propaganda about the threat from Spain. This appreciation would still have appeared sound even after Mary had announced that she intended to stay and fight. If she failed, as the council was confident she would, her flight to the arms of Charles V would be immediate. That this was the thinking of the councillors is confirmed by their decision to deploy six warships off the Suffolk coast, perhaps three of two to three hundred tons and the others smaller pinnaces.[40] A force of this size and strength was enough to control the required area of the coast and more than enough to deter an imperial invasion fleet.[41] Precisely when the ships sailed is not clear. Two days before Edward's death the imperial ambassadors reported that they were lying in the Thames from Limehouse to Greenwich ready for sea but without crews.[42] The fleet was certainly off the Orwell on 13 or 14 July and so had probably been despatched as reinsurance at the same time Robert Dudley marched out to capture the princess. Sir Richard Brooke, the overall commander, was a man Northumberland must have thought he could count on. He had played a major role in the 1544 invasion of Scotland and in 1545 had commanded *The Unicorn*, one of the prizes from that raid, in the duke's division of the fleet for the operations which followed the loss of the *Mary Rose*.[43] Between the duke's guns and cavalry advancing from the west and Brooke's ships at her back Mary would be helpless. With reasonable luck there need be no battle. Northumberland's force was intended to serve more as a posse than an army.

If this analysis of the strategy of Jane's government is correct, by the time Northumberland reached Cambridge he must have recognized that things were not going entirely as planned. Risings in favour of Mary were being reported from several of the counties west of London, and the morning after he arrived at Cambridge the council in London decided that the threat in Buckinghamshire was serious enough to necessitate more support.[44] How soon the duke had been informed of this is not known, but a recognition that he was now effectively on his own could well explain his grim joke to the vice-chancellor, Edwin Sandys, and other Protestant clerics over supper on the Saturday: 'Masters, pray for us that we speed well: if not you shall be made bishops and we deacons', that is 'you will have mitres (flames) on your heads [i.e. be burned] and we shall be tonsured [i.e. beheaded].'[45] Challenged to preach the next day, Sandys produced at the shortest of notice a sermon on the text:

> They answered Joshua saying, 'All that thou commandest us we will do, and whithersoever thou sendest us, we will go. According as we hearkened unto Moses in all things, so will we hearken unto thee: only the Lord thy God be with thee, as he was with Moses. Whosoever he be that doth rebel against thy commandment, and will not hearken unto thy words in all that thou commandest him, he shall be put to death: only be strong and of a good courage'.[46]

According to Foxe, Sandys gave a bravura performance, brandishing a missal and a Catholic chalice looted from Sawston, and Northumberland and the other peers ordered him to publish his sermon at once![47]

A morale-boosting exhortation did not, however, change the reality. Northumberland could no longer expect a second wave of support from the council and when he marched to the planned rendezvous at Newmarket he would find not reinforcements but further 'discomforting' letters from London.[48] Not that we can suppose the duke despaired because the odds had shortened somewhat. He was renowned for his (justifiable) self-confidence and his 'high courage', and might rightly feel that he still held the initiative. Sympathizers with Mary elsewhere in the country would disappear overnight once he had dispersed her forces at Framlingham. Stories that her supporters there had risen to huge numbers could be dismissed as obvious exaggerations, and with very few exceptions the leaders of the country who counted were still active for Jane. The duke must have been concerned that once the supportive presence of Robert Dudley had been removed the earl of Sussex succumbed to pressure and took his military expertise over to Mary, but otherwise the aristocrats with the princess were a handful of nonentities.[49] Even the defection of the earl of Oxford (news of which reached the duke on the 18th) brought the princess only the prestige of England's second-ranking earldom, not a leader of any real competence. The duke still had a reasonable hope that reinforcements on the way from Lincolnshire would arrive before any battle and his son Robert was achieving real progress around the Wash. As well as Wisbech, which he made his base, Robert seems to have secured support for Jane in Thetford – the mayor felt it necessary to appeal to Mary for troops on 16 July.[50] Boston probably declared for Jane – the relevant pages have been torn out of the town records and the mayor and aldermen were exempted from Mary's coronation pardon.[51] On 18 July Robert achieved his greatest success by bringing King's Lynn, Norfolk's second-largest town and the metropolis of the Fenland, over to Jane Grey's side.[52] Even after Mary's victory, opposition to her persisted in the marshland possibly for weeks.[53]

The duke of Northumberland therefore marched out of Cambridge on the morning of Tuesday 18 July giving no signs of undue concern. The army resumed its smart pace and reached Bury the same day, though again the guns must have lagged behind. We can assume that as soon as possible patrols were sent out, but there was no action that evening. Nor was there action on the Wednesday. Instead the campaign stalled in uncertainty until late in the day the retreat to Cambridge began. If we reject the story that when Northumberland's army left Cambridge it was already rotten with disaffection, the problem is to explain why, having come within twenty miles of his objective, the duke decided without warning to retreat. There is no first-hand evidence to help us – after the event those involved probably thought that wisdom lay in the cover story of a rabble driven on by the manic force of the duke's personality but just waiting to fall apart. A distant possibility is a lack of provisions; Mary had stripped the area of cattle.[54] The principal explanation must, however, lie in what the duke discovered once he was near enough to replace rumour with good intelligence of the actual status of Mary's army. He would have expected his patrols to report that he was outnumbered but the extent of this may have been worrying. In contrast to her escort from Framlingham of only a few hundred, Mary had perhaps 10,000 men and, even granted the superiority of quality troops, 3:1 against is a tall order, particularly as the Marian forces had chosen to dig in.[55] More important, scouts would also have told the duke that the assessment of the enemy as 'ill-armed peasants' was no longer valid. A significant stiffening of local gentlemen had come in with their 'powers' and the earl of Sussex had worked wonders, turning a confusion of loyalty into what would pass for an army. By 20 July (before the news of Northumberland's retreat arrived) the earl was able to muster Mary's supporters in two divisions showing some semblance of order and discipline and even to mount a demonstration cavalry charge.[56]

This intelligence would have been sufficient to convince Jane's commanders that an attack on Mary's army would be far more of a risk than had been expected, even if they waited for the troops from Lincolnshire. But waiting was not an option – time was not on the queen's side; they were well aware of the increasing support for Mary elsewhere in the kingdom. Given such considerations, the right – indeed the only – policy was to continue the advance. That instead of doing this and putting pressure on Mary, Northumberland chose to retreat and to retreat precipitately argues that there was something else in the intelligence he had received which was wholly disastrous and a complete surprise. And we can guess what that was. Mary had artillery. His scouts should, indeed, have reported that her forces were possibly superior in that arm, even though the duke knew that his was the only force in the country which could have had access to such heavy weapons. Yet wherever they had come from, Mary did have guns and the duke's intended tactic of combining cavalry and artillery had become wholly unrealistic. Far from counting on the royal gunners to terrify peasants at long range, he knew they would face counter-battery fire.

Mary Tudor was dealt the trump card of artillery support not by supplies from her Habsburg cousin but by courtesy of the fleet which had been sent to prevent such support getting through. While Northumberland was imagining Brooke running an effective patrol line from Lowestoft to the River Orwell – his six ships would have allowed a blockade at two or three times the minimum density – North Sea weather had intervened. Before the blockade was even set up a north-easterly had forced five of the fleet to take shelter in the estuary of the Orwell. Framlingham was only twenty-five miles away and Mary's agents were very active along the river. Communication was opened with the ships, and the officers and crews came over to Mary. Guns were put ashore and taken to Framlingham, no doubt along with the trained gunners and a plentiful supply of ammunition plus the complement of soldiers the ships carried.[57] No attack from Jane's forces thereafter had any hope of success.

As Northumberland rode back to Cambridge he must have asked himself whether he could have done anything different. His most bitter regret would have been for the days lost before he set out from London. If the army had been at Bury on the 14th matters could have been quite different. They might also have been different if at the start he had been able to send out more parties of the kind Robert Dudley had led. What his son achieved with a very small force indicates that active patrolling on a larger scale would have checked the unexpected rapidity of the recruitment to Mary and, in particular, have caused the gentlemen to weigh loyalty to her claims against the probability of arrest and the certainty of losing their property. We shall see that Sussex's change of sides came only after Mary's forces had captured his son and heir and that Oxford only switched allegiance when the force sent to Castle Hedingham to recruit his men to serve Jane became outnumbered.[58]

In reflecting on the campaign, Northumberland had little reason for self-reproach. Once started he had moved fast, kept his force together and made contact with the enemy with a tactical plan ready which on his best intelligence should have worked. The artillery he could not have anticipated – nor could any action of his have brought Jane's army to Bury before the guns had changed the balance so disastrously. We do not know when they actually reached Framlingham, but reports point to Saturday 15 July as the date on which Richard Brooke rode to Mary to present the loyalty of the ships, and it is possible that he brought some with him.[59] Instructions to bring the rest were issued on the 16th, and these were possibly there on the 17th, certainly by the 18th.[60] On the 17th, too, guns were ordered to be landed from the sixth ship, the *Greyhound*, which had taken shelter in Yarmouth.[61] Even if the duke had not paused at Cambridge he must still have found Mary in an unassailable position. Where Northumberland should, perhaps, have blamed himself was for falling into the old error of setting out to fight the previous war. Mary Tudor was not Robert Ket, even if most of her men were again East Anglian peasants. Sending a small, fast, elite force to sweep aside inadequate opposition and capture Mary offered the chance to nip opposition to Jane in the bud, but it was a high-risk strategy which had to be executed quickly and it allowed no margin for failure. Again lack of time and lack of forward planning were to blame. If only Northumberland had had at Bury the fourteen hundred German hackbutters he had had with him at Dussindale, Brooke's guns might have been dealt with.

Once Mary was safe behind the guns of the fleet, the royal commanders had only one option left. This was to retreat but hold the army together in the hope of giving the privy council some bargaining power. That illusion only lasted until letters arrived from London announcing the change of sides in London. At that point the duke bowed to the inevitable. When he came away with Sandys from proclaiming Mary at Cambridge on Thursday, he said that Mary was a merciful woman and that he looked for a general pardon. Sandys, however, told him the truth: 'My life is not dear unto me, neither have I done or said any thing that urges my conscience ... But be you assured, you shall never escape death; for if she would save you, those that now shall rule, will kill you.'[62] A scapegoat carries other men's sins and, once identified, it must not be allowed to escape.

21

A SECOND FRONT

FAILURE is never pleasant, but as he waited at Cambridge John Dudley could have reflected that success would have been worse. Capturing Mary would have left him facing a council and a capital which had declared for a claimant he had just defeated. Indeed, is the truth that events elsewhere in the country had made all his efforts irrelevant?

Two facts make it difficult to get to the bottom of what went on after Northumberland left London. In the first place there is precious little evidence and it is very confused – the equivalent of a modern crisis obscured by discrepant media reporting. In the second, much of what there is has yet again been spun in an effort to obscure responsibility. The earl of Arundel even had the gall to reduce the crisis to a confrontation between Mary and the duke and say that it was up to the council to decide which of them to support.

> Now seeing we are to suppress one of these two factions, consider I pray you which is most fit to be abandoned and which you are to adhere unto. I assure myself ... you will say that of the duke's as being contrary to all reason, unjust and fit to breed infinite mischiefs and inconveniences, which if you well understand, it shall not be amiss to take order accordingly.[1]

Mary herself found it wise not to question too publicly the council's explanation that

> We your most humble, faithful and obedient subjects having always (God we take to witness) remained your Highness's true and humble subjects in our hearts ever since the death of our late sovereign lord and master, your highness's brother whom God pardon; and seeing hitherto no possibility to utter our determination herein without great destruction and bloodshed both of ourselves and others till this time, have this day proclaimed in your

city of London your majesty to be our true, natural sovereign liege lady and queen, most humbly beseeching your majesty to pardon and remit our former infirmities and most graciously to accept our meanings which have been ever to serve your highness truly.[2]

Unusually for a Tudor event, the one certainty is the timing and the circumstances of the ending of Jane Grey's reign. On the morning of Wednesday 19 July the council sent a letter to Lord Rich urging him to remain loyal to Jane.[3] It was signed by sixteen privy councillors including the earls of Arundel and Pembroke and all the other seniors available, along with Lord Paget, restored to the council after being out of public life for effectively two years.[4] But later that morning a majority of councillors left the Tower and moved to the earl of Pembroke's accommodation at Baynard's Castle. There they agreed to abandon Jane and proclaim Mary.[5] The earl of Shrewsbury and Sir John Mason then went in search of the lord mayor of London and, finding him in the early afternoon at Paul's Wharf, instructed the mayor to collect what aldermen he could and join the privy council at Baynard's Castle within the hour.[6] Shrewsbury and Mason went next to the lodgings of the imperial ambassadors and informed them that

> though it had been said that the late King Edward's devise touching the succession had received the assent of the Council, only three or four of them had given their willing assent and the rest had been compelled and treated almost as if they were prisoners. The earls of Pembroke and Shrewsbury, the Lord Privy Seal [the earl of Bedford], the earl of Arundel, Mason, the three secretaries and Paget ... with the Treasurer [the marquis of Winchester] whom they knew to be of their opinion, had been persuaded that the Lady Mary was rightful queen, and had decided to proclaim her as such this very day.[7]

When the mayor and his colleagues arrived at Baynard's Castle, they were told about the U-turn and accompanied the council to hear the earl of Pembroke proclaim Queen Mary. With Garter King at Arms and the trumpeters already at the Cross in Cheapside, rumour flew like wildfire and the councillors and aldermen had difficulty in forcing their way through the huge crowd.[8] When Pembroke got to the name Mary, London erupted and drowned out the rest: 'The content and joy of all were such that almost all cast up their caps into the air without caring to recover them, and all who had money in their purses threw it to the people. Others, being men of authority and in years, leaping and dancing as though beside themselves.'[9] Another eyewitness reported that 'The earl of Pembroke threw away his cap, full of angelets [jewels]. I saw myself money was thrown out at windows for joy. The bonfires were without number and what with shouting and crying of the people, and ringing of the bells, there could no one hear almost what another said, besides banquetings and singing in the street for joy.'[10] Leaving a near-riot behind – Sir John York narrowly escaped lynching – the aldermen and the council led the way to St Paul's to hear evensong and 'the choir sing *Te Deum* with the organs going and the bells ringing'.[11] Finally Arundel and Paget rode off through the night to take the council's contrition to Framlingham.[12] Behind them London reacted in a celebration fuelled by 'wine, beer and ale in abundance' which exhausted itself about mid-day on Thursday.[13]

Where in all this treachery was Queen Jane? As before, stories disagree – those, that is, that even bother to mention her. The resident Spanish merchant, Antonio de Guaras, says that Jane and her father were warned about the volte-face on 18 July, but the council letter sent to Lord Rich the next morning disproves that.[14] An Englishman who was present at the proclamation says that Suffolk was in the Tower and 'as some say did not know of it', but that as soon as the duke realized, he ordered his men to leave their weapons, and with a comment 'that he himself was but one man.', went to proclaim Mary on nearby Tower Hill. He then abandoned the Tower and Jane.[15] The picture of the young queen being deserted is certainly what comes out of the autobiographical narrative by Edward Underhill, the staunchly Protestant man-at-arms who had refused to march with Northumberland.[16] His six-day-old son was due to be christened on 19 July in the church of All Hallows Barking-by-the-Tower and Queen Jane had agreed to act as godmother. Lady Anne Throckmorton, the wife of Sir Nicholas, deputized for the queen (the usual arrangement), but the godmother selected the name and Jane chose to call the boy Guildford, after her husband.[17] But, says Underhill, 'immediately after the christening was done, Queen Mary was proclaimed in Cheapside, and when my Lady Throckmorton came into the Tower the cloth of estate was taken down and all things defaced: a sudden change. She would have gone forth again, but could not be suffered [allowed].' This to a degree chimes in with the report sent to Charles V on 22 July that as soon as Suffolk realized that the council was going over to Mary he went to Jane, who was at supper, and took down the cloth of estate with his own hands, telling her to accept Mary. She replied that this was much better advice than when he had urged her to take the crown. Later her mother was told that she could leave, and also her ladies-in-waiting, 'and they left for their own homes, abandoning Jane'.[18]

When Shrewsbury and Mason went to the imperial ambassadors that Wednesday afternoon, they went with excuses ready prepared. 'Only three or four of them [the councillors] had given their willing assent and the rest had been compelled and treated almost as if they were prisoners.' As soon as Northumberland and the army were out of sight, they had begun looking for the chance to pull the rug from under him.[19] This rapidly became the accepted story. Three weeks after Mary's triumph Cardinal Commendone arrived in England and what he picked up was that

> Although the duke of Suffolk remained as [Northumberland's] deputy, as he was not held as [a] man of great valour and therefore lacked authority, several lords of the council freely discussing this matter, reached the conclusion that it was iniquitous and contrary to their duty to permit that the legitimate heir, by law of God and of the country, be robbed of the crown, submitting so abjectly to a public tyrant, failing to do their duty to their sovereign, to their own reputation and to the love of their country.[20]

As we have seen, Edward had feared something of the like.[21] Northumberland too may have had doubts.[22] At the final dinner with the rest of the council before he left with the troops against Mary, Dudley spelled out bluntly that he and those with him were risking everything on the faithfulness of their colleagues left behind: 'If we thought you would through malice, conspiracy or dissension leave us your friends in the briars and betray us, we could as well sundry ways foresee and provide for our own safeguards as any of you by betraying us can do for yours.' His own life and that of 'these other noble personages and the whole army', the 'conservation' of their children and families, continued religious reform and resistance to popery depended upon the 'constant hearts, abandoning all malice, envy and private affection' of those in London. There was even a sign of feeling for Jane: 'God shall not acquit you of the sacred and holy oath of allegiance made freely by you to this virtuous lady the queen's highness, who by your and our enticement is rather of force placed therein than by her own seeking and request.' It is hardly the voice of a man confident in his support.

The picture of a council lukewarm from the start is easily amplified. On the day the duke left, De Noailles reported that there was anxiety in the council and he coupled this with fear for his own safety should Northumberland fail.[23] Sunday evening saw a security clampdown; at 7 p.m. the Tower was suddenly closed and messengers sent to fetch back the marquis of Winchester, who had left for his own house. The announced reason was that a seal had gone missing, but Paulet only returned at midnight and rumour had it that Jane 'feared some packing in the lord treasurer'.[24] We cannot know, but the episode at the least suggests increasing nervousness. The Tower resident names Pembroke and Cheyne as being anxious to get out of the fortress.[25] According to Cecil's own attempt at exculpation, he was in the thick of this. He plotted with the marquis of Winchester to get control of Windsor Castle by winning over the earl of Bedford whose son, Lord Russell, was the governor there. The hope was that father and son would then use the Russell status in the south-west to raise an army for Mary. In case they would not bite, Cecil arranged a bolt-hole with Winchester's son, a supply of blank passports and even an alias – 'Mr Harding'. And all this went along with issuing orders to supply men and horses to the duke's army which he then secretly blocked.[26] Less cloak and dagger, he also claimed that – with the approval of Sir William Petre, his fellow secretary – he won over the earl of Arundel and Lord Darcy. The inevitable result of a council so rotten with doubt was the move to Baynard's Castle – disguised, it was said, as a visit to consult the French ambassador over the duke's wish to recruit mercenaries in Picardy.[27] Before the duke left, Arundel had assured him that 'he was very sorry it was not his chance to go with him and bear him company, in whose presence he could find in his heart to spend his blood, even at his foot'.[28] Now he took the lead in calling for a return to Mary:

> For my own part I see not what course can be taken more reasonable and lawful than for us all jointly with one consent to render obedience to our queen, peace to the people and liberty to ourselves; to take from the tyrant his authority, depriving him of his forces and giving the crown to whom it by all right belongs.[29]

Pembroke followed, promising to back Mary with force. Giovanni Commendone has it that some councillors argued for a pause to allow Northumberland to be informed and a general pardon negotiated, but the majority was for proclaiming Mary without delay.[30]

The story of a council which could hardly wait to endorse Mary has passed into general currency, but it deserves at least a raised eyebrow. Arundel's speech is clearly a literary construction. It is found in a fulsome posthumous tribute to the earl and so might be dismissed as imaginative embellishment of the earl's supreme moment of loyalty. It is, however, not retrospective. Arundel's oration and Pembroke's militant challenge circulated at the time – Commendone had a copy – so evidently they were prepared as *pièces justificatives* to cover up council complicity.[31] Cecil's evidence is not entirely trustworthy, either. It is, as Stephen Alford puts it, 'the authorised story

Cecil wanted to be told. Readers will have to judge for themselves'.[32] His petition written at the time implies that he was prevented from leaving the Tower whereas others 'had liberty after their enforcement to depart, ... [and] both like noble men and true subjects show their duties to their sovereign lady'.[33] The 1573 letter from his servant Roger Alford has it that Cecil was sent to Mary at Ipswich in the wake of Paget and Arundel. Roger Alford also shows that Cecil took the precaution of sending Alford ahead to present his excuses and support the solicitations of his sister in law, Lady Anne Bacon. The most dangerous evidence against Cecil was the armed horsemen he had sent from his Northamptonshire estates against the queen, but Alford 'being privy to the matter before' was ready with a laugh and the explanation that Cecil had stopped the group secretly. Thanks to Alford and Lady Bacon, Cecil was admitted to present his apologia to Mary in person and was allowed to kiss her hand.[34]

Mary certainly took with a sizeable pinch of salt the story of a council just waiting to return to its longed-for loyalty. She might allow Cecil the benefit of the doubt, but not the bigger fish. Winchester, Shrewsbury and Pembroke got the rough edge of her tongue and may even have been briefly under house arrest.[35] Clinton, Grey and Montagu were heavily fined.[36] But what of Northumberland's call to his colleagues to stay loyal? Is that not conclusive evidence for the traditional story of a council ready to desert?[37] In fact the speech is entirely in character – precisely what one might expect of a man who, as we have seen, was plagued through his whole career by insecurity and the fear of being left in an exposed position, just like his father. He knew perfectly well that he was taking a gamble; as Holinshed put it, he was setting 'apart the fear of all perils (which in lesser cases he never used)'.[38] The imperial ambassadors certainly did not detect a council on the point of collapse. At the very moment Shrewsbury and Mason arrived with news of the volte face, the ambassadors were in process of compiling a report to the emperor which commented on the brave bearing of Jane and her council in the face of Mary's growing support. Even after the visit, the envoys were not wholly convinced that some subtle treachery was not in hand.[39] The few surviving government documents also suggest a council with some backbone.[40] Two letters addressing the crisis were sent on behalf of the queen before Northumberland left with the army; every councillor he was leaving in London and who mattered signed at least one. In seven letters signed after the army had left, support for Jane continues. Four signatures appear every time – Cranmer, Winchester, Bedford and Shrewsbury. Suffolk, Arundel, Pembroke and the chancellor signed on six occasions, Rich signed on four, Darcy and Cobham three, Cotton and Cheyne one. And support does not fade towards the end. Except for Rich who had left London, the final letter lacks only the signature of Lord Cobham. The public, too, detected no lessening of support for Jane. Holinshed recalled the 'speeding and sending forth [of] ordinance out of the Tower, yea, even the same day that Queen Mary at even was proclaimed queen'.[41] Nothing here prepares us for the traditional story of premeditated conciliar treachery. It seems far more probable that although events after the army left may have begun to sap confidence, the final collapse was sudden. That would certainly explain why in the morning of 19 July there was unanimity on the letter to Lord Rich but, as Underhill put it, 'a sudden change' in the afternoon.

What, therefore, has to be explained is not just a collapse but a sudden collapse. The factor which contemporaries commonly point to is the news of the fleet deserting to Mary. The Tower resident wrote that after this 'each man began to pluck in his horns'.[42] De Guaras agreed about the significance of the ships; so did Charles V's ambassadors.[43] On the other hand, the surrender of the fleet to Mary took place on 15 July and was probably known in London late that night or early the next day.[44] That is too soon to account for the U-turn at Baynard's Castle four days later. It would, however, explain why Cecil made plans to hedge his bets still further.[45] On Sunday 17 July he sent instructions to Richard Troughton at Stamford to have horses ready for him at Royston at noon on the following Wednesday. He was not yet ready to run but by Wednesday he would know which way to jump. As well as seeing the desertion of the ships as a turning point, imperial ambassadors also mentioned 'the popular rising, [and] the increase of the Lady Mary's force'.[46] De Guaras, writing six weeks after the event, has it that concern among the councillors that Mary might after all win raised the fear that 'they would be liable to many troubles in their persons and possessions'.[47] Raphael Holinshed agreed. He wrote later but had probably been in London at the time: 'the council ... began to suspect the sequel of this enterprise, so that providing for their own surety without respect of the duke ... they set to a new counsel [policy] and lastly, by assent, made proclamation at London in the name of the lady Mary'.[48] John Foxe, who had been close to the Protestant establishment, suggests another factor at work: 'when the council at London perceived that the common multitude did withdraw their hearts from them to stand with her and that certain noble men began to go the other way: they turned their song and proclaimed for queen the Lady Mary, ... and so the duke of Northumberland ... was left destitute and forsaken alone at

Cambridge.[49] For 'certain noblemen' read the nation's 'natural' governors. Elite loyalty, the bedrock of social and political control, could no longer be depended on.

This is made very clear by the response of the intended recipients of William Cecil's circular, announcing the arrival of the lords lieutenants.[50] Some of the gentlemen he named did indeed support Jane, but many, possibly a majority, opted for Mary. Others remained neutral. For example, of the seven men Cecil listed for Suffolk, Sir John Clere was active for Jane, five were enthusiastic for Mary and the seventh dithered.[51] In nearby Norfolk, Christopher Heydon supported the queen, Richard Southwell and Henry Bedingfield backed Mary while Thomas Woodhouse and Nicholas Strange appear to have sat on their hands.[52] A similar inconsistency is seen in the response to council instructions to proclaim Queen Jane. There was compliance. Jane was proclaimed in York, Oxford, Wells, Frome, Shaftesbury, Cornwall, Exeter, Ipswich, Worcestershire and Gloucestershire, probably in the town of Boston, and in Essex, Denbighshire and Nottingham and Derby and possibly as far away as Berwick.[53] There was also resistance. The Wiltshire JPs appear to have ignored Jane's nominee as sheriff.[54] In many places both Jane and Mary were proclaimed by their respective supporters.[55] The importance of individual influence is also clear. At Coventry the recorder backed Mary; at Wells the bishop supported Jane.[56] Jane was proclaimed at Shaftesbury following a special journey by a prominent Dorset official and JP, William Thornhill.[57] The bishop of Salisbury delayed proclaiming Jane until 19 July and had to backtrack the next day.[58]

At Warminster, near the Wiltshire–Somerset border, a squabble over being the first to demonstrate loyalty by proclaiming Mary reveals a good deal about the previous fortnight.[59] George Lord Stourton was the most die-hard of Catholics, but he was also Northumberland's nephew. What the claims and counter-claims suggest is that although he received the plea for assistance which Mary sent out on 8 July, he took no action. Instead he played host to William Thornhill on his mission to proclaim Jane. But, with the duke safely in custody, he produced Mary's letter on 22 July claiming that the now queen had made him lord lieutenant of Wiltshire, Somerset and Dorset. Stourton was opposed by Sir John Thynne and Sir John Bonham whom he referred to as 'spotted persons', deriding as 'mustard after the meat' their claim to have been ready to support Mary with horsemen – and certainly Thynne was close to Cecil and Winchester and at least in touch with potential activists for Jane.[60] However, the response by Thynne and Bonham suggests hardly more enthusiasm for

Mary than Stourton's ignoring her call for help. What had held them back, they said, was fear that Stourton would then 'have entered and rifled' their houses.[61] Quite clearly, those concerned were motivated less by their respective loyalties than a concern to ensure they would stand well however the crisis turned out. With the county of Kent, one suspects jumping on a bandwagon. Led by Lord Bergavenny and Charles Neville, the son and heir of the earl of Westmorland, a powerful group of gentlemen proclaimed Mary queen 'as of right she is, as well by descent of royal blood as by lawful succession granted, ratified and confirmed by the nobility and the whole realm' (a clear reference to the 1544 statute).[62] Jane was denounced as 'a queen of new and pretty invention', her local supporters urged to abandon her and a message sent advising London to 'recant' the proclamation of Jane and expressing a willingness to follow city advice on supporting Mary. Yet Bergavenny had signed Edward's 'deuise', and this resounding endorsement of Mary only surfaced on 19 July. As for the appearance of Charles Neville, we have seen that his father marched with Northumberland. Did his son endorse the Kent letter spontaneously or was it a calculated attempt to hedge the family's bets? Even a letter which arrived after the event could make a good impression.[63] Towns, too, preferred to wait on events. Norwich, on Mary's doorstep, was at first uncertain about accepting her.[64] At Yarmouth Jane had significant support, although eventually it followed its big neighbour.[65] King's Lynn took several days and the presence of Robert Dudley before deciding to back 'the wrong horse', and we have seen how the marshland was slow to accept Mary.[66]

What was going on was one of the periodic demonstrations that Westminster could not take for granted the uniform, unquestioning loyalty of the English elite. That had been the lesson of the Lincolnshire Rising and the Pilgrimage of Grace in 1536 and Charles I would discover it for himself a century later. And not only the loyalty of the gentry and the town elites. Soon after the news of the ships deserting, the Tower was buzzing with 'word of a greater mischief . . . the noblemen's tenants refused to serve their lords against Queen Mary'.[67] One documented example of this involved the earl of Oxford.[68] John de Vere was a pretty ineffective individual, but he had prestige as England's second ranking earl and could call up significant manred. But when Sir Henry Gates, Sir Robert Stafford and the earl's brother-in-law, Sir Thomas Golding, arrived from Northumberland expecting to muster the de Vere 'power' for Jane, 'a hundred common servants' told the previously complicit earl that unless he backtracked and supported Mary, they would throw off their liveries and go to her without him. De Vere caved in,

Northumberland's envoys were locked up along with members of the household who did favour the queen, and, says Wingfield, Oxford and his men set off to join the princess.[69] Nor was this an isolated episode. Once the July crisis was over, a group of East Anglian peasants felt entitled to ask Queen Mary to protect them against unreasonable landlords on the ground that 'the said gentlemen had not us your said subjects and commonalty at their commandments in their proceedings against your most honourable grace'.[70] The implied consent which bound English society together meant that 'the men of power' could no more take for granted 'their servants, tenants and others under your rules and offices' than the sovereign could take the nobility and gentry.

Had Jane Grey's government survived, it would clearly have faced serious problems, with opposition expressed as far afield as Leominster in Herefordshire and Lichfield in Staffordshire, yet once again there is nothing in this patchy response to account for the suddenness of the collapse at Westminster.[71] Was a more substantive threat the concentration of support for Mary which developed in the counties to the west of London? This, as we shall see, was not accidental; it was triggered by the same direct appeal from Mary which Lord Stourton had finessed.[72] It seems to have begun in Buckinghamshire, where, by the time the duke left for Cambridge, Lord Windsor, Sir Edmund Peckham, and Sir Edward Hastings had already proclaimed Mary queen.[73] The three were very much the elite of the area. Windsor was a veteran of the Tudor aristocracy and related by marriage to the marquis of Winchester, Peckham was treasurer of the mint and a former privy councillor, Hastings was the brother of the earl of Huntington. Moreover they were backed up by the leading citizens of Aylesbury, High Wycombe, and Buckingham, the county town.[74] Sir John Williams raised men in Oxfordshire – allegedly six or seven thousand – while Banbury, in the north of the county, was also active for Mary.[75] Northamptonshire was divided. 'Sir Robert Tyrwhitt mustered in Northamptonshire to go to my lord of Northumberland as many men as he could get' but Sir Thomas Tresham refused to obey council instructions and led the citizens of Northampton in proclaiming Mary.[76] Tresham then joined forces with Lord Windsor.[77] According to news reaching Mary on Sunday 16th, her supporters had planned to be at Lord Paget's house at Drayton, fifteen miles west of the city, on the previous evening with ten thousand men, and the intention of marching to Westminster that day to arm themselves from the stores there.[78]

Yet although so near to London, these risings in the Thames Valley cannot have been the decisive factor in Mary's victory. They may explain why councillors did not 'send their powers after' Northumberland, yet the severity and immediacy of the threat they posed has to be doubted. The muster at Drayton was clearly optimistic – there was no raid on Westminster on Sunday 16 July or on any other day – and Sir John Williams's six or seven thousand men seems equally exaggerated; other evidence suggests that he and Leonard Chamberlain may have been able to raise 750.[79] The council, for its part, paid no attention to Lord Windsor and the rest until Tuesday 18 July, the day before it collapsed. Only then did it issue letters to raise forces to suppress 'certain tumults and rebellions' in Buckinghamshire. Two copies have survived. Both were to Gloucester recipients, one to Sir John Brydges and Sir Nicholas Poyntz and the second to Sir John St Loe and Sir Anthony Kingston.[80] As Brydges is named among Mary's supporters in Buckinghamshire he may never have received the letter, but the other three were probably likely allies for Jane; they would later be active opponents of Mary's policies.[81] The letters emphasize the social threat even more than previous communications, referring directly to the 1549 rebellions – seditious people 'seeking the destruction of their native country, and the subversion of all men in their degrees, by rebellion of the base multitude, whose rages being stirred, as of late years hath been seen, must needs be the confusion of the whole commonwealth'. But effectively written or no, the letters came too late. As St Loe and Thynne were conferring at Longleat on Friday morning 21 July, a hasty note arrived from Poyntz saying that, very late the previous night, news had arrived from London that Mary had been proclaimed queen.[82]

Abortive though the circulars of 18 July were, a detail in them does at last provide the clue to explain the suddenness of the switch to Mary. The gentlemen had been called on to 'raise all the power that you can possibly make', but with a significant proviso: 'reserving to' the earls of Arundel and Pembroke their 'tenants, servants and officers'. Then they were to take the forces raised and join the earls for a march on Buckinghamshire.[83] Evidently the plan on 18 July was for Pembroke and Arundel to muster the significant 'manred' they had on the nearby Welsh border, and unite with a Gloucestershire/Wiltshire contingent to march on the Thames Valley from the west. This would pin Mary's supporters against council forces in London in a move reminiscent of Pembroke's decisive intervention in the crisis of 1549.[84] It was an obvious strategy, but a strategy which introduced a new factor into the situation. It required Arundel and Pembroke to take personal action against the princess, a level of commitment which was beyond anything either had risked so far. Early on Wednesday

19 July the loyalist letter to Rich was sent off, but Cecil, who had 'opened' himself to the earl of Arundel, felt secure enough to send his own message cancelling the appointment at Royston, saying that 'all was well'.[85] At Baynard's Castle later in the morning, Arundel and Pembroke broke cover, seized the initiative and brought the council over to Mary.[86] The most convincing explanation of the dramatic collapse of Jane's privy council is that two key earls drew back from committing themselves to military action. Called on to up their stake in Queen Jane, Arundel and Pembroke chose to fold.

22

THE REBELLION
OF MARY TUDOR

TUDOR England called on the great Christian hymn *Te Deum Laudamus* ['We praise you, O God'] at moments of deliverance, not at moments of rejoicing. Sung by the choir of St Paul's Cathedral immediately after the proclamation of Queen Mary and repeated the following day in church after church throughout London, it was a sigh of the most profound collective relief: 'In thee, O Lord, have we trusted; let us never be confounded'.[1] It was a prayer which Mary herself had repeated again and again during the crisis but with the comforting addition, 'Si Deus pro nobis, quis contra nos?' – 'If God be for us, who can be against us'.[2] It had been a miracle. Historians are not by and large inclined to supernatural explanations, but they are addicted to a near equivalent – 'inevitability'. From the comfort of centuries, it is all too tempting to demonstrate that though at the time anxiety was rampant, this or that outcome was in fact inescapable. Mary's victory has long been interpreted in this way.

> cruelty and wrong never stand secure … The duke by piercing his ambitious purpose with his unjust policy, did no otherwise than often doth a foolish, greedy gamester, who by stealing a card to win a stake, forfeits the whole rest.[3]

Mary's movements in the first week in July 1553 are surrounded with a deal of myth. At the start of the month she was at her house at Hunsdon. Edward died at Greenwich about 9 p.m. on Thursday evening 6 July, and by Saturday 8 July Mary was issuing letters from her Norfolk manor of Kenninghall, calling for support.[4] The most detailed account is by Robert Wingfield. He has it that the princess was secretly warned that Edward was near the end, and 'to escape as soon as possible the jaws of her enemies' left her house at Hunsdon by night, accounting for the sudden move by a story that infection had broken out.[5] After spending some hours at Sawston Hall near Cambridge, she rode on to Euston Hall, near Thetford, where the first news of Edward's death reached her. Since Euston is ninety miles from London, this information cannot have reached her earlier than the evening of Friday 7th which, reading back, indicates that on Wingfield's timing she can only have left Hunsdon at about the time Edward died or even somewhat later. From Euston she went a further thirteen miles to Kenninghall and would thus have arrived there either late that same night or in the course of Saturday morning 8 July, the day the council in London warned county magistrates against her.[6] The story is dramatic, but the route and timing are both credible. Mary could have travelled the twenty-one miles to Sawston, arriving in the small hours of Thursday–Friday, and the further twenty-seven to Euston during daytime on Friday. The messenger, too, could have reached Euston in the time by riding hard and changing horses on the way.[7] Cardinal Commendone who obtained his information in August/September 1553 understood that Mary had left after Edward's death, but again he picked up the night ride and he also knew of the sickness cover story.[8] The resident Venetian ambassador reported that Mary took flight when Edward was at the point of death, by night, and with two maids of honour and only four gentlemen.[9] Romance has it that the princess left Sawston accompanied by only one servant and in disguise (traditionally, as a dairy maid).[10]

Unfortunately for romance, the privy council letter to the lords lieutenants throws cold water on this derring-do.[11] It agrees that the cover story was that Mary had to move because of infection, but states that she left on Tuesday 4 July, two days before Edward's death.[12] That is confirmed by Antonio de Guaras and supported by the imperial ambassador.[13] His report of 4 July is that the previous day a 'friend' had warned the princess to move.[14] That despatch also gives the destination of the princess as Framlingham in Norfolk, which revealingly conflates her immediate goal, Kenninghall in Norfolk, with Framlingham in Suffolk, which she did move to on 12 July. That can only mean that the ambassadors had some prior knowledge of her intended movements and hence Mary's flight was definitely not on the spur of the moment. The source of the information was no doubt Mary's comptroller Robert Rochester on one of his secret visits to the embassy in what the privy council later described as 'the night seasons'.[15] Framlingham was, in fact, nearer to Hunsdon and the castle there a better place to make a stand, but the need to assemble a garrison first explains the choice of the more distant Kenninghall as the initial recruiting base. Advance planning also explains how when Mary arrived there she found sixty servants waiting.

It can, however, be objected that the tale of a princess travelling by night is too unusual to have been fabricated, certainly not in time for Antonio de Guaras to retail it at the beginning of September 1553.[16] The probability is, therefore, that along with Mary moving or being lured to Hunsdon, a contingency plan had been put in place, and that something triggered this on Tuesday 4 July. What spooked Mary was most probably the warning from a friend on Monday 3 July which, according to the ambassadors, seems to have included details of her brother's 'declaracion'.[17] Who told the princess (and presumably the ambassadors) we do not know. According to Cardinal Commendone she was 'secretly informed by some members of the council of the machinations of the duke', but he identifies no-one.[18] The Catholic historian Lingard names the earl of Arundel, but cites no evidence and in any case by early July scores of men had witnessed Edward's plan.[19] But even so, why flee by night? Conjecture suggests that although the warning arrived on Monday, preparations were not complete until late Tuesday when, despite the hour, it was thought prudent not to wait until morning. Abandoning Hunsdon meant, of course, losing touch with the court and the imperial embassy, but it appears that Mary left behind Thomas Hughes, her physician, to bring the news of Edward's death; medical men, by the nature of their profession, could move around the court and the city without arousing suspicion.[20] The concern was that false news of her brother's death might be fed to Mary in order to trap her into making a premature claim on the crown and thus commit high treason.[21] In the event, although Nicholas Throckmorton sent her gold-smith with the news, Mary still waited for Hughes to bring confirmation because, as Throckmorton complained, she did not trust his avowed Protestantism.[22]

Mary's plan of retreat is not the only evidence of forethought. Wingfield tells how, when she arrived at Kenninghall, Mary consulted her advisers, summoned her whole entourage, told them of Edward's death, asserted her right to the throne, and declared that she 'was most anxious to inaugurate her reign with the aid of her most faithful servants as partners in her fortune'.[23] They cheered to the rafters what was, Wingfield says, an act 'of Herculean rather than of womanly daring' since 'she was entirely unprepared for warfare and had insignificant forces'. The reality, however, was otherwise. This household of sixty was straining at the leash to leap into action as a secretariat or mini-chancery. For evidence of this we are dependent on accidental survivals, but the overall picture is compelling.

Thus a single surviving copy shows that on Saturday 8 July letters were sent to Sir George Somerset, Sir William Drury, Sir William Waldegrave and Clement Heigham calling them to ignore the council in London and come to Kenninghall immediately, with whatever force they could muster.[24] No doubt there were other similar letters. By next day the letter for the privy council was ready for Hungate to take to London and copies to go out generally.[25] Direct appeals for help also continued. Another letter of 9 July which has survived is the crucial summons to the Sir Edward Hastings who played a major role in rallying support for Mary in the Thames Valley.[26] Towns were targeted too; we have copies of the messages to Great Yarmouth (dated that same day) and to Chester shortly after.[27] What is more, some of the drafting looks professional and someone at least had a notion who should be canvassed and what public instruments were urgent. As we have seen, Lord Stourton was not only ordered to proclaim Mary but was appointed lord lieutenant of Wiltshire, Somerset and Dorset, and that authorization was dated 8 July.[28] The other lieutenancies must also have been covered. Moreover, distributing the letters required a rudimentary courier service to be in place. Without question, Mary's entourage was prepared in advance, not least in having a schedule of tasks and enough literate manpower for the sheer physical burden of writing this volume of letters by hand. All this is in the greatest contrast to the lack of forethought in London. Mary's victory was won at the writing desks of Kenninghall.

Given Mary's psychology there can be no doubt that the decision to challenge Jane was Mary's own. To do anything else would have been to deny truth and dishonour her mother a second time. Yet that does not mean that Mary was responsible for the contingency plan to move from Hunsdon to East Anglia, or for preparations to make a contested claim to the throne. When the earlier episode of her abortive attempt to flee the country had seen her paralysed by doubt, Robert Rochester had rescued her. Since it was Rochester who informed the imperial ambassadors about Kenninghall and Framlingham, he seems the likely mover in July 1553.[29] This need for others to mind her is confirmed by Wingfield's reference to the advisers she consulted before announcing her claim.[30] In addition to Rochester, these were most probably her steward, Edward Waldegrave, and Henry Jerningham, possibly the princess's vice-chamberlain.[31] All would be appointed to her privy council (along with Sir Francis Englefield, probably her chamberlain), and Rochester, Jerningham and Waldegrave were awarded major offices in the new queen's household.[32] The loyalty of the four was total. It had cost Englefield, Rochester and Waldegrave months in a Tower cell and it was Jerningham who would persuade Northumberland's sailors to change sides.[33] Englefield was not involved in the Kenninghall decision because at some point in the summer Northumberland had him arrested. Is it possible that he had been monitoring events at court and left it too late to leave for Hunsdon?[34]

Almost certainly it was thanks to men such as these that Mary escaped from Hunsdon and not only arrived at Kenninghall but arrived with machinery poised to summon possible sympathizers.[35] Yet who would respond?[36] The initial answer is the network to which the very men belonged who were so busily sending out recruiting letters. Robert Wingfield records the names of twenty-nine gentlemen servants at Kenninghall led by Rochester, Jerningham and Waldegrave, almost as a roll-call of Marian loyalists.[37] The first thing which the list reveals is that the majority of those who can be identified came from Norfolk, Suffolk and Essex. This was no accident. Until her father's death Mary had a personal staff or 'chamber' but no full establishment of her own; she resided either at court or in one of the royal palaces. Henry VIII, however, had bequeathed her the net income of £3,000 a year until she married and this was not discharged as an annuity but by assigning property to her which would yield the desired amount in rents and the like. For the first time she could set up a noble household of her own.[38] In the event the estate she was allocated produced twenty per cent more than her bequest and that made her establishment one of the six wealthiest in the country.[39] The lands granted her were mostly in Norfolk, Suffolk and Essex and at a stroke made her the principal employer and the major patron in the area. No wonder her household was staffed by local men. Robert Rochester came from Stansted in Essex. He had made his career in the service of the earl of Oxford whose principal seat was at Castle Hedingham, just across the border from Suffolk, but when Mary assembled her household in 1547, he joined the princess.[40] Henry Jerningham came from east Suffolk. Others from Suffolk were, for example, her receiver, Thomas Poley of Badley, and a second Poley in Wingfield's list, almost certainly a relation. Family played a part as well as location. George Jerningham was Henry's nephew. Edward Waldegrave, from Sudbury in Suffolk, was Rochester's nephew. George Whyte from Essex was the nephew of Susan Clarencius, one of Mary's longest-serving ladies.[41] The three Tyrells in Mary's service were also Susan's relatives.

Mary's gentlemen could thus appeal to their connections in East Anglia and Essex, but the address list for the letters they were sending out on her behalf was affected by other factors too. The majority of the lands granted her had for many years been in the hands of England's premier noble family the Howards, and had only been forfeited in the final weeks of Henry VIII's life when Thomas Howard, 3rd duke of Norfolk, and Henry his son, the earl of Surrey, were condemned for high treason. As summed up by one duke, the Howard position was: 'next the king our sovereign lord, by his good grace and licence we will have the principal rule and governance through all the shire of which we bear our name while that we be living as far as reason and law requireth'.[42] And not only the shire of Norfolk; the family was big in Suffolk too. With Mary now in place of the Howards, much of this local status and importance was hers. She had acquired what in Tudor parlance was an 'affinity' – her household plus her immediate tenants (with the manred that implied) and her 'well-wishers', gentlemen and yeomen in the area who looked to her for leadership and 'the principal rule and governance' which the Howards no longer provided. It was to summon this wider affinity that quills were so busy at Kenninghall.[43]

The letter to Somerset, Drury, William Waldegrave and Clement Heigham provides a good example.[44] All four lived within twelve miles of Mary's substantial Suffolk estate of Long Melford. Drury was related to Henry Jerningham. Waldegrave had been a 'well-wisher' of the Howards. Heigham was his brother-in-law. The first person to arrive at Kenninghall was another client of the Howards, Sir Henry Bedingfield, along with his two brothers. The earliest list of those 'sworn to the Queen's Majesty' (Mary) is dated 14 July (Friday), but clearly includes earlier arrivals.[45] There are forty names, thirty-two of them gentlemen or above, and fifteen of them at least are plausibly from East Anglia. Francis Jenney is there from the Jenney clan of Knodishall in Suffolk, Bedingfield and his two brothers, Sir Thomas Holis from Norfolk. From Dunwich came a former Howard client, Sir Edmund Rouse (along with a relative). Thomas Timperley of Hintlesham who swore allegiance the same day was a grandson of the disgraced duke, and so the list goes on.

Mary, however, had not simply stepped into Howard shoes. Before the July crisis she had held her premier place in East Anglia for six years and in that time she had made her affinity distinctive. This was a consequence of her deliberate opposition to Edwardian religious reform. We have seen something of the long-running guerrilla warfare between the council and the princess over the mass and the attempts that were made to force her household to conform. But Mary did not simply disobey, she made her household a defiant witness to the old faith. Her choice of Rochester as her comptroller was undoubtedly helped by the fact that his brother John had been one of the most defiant of the Carthusians monks who refused to accept Henry VIII's breach with the pope. After challenging the king to allow him to demonstrate face to face that the royal supremacy was 'directly against the laws of God, the faith catholic and the health of his Highness's body and soul' John Rochester was drawn, hanged and quartered, defiant to the last.[46] Edward Waldegrave was the son-in-law of Sir Edward Neville, executed for high treason in 1538 for his association with Henry's conservative critics, among whom had been Mary's former governess, the Countess of Salisbury, who was herself executed three years later. Of the five senior household servants listed by Wingfield who can be followed after Protestantism returned in 1558, each refused to abandon traditional Catholicism. Waldegrave would die in the Tower, convicted on charges of hearing mass and harbouring priests. Sir Francis Englefield abandoned his estates and went into exile, dying in Spain in 1596. Personal affection seems to have allowed Mary to keep Anne Bacon (née Cooke) as one of her ladies, despite her reformed opinions, but the house rules obliged 'every gentlemen, yeoman and groom not having reasonable impediment' to attend matins, mass and evensong each day.[47] 'To be in Mary's service was to live as a Catholic.'[48]

The princess had not the authority to prevent church wardens from complying with Edwardian decrees on the removal of images, religious books and church plate, but as soon as liturgical changes came in, 'wherever she had power [i.e. property and influence] she caused the mass to be celebrated and the services of the church performed in the ancient manner'.[49] She simply ignored the restrictions in her personal permission to hear mass privately (which she had won after her public defiance of the First Prayer Book); denying anyone access to the miracle of the mass was a grave sin.[50] In March 1551 no less than a person than Sir Antony Browne, the future Lord Montagu, took the chance to hear mass at Romford 'as my lady was coming hither about 10 days past' even though, as we have seen, it cost him a spell in the Fleet prison.[51] That was the visit we have already noted when Mary mustered a retinue of fifty knights and gentlemen and eighty gentlemen and ladies to parade through London telling their illegal rosary beads.[52] The Howard affinity the princess inherited seems also to have been substantially conservative. Thomas, the 3rd duke, had hated religious change – 'I have never read scripture nor ever will read it'.[53] Sir Richard Southwell rallied to Mary in July 1553 'amply provided with money, provisions and armed men'.[54] Southwell, from Wood Rising, fifteen miles from Kenninghall, was a former client of the Howards and his view of Protestants was 'to the rack with them, one of these knaves is able to undo a whole city'.[55] Another conservative arriving at Kenninghall was the earl of Bath who had already entertained Mary at Euston.[56] The Howards regarded him as their man, though Wingfield's claim that he arrived with 'a large band of soldiers' seems excessive for a parvenu in the area.[57]

Catholic supporters also arrived from further afield.[58] The son of Lord Mordaunt came from Turvey in Bedfordshire; his wife was a former lady to the princess. The lawyer Richard Morgan came from London and would go on to be her chief justice of the common pleas.[59] He pronounced the death sentence on Jane Grey and three years later died insane – according to Foxe, crying 'out continually to have the lady Jane taken away from him'.[60] Mary's appeal to the Thames Valley for support was likewise spread through her Catholic links. Sir Edward Hastings was vehemently opposed to reform, even though he was the brother of the Protestant earl of Huntingdon. His bête noire was Edward Underhill who, to the earl's delight, had worsted Hastings in theological argument while on garrison duty at Calais.[61] Sir Thomas Tresham, who proclaimed Mary at Northampton, was a die-hard, but cautious. On the return of Protestantism under Elizabeth, a servant commented that Tresham would 'remain a good Christian, as he always was at the time of the other schism, but he will remain in the country and will observe the old rite secretly'.[62] The opinions of Sir Leonard Chamberlain who helped raise Oxfordshire and Berkshire are clear from the request in his will for 'solemn exequies to be sung and done for me, according to the order of the holy Catholic Church'.[63]

We would, however, be wrong to assume that support for Mary meant support for Rome. During Ket's Rebellion in 1549, the peasantry of Norfolk and Suffolk had demonstrated support for the religious reforms of Edward's reign, and according to John Foxe, the rally to Mary four years later was conditional on her agreeing to make no innovation in religion: 'Thus Mary being guarded with the power of the gospellers did vanquish the duke'.[64] The story is repeated by Holinshed but at first sight it seems entirely out of character given Mary's previous intransigent Catholic commitment and the persecution which would mark her reign.[65] Yet some understanding with Protestant supporters would certainly explain the mild language of her first pronouncement on religion – a proclamation stating that while she wished her subjects to follow the faith which 'she hath ever professed from infancy', she 'mindeth not to compel any of her subjects thereunto until such time as further order by common consent [i.e. parliament] may be taken therein'; what is more, she forbad the 'new-found devilish terms of papist or heretic', prohibited unlicensed preaching and printing and commanded everyone to 'live together in quiet sort and Christian charity'.[66] The Protestant clergy rapidly discovered that this did not prevent the conservatives who were now taking over the church machine from pressing on them very heavily; reformed preaching was treated as sedition, and Catholic restorations were allowed to go ahead. Yet no public 'order' was issued until parliament had met, so if Mary had promised the peasants anything, within legalistic limits she did keep her word.

Be the truth of the *Acts and Monuments* story what it may (and we have seen that solid support for Mary did not extend to the west Norfolk peasantry), Foxe points out that the Suffolk peasants also had a very secular motive – hatred of the duke of Northumberland.[67] This was widespread. The comment of de Noailles was that 'All these things have happened more because of the great hatred felt towards the duke who wished to keep everyone in fear, than for love of the queen, despite the united show of a desire to honour and obey her.'[68] However justified, the duke's law and order policy and his insistence on retrenchment were extremely unpopular, and he could never live down the accusation that he had judicially murdered the hallowed duke of Somerset. Whatever informed observers might say and modern analysis may suggest about the real John Dudley, masses of common people in 1553 heartily disliked what they knew of the duke of Northumberland. But in Suffolk it was not just dislike, it was vitriolic hatred, driven by the memory of the brutality meted out to Robert Ket and his supporters four years before – to men who had set out not to rebel but to act in the king's name against what John Foxe called 'uncharitable dealings between landlords and tenants'.[69] Resentment against the East Anglian gentry who had supported the duke was equally bitter and the peasants who rallied for Mary did so in full awareness that they were defying their landlords too.[70] Another consideration to bear in mind is that for the great majority of Tudor Englishmen and women, local issues were more immediate than issues of state. A clear instance of this occurred in the important shipping town of King's Lynn.[71] Thomas Waters and William Overend were key figures in the borough; between them they sat ten times as MP and served five terms as mayor and fifty-five years as aldermen, and they were prominent in the decision of the town on 18 July to support Jane. Mary's council had them arrested, imprisoned for several weeks and only released on payment of a £200 fine. Waters's rival in the grain trade was a gentleman from outside the borough named Osbert Mountford (or Monford). He rallied to Mary and become the principal supplier of grain to her men.[72] On the same day that orders were given to arrest Overend and Waters, Mountford was sent into King's Lynn 'for the better order of the town' and on 7 August he was formally given 'the governance' of the town.[73] He was very probably a Catholic but there is no evidence that his rivals were reformers. It was a case of old rivalries continued. There is even a possibility that King's Lynn only decided for Jane because the outsider Mountford had cornered the grain supply to Framlingham.[74] The little this had to do with Jane or Mary becomes still more obvious in the decision of the town (once it got its powers back) to pay the fine on Waters and Overend by public subscription – a gesture of local independence which the privy council stamped on heavily.

If factors other than religion affected the popular support for Mary, is the same true of their betters? Sir John Harington of Exton was certainly a Catholic traditionalist, yet he stood on the 1544 statute.[75] Mary, indeed, was careful to avoid making Catholicism a rallying cry. In marked contrast to the appeals to resist popery which were made for Jane, the letters sent out by the princess's household asserted her right 'by act of parliament and the testament and last will' of Henry VIII.[76] Was this tactic successful in bringing Protestant and centrist gentlemen to rally to Mary? The princess certainly did have such support. Among those swearing allegiance on or before 14 July was Owen Hopton from Yoxford in east Suffolk. His religious views have been described as 'difficult to assess', but since he went on to become Elizabeth's lieutenant of the Tower and as such to supervise the torture of Catholic priests, not religion but the rightness of Mary's claim to the crown must have been what motivated him.[77]

Another powerful incentive was self-preservation. An important arrival at the princess's camp was Thomas Lord Wentworth. He was joint lord lieutenant for Suffolk and he brought with him 'several gentlemen of the county who were wont to go in his company', some, like him, staunch reformers.[78] Wentworth had signed Edward's 'declaracion' and on Tuesday 11 July had attended a discussion at Ipswich, convened by the sheriff, Sir Thomas Cornwallis, which ended in the leading men of east Suffolk agreeing to proclaim Jane. However, on 14 July, Mary sent two envoys to Wentworth warning that 'he should take good care for himself and for his family not to forsake the queen's cause which would be to the perpetual dishonour of his house'.[79] After 'a little reflection as to what to do best', Wentworth abandoned Jane saying that 'his inner conscience constantly proclaimed that Mary had a greater right to the throne'. In truth he had little choice; the day after the Ipswich meeting, Mary and her (by now) significant force had moved to Framlingham, less than twenty miles away. Self-interest also brought the princess her biggest prize – Henry Radcliffe, earl of Sussex. He too was a reformer and had signed the 'declaracion', and as joint lord lieutenant for Norfolk was in active communication with the Council in London. His son was the courier but on the way south the young man was captured by John Huddleston. With his second son a prisoner and the contents of his letters known to Mary, the earl hurried to the princess, 'defending himself as well as he could' by a somewhat thin cover story: he would have come earlier but Robert Dudley (his colleague as lieutenant for Norfolk) had lied and convinced him that Edward was still alive.[80] Just like Wentworth, Sussex appears more concerned to secure himself and his family than to advance Mary's rights. The same seems to be the case with Cornwallis, the sheriff of the joint counties of Norfolk and Suffolk. He had called the Ipswich meeting after receiving letters from both Mary and the privy council. But after he had implemented its decision and proclaimed Jane, Thomas Poley, Mary's receiver, arrived with orders to proclaim the princess, which he did hurriedly in Ipswich market place before scurrying off to avoid Jane's supporters. That put Cornwallis in a quandary and 'in grave peril of his life', so the next day he set off to London to seek advice. On the way the sheriff met a friend coming from the city who convinced him that 'everything pointed to violence and an uprising', so Cornwallis returned to Ipswich with the friend and proclaimed Mary. When the sheriff arrived at nearby Framlingham, the princess gave him a very cold reception, berating him 'for being somewhat slow and stubborn and less mindful of his duty than he ought to have been despite the repeated requests of her letters'.[81] This was in marked contrast to the welcome accorded to Wentworth and Sussex. Was it because Cornwallis was a Catholic and should have known better?

The picture of Mary's support outside the eastern counties is again of a mainly Catholic core surrounded by men motivated by a variety of reasons. A handbill distributed through London in early August named Rochester, Waldegrave, Englefield, Hastings and Weston 'hardened and detestable papists all', supported by two archpapists, the earl of Derby and Lord Stourton, with Arundel as a third.[82] The imperial ambassador reported that Derby had marched to Mary's aid with 15 or 20,000 men, although he seems to have got no further than mustering about two thousand.[83] Reformers who might have been expected to support Jane supported Mary instead – even the future martyr, John Hooper, bishop of Gloucester. He claimed that when there were both commandments and commissions out against her whereby she was ... the more in danger and the less likely to come to the crown ... I rode myself from place to place (as is well known) to win and stay the people for her parties [*sic*]. And whereas another [Jane] was proclaimed, I preferred her notwithstanding to the proclamation; and to help her as much as I could, when her highness was in trouble, I sent horses out of both shires, Gloucestershire and Worcestershire, to serve her in her danger.[84]

As we have seen, in Wiltshire the Catholic Lord Stourton lay low in case his Protestant uncle Northumberland came out on top.[85] In Oxfordshire the ultra-loyalist Sir John Williams showed no hesitation in backing Mary despite being cautiously inclined to reform.[86] Sir Peter Carew was a prominent evangelical with, according to his biographer, eyes wide open to the religious threat Mary presented. But despite Jane having already been proclaimed in Devon, 'respecting his faith [loyalty], duty and allegiance to his natural prince' he engineered counter-proclamations for Mary at Dartmouth and Newton Abbot and was among those she thanked for 'your diligence, your faithfulness and true hearts'.[87] As well as men who apparently went against their interests, there are others who simply bewilder us. We have seen how the earl of Westmorland marched with Northumberland while his son opted for Mary. On 23 July Mary's council wrote to the earl 'thanking him for his coldness in prosecuting the causes of the usurper with a commendation of his indifferency towards the Queen's Majesty, with exhortation of a more ferventness and request to see the country in good quiet'.[88] What behaviour had earned this backhanded compliment we do not know. Had a council of war preceded the retreat from Bury St Edmunds at which the earl told Northumberland that the game was up? There were odd rumours too about the behaviour of Lord Wharton, Northumberland's deputy as warden general of the Scottish Marches. He is always thought to have been conservative in religion and his son was in Mary's household, but one of the earliest actions of Mary's council was to protest about the force he was said to be raising against Lord Dacre 'in the defence of the usurper's quarrel'.[89] The letter was countermanded later, but Wharton had been in frequent communication with the duke and the story had been taken seriously.[90] One of the oddest stories concerns Sir Nicholas Throckmorton. In May 1553 he was licensed to keep twenty-five retainers, a clear sign of Northumberland's trust.[91] A gentleman of the privy chamber, he signed Edward's 'declaracion' and we have seen how his wife was in the service of Queen Jane right to the end.[92] Despite this, Nicholas sent word to

Plate 1 Anon., *Jane Grey* (c.1590) [the 'Houghton Jane']

Plate 2 Anon., *Lady conjectured to be 'The Lady Jane Graye executed'* [the 'Northwick Park Jane']

Plate 3 Marcus Gheeraerts (attrib.), *Katherine Grey*

Plate 4 Hans Eworth, *Mary Grey*

Plate 5 Willem and Magdalena de Passe, *Jane Grey* (engr. c.1620)

Plate 6 Levina Teerlinc, *Lady conjectured to be Jane Grey*

Plate 7 George Vertue, *Jane Grey* (engr. J. Basire)

Plate 8 Anon., *Lady conjectured to be Jane Grey* [the 'Wrest Park Jane']

Plate 9 Hans Eworth, *Portrait of a Lady*

Plate 10 *Bradgate Park*, engr. Johannes Kip (c.1715)

Plate 11 John Throsby, *Bradgate Park*, engr. Walker (1777–8)

Plate 12 Anon., *Henry Grey, marquis of Dorset, duke of Suffolk* (engraving of lost portrait 1826)

Plate 13 Hans Holbein the Younger, *The Dutchess of Suffolk* (1532–43)

Plate 14 Anon., *Katherine Parr* (1545)

Plate 15 Hans Eworth, *Mary I*

Plate 16 Anon., *Edward VI and the Pope* (c.1570)

Back row left to right: Henry VIII, Edward VI, Edward Seymour duke of Somerset; Thomas Seymour Lord Sudeley, Thomas Cranmer; John Russell, earl of Bedford; William Paget (?)

Front row left to right: John Dudley, earl of Warwick; Cuthbert Tunstal; William Paulet, Lord St.John (?)

Plate 17 Anon., *John Dudley, earl of Warwick, duke of Northumberland*

Plate 18 Hans Eworth, *Henry Fitzalan, earl of Arundel*

Plate 19 Sudeley Castle

A summary of matters to be concluded. 19

1. How a masse of mony may be gotten, to discharg the summe
of 300000li. both for discharg of the dettis, and also
to get 50000li of treasur mony for al euentis.

2. Deminishing of the charges. of the pensionars
table. the L preuyseals, the phisitions, and the 4tr of Hous-
hold, giueng the reasonable recōpes.

3. Redeming the lesses partaineng to the Lurees at
westmynster (whalta and R eding, and Saint Albōs

4. Discharging int thadmiralie.

5. Prouision to be made for the wardrobe,
whearby the charg may be the lesse.

6. Discharg of the postes

7. Discharg of ceirtein bulwarkes on the seaside
wich be thought supfluous.

8. Discharging the 1000 men in Irlande mo thā be yet

9. Discharg of 500 mē at Barwike (whē the
fort shal be rearid, and 200 at guisnes for this
winter.

10. Bringing thaugmētation court into thexchequer
and likwise the court of first fruites and
tenthes, and sauing al thos fees that may
be spared.

11. Examing wither by their parētes they haue
portage mony alowed the, and if they haue it, how they

12. Discharging the sunfluous fees in thaugm̄
rat the duchie, and the wardis, and also in
the mintes

13. Gathering and coining of the churchpiate

14. Sale of certein landis of chauntries, colleges houses, ad
Beaumonts landis to the sōme of the 5000li

15. Bringing in the remnaū of my dettis.

16. Taking accoumptes of al thos that haue had
to doe w mony sins the 36 yeare of k. h. 8

17. The stay of lead

18. The sale of the belmetal.

19. Thexecution of penal lawes, touching horses, ploughs, pasture

Plate 21 William Theed the Younger, *Lady Jane Grey at her studies* (relief from the Prince's Chamber, Palace of Westminster)

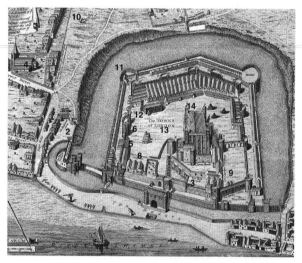

1. River Stairs	8. Lieutenant's Lodging
2. The Lion Gate	9. The Queen's Garden
3. Royal Apartments	10. The Scaffold on Tower Hill
4. All Hallows Barking-by-the-Tower	11. The Devil's Tower
5. Partridge's House	12. St.Peter ad Vincula
6. The Beauchamp Tower	13. Where Guildford's body was seen by Jane
7. The Bell Tower	14. Site of the Scaffold

Plate 22 The Tower of London (engr. 1742)

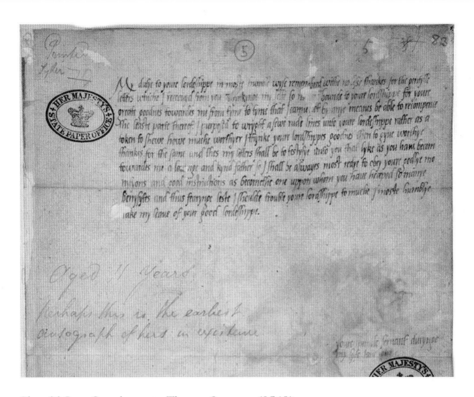

Plate 23 Jane Grey, letter to Thomas Seymour (1548)

in Christo seruatore meo fidem amplectar tibi in hac parte. Οὐδὲ θεὸς ἄνευ conitar satisfacere. sed donum dei agnosco eam esse & proinde tantum polliceri debeo quantum Dominus impertierit. neq tamen cum Apostolis orare desistam: ut eam mihi sua benignitate indies augere uelit. Huc etiam eam deo iuuante ut iubes adiungam uitæ puritatem quam mea heu nimium infirmæ uires præstare poterint. Tu interea pro tua pietate in oratione tua mei quotidie facias mentionem rogo. Ad Hebraicæ linguæ studium eam ingrediar uiam quam tu fidelissime monstras. vale. Et Deus te in hac suscepta abs te prouincia tueatur & proueh at æternum.

Tibi ad omnia pietatis
officia paratissima
Joanna Graia.

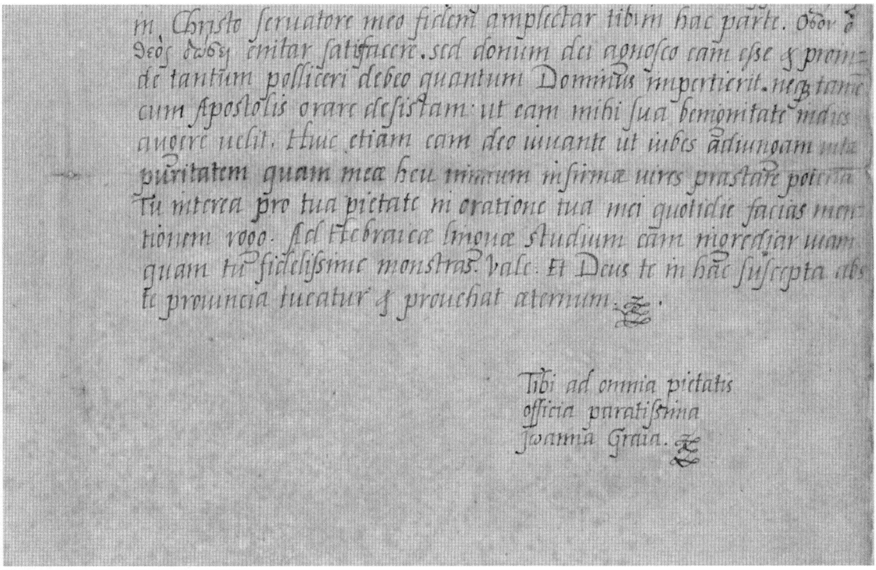

Plate 24 Jane Grey, letter to Henry Bullinger (1552)

Plate 25 M. Florio, copy of *Regole de la lingua thoscana* dedicated and presented to Jane Grey (original binding)

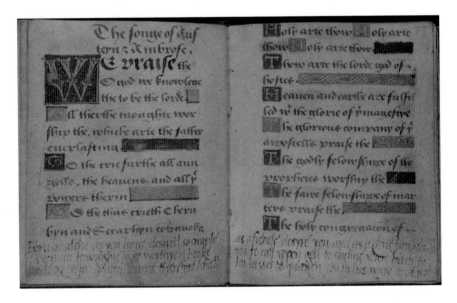

Plate 26 Jane Grey's Prayer book, inscribed to Sir John Brydges

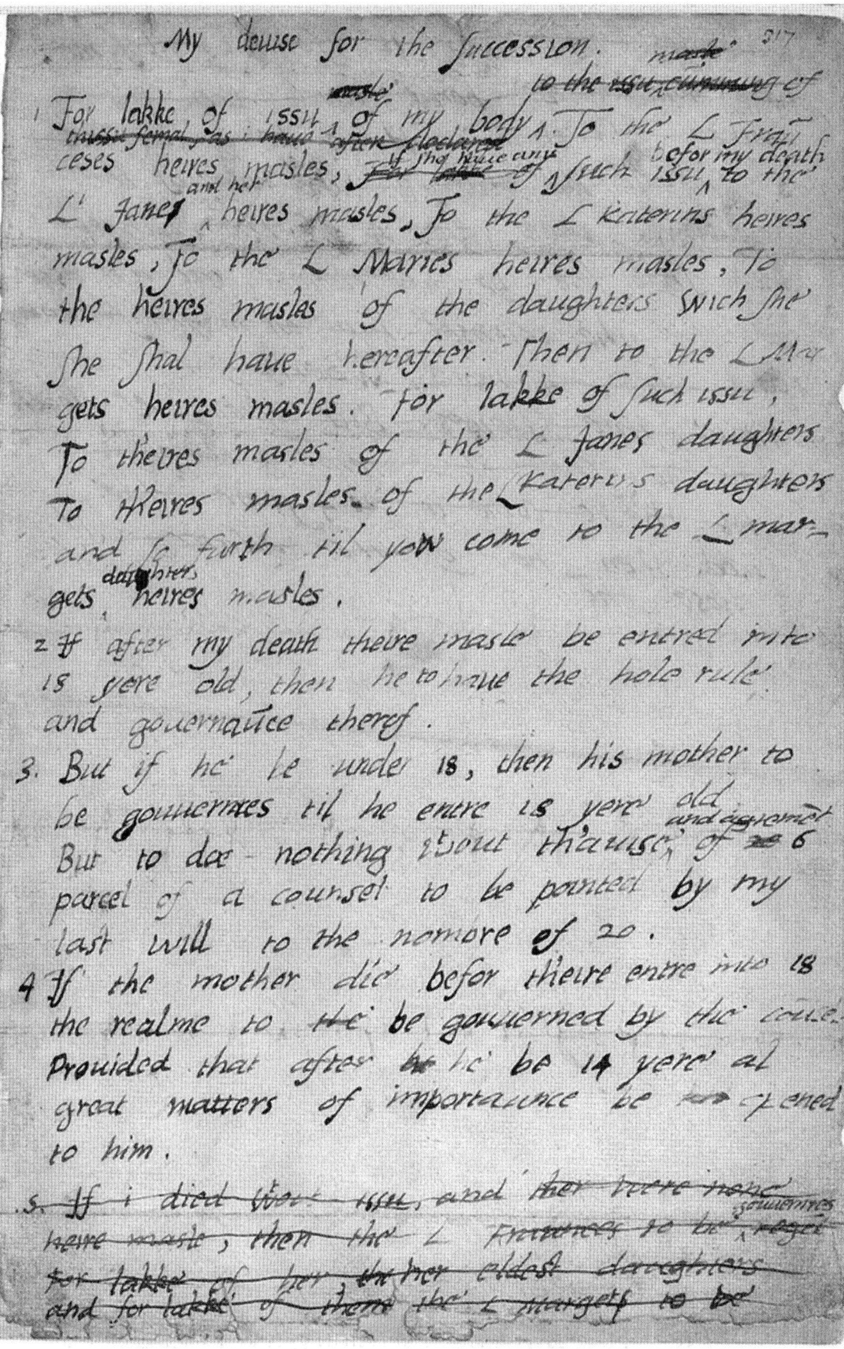

My deuise for the succession. ~~masle~~ 217

1 For lakke of issu ~~masle~~ of my body ~~to the issu masle cumming of thissu femal, as i haue after declared~~ To the L Fraunceses heires masles, ~~for lakke~~ if she haue any ~~of~~ such issu befor my death to the L' Janes and her heires masles, To the L Katerins heires masles, To the L Maries heires masles, To the heires masles of the daughters wich she shal haue hereafter. Then to the L Margets heires masles. For lakke of such issu, To theires masles of the L Janes daughters To theires masles of the L Katerins daughters and so forth til yow come to the L Margets daughters heires masles.

2 If after my death theire masle be entred into 18 yere old, then he to haue the hole rule and gouernaunce therof.

3. But if he be under 18, then his mother to be gouuernres til he entre 18 yere old But to doe nothing w'out th'auise and agrement of ~~20~~ 6 parcel of a counsel to be pointed by my last will to the nombre of 20.

4 If the mother die befor theire entre into 18 the realme to ~~the~~ be gouuerned by the counsel Prouided that after ~~he~~ he be 14 yere al great matters of importaunce be opened to him.

5. ~~If i died wout issu, and ther were none heire masle, then the L Fraunces to be gouuernres regent for lakke of her, the her eldest daughters and for lakke of them the L Margets to be~~

Plate 27 Edward VI, 'My deuise for the succession'

Plate 28 Paul Delaroche, *The Execution of Lady Jane Grey* (1833)

Mary that Edward was dead – because, according to his verse biography, 'that wicked notion right heirs for to displace I did detest' – although subsequently he had the altercation with Sir Thomas Tresham at Northampton over proclaiming Mary, behaviour which the crowd clearly thought was an attempt to maintain Jane.[93] Either they were wrong or the matter was glossed over, since on 24 July he and Tresham were instructed to muster an escort for the new queen.[94]

The persuasive conclusion about the rebellion of Mary Tudor is that it was inspired by her Catholic household, well planned, supported by her (substantially traditionalist) affinity, and spread through a wider network of religious conservatives but also backed by Protestants and neutrals for a wide variety of reasons. All this is summed up in that most crucial of episodes in the rebellion, the fleet deserting to Mary. According to Wingfield, Sir Henry Jerningham went to Ipswich on Friday 14 July to see how Mary's agents had fared with Lord Wentworth and what should be done to hold Ipswich. At the inn he was told about Northumberland's ships sheltering from the bad weather in the mouth of the Orwell and learned that the crews had mutinied in support of Mary.[95] The next morning he travelled the twelve miles or so to Languard Point and summoned Richard Brooke, the overall commander, to meet him, and together Jerningham and Brooke rode to Framlingham 'to bring news of this happy and unexpected arrival to the queen'. That there was more to this than Wingfield tells is clear. In the first place, although Brooke, as we have seen, had a long record of service with the duke, he was also a knight of the Order of St John of Jerusalem which had been suppressed in 1540 for, allegedly, maintaining 'the usurped power of the bishop of Rome'.[96] He is, thus, unlikely to have given Jerningham much trouble. On the other hand, the mutiny of the crews was only partly, if at all, motivated by love of Mary. The story came out some years later. The sixth ship in the fleet, the *Greyhound*, did not make the Orwell and had been driven instead into Lowestoft Roads.[97] Gilbert Grice, the captain, went ashore in search of news but was arrested, leaving the ship's master to grapple with messages from his captain and pleas from supporters of Jane and pleas from supporters of Mary. Even when Mary's receiver Thomas Poley got on board, he was unable to secure the ship for the princess. Instead it sailed south to join the rest of the squadron in the Orwell. There the real cause of the fleet standstill became clear as the sailors broke into the captain's chest and took their overdue wages. It was then Jerningham arrived and was asked by the sailors to arrest the captains 'or else we shall throw them to the bottom of the sea'. Faced with this the captains said that they would be only too glad to serve Mary. The two stories do not entirely agree, but the essentials are the same. Mary's Catholic agents at work, commoners with an agenda of their own and gentlemen officers appointed by Northumberland who were forced by circumstances and conviction to recognize on which side their bread was buttered.

PART IV

CONSEQUENCES

23

Every Man for Himself

ONCE the London council had proclaimed Queen Mary, the single issue in the minds of those who had been promoting Jane Grey was how to escape punishment.[1] 'Ceste pauvre royne', as de Noailles called Jane, was left to fend for herself, abandoned in the Tower with her husband Guildford Dudley and her mother-in-law, the duchess of Northumberland.[2] One story has it that she asked to go home and it is not clear why she and the duchess were not allowed to leave. Once the duke of Suffolk had walked out on his daughter, responsibility for the fortress reverted to the lieutenant currently in post, Sir Edward Warner, and he was a Dudley sympathizer. But that was now the mark of Cain and very probably Warner was desperate to avoid doing anything which might antagonize the new regime – as it was he would lose his job within days.[3] Another possibility is that the Tower garrison simply anticipated the instruction they received on or before 23 July.[4] Or again, Jane and her mother-in-law could have been detained as the wife and mother of a Dudley who had begun to ape the style of a 'king', even being addressed as 'your majesty'.[5] The imperial ambassadors particularly relished the boy's humiliation and when the bishop of Winchester was told that Underhill's son had been christened 'Guildford' 'he was much offended'.[6]

We have no eyewitness descriptions to tell us what happened at Cambridge after the return of Northumberland and his men from Bury on the evening of 19 July, and the second-hand narrative accounts do not agree in detail.[7] However, it appears that a copy of Mary's proclamation reached the duke from London in the late afternoon of Thursday 20 July. He thereupon called his officers and, pointing out that everything done so far had been on the orders of the privy council, called on them to continue to obey and thus accept Mary. He then went to the market place along with his son, the earl of Huntingdon, the Gates brothers and Edwin Sandys, the vice-chancellor, and proclaimed Queen Mary. As Sandys remembered it years later, the duke threw the ritual hat into the air and 'so laughed that the tears ran down his cheeks for grief'; he, John Dudley, after a lifetime's caution, had been caught exactly as his father had been.[8] Shortly afterwards a herald arrived with a message from the council ordering him to disarm his troops and to return to London only on the queen's express instructions. It offered superficial assurance that if the duke 'will shew himself like a good quiet subject we will then continue as we have begun as humble suitors to our sovereign lady the queen's highness for him and his as for ourselves', but reality lay in the order to the herald that 'in all places where ye come, notify it [that] if the duke of Northumberland do not submit himself to the queen's highness, Queen Mary, he shall be accepted as a traitor. And all we of the nobility that were counsellors to the late king will to the uttermost portion, persecute him and his to their utter confusion.'[9] 'We that were counsellors' – already the duke's erstwhile colleagues were asserting 'some difference from others that have more plainly offended'.[10] John Stow has it that when the orders arrived 'every man departed', but those with a lot to lose had not waited.[11] Their minds were on the sixty miles between them and Framlingham and the need to throw themselves on the new queen's mercy as soon as possible. At Framlingham on that Thursday, Mary was, in fact, busy reviewing her forces. This had started at 4 p.m. with a slight contretemps when her horse took fright at the massed ranks, so reducing her to reviewing them on foot. In all she spent three hours very happily with her men and it was as she returned to the castle that news came of Northumberland's retreat from Bury the evening before.[12] Soon afterwards Arundel and Paget arrived bringing the loyalty of the privy council in London, and then the fugitives from Cambridge began to appear. The first was Sir John Clere, the one name on Cecil's Suffolk list to have endorsed Jane.[13] Mary's men had already commandeered his armour and he was anxious to minimize additional penalties for having attempted to hold Great Yarmouth for Jane.[14] Lord Clinton arrived next, then a prominent Dudley supporter, Sir James Croft, followed by a stream of 'other men of consequence' including Lord Grey.[15]

In Cambridge itself, the rank and file began to drift homewards as best they could, but not the royal guard. Their names were on record and they could not melt into general anonymity. The city and the university also felt vulnerable because they had given the duke 'a splendid welcome'. So the mayor raised a large posse of townsmen and scholars and surrounded King's College where the duke and those still with him were staying.[16] Then they sent in a serjeant-at-arms to arrest Northumberland and hold him until Mary's wishes were known. The duke made no resistance although his son and the earl of Huntingdon did; also taken were the Gates brothers, the duke's brother Andrew, Sir Richard Sackville, Sir Robert Stafford and the duke's brother-in-law, Francis Jobson.[17] Why in particular Sackville had not left for Framlingham is hard to say. He was a senior government officer – chancellor of the court of augmentations – and stood to lose a great deal.[18] At this point a further letter arrived from the council clarifying matters and the duke seized on it to get rid of the men guarding him. 'You do me wrong to withdraw my liberty; see you not the council's letters, without exception, that all men should go whither they would?'[19] While this was going on, a powerful move was afoot within the university to oust the vice-chancellor. Sandys was rescued from vigilantes by Sir John Gates who told him 'to walk in the fields', but when the bell rang to summon Congregation, he came back and attempted to preside. A rough-house ensued and Sandys was stripped of his office.[20] The men of the guard, meanwhile, had concluded that their best defence was to say that they were only obeying orders. So in the small hours of Thursday–Friday they detained first Sir John Gates, their captain (he was lodging with the vice-chancellor), and then the duke himself.[21] One story has it that Northumberland was dressed and ready to escape, another that his son was about to leave.[22] Thereafter there was nothing to do but wait for Framlingham.

Individual survival in the collapsing regime of Queen Jane was heavily dependent on luck and good contacts. The men who arrived early at Framlingham seem to have been greeted by the queen with relief. They would still have to buy pardons for their misdeeds – Clinton was later reported as compounding for £6,000 – but Mary did extend her royal favour to them, which meant that they would not face trial.[23] They expressed their relief by turning on their erstwhile colleagues, a reaction which was evident again in the August treason trials.[24] Thus it was Arundel who led the party Mary sent to take charge at Cambridge, an earl whose last words to the duke a week before had been a wish to spend his blood alongside him.[25]

As soon as ever he saw the earl of Arundel [Northumberland] fell down on his knees and desired him to be good to him for the love of God:

> DUKE: And consider that I have done nothing but by the consents of you and all the whole council.
>
> ARUNDEL: My lord, I am sent hither by the queen's majesty, and in her name I do arrest you.
>
> DUKE: And I obey it, my lord, and I beseech you my lord of Arundel, use mercy towards me, knowing the case as it is.
>
> ARUNDEL: My lord, you should have sought for mercy sooner.

Alongside Arundel stood Lord Grey. There are stories that he and the duke did not see eye to eye, but forty-eight hours before he had held high command in the duke's column. Now he was an enthusiast for Mary, although he was as yet unaware that this would cost him £7,000 by way of composition.[26] Also heading the Framlingham team was the Marian loyalist Sir Henry Jerningham, but with him was the erstwhile paymaster of Northumberland's troops, Thomas Mildmay. Their orders were to arrest the vice-chancellor on account of the sermon he had preached the Sunday before at Northumberland's request.

> Mr Mildmay said he marvelled that a learned man would speak so unadvisedly against so good a prince and wilfully run into such danger. Dr Sandes answered, "I shall not be ashamed of bonds. But if I could do as Mr Mildmay can, I needed not fear bonds. For he came down in payment against Queen Mary, and armed in the field, and now he returneth in payment for Queen Mary, before a traitor and now a great friend. I cannot with one mouth blow hot and cold after this sort.[27]

The *ad hominem* fate of Jane's supporters remained the pattern as prisoners not offered favour began to flood into the Tower. The duke arrived under escort on 25 July along with his three sons and his brother Andrew, Francis Hastings, earl of Huntingdon, and his son Lord Hastings, the Gates brothers, Sir Thomas Palmer and Dr Sandes (and others would follow, including Jane Grey's father).[28] Henry Lord Hastings was, however, promptly discharged into the keeping of the earl of Arundel; his mother was the granddaughter of Mary's governess the Countess of Salisbury, and one of the only two living relatives of Cardinal Pole, who was already pencilled in to become Mary's archbishop of Canterbury. As Mary herself progressed towards London the story continued of favour extended or refused.[29] At Ipswich Sir Thomas Heneage, at one time Henry VIII's most intimate attendant and now in his seventies, received a kindly welcome even though he had sat on the fence, and in view of his service to her father the queen extended her favour to his son-in-law William Lord Willoughby who had actually backed the duke.[30] At Ipswich, too, William Cecil and his brother-in-law Nicholas Bacon arrived to sue for grace. Mary then moved via Wingfield's house to Newhall, where Frances Grey, Jane's mother and the queen's old friend arrived.[31] As a result of her plea, her husband the duke of Suffolk was released from the Tower after only three or four days, but not Jane.[32] Had Frances interceded for her daughter and been turned down, or had she simply written Jane off? William Petre's house at Ingatestone was Mary's next stop and there, thanks to the intercessions of Anne Bacon and his own persuasive tongue, Cecil was restored to grace.

Others were not so fortunate. After her release, the duchess of Northumberland went to the queen to plead for reprieves but was refused audience.[33] She thereupon lobbied Lady Anne Paget to persuade Susan Clarencius and the marchioness of Exeter to intercede for the duke, but again without success.[34] Nicholas Ridley had even more misfortune. He was arrested before he could even reach the court.[35] If Bishop Ridley had really thought he had a hope of grace he was much mistaken, for he was one of a clutch of men against whom Mary herself had determined to take revenge. Chief Justice Montagu was another. We have seen his attempt to excuse his part in drawing up Edward VI's 'deuise', but it was to little effect. He was imprisoned in the Tower for six weeks, dismissed from his post of chief justice of the common pleas which brought in £400 p.a., forced to surrender lands granted by Edward VI to him and his heirs (worth £52 4s. p.a.), and fined £1,000.[36] He was most aggrieved at this treatment because all his actions were in Edward's reign and he had sent his son with twenty of his servants to support the rising for Mary in Buckinghamshire. Royal vindictiveness was especially directed at those who had insulted her legitimacy. The royal printer was sacked for producing Jane's proclamation.[37] Chief Justice Cholmley, like his colleague Montagu, spent six weeks in the Tower, lost his post and paid 'a great fine'.[38] We do not know how prominent he had been in preparing the 'deuise', but he had been responsible for convincing the guard of Jane's right to the crown.[39] Royal vengeance was not confined to the prominent, either. John Lucas and John Coke held middle-ranking posts as masters of requests but they were specifically sought out and imprisoned in the Fleet; Coke, indeed, may have been briefly in the Tower. Both men lost their jobs.[40] A possible reason for this is suggested by the appearance of Lucas's signature among the otherwise more significant names on the 'engagement'. Had he and Coke drafted Edward's documents? John Throckmorton who did draft Jane's proclamation was almost immediately appointed by Mary to one of the confiscated masterships, but he had been able to reach her at Framlingham and was, indeed, given a £20 reward for his services.[41] One of the most unfortunate victims was John Cheke whom Mary clearly loathed. This was thought to be quite unreasonable; Cheke had been junior secretary to the council for less than two months.[42] Gossip did suggest that he may have had a part in advising Edward about the succession, but his more obvious offence was having written the council's robust reply on 10 July which told Mary she was illegitimate, and he may well have drafted other council documents which she found offensive. In this, however, Cheke was simply the fall guy. Cecil had deliberately 'shifted ... all dealing in those matters'.[43] Mary's biggest target for revenge was, however, Thomas Cranmer, and it was a dish she consumed slowly. Not until 14 September was he put in the Tower, into the very cell which Northumberland had occupied.[44]

Cells full of prisoners did not, however, mean business for the executioners. Francis Bacon wrote of Henry VII that 'the less blood he drew, the more he took of treasure', and this was certainly true of his granddaughter Mary. Over the first months of her reign the Tower and other prisons gradually emptied as compositions were agreed, but only three men were executed – Northumberland, John Gates and Thomas Palmer. Two factors explain this leniency. In essence, earlier rebellions in the century had been popular uprisings directed against government policy, and had been put down by force and martial law. In 1553 the division was within the country's ruling elite. There had been no fighting and the rank and file on Jane's side had done little more than follow their leaders on a week's perambulation through eastern England. In the second place, the purpose in Mary's rebellion had been to oust the reigning monarch, not to fracture the ruling class without which she could not govern. Thus her priority was to turn dissidents into loyalists. Vengeance may nevertheless explain an apparent oddity in the executions which did take place. The heads of the duke (the country's principal minister) and Gates (the individual directly responsible for the security of the sovereign) were the minimum forfeit if Mary was to be respected, but Palmer? Sir Thomas was nearly sixty, a tall, hugely experienced soldier, most recently a senior commander and expert in fortification in Edward VI's Border wars.[45] Known as 'buskinned Palmer' (i.e. Palmer the extrovert), he had been Henry VIII's gambling companion and clearly cared for nobody. When put on trial with the Gates brothers and Andrew Dudley, he had protested violently at his judges – Winchester, Bedford, Shrewsbury, Rich, Paget and others of Jane's council – they deserved punishment as much as he did. Not until he had calmed down could the trial proceed.[46] Unlike the other three defendants he had then insisted on pleading not guilty, pointing out that he had never taken any armed action against Mary. The lawyers asked 'Can you deny that you were there?' 'No.' 'Then it cannot be but that you are culpable' – to which Palmer replied, 'Well then, since it is so, I confess.'[47] The last of the three to be executed, he climbed the blood-soaked scaffold, shook hands with everyone there, doffed his hat to the crowd and said 'God give you good morrow', to which many gave the conventional response 'Good morrow to you'! Palmer responded, 'I do not doubt but that I have a good morrow and shall I trust have a better good even.' He then proceeded to tell of the spiritual transformation the Tower had produced in him so that in God 'I trust to live eternally'.[48] Why such a man was selected to die is a puzzle. Nothing is known of any action against Mary except 'being there', as were thousands of others. There are three conjectures. Had the embarrassing attack on his judges cost him a reprieve? Had complaints been made against him at Framlingham because of the part he had taken in the suppression of the rising led by Robert Ket? Or is there significance in the presence of the two sons of the duke of Somerset in the Tower chapel on 21 August and also before the executions the next day?[49] According to the imperial ambassador Palmer admitted to the brothers that his written testimony which had helped to destroy their father had been invented by Northumberland and was false.[50] This was a common practice in political treason trials but Sir Thomas had hated the protector whom he blamed for a major humiliation suffered at the hands of the Scots.[51] If either of these last guesses is correct, Palmer's execution had nothing to do with supporting Jane but was stage-managed to demonstrate that under Mary even past wrongdoing would not be condoned.

By the end of August, Jane and Guildford were two of only a handful of prisoners remaining in the Tower. [plate 22] The couple had been indicted on 12 August, but not until November would steps be taken to bring them to trial.

24

THE TOWER

L EAVING Jane Grey in limbo for four months before bringing her to trial did not mean that she had been forgotten. Certainly not by Simon Renard, who from September 1553 became Charles V's sole accredited representative in England.[1] He was able to get close to Mary because she had long seen herself as a protégée of the emperor and because so many of her most prominent advisers had supported Jane and had still to gain her full confidence. The ambassador was therefore able to act as an *éminence grise* exploiting her naivety in government and the Catholicism she shared with Habsburg relatives, and his instructions were to persuade her to marry the emperor's son, Philip.[2] Renard deluded himself about the extent of his influence, but almost the only evidence we have of Mary's thinking in the first months of her reign is found in his reports to his imperial masters. The earliest hint of anything affecting Lady Jane comes in his letter to Charles dated 8 August, with the suggestion that Mary needed to be encouraged 'to have justice done'.[3] A week later in a private audience with the queen at Richmond, Renard was more specific.[4] The authors and inventors of the plot should be tried as soon as possible. Mary responded that she had not pardoned anyone as yet and

> as to Jane of Suffolk whom they had tried to make Queen, she could not be induced to consent that she should die .... Three days before they went to fetch her from Syon House to take her to the Tower and make her entry into the town as usurping Queen, she knew nothing of it, nor was she ever a party, nor did she ever give her consent to the duke's intrigues and plots. Her conscience, [Mary] said, would not permit her to have her put to death.

This echoes the explanation which Jane had given to the queen in her letter, so proving that Mary had received it and accepted it as true.[5] People outside the palace, even supporters of Jane such as Florio, also knew that the queen believed her innocent.[6] Renard tried to shift Mary by arguing that there was sufficient 'semblance of foundation' in Jane's claim to the throne to cause trouble in the future, and he quoted the example of the fourth-century emperor Theodosius, who executed both his rival Maximus and his rival's young son 'because of the scandal and danger which might have followed'.[7] Mary's only reply was that she would take the greatest care before freeing Jane. Given this the ambassadors fell back on recommending confinement 'in a safe place', but their disagreement about a policy of clemency kept cropping up.[8] On 19 September Renard was claiming that Mary's preferred policy of financial penalties had made her a laughing stock and that, to counter this, Jane and the four Dudleys were to be tried and executed.[9] This is a good example of Renard's failure to understand the English. Holinshed remembered the commission to compound with offenders and described its impact as 'very grievous'.[10] Nor, when at last it did take place, was Jane's trial triggered by Renard's call for blood. The government had got itself into a muddle. In a desire to avoid a trial entirely, a bill of attainder was put through parliament, in which clause 2 ordered that Jane, Guildford, Cranmer and the Dudley brothers 'shall suffer death'.[11] However, the previous clause lumped them together with those tried in the previous August and stated that they had already been 'justly, lawfully and according to law' convicted and attainted of high treason. Thus if the bill was to make sense, trying them became unavoidable. However, the choice of 14 November as the date to put things right is probably explained by a quite separate piece of parliamentary legislation: the bill to repeal Edward's Protestant settlement. This finally passed on 8 November, despite vocal resistance, and nothing could more publicize that victory than, a week later, parading the survivors of the Edwardian regime in disgrace.[12]

The circumstances of Jane's imprisonment in the Tower were not harsh. She lived in the house of Nathaniel Partridge, the gentleman-gaoler, and was attended by three gentlewomen (possibly on a rota) and a manservant; after all, she was still the queen's cousin.[13] On Tuesday 29 August, a week after the execution of Northumberland, Gates and Palmer, Partridge invited 'Rowland Lea', his friend from the mint, to dinner.[14] Jane normally ate in her own rooms, so the men and Partridge's wife were taken aback to walk in and find Jane dining below, with her gentlewoman and her man. Caps came off hastily, but Jane told them to put them on again. She said that Lea was 'heartily welcome' and drank his health a couple of times. Being so near a 'royal' was clearly a major experience and he noted down parts of the conversation. The only reference he has to Jane's situation is her remark that 'The queen's grace is a merciful princess; I beseech God she may long continue and send his bountiful grace upon her', which could imply that she had received some assurance that she would not follow her father-in-law. Talk then turned to religion and in a way typical of every prisoner, Jane was hungry for news. Who preached at St Paul's on the previous Sunday and was the mass back in London? The answer 'in some places' led her to the events of the previous week and to remarks which strip Jane's personality bare.

> JANE: [The mass in London] is not so strange as the sudden conversion of the late duke. For who would have thought he would have so done?
> LEA or PARTRIDGE: Perchance he thereby hoped to have had a pardon.
> JANE: Pardon? Woe worthy him! He hath brought me and our stock [family] in most miserable calamity and misery by his exceeding ambition. But for the answer that he hoped for life by turning, though other men be of that opinion, I utterly am not; for what man is there living, I pray you, although [even if] he had been innocent, that would hope of life in that case, being in the [battle]field against the queen in person as general [in command] and after his taking, so hated and evil spoken of by the commons? And at his coming into prison so wondered [gaped] at as the like was never heard by any man's time. Who was judge that he whose life was odious to all men should hope for pardon?

Contempt burns on the page. A man as rational as John Dudley must have known that a pardon was not remotely possible.

> But what will ye more? Like as his life was wicked and full of dissimulation, so was his end thereafter. I pray God, I, nor no friend of mine die so. Should I, who [am] young and in my few years, forsake my faith for love of life? Nay, God forbid! Much more he should not, whose fatal [life's] course, although he had lived his just number of years, could not have long continued. But life was sweet, it appeared; so he might have lived, you will say, he did [not] care how. Indeed the reason is good; for he that would have lived in chains to have had life, belike would leave no other mean attempted.

Northumberland had stripped himself naked of every vestige of honesty and pride, and in hope of just a few short years more – the authentic voice of the young through the ages on the value of life to the old. Then finally the intolerant certainty of the martyr:

> But God be merciful to us, for he says, Whoso denies him before men, he will not know him in his Father's kingdom.[15]

'Much like talk' continued during the rest of the dinner, but we also get a sense of Jane evidently relaxed and at home with people she would not normally have socialized with. When the meal was done,

> 'I thanked her ladyship that she would vouchsafe to accept me in her company; and she thanked me likewise, and said I was welcome. She thanked Partridge also for bringing me to dinner. "Madam," said he, "we were somewhat bold, not knowing that your ladyship dined below until we found your ladyship there". And so Partridge and I departed.'

We do not know what Lea's religious opinions were, but the meeting with Jane may be responsible for the considerable interest his account appears to have taken in her future.[16]

When eventually it came, Jane's trial was deliberately demeaning. She and the other accused were commoners. Not for them the privacy of a boat to Westminster; their trial was set for London's Guild Hall. This meant a mile walk through the busy streets of the city and gave the government an opportunity to make the most of the humiliation of defeat. Four hundred halberdiers were on duty, not to guarantee security but to demonstrate power.[17] First on this *via dolorosa* came the officer carrying the great axe with the blade turned away from the prisoners to show that for a short time they would still be innocent in the eyes of the law. Cranmer and his keepers came first, next Guildford and his escort, then Jane between two guards and with two gentlewomen behind her and finally the Dudley brothers.[18] Jane had dressed carefully, in black from head to toe – a cloth gown and a furred cape and a French hood where even the decorated edge, the 'billement', was of jet. From her girdle hung a book bound in black and she carried another, almost certainly a Bible, and it was open. The proceedings opened with a Catholic liturgy, and the commission to try the accused – headed by Sir Thomas White, the lord mayor, and the veteran Duke of Norfolk – was overwhelmingly Catholic in sentiment.[19] Indeed, all but one or two had been active in the rebellion against Jane. This display of religious conviction was probably more because of Cranmer than the deposed queen; the old archbishop was to be denied even a flicker of sympathy.[20] The accused were all charged with high treason: the archbishop for entering the Tower on 10 July and proclaiming Jane, and also for sending troops to Cambridge; Jane and Guildford for taking possession of the Tower and proclaiming Jane while she faced the additional charge of 'signing various writings'.[21] Thomas Cranmer pleaded 'not guilty', which meant that a trial jury had to be empanelled and the case presented, but before the jury returned its verdict, he changed his plea and joined the others in confessing the indictment.[22] The men were sentenced to be drawn, hanged and quartered. Jane was condemned to be 'burned alive on Tower Hill or beheaded as the Queen should please'. Observers expected her to go white at this point but the sentence brought not the slightest reaction.[23] Then back to the Tower with the axe blade turned towards the tiny group – guilty as charged – the last walk Jane would ever take outside prison walls.

Despite this show of rigour, there was no thought of executing Jane; she was to be kept in prison. Initially confinement was close. After she was removed from the royal apartments, Jane was for many weeks denied exercise, or so it would seem. Not until 17/18 December was she given 'the liberty of the Tower' so that she could walk in the queen's garden.[24] That may also have brought some supervised contact with the other prisoners, because at the same time the lieutenant of the Tower was empowered to allow Cranmer and the Dudley brothers, including Guildford, access to the garden 'for want of air'. Even if Jane was not allowed to speak with her husband, she undoubtedly saw him for he seems to have been moved to the Bell Tower where more prestigious prisoners were accommodated and fed from the lieutenant's kitchens, and his route to the garden may have passed Jane's door.[25] The Dudleys had, in fact, been privileged weeks earlier. In September two were permitted visits by their wives, and John, Ambrose, Henry and Guildford were allowed to walk on sections of the Tower leads.[26] Why Jane had to wait the extra months is not clear. Was it until many of the issues which had disturbed the first months of Mary's reign had been, or were on the point of being, resolved? The coronation had been a triumph, parliament had been successfully negotiated, the queen declared legitimate, the religious changes of Edward's reign reversed, and her marriage to Philip of Spain agreed. Alternatively, was it an attempt to put pressure on Jane's father whose refusal to conform to the new religious settlement was seen as encouraging dissent?[27] Or was Jane herself as intransigent as Florio suggests? Was she saying that her offence had been very slight and her attendants were not to weep for her – the people who needed to come to terms with their

consciences were her judges?[28] Also the September relaxations had
included permission for the marquis of Northampton, the earl of Huntingdon and even Bishop Ridley to attend the Tower chapel on mass days,
and it is hard to believe that Jane would not have secured more lenient
treatment by also giving that minimum recognition to Catholic services.[29]

According to Florio Jane occupied her time in studying the Bible.
Whether she had classical texts in addition to her Greek New Testament
and a prayer book is not known. She also had access to pen and paper and
it was probably only in a desire for permanence that at one point she is
reported as scratching some verses with a pin.

> Non aliena putes homini quae obtingere possunt:
>   Sors hodierna mihi, tunc erit illa tibi
>
> Do never think it strange,
> Though now I have misfortune.
> For if that fortune change,
> The same to thee may happen.
>
>   Jane Dudley
>
> Deo juvante, nil nocet livor malus:
> Et non juvante, nil juvat labor gravis
>
> If God do help thee,
> Hate shall not hurt thee;
> If God do fail thee,
> Then shall not labour prevail thee.
>
> Post tenebras spero lucem[30]

She did have occasional visitors and the lieutenant of the Tower encouraged his most prestigious prisoner to hope for a pardon. Jane's public
response, however, was to say that now her mind was fixed on heaven.[31]

It was, nevertheless, during her months in the Tower that Jane revealed
more about herself than ever before. She had written to Thomas Seymour
when she was barely eleven; in addressing Bullinger she had been as much
or more concerned to demonstrate literary skill as to reveal her mind; her
letter to Mary was a petition. What she wrote in the Tower she wrote from
passion and conviction, bringing us closer to the real girl than anything
bar her speech from the scaffold. This is particularly true of the letter to
Thomas Harding. Clearly it was written immediately Jane heard that her
former chaplain – 'a most active preacher of the gospel' – had reneged on
his beliefs, but when she learned of the apostasy can only be guessed. The
probability is the late autumn of 1553, by which time other reformers in

Oxford had conformed to the new regime.[32] Given her upbringing, it is no surprise that the letter is redolent of scripture.[33] Old Testament references are in a minority, but three of the four Gospels are cited and at least eight of the other New Testament books. None of the score of direct quotations is surprising given that treachery was her concern. For example, she quoted both of the warning passages from the Epistle to the Hebrews which promise that all an apostate can look forward to is 'the terrible expectation of judgement'.[34] Equally expected are the examples she cites of penitents: the return of the prodigal son who had wasted his inheritance and the tax collector who prayed 'Lord, be merciful unto me, a sinner'.[35] But what reveals the extent of Jane's intimacy with scripture are the biblical terms and phrases which occur time and time again in what she wrote. For example:

> Wherefore hast thou instructed other ... when thou thyself doest abuse the law of the Lord and preachest, not to steal and yet most abominably stealest not from men but from God as a most heinous sacrilege; robbest Christ of his right members, thy body and soul when thou doest choose rather to live miserably with shame to the world than to die and gloriously with honour reign with Christ even in whom in death there is life?[36]

In sequence the passage cites 1 Corinthians 9:27; Amos 2:4; Malachi 3:8 and Romans 2:21; Hebrews 6:6; 1 Corinthians 6:15; Matthew 16:25, Romans 14:8 and Hebrews 11:25; Revelation 20:6; John 11:25 – one biblical echo every nine words. Alongside this familiarity with canonical scriptures, Jane evidently knew the Apocrypha, which Cranmer's Forty-Two Articles of 1553 had endorsed to be read 'for example of life and instruction of manners, but ... [not] ... to establish any doctrine'.[37] Thus she included a lengthy paraphrase of a passage which warned Jews exiled in Babylon against being sucked into idolatry.[38] She could easily have found similar passages in the Old Testament but what would have attracted Jane to the Apocrypha was its specific warning against 'gods of gold, silver, wood and stone borne upon men's shoulders'.[39] Mary's victory had brought back with a vengeance the Catholic practice of venerating and parading sacred objects, in particular the host, the consecrated wafer which Catholics saw as the body of Christ but which Jane denounced as 'the invention of man, the golden calf, the whore of Babylon, the Romish religion, the abominable idol, the most wicked mass'.[40] Later in the letter Jane turned to the Apocrypha for most of her examples of godly suffering – the song of Daniel's three friends in the burning fiery furnace, the ninety-year-old Eleazar who was flogged to death for refusing to break Jewish dietary law and seven brothers who were mutilated and roasted to death for the same offence.[41]

In this reference to scripture, canonical and otherwise, the passage which came back to Jane's mind more than any other was the tenth chapter of the Gospel of Matthew. In this Jesus Christ warned his disciples of the hostile reception they should expect. Jane's first quotation was 'whosever seeketh to save his life shall lose it: but whosoever will lose his life for my sake shall find it'.[42] With this she joined 'whosoever loveth father or mother above me, is not meet for me. For he that will be my disciple must forsake father and mother and himself and take up his cross and follow me'.[43] Jane then asked 'What cross?' and answered 'The cross of infamy and shame, of misery and poverty, of affliction and persecution, for his name's sake'.[44] Later she quoted the passage: 'I am not come to bring peace on the earth but a sword. That is, Christ came to set the son against the father and the daughter against the mother-in-law'.[45] The Gospel text actually reads 'daughter against her mother and daughter-in-law against her mother-in-law', so was the crossing of the relationships a Freudian slip? Jane and the duchess of Northumberland? Four sentences later comes the Matthew quotation she had used during dinner with Lea and Partridge: 'He that denies me before men, I will deny him before my Father in heaven.'[46] Her final citation is from earlier in the chapter: 'Fear not them (saith Christ) that have power over the body only, but fear him that hath power both over soul and body'.[47] To this Jane added from the Gospel of John: 'The world loveth her own. If ye were of the world, the world would love you; but you are mine, therefore the world doth hate you.'[48] The relevance of all this to Harding's apostasy is clear, but it is hard not to see the choice of verses as indicative of the way Jane increasingly saw her own plight. In August she had accepted that she was in prison for offending against the English crown. Is she now seeing herself as suffering for Christ? That would certainly explain references in the letter to being loyal to Christ even in the face of death and her clear implication that Harding had been motivated by fear. We know that Mary attempted to convert Jane just before her death. Perhaps reformers were right when they imply that there had been a campaign to persuade her to recant.[49]

The Harding letter offers other insights too into the mind of Jane Grey. There is a flash of the humanist in a quotation from Cicero – '*amicitia non est, nisi inter bonos*', while her mention of 'the lamentable case of Francis Spira of late' reflects her interest in continental reformers.[50] Spira was an Italian lawyer who converted to Protestantism in the 1540s but, after being forced to recant, became suicidally convinced that he was damned.

The story had been published in England in 1550 with a preface by Calvin.[51] If Jane did not read the story there, Florio would undoubtedly have told her. The Harding letter also reveals how well Jane had absorbed tuition in rhetoric – that art of effective communication which humanists prized even more than the fluency in classical languages in which she excelled. In a formal Renaissance accusation, six stages were expected: I announcing the issue; II specifying the charge; III analysing the charge; IV proving the charge; V countering any defence; VI attempting to win over the accused.[52] Jane's letter to Harding follows this structure exactly:

I The issue	'So oft as I call to mind the dreadful and fearful saying of God … and on the other side the comfortable words of our Saviour … I cannot but marvel at thee and lament thy case.'
II Specifying the charge	'I cannot but speak to thee and cry out upon thee … whom the devil hath deceived, the world hath beguiled and the desire of life subverted, and made thee of a Christian an infidel.'
III Analysing the charge	'wherefore … wherefore … wherefore'
IV Proving the charge	'Wilt thou honour a detestable idol invented by the Romish popes and the abominable college of cardinals?
V Countering any defence	'But thou wilt say thou doest it of good intent. O wicked man, the sink of sin, the son of perdition … But ye will say ye will not break unity … But what unity? As Cicero says of amity: "Only among good men is amity possible." … The agreement of ill men is not unity but a conspiracy.'
VI Winning over the accused	'If these terrible and thundering threatenings cannot stir thee to cleave unto Christ and forsake the world; yet let the sweet consolations and promises of the Scriptures, let the example of Christ and his apostles, holy martyrs and confessors encourage thee to take faster hold by Christ.'

What is noticeable is that a quarter of the letter is taken up with the defences Harding might use, and this prompts the speculation that Jane was responding to a letter from Harding urging her to follow his example. Personal response or no, the care she gave to constructing the letter suggests that Jane was hoping for a general circulation. If so, over the next 250 years, that wider readership would be amply realized.[53] As well as following the 'canons of rhetoric', Jane's letter also followed the rules in respect of style. She began in the 'grand' style designed to move the hearer or reader, changed to the 'low' style for the argument, and finally used the 'middle' style to woo Harding back from his errors.[54] She also picked up the trick that in making the final appeal it was effective to exploit pathos: 'Christ who now stretcheth out his arms to receive you, ready to fall on your neck and kiss you'. Jane also employed some of the countless available rhetorical figures: 'rhetorical questions' – 'wherefore', 'wherefore', 'wherefore'; *anaphora* – 'sometime the beautiful temple of God', 'sometime the unspotted spouse of Christ', 'sometime my faithful brother'; *procatalepsis* – 'but wilt thou say'; 'transferred epithets' – 'thundering threatenings'; perhaps most of all, *gradatio*, piling up phase upon phrase to the climax.

If the Harding letter may have been intended for circulation, that was certainly the case with the account Jane prepared of her discussion with Feckenham.[55] Given the little time she had to write between his final visit and the end, this says much for her determination that her death should have meaning. In a twenty-first century accustomed to the statements of suicide bombers such a motivation is increasingly intelligible. Indeed the fact that the printers had Jane's text 'word for word' may hint that she even had it smuggled out direct to them.[56] The monk and the sixteen-year-old began by sparring over salvation by faith alone. To Feckenham's insistence that good works were necessary for salvation Jane responded that 'faith only saveth'. On the scaffold she would say that this was the certainty she died in. A life of virtue was not a means to earn God's favour. Virtuous living was the outworking of faith. Then the subject moved to the eucharist which Jane insisted on describing by the reformers' favoured term 'the Lord's supper'. Already in her letter to Harding she had passionately attacked the notion of transubstantiation. 'Wilt thou torment again, rend and tear the most precious body of our saviour Christ with thy bodily and fleshly teeth?'[57] Equally obnoxious was the belief that in conducting mass the priest offered up the sacrifice of Christ: 'Wilt thou take upon thee to offer up any sacrifice unto God for our sins considering that Christ offered up himself as Paul says upon the cross, a lively [living] sacrifice

once for all?'[58] Now she insisted to Feckenham that the purpose of the
sacramental bread and wine was to 'put me in remembrance how that for
my sins the body of Christ was broken and his blood shed on the cross'; in
no way did they did become the actual body and blood of Christ. In
response the monk advanced the customary proof text: 'Doth not Christ
speak these words, "Take, eat, this is my body"? Require you any plainer
words?' Like a flash Jane came back, 'And so he saith, "I am the vine, I am
the door", but he is never the more for that, the door or the vine.' Then
she went on the offensive:

> I pray you answer me to this one question: Where was Christ when he said,
> 'Take, eat, this is my body?' Was he not at [the supper] table when he said so?
> He was at that time alive, and suffered not until the next day. What took he
> but bread? What brake he but bread? And what gave he but bread? ... yet all
> this while he himself was alive and at supper before his disciples.

Both the arguments Jane produced were standard in the reformist/tradi-
tionalist debate, but this was not some coolly held intellectual opinion.
Jane had long abhorred Catholic teaching – she had clashed with Anne
Wharton about it years earlier – but her hostility was now vehement. This
personalization is probably explained by the influence of the German
theologian Martin Bucer, the regius professor of divinity at Cambridge.[59]
As we have seen, he had been something of a spiritual director to Jane and
one of Bucer's great emphases was the importance of a true understanding
of the eucharist and the absolute evil of the Roman Catholic mass.[60]

Feckenham's reply was to cite the authority of the church 'to whom ye
ought to give credit'. Jane retorted, 'I ground my faith on God's word
[i.e. the Bible], and not upon the church. For if the church be a good
church, the faith of the church must be tried by God's word, and not
God's word by the church, neither yet my faith.' The Catholic church was
not just in error, it was an evil church. For a demonstration Jane turned
again to the eucharist, this time the Catholic refusal to allow the laity to
receive wine as well as bread:

> Shall I believe the church because of antiquity or shall I give credit to the
> church that taketh away from me the half part of the Lord's supper and will
> not let any man receive it in both kinds? ... I say that it is an evil church and
> not the spouse of Christ, but the spouse of the devil that alters the Lord's
> supper and both takes from it and adds to it.

This was a remarkable assertion of the supremacy of the individual conscience, and according to Florio Jane elaborated on it by saying that Mary

of all people would not want her to violate her conscience. After all, even 'pagans' [i.e. classical writers] accepted 'good conscience' as the ultimate authority.[61]

So much for the writings she prepared for circulation. The prayer she wrote in the Tower is in marked contrast.[62] Here we have evidence of Jane's state of mind during her imprisonment fit to be measured alongside the more intimate of Thomas More's Tower writings. Some scholars date the prayer shortly before the final catastrophe, but against this is the phrase 'assuredly knowing that as thou canst, so thou wilt deliver me, when it shall please thee'; Jane had not abandoned the possibility of release. On the other hand, she also wrote that without divine 'mercy and help ... so little hope of deliverance is left, that I may utterly despair of any liberty'. Taken together, the sentiments suggest that the prayer was composed in the aftermath of her trial but before the conditions of her imprisonment were relaxed in December. Mary may have accepted that Jane was innocent of intent and might have no plans to execute her, but the legalities of the trial had demonstrated that she was to be left with the death penalty hanging over her. For how long? The recently released earl of Devon had been held in the Tower for sixteen years from the age of ten. In such uncertainty Jane's only resource was the Bible, and the result is a prayer in which references and allusions to scripture are even more dense than in the Harding letter. Interestingly, a mistake which Jane makes at one point reveals how deep – almost instinctive – this biblical cast of mind had become. The book of Proverbs was supposed to have been composed by Solomon, so she automatically credited a quotation to him, whereas checking with a Bible would have revealed otherwise.[63] Matthew chapter 10 does not figure in the prayer, but Jane did return to Ephesians chapter 6, which spells out the spiritual armour of the believer. What she had advocated to Harding, she now prayed for herself.

Jane's prayer also gives an insight into the way she reconciled her misfortune and her Christian belief.

> Albeit it is expedient that, seeing our life standeth upon trying, we should be visited sometime with some adversity, whereby we might be tried whether we be of thy flock or no, and also know thee and ourselves the better: yet thou that saidest thou wouldest not suffer us to be tempted above our power, be merciful unto me now, a miserable wretch.[64]

On one level this reflects passages in the Bible which see suffering and hardship as a way by which God teaches believers: 'whom the Lord loves he disciplines'.[65] It is as if Jane wrote: 'Trials are part of life, but there is value in sometimes experiencing adversity which will test (and so strengthen) our faith and also build an understanding of God and of ourselves.' But Jane meant more than that, for she included the highly significant phrase 'be tried [tested] whether we be of thy flock or no'. The reformers (like those medieval theologians who had followed the tradition of St Augustine) believed that human beings fell into one of two categories. On one side were those who had faith and belonged to God, and on the other those who did not and belonged to the devil, and where one stood was decisive not just for this life but for the life to come. What is more, faith was not a matter of human decision; it was given by God to some, 'the elect'. No-one could be categorical about being one of the elect, and later theologians developed rigid ideas about predestination, but Jane had evidently been taught that awareness of being chosen by God was, as the Forty-two Articles said, a 'sweet, pleasant and unspeakable comfort'.[66] Not that this encouraged smug satisfaction. The proof of election was, the Article said, 'the working of the Spirit of God, mortifying the flesh ... and drawing up [the] mind to high and heavenly things'. In other words, how she responded to imprisonment in the Tower was a test of her election. That this was how Jane rationalized what was happening to her is specifically confirmed by Florio.[67] In this she was in all probability once more living out what she had been taught by Martin Bucer, who made a great deal about the blessings of election and its consequent responsibilities.[68]

Jane faced imprisonment in the Tower positively. The loss of liberty was irksome, but the more she could, by God's grace, triumph over hardships, the more confident she could be of her eternal destiny.

25

NEMESIS

A S Christmas 1553 approached, the recent relaxation in her confine-ment must have encouraged Jane to hope that she might soon be moved to house arrest in a less overpowering place of confinement. She must have heard – possibly even seen – Mary leave the Tower at the start of her triumphant coronation. She knew of the revival of the mass and was probably well aware that parliament and the country had accepted – in many cases welcomed – a retreat from Edward's religious reforms to the familiarity of Henry VIII's last years. Given all this endorsement, surely Mary would be kind.

What, however, Jane was almost certainly ignorant of was the unease which was growing over the issue of Mary's marriage. The queen had to marry – that was obvious. She needed a man to rule for her and a husband to beget an heir, and given Mary's years that need was urgent. The country was unanimous that it did not want a foreigner and the best-qualified Englishman on offer was Edward Courtenay, whom the queen had just restored to the earldom of Devon, forfeited by his father, one of Henry VIII's victims. Despite this, barely three months after her triumph over Jane, Mary had settled privately on marrying Charles V's son, Philip of Spain.[1] When her choice began to be discussed in confidential government circles it immediately became plain that there was opposition. By the beginning of November the secret was out more generally, and when a parliamentary delegation requested that she marry within the realm, Mary lost her temper.[2] Negotiators arriving from Spain were pelted with snow-balls by the London apprentices and when on 14 and 15 January the terms of the marriage treaty were made public to the court and to the city of London, 'almost each man was abashed, looking daily for worse matters to grow shortly after'.[3]

In reality, 'worse matters' were already afoot.[4] A small group of MPs and former MPs had concluded at the end of November that Mary would not be deterred by the overwhelming dislike of her subjects for a foreign prince. She had to be stopped. They had wide connections which led to hopes that major members of the nobility might support them, and they built close ties with de Noailles, the French ambassador, but in the end the only aristocrats to join the conspiracy were Edward Courtenay and Jane Grey's father, the duke of Suffolk, along with his two brothers, Lord Thomas and Lord John.[5] Precisely what their object was other than stopping the Spanish marriage seems never to have been agreed. Under questioning the conspirators denied any wish to harm the queen, but had they succeeded she must at least have been deposed, with Princess Elizabeth the obvious alternative and Courtenay as her husband. When the princess herself was interrogated she stoutly asserted her innocence and rivers of ink have failed to settle the extent of her involvement. Elizabeth's own words were: 'Much suspected by me, Nothing proved can be'.[6] Despite the lack of a positive objective, on 22 December a plan was agreed for a four-pronged march on London, Sir Peter Carew from the West Country, Sir Thomas Wyatt from Kent, Sir James Crofts from Herefordshire and the Grey family from Leicestershire. Palm Sunday, 18 March, was to be D-Day.[7]

Luck did not favour the conspirators. Carew went off to Devon but on 2 January the council summoned him to appear before them. Why is not clear, although rumours of trouble were rampant. Assuming that the cat was out of the bag, Carew did not obey, Courtenay broke down and confessed and the conspiracy went off at half-cock. Wyatt did manage to raise an army in Kent which was able to threaten London, but the city stood firm for Mary and the rebels surrendered on 7 February. By then Carew's efforts in the West had proved ineffectual and he had fled to France; Crofts achieved nothing on the Welsh Marches and was soon arrested. As for Jane's father, in January 1554 he was at the family's house at Sheen, unwell, but, of course, totally exposed should the details of the plot become known – as they were bound to. Precisely what ensued is confused. The earl of Shrewsbury reported that 'on Friday' (i.e. 26 January) Suffolk had 'stolen away from his house at Sheen and run away with his two brethren to Leicestershire'.[8] The confession which the duke wrote afterwards 'with his own hand' said that he moved on hearing of the arrest of Sir Edward Warner, and that did take place on the 26th.[9] The Tower resident had a different story. On the morning of Thursday 25 January (the day Wyatt raised his standard at Maidstone), there came a messenger to [the duke] from the queen that he should come to court. 'Marry,' quoth he, 'I was coming to her grace. You may see I am booted and spurred ready to ride, and I will but break my fast and go.' So he gave the messenger a reward and caused him to be made to drink, and so thence departed himself, no man knows wither.[10]

Both stories are, however, contradicted by the testimony of John Bowyer, the duke's secretary.[11] According to Bowyer, early on the morning of Wednesday 24 January the duke sent him to London to tell his brothers to leave by 6 p.m. that day, and in the early hours of Thursday 25th, Bowyer and the brothers caught up with Suffolk at Lutterworth in Leicestershire where the duke was spending the night in the house of a servant named Johnson. This means that Suffolk left Sheen on 24 January and establishes that the story of his receiving a message from the queen was simply rumour.[12] From Lutterworth the party seems to have gone to the family home at Bradgate to issue letters summoning support from at least Northampton and Coventry.[13] The duke may also have been putting out propaganda. According to Renard, one of his servants was caught carrying a placard calling for an uprising to resist 12,000 Spaniards massed at Calais and as many in the west country, all ready to conquer England.[14] On Monday 29 January Suffolk moved to Leicester where the next morning he summoned the town to rise against the Spaniards. His proclamation fell on deaf ears and his attempts to rally support by offering 6d. a day were hardly any more successful there than they had been en route, so that when he moved to Coventry he had only 140 men. By then the three brothers had been proclaimed traitors and the earl of Huntingdon sent to arrest them, so they arrived to find the city gates shut.[15] The duke – apparently sighting Huntingdon's advancing posse – withdrew a few miles to his Warwickshire house at Astley and dismissed the fifty men still with him 'to make the best shift each one for his own safeguard that he might, and distributing to every of them a portion of money, according to their qualities [status] and his store at that present'.[16]

What ensued was akin to farce. The duke himself decided to flee into Wales with Denmark as an ultimate refuge – Florio said Scotland – but he was let down by a servant and, with his younger brother John, was reduced to hiding 'in secret places within Astley Park'.[17] According to the imperial ambassador, the duke took refuge in a large hollow oak tree where he was betrayed by a dog barking.[18] The chair and table the duke is supposed to have used while in hiding are today displayed in the Long Gallery of Arbury Hall.[19] Lord John was found under a pile of hay. Later English sources held that the duke, after some days, was betrayed for a reward by the park-keeper, named Underwood, but the concealment did not last that long for Grey was under arrest on 2 February.[20] The two brothers spent three days in custody at Coventry but by 10 February Huntingdon had conveyed them to the Tower under heavy escort.[21] Thomas Grey, meanwhile, had got away towards Wales, intending to reach the coast and a ship to France, but in a fortnight he only managed to get as far as Oswestry. There he was arrested and handed over to the Council for the Marches of Wales. That arrest, too, had elements of the ridiculous. His servant left the bag containing their money at the inn in the town and going back for it found himself interrogated and the truth came out. Lord Thomas arrived at the Tower under escort on 21 February.[22]

Despite the ludicrous end, the uprising Jane's father had planned for Palm Sunday had more substance than history usually allows.[23] Bowyer and the younger Grey brothers knew the route from London to Leicester along Watling Street like the back of their hands, yet on 24 January they took the road to Cambridge. Ostensibly this was to avoid Barnet but the real reason was to call on Sir Thomas Wroth at Cheshunt.[24] By then it was 9 p.m. and dark, but they were not invited in. Instead Wroth, a staunch Protestant and a former supporter of Jane Grey, came out with Sir John Harington, Thomas Seymour's erstwhile retainer. A long discussion ended with Wroth and Harington 'saying it was too late to move' and a servant being sent to guide the Greys back to Watling Street. On Saturday evening Bishop Gardiner arrested Harington and by Sunday evening Wroth was at Leighs Priory in north Essex, the home of the Marian loyalist Lord Rich, to lay information about the visit of the Greys on the previous Friday. Bishop Gardiner was not taken in; he called for Wroth's arrest and Sir Thomas fled abroad.[25] Harington spent many weeks in the Tower under suspicion. Another sign of planning is that the duke genuinely believed that the earl of Huntingdon was coming to join him; after all he had been one of the most intransigent of Mary's opponents in July 1553. Yet what Huntingdon did when Suffolk's move became known was to go to Mary and beg to be sent to arrest the duke. The fact that the Hastings and the Grey families had long been rivals for local status convinced Renard that this was a genuine demonstration of loyalty, but it looks more like an attempt to create an alibi, akin to Wroth running to Lord Rich.[26] It is clear, too, that the duke fully expected Coventry to rally to his call. His agent had been assured that 'the whole of this town is my lord's and at his commandment, unless it be certain of the counsel of the town'. That caveat was, however, fatal. The mayor closed the city on the urgings of the recorder Edward Saunders, who the previous July had swung Coventry to support Mary. Taken all in all, it looks very much as though the earl of Huntingdon, Sir Thomas Wroth, Sir John Harington and significant numbers of the citizens of Coventry were complicit in Suffolk's plans. The duke's journey to Leicestershire was not the flight triggered by the arrest of Warner which he claimed in his confession. Nor had he, as he implied at his trial, acted almost on impulse when his brother Thomas 'persuaded him rather to fly into his country [Leicestershire and Warwickshire] than to abide, saying that "it was to be feared he should be put again into the Tower, whereas being in his country and among friends and tenants, who durst fetch him?" '[27] Once Wyatt had moved, the duke's only hope was to ride to the Midlands and implement what he could of the plans he had laid.

In all of this no-one was less involved than Jane Grey. She knew nothing, and none of the conspirators ever said a word in her favour. Far from it. Northumberland's treachery meant that Jane's was the last name to invoke. Yet if her father did not join the plot in order to advance his daughter, why did he listen to the conspirators? As he admitted, he had been leniently treated in July 1553 and common sense alone would suggest either keeping his head down or at least waiting until others had moved effectively.[28] Renard says that Suffolk stated that he had been brought into the plot by Croft and Carew who had convinced him that Mary had to be replaced by Elizabeth. Since, at that moment, the ambassador was doing all he could to implicate the princess, this last might be suspect, but at his trial the duke admitted having said that if necessary he would undertake, with a hundred gentlemen, to put the crown on Courtenay's head – evidently as king consort.[29] Another story was that the government flushed out the duke by choosing him to command the forces against Wyatt.[30] One factor must have been Suffolk's Protestantism. On 1 November Renard reported that 'the duke of Suffolk is doing bad work in connection with religion and the queen is angry with him for his manner of abusing her clemency and good nature', and on 14 November that the queen was 'truly irritated against the duke of Suffolk'.[31] What Renard was referring to can only be guessed at. Parliament had opened on 5 October. Had he taken his seat in the Lords in time to speak against the repeal of the Edwardian reforms?[32] Was Suffolk giving aid and comfort to reformist clergy in the public disputation on the sacrament which had opened in St Paul's on 18 October?[33] Perhaps his protégé Ralph Skinner had been a leader among the sixty MPs who 'stood for the true religion'. But if Suffolk's underlying motives were religious, once talk began about positive action against the Spanish marriage a significant change came over his behaviour. On 17 November the ambassador reported that 'The duke of Suffolk has made his confession as to religion' – whatever that may mean – 'and the queen has therefore remitted his composition of £20,000 and reinstated him by means of a general pardon'.[34] Ten days later Renard commented that the clemency Mary had shown to the duke and others 'has done much good and won over numbers of the nobility who have heard of these lords' devotion to the queen'.[35] As Christmas approached Suffolk even let it be known that he was in favour of the impending Spanish marriage.[36] Henry Grey was covering his tracks.

Suffolk himself explained his alienation from the crown not by religion but by his arrest in July 1553 and 'the small esteem in which the council held him'. Evidently he did not see why, of all those who had supported and then abandoned Northumberland, he should have been treated as he had been. Six senior peers had switched allegiance to Mary: Suffolk, Winchester, Bedford, Arundel, Shrewsbury and Pembroke. Suffolk alone had suffered the disparagement of arrest and incarceration in the Tower – if only for a couple of nights. Suffolk alone had not been appointed to Mary's privy council. Suffolk alone had not received a summons to Mary's first parliament and had to be admitted after the session had begun.[37] He, the only English duke. Clearly he did not see that being Jane's father should have made any difference. Holinshed was evidently right when describing the duke as 'of stomach stout and hardy, hasty and soon kindled ... [not] well able to bear injuries, but yet forgiving and forgetting the same if the party would seem but to acknowledge his fault and seek reconcilement'.[38] Perhaps Mary could have handled him better, but he was being wholly unrealistic if he imagined that the crown would make the first move.

If this reading of Henry Grey is correct, arriving in the Tower on Saturday 10 February to be told that his daughter was to die on Monday 12 February must have been a total shock. What had she to do with his recent activities? Incarcerated in the Tower, how could she be guilty of anything? The chronology of the decision to execute Jane is unclear. A new trial was not necessary; the condemnation of November 1553 still stood. According to the observer in the Tower the sentence was initially scheduled for Friday 9 February and he conjectured that the respite was because Suffolk had not by then arrived.[39] That seems unlikely. On 21 January the government knew something of Suffolk's involvement in the plot; his hurried move to Leicestershire confirmed this; on 2 February news of his capture was received.[40] What more would his presence in the

Tower add? Commendone's account supplied the real explanation for the delay. Once the execution had been agreed, the Benedictine John Feckenham had been sent to interview Jane, and he secured a three-day reprieve, i.e. Friday, Saturday and Sunday, to allow time to convert Jane to the Roman church.[41] This means that Thursday 8 February is the latest date for the monk's initial visit and thus of the decision to execute. *An Epistle* puts the meeting on Wednesday 7 February. Simon Renard reported that the execution had been planned for Tuesday.[42] What is important in this is that whatever the differences, Commendone, Renard and *An Epistle* each point to a decision to execute taken in the middle of the week or possibly earlier, in other words at the very height of the Wyatt threat. On the previous Saturday his rebel forces had arrived at the Southwark end of London Bridge, which was held by loyalists, but on 6 February Sir Thomas suddenly executed a night flanking move aiming to enter the city via Fleet Street. The court took fright. While she was still in her bedchamber the Queen held an emergency council meeting and not until late afternoon were her forces victorious. Given this, the decision to execute Jane and Guildford looks like panic.

There are, on the other hand, hints of an old score being settled. On 28 January the council sent a letter to county officers claiming that the duke and his brothers, with Carew and Wyatt, had 'conspired to stir our subjects to rebellion pretending upon false promises that the Prince of Spain and the Spaniards should come over to conquer this said realm, while indeed they traitorously purpose to advance Lady Jane his daughter and Guildford Dudley her husband'.[43] This was undoubtedly false.[44] Moreover the crown knew that it was false. A royal letter sent out the day before had stated that the Greys and others were directing their actions 'against us and the laws lately made by authority of parliament for the restoration of the true Catholic Christian religion, making their only pretence, nevertheless (though falsely) to let [prevent] the coming in of the Prince of Spain and his train, spreading most false rumours that the said Prince and the Spaniards intend to conquer this our realm'.[45] Circulating the lie that the rebels were resurrecting Jane's claim could have been a propaganda ploy to blacken them by association with the hated Northumberland.[46] Alternatively, it could have been intended to make it impossible for Mary to continue to protect Jane; a second rising in her favour had to mean death. Ambassador Renard certainly used the occasion to press again for her execution and he was very concerned lest Mary gave way to her instinct for mercy.[47] Not until 17 February did he have the satisfaction of assuring Philip of Spain that 'At present there is no other occupation than the cutting off of heads and inflicting exemplary punishment. Jane of Suffolk who made herself queen and her husband have been executed.'[48] Commendone has it that Mary was on the point of having Jane reprieved 'but judging that such an action might give rise to new riots, the Council ruled it out'.[49] Florio, who was sympathetic to Mary, believed that she was persuaded by 'papist' warnings about security and urged on by Habsburg advice from Brussels.[50] As we have seen, John Ponet blamed the council, accusing former supporters of Jane 'at this present in the highest authority in the queen's house, and the chiefest officers and doers in the common wealth' of being 'counsellors (I will not say procurers) of the innocent Lady Jane's death'.[51] John Knox, in what surely must be a reference to the deaths of Jane and Guildford, saw the influence of Gardiner and papists on the council corrupting Mary 'for who could have thought that such cruelty could have entered into the heart of a woman and her that is called a virgin, that she would thirst the blood of innocents and of such as by just laws and faithful witnesses can never be proved to have offended by themselves'.[52] Why it should have been thought important to destroy Jane is strange. It did eliminate her as a claimant to the throne but the place of the other Grey sisters in the succession was unaffected. Would her death remove an uncomfortable reminder of earlier treachery? Was it revenge on Suffolk for endangering the settlement of the year before? Or were the executions unfinished business and Guildford Dudley the real target? Certainly Stephen Gardiner felt it necessary to keep up the pressure for Jane's death until the last. On the day before she was to die, he preached a sermon at court which attacked the whole reformist agenda and ended with a plea to Mary not to grant mercy to erring individuals but instead 'be merciful to the body of the commonwealth and conservation thereof, which could not be unless the rotten and hurtful members thereof were cut off and consumed'.[53] Mary was ultimately responsible for what was both a crime and a folly, but the guilt may well lie elsewhere.

Jane expressed no pleasure at the initial visit of John Feckenham.[54] But the stocky, red-faced Midlander had considerable tact and held back on his real mission. 'Madam, I lament your heavy case; and yet I doubt not but that you bear out this sorrow of yours with a constant and patient mind.' Jane's response hardly suggested pliability:

> You are welcome unto me, Sir, if your coming be to give me Christian exhortation. And as for my heavy case, I thank God, I do so little lament it, that rather I account the same for a more manifest declaration of God's

favour toward me, than ever he showed me at any time before. And therefore there is no cause why either you or others which bear me good will, should lament or be grieved with this my case, being a thing so profitable for my soul's health.[55]

Commendone simply says that when Feckenham explained that he was there to 'free her from the superstition in which she had grown up' she replied that 'it was too late for such an office as there was not sufficient time to attend to so many matters'.[56] Pollini has it that she sat in silence while Feckenham expounded 'the truth of the old religion' and the mistakes of the new, and that her response was that to change religion 'concerned the entire health of one's soul' and required time and thought.[57] Either way the reply was enough to give Feckenham the lever to secure the reprieve. Florio records things differently.[58] Jane did discuss changing religion, but only to make the point that this must not violate good conscience but must reflect genuine conviction. Also she did ask for more time, but only 'for one day of life to thank God for his grace given me'. When Feckenham returned with the news that Mary had granted three days 'to enable her to amend her errors', Jane was not best pleased. She had not asked for that and 'during his absence she had taken leave of all earthly matters so that she did not even think of the fear of death'; her mind was now on 'the eternal light'.[59] Yet when the Benedictine explained that he was following the queen's instructions, Jane accepted and was rapidly seduced by the old lure of a cut-and-thrust argument. Very probably too, debating with Feckenham was a relief, something of an analgesic, and the account which Jane then wrote out kept her mind occupied even longer. It was what she was good at. As she told the monk, her great pleasure was in good letters and the scriptures.[60] The account of the discussion which she wanted to preserve for posterity ended, as we have seen, with the words, 'There were many more things whereof we reasoned, but these were the chief, by me Jane Dudley'.[61] But the English sources continue with an exchange 'spoken openly', i.e. overheard by others:

> After this Feckenham took his leave saying that he was sorry for her, 'For' (said he) 'I am sure we two shall never meet.'

(Between the heaven of the believer and the hell of the unbeliever was a great gulf fixed.)

> 'True it is' (quoth she) 'that we shall never meet unless God turn your heart, for I am sure (unless you repent and turn to God) you are in an evil case and I pray to God in the bowels of his mercy to send you his Holy Spirit.'

Not she but Feckenham was in an 'evil case'. But then the girl in Jane broke through and she added: 'For [God] has given you his great gift of utterance, if it please him to open the eyes of your heart to his truth.'[62] Intellectually she had yielded not an inch, but kindness can pierce the strongest defences. In a meeting of minds which Protestant sources refused even to mention, Jane agreed that Feckenham could accompany her to the scaffold – perhaps she even asked him.

26

THE RIVER OF JORDAN

WITH Feckenham's visits behind her, Jane faced the last hours of her life. She passed much of the time in prayer, meditation and reading her Bible, and with thoughts of her family.[1] If she did write to her mother, as Florio states, all trace of it has disappeared, but we do have printed texts of the letter to her sister Katherine which Jane wrote in her copy of the Greek New Testament.[2] Nothing has survived to tell us of the relationship between Jane and the thirteen-year-old. The two were presumably educated similarly. Katherine knew Latin and some Greek, and was later in the reformist camp, but nothing suggests that the younger sister shared Jane's intellectual interests or her all-consuming religious commitment.[3] One possibility, therefore, is that Jane had little in common with the girl she wrote to, and from that it is easy to jump to the conclusion that her letter was a ponderous sisterly admonition to someone who may already have shown signs of her later propensity to allow emotion to rule her head.[4] Jane began,

> I have here sent you, good sister Katherine, a book the which, although it be not outwardly trimmed with gold, yet inwardly it is more worth than precious stones. It is the book, dear sister, of the law of the Lord. It is the testament and last will, which he bequeathed unto us wretches which shall lead you to the path of eternal joy. And if you with a good mind read it, and with an earnest mind follow it, it shall bring you to an immortal and everlasting life. It shall teach you to live and learn you to die.[5]

This would certainly not be the way to write to a teenager today, but earlier generations accepted that the more mature had a responsibility to guide those who were younger. The shadow of the scaffold must have made that responsibility even greater. Equally, however, we must recognize that Jane was also addressing herself. The comforts and certainties she was urging on Katherine were the comforts and certainties which she had to hold on to through the ensuing hours.

> [T]rust not the tenderness of your age shall lengthen your life for as soon, if God will, goes the young as the old. Wherefore labour always to learn to die. Defy the world, deny the devil and despise the flesh and delight your self only in the Lord. Be penitent for your sins and yet despair not. Be strong in faith and yet presume not and desire with St Paul to be dissolved and to be with Christ, with whom even in death there is life.[6]

Then the personal becomes specific:

> Rejoice in Christ as I trust I do and seeing that you have the name of a Christian, as near as you can follow in the steps of your master, Christ, and take up your cross. Lay your sins on his back and always embrace him. And touching my death, rejoice as I do, good sister, that I shall be delivered of this corruption and put on incorruption, for I am assured that I shall for losing of a mortal life win an immortal life.[7]

Finally, real feeling for Katherine does break through, and a desperate concern for her eternal future. Would she be strong enough to stand up to the likes of Feckenham? '[Immortal life] I pray God grant you, and send you of his grace to live in his fear and to die in the true Christian faith from the which in God's name I exhort you that you never swerve neither for hope of life nor for fear of death.' It was the message to Harding again. Compromise was not an option:

> if you will deny his truth [in order] to lengthen your life, God will deny you and yet shorten your days. And if you will cleave to him he will prolong your days to your comfort and his glory to the which glory God bring me now and you hereafter when it shall please him to call you. Fare well good sister and put your only trust in God who only must help you. Amen Your loving sister, Jane Dudley.[8]

There is no external evidence to indicate that Katherine had had any direct contact with Jane, but the urgency which builds up during the letter could reflect something of the kind: a visit or at least a letter? That would certainly explain a remarkable comparison which Jane used to extol the value of the gift of her New Testament:

> It shall win you more than you should have gained by the possession of your woeful father's lands. For as if God had prospered him, you should have inherited his lands, so if you apply diligently this book, seeking to direct your

life after it, you shall be an inheritor of such riches as neither the covetous shall withdraw from you neither the thief neither yet the moth corrupt.[9]

Had Katherine lamented that her father's actions had destroyed not only Jane but her future as well?

Writing in her Greek New Testament was possibly the only way Jane could hope to send her sister a keepsake.[10] In law the erstwhile queen now owned nothing – even her clothes would become the property of the executioner. Alternatively, it could be that in the final days the security around her tightened and she was denied paper to write on. Certainly her final message to her father had to be written in the prayer book she was to carry to the scaffold, and to get that to Suffolk clearly required the collaboration of Sir John Brydges, the lieutenant of the Tower. Soldier and courtier though Brydges was, and 'much addicted to the old religion', in the months Jane had been his responsibility the sixty-one-year-old had become fond of his remarkable prisoner. He agreed to show the duke her message, but asked if he could himself retain the book as a memento.[11] The duke would not live to keep it; neither Jane nor the lieutenant could have had any expectation of that. Nevertheless Jane's message to her father was not despairing. It was positive and redolent of the faith they shared:

> The Lord comfort your grace, and that in his word wherein all creatures only are to be comforted. And though it has pleased God to take away two of your children [herself and Guildford], yet think not, I most humbly beseech your grace, that you have lost them, but trust that we, by leaving this mortal life, have won an immortal life. And I for my part, as I have honoured your grace in this life, will pray for you in another life.
> Your grace's humble daughter, Jane Dudley[12]

The conventions are still in place, but it would be hard to deny the underlying affection.

With her letters written, it is probable that Jane sat down to compose what was in effect her own epitaph. She had told Feckenham on his initial visit that her greatest joy had been to study Latin, Greek and Hebrew and to engage with good letters and especially holy scripture.[13] Now, with the hours ticking away, she turned for refuge to the one reality which had given her identity and never let her down. The result was a series of epigrams, the first in Latin, the next in Greek and the last in English.

> [Latin] If Justice is done with my body, my soul will find mercy in God
> [Greek] Death will give pain to my body for its sins, but the soul will be justified before God.

[English] If my faults deserve punishment, my youth at least, and my imprudence were worthy of excuse; God and posterity will show me favour.[14]

These sentences are only found in the Italian writers, and they confuse them with what Jane would write in the prayer book promised to Brydges.[15] For that reason they have been dismissed as apocryphal, but that seems unlikely.[16] Commendone had them within months of Jane's death, and not only are the sentiments right in context, it would be entirely in character for Jane to take refuge in scholarship. What is more, the fact that they have come down to us via Catholic sources suggests that it was a Catholic who preserved them and a rational speculation would point to John Feckenham. It would be wholly in accord with the empathy which had grown up between them for the monk to request or Jane wish to compose a valedictory for him.[17]

The decision was that the husband should die first on Tower Hill and then the wife inside the fortress, on Tower Green. Tower prisoners were normally executed early in the day, but it was February, and no doubt a mist from the river. Thus not until 10 o'clock was Guildford brought out of the fortress and handed over to Thomas Offley, the sheriff of London who had responsibility for that execution.[18] There had been no farewell to Jane. According to Commendone Guildford did ask to see her but Jane had refused.

> If their meeting could have been a means of consolation to their souls she would have been very glad to see him, but as their meeting would only tend to increase their misery and pain, it was better to put it off for the time being, as they would meet shortly elsewhere, and live bound by indissoluble ties.[19]

Some have seen this as the response of an ice maiden who despised her weak husband. More probably it reveals the struggle Jane was having to retain her own focus. The poise she maintained through the last hours of life was not bought easily, but as Guildford left under escort, she did watch from a window of the lodgings where she had lived alone for the last months.[20]

At the outer gate Dudley found himself surrounded by well-wishers, and begged them to pray for him.[21] We know the names of two of those he shook hands with, and, interestingly, both were supporters of Queen Mary. John Throckmorton is explicable. Although he joined her forces at Framlingham he had worked for Guildford's father and the council in 1553.[22] The other, Sir Anthony Browne, presents problems. He had been imprisoned in 1551 for hearing mass in Princess Mary's household, had carried her train when she entered London and would soon be appointed master of the horse to King Philip.[23] Does coming to say farewell to the young Dudley indicate that some at least of Mary's courtiers were unhappy with the decision to carry out the sentences? Observers noticed also that no priest accompanied the prisoner to the scaffold and this implies that Guildford had remained staunch to reform, unlike his father (who had been supported by the bishop of Worcester).

The short walk over, Guildford spoke to the crowd. He was brief and what he said has not come down to us. The marquis of Northampton, who was watching from the Devil's Tower, was too far away to hear.[24] Next Guildford kneeled down and prayed, 'holding up his eyes and hands to God many times', then he turned to the crowd and asked the people to pray for him. Finally he put his neck on the block and the executioner killed him with a single blow.[25] Recourse to the axe did not win the Queen many friends. Richard Grafton, who very probably had known Guildford, recalled ten years later that 'even those that never before the time of his execution saw him, did with lamentable tears bewail his death'.[26] The body was put on a cart and brought back into the Tower where Jane saw it being unloaded and taken into the Tower Chapel.[27] Holinshed's *Chronicle* says that she actually encountered the cart when she herself was being brought out to die, a 'miserable sight ... to her a double sorrow and grief', and many artists have been drawn to the emotion of that supposed meeting.[28] The reality is that Jane insisted on watching from a window, despite the efforts of her ladies to dissuade her.[29] She said 'Oh Guildford, Guildford' and perhaps something about the bitterness of death, but hardly the contrived conceit which Florio reported about the executions being the *antepasto* to the heavenly banquet.[30]

Waiting with Jane was the lieutenant of the Tower, Thomas Brydges his brother (and deputy), and Jane's two ladies, Mistress Ellen and Mistress Elizabeth Tilney.[31] Feckenham was also there, as promised. Executions in the Tower were the lieutenant's responsibility, so Sir John arranged that Jane would give her prayer book to his brother to be taken to her father and then kept by him. 'But please will you write in it for me?' Jane took a pen and wrote:

> Forasmuch as you have desired so simple a woman to write in so worthy a book, good Master Lieutenant, therefore I shall as a friend desire you, and as a Christian require you, to call upon God to incline your heart to his laws, to quicken you in his way, and not to take the word of truth utterly out of your mouth.[32]

Despite what lay ahead of her, Jane still felt compelled to urge even this
staunch traditionalist towards a more personal religious experience. Had
Jane discussed 'the word of truth' with Brydges during the past months?
And what made it imperative for him to respond was the death she and he
each faced:

> Live still to die, that by death you may purchase eternal life, and remember
> how the end of Methuselah, who, as we read in the scriptures, was the
> longest liver that was of a man, died at the last: for as the Preacher [Eccle-
> siastes] says, there is a time to be born and a time to die; and the day of death
> is better than the day of our birth.
> Yours, as the Lord knows, as a friend, Jane Dudley [plate 26]

By that time the executioner was back from Tower Hill and waiting.[33]
The lieutenant led Jane out followed by Feckenham and the others. The
diminutive former queen was in total command of her emotions, unlike
her two ladies who 'wonderfully wept'. Dressed as for her trial, all in black,
she carried her prayer book which she read from all the way: perhaps 'the
prayer of Queen Esther for help against her enemies', 'the Lord's Prayer
and holy ejaculations suitable to the condition of a person in tribulation',
the 'prayer for strength of mind to bear the cross', certainly the prayer 'for
grace to believe and trust in Christ Jesus'.[34] How many people watched
her we do not know; certainly not the thousand who saw Anne Boleyn die
at the same spot.[35] Jane's death was little more than an exercise in refuse
disposal. The party climbed the scaffold and Jane said to Thomas Brydges.
'Can I speak what is in my mind?' 'Yes, Madam.' She turned to those
watching. 'Good people, I am come hither to die, and by a law I am
condemned to the same; the fact indeed against the Queen's Highness was
unlawful and the consenting thereunto by me.'[36] Jane was observing the
convention that those about to die should concede the legality of their
sentence. But being condemned was not the same as being guilty, and she
continued: 'touching the procurement and desire thereof by me or on my
[be] half, I do wash my hands thereof in innocency before the face of God
and the face of you good Christian people this day'. And she wrung her
hands accordingly. Jane then spoke of death: 'I pray you all good Christian
people to bear me witness that I die a true Christian woman and that I do
look to be saved by no other mean, but only by the mercy of God, in the
merits of the blood of his only son Jesus Christ.' No-one must be in any
doubt. She was dying confident in salvation by faith alone. Catholics, of
course, would see that as arrogance and human pride, so Jane continued:
'I confess when I did know the word of God I neglected the same and

loved myself and the world, and therefore this plague or punishment is happily and worthily [deservedly] happened unto me for my sins.' But even in that there was divine mercy: 'I thank God of his goodness that he has thus given me a time and respite to repent.' Finally she asked for prayers, but with a defiant Protestant twist: not 'now good people, I pray you to assist me with your prayers' but 'now good people, while I am alive, I pray you to assist me with your prayers'. Only faith in this life secured salvation in the next; once the axe had fallen, she would be past being prayed for – praying for the dead was a Catholic superstition. To the last Jane was determined to witness to the truth – and in Greek, her beloved Greek, the word for 'witness' was 'martyr'.

Then Jane knelt and, with the first sign of uncertainty, pointed to Psalm 51 in her prayer book and asked Feckenham, 'Shall I say this psalm?' It was the Miserere: 'Have mercy upon me O God, after thy great goodness: according to the multitude of thy mercies, do away mine offences.' 'Yes', said Feckenham, so Jane said the psalm 'in English in a most devout manner to the end', possibly with Feckenham saying it with her in Latin.[37] Then she stood up to thank the monk for keeping her company, and gently tease him that during those few days she was more bored by him than frightened by the shadow of death.[38] It was said with affection for she then embraced him and said 'Go and may God satisfy every wish of yours'.[39] Next the preliminaries. Gloves and handkerchief to Mistress Tilney; prayer book to Thomas Brydges; gown – though when the heads-man moved to help her she said 'let me alone' and turned to the two women.[40] Headdress next and her collar. The executioner then knelt to ask her forgiveness which she gave 'most willingly' and he told her to move on to the straw. Only then she saw the block and said, 'I pray you, despatch me quickly.' But when she knelt down she asked anxiously, 'Will you take it off before I lay me down?' 'No madam.' Jane then tossed her hair forward to bare her neck and tied it with the blindfold she had been given. And with darkness panic. 'What shall I do? Where is it?' The rest of the scaffold party froze and a bystander had to guide Jane to the block. She put her neck on it. 'Lord, into thy hands I commend my spirit.' And the horror was over.

Or perhaps not quite. The shock drained the Tower of all resolution. Hours later Jane's headless body still lay on the scaffold in a welter of blood.[41]

27

AFTERLIFE

TODAY Jane Grey lives thanks to one iconic image. *The Execution of Lady Jane Grey* by the French artist Paul Delaroche caused a sensation when first exhibited in Paris in 1834 and, more than four hundred and fifty years after her judicial murder, still stuns the crowds as it hangs in the National Gallery. [plate 28] For many years art critics dismissed Delaroche, labelling his historical paintings with their painstaking attention to realism as 'romantic', 'sentimental', 'melodramatic'. He was, however, 'perhaps the most famous (and consequently the most collected) painter of the day' and now he is taken more seriously.[1] Public taste is not always wrong.

Delaroche's search for the dramatic led him to the most poignant moment in the execution when Jane had to be helped to find the block, but there is more to the painting than drama. His Jane is a victim. She is young and helpless. She is innocent – her pallor, her dress and the blindfold provide the only light in the painting – and her fragility contrasts with the strength of the male figures. This is rape. To emphasize darkness, Delaroche deliberately translates the execution from the open air. Jane is alone (her ladies have collapsed), she is in the grip of a merciless system (the executioner is merely curious); only a casual kindness helps her to the death she voluntarily accepts. The painting is a perceptive attempt to penetrate some of the emotions in one of the world's most repulsive individual atrocities, along with the fate of the daughter of Sejanus in first-century Rome, Prince Arthur in the reign of King John, the Princes in the Tower, Louis XVI 's son, Napoleon's son and the children of the last Tsar – children slaughtered not for what they had done, not even in the course of genocide, but specifically because of the bed they were born in.

Delaroche was not the first artist to respond to Lady Jane's story.[2] From the early seventeenth century, portraits supposedly of Jane figured regularly in histories in Britain and in Europe. The events in her life were less often depicted, but in the eighteenth century scenes from Jane's life become more common, although portraits do continue to dominate.[3] This was particularly true in popular play texts and editions of John Foxe's martyrology.[4] Then from the 1760s 'history painting' came to dominate the artistic scene, that is painting which demonstrated noble actions in an increasingly British (not classical) past, depicted for the instruction of subsequent generations. Jane was an immediate favourite.[5] Advised increasingly by antiquarian studies, painters began to pay attention not just to the subject but to historical verisimilitude – no longer, therefore, Jane in eighteenth-century costume with no reference to her supposed portraits – and from the 1820s canvases presenting the 'historic' Jane came thick and fast. Between 1827 – the date of Charles Robert Leslie's *Lady Jane Grey prevailed upon to accept the Crown* – and 1877, twenty-four paintings featuring Jane were exhibited at the Royal Academy.[6] The apotheosis was reached in 1855 in the rebuilt Houses of Parliament. Twelve Tudor subjects were selected to decorate the Prince's Chamber in the House of Lords and one of these was '*Lady Jane Grey at her Studies*'. The 760 mm□ bronze bas-relief by William Theed shows her with a copy of Plato in her hand, her lute resting nearby, interrupted in her reading by the arrival of Ascham. Jane Grey in the pantheon of British glory.[7] [plate 21] Delaroche was, thus, very much in the fashion, and he was not the only foreign artist drawn to Jane's story. Henri Jean-Baptiste Victoire Fradelle from Lille settled in London and painted an earlier attempt at the meeting of Jane and Roger Ascham.[8] Commissioned by the New York businessman Lumen Reed, George Whiting Flagg set out to paint *Mary Queen of Scots Preparing for Execution*, only to change to Jane when he discovered that Mary was 'too old at the time of her execution to make an interesting picture'.[9]

Much of this nineteenth-century artistic output reflected the Victorian obsession with 'the victimized child woman', but Jane Grey as the suffering innocent already had a long history.[10] Within months of her death, George Cavendish imagined her ghost complaining:

> I was your instrument to work your purpose by;
> All was but falsehood to blear withal my eye.

> O ye counsellors, why did ye me advance
> To a queen's estate, full sore against my mind,
> Assuring me it was my just inheritance.
> Now, contrary to your suggestion, I perceive and find
> All was in vain, your wits were too blind
> Me to delude against the form of law;

Forsooth, you were to blame, and all not worth a straw.

> Your creeping and kneeling to me, poor innocent
> Brought me to weening [agreeing] with your persuasions
> That all was truth which you untruly meant.
> Such were your arguments, such were your reasons
> Made to me sundry times and seasons
> Your subtle dealing deceived hath both you and me.
> Dissimulation will not serve, now may you see.[11]

In 1562 a broadsheet appeared in the streets of London entitled *The lamentacion that Ladie Jane made, saiying for my father's proclamacion now must I lese my head*.[12] Its sixteen verses also stress Jane's vulnerability and innocence:

> The headsman kneeled down to her
> To forgive him her death.
> 'Friend,' she said, 'God forgive thee,
> With all my heart and faith.'
>
> She kissed him, and gave him a reward
> And said to him, incontinent,
> 'I pray thee yet remember afterward,
> That thou hast headed an innocent.

The next verse even linked her treatment to the betrayal of Christ:

> She gave the Lieutenant her book
> Which was covered all with gold,
> Prayed him thereinto to look
> For his sake that Judas sold.

At the opposite end of the market was the Latin of the polite society poets, for example the elegy by Sir Thomas Chaloner entitled 'A lament on the death of that most eminent heroine, Lady Jane Grey, daughter of Henry, duke of Suffolk who was smitten with the axe and died in most steadfast spirit'.[13] Famous for his skill in classical verse, Chaloner had been cautious in expressing public support for reform during Mary's reign, but in verse he presents Jane (whom he had known) as 'a heroine fearlessly suffering an undeserved death', and mounts a fierce attack on those responsible for killing such a paragon, specifically Queen Mary.[14] Indeed Chaloner declares that Mary's shortened life and her 'sickly feelings in her long-failing body' were God's judgement on her pitiless conduct.[15] He attributes this not to the queen's bigoted Catholicism but to a denial of human, specifically feminine sympathy:

> Oh Jane ... should not at least the feelings of your kinswoman have been swayed by you? Or indeed the emotion of any woman? Despite knowing full well [where blame lay] for the trouble you were in, she did not pity you as you lay prostrate. Supposedly pious, her own actions showed her savage. Should not a lady once cultivated herself have been moved by another so cultivated as Jane?[16]

A generation later, the rising poet Michael Drayton included in his most popular work, *England's Heroicall Epistles* (1597), an imaginary letter from Jane to Guildford and his reply. This added love to the theme of innocence. There is reference to 'the days of idolatry and sin' of Mary's reign and ritual praise of Elizabeth, but the emotion between the couple and their artlessness is the main concern: 'Farewell sweet Guildford, know our end is near. Heaven is our home; we are but strangers here.' An appended historical note says: 'Seldom hath it ever been known of any woman endued with such wonderful gifts as was this lady, both for her wisdom and learning.'[17] With the growth of a professional theatre, Jane Grey the innocent was an obvious subject. Philip Henslowe, the impresario who ran two London playhouses, the Rose and the Fortune, paid eight pounds to a group of playwrights in October 1602 for the first of two plays about her and a down payment of five shillings on a sequel.[18] Neither part has survived, but it is possible that John Webster and Thomas Dekker cannibalized them to produce *The Famous History of Sir Thomas Wyatt*, a version of which was printed in 1607 and again in 1612. The play is a historical hotchpotch but the interest in Jane is again on her relationship with Guildford: 'In truth, I do enjoy a kingdom, having thee.'[19] Together they are the victims of parental ambition, and the play ends 'Thus much I'll say in their behalfs now dead, Their fathers' pride their lives have severed'.[20]

The idealization of Jane Grey did not fade as events receded still further. In his *Life and Raigne of King Edward the Sixth* [1630] John Hayward described her as 'a woman of the most rare and incomparable perfections' and referred to 'her excellent beauty adorned with all variety of virtues as a clear sky with stars, as a diadem with jewels'.[21] Fifty years later Bishop Burnet effused: 'as she was a beautiful and gracious person, so she had great parts and great virtues ... so humble, so gentle and pious that all people both admired and loved her. She had a mind wonderfully raised above the world. . . . the wonder of her age. She had a sweetness of temper as well as a strength of mind that charmed all who saw her.'[22]

Increasingly, Drayton's imaginative reconstruction was imitated. In 1715 there appeared a cantata, *The Meditation*, which explored Jane's emotions as she faced death.

> Not all thy Riches, Pomp or Power
> Th'Ambitions can relieve;
> He that hath least, and asks no more,
> Has all the World can give:
> Withdrawn from thee, my soul's at rest,
> And while to Heaven resign'd,
> By Conquer'd Passions, I'm confess'd
> The Monarch of my Mind.[23]

James Cawthorn, the headmaster of Tonbridge School, produced 'an epistle' from Jane to Guildford 'in the manner of Ovid' to be declaimed at speech day in 1753. Although it includes some lines of patriotic anti-Catholicism, the principal thrust of the imagined letter is the attempt of Jane to provide wifely comfort to her husband.

> What comforts can a wretched wife afford
> The last sad moments of her dying lord?
> With what fond tear, what love-impassion'd sigh,
> Soothe the dear mourner ere he reach the sky?
> [. . .]
> While Heav'n shall leave one pulse of life
> I still am woman, and am still a wife.[24]

When four years later George Keate, the friend of Voltaire, also published a lengthy verse, *Epistle from Lady Jane Grey to Lord Guildford Dudley*, he explained in a preface the principles behind such pieces. Having sketched Jane's life, he wrote:

> Such were the Distresses that surrounded her, when I ventured to put the pen into her hand: awake as she was, to every Passion and Delicacy of Sentiment, which Love, Disappointment, and Calamity could give Birth to; yet, by the Force of Religion, subduing their Poignancy, and at last totally triumphing over them. I much doubt whether I may have done sufficient Justice to the Character of this virtuous Lady; but hope at least, that I have not departed from Nature, in any Sentiment which I have attributed to her.[25]

However, not all treatments were so serious. The *Opera Epilogue to the Tragedy of Lady Jane Grey* put on in Dublin in 1729 has Jane return as 'a restless ghost' and lead an attack on erring husbands.

> You Husbands, too, who follow lawless Pleasures,
> And dare, at Home, neglect your Bosom-Treasures:
> Know, I shall rise t'assert the Female Cause,
> The Guardian Genius of connubial Laws:
> I'll make ye, ev'ry Night your Crimes atone;
> Nor Wifes in sep'rate Beds shall sigh alone:
> Like Marg'rets grimly Ghost, I'll haunt such Hectors:
> And shake their Beds with thund'ring Curtain-Lectures.
>
> Fond Husbands, I charge ye, to Night,
> Each Cherish his Fair in his Arms;
> When closely for fear of a Spright,
> They hug ye with tender Alarms.

The piece ends by warning each husband 'to avoid a Wife's Curse, Still take his own *goose* for a *swan*'.[26]

The romantic emotions in Jane's story attracted attention abroad. Her letters were published in Tartu, Rouen and Zurich[27] A biography appeared in Philadelphia.[28] In Dresden in 1832 Edw Sommer published *Johanne Gray. Trauerspiel in fünf Acten*.[29] In Paris in 1844, the poet Alexandre Soumet and his daughter Gabrielle d'Altenheym matched this with *Jane Grey*, a tragedy also in five acts.[30] There were imaginative pieces, as in Christian Barth's *Bilder aus dem innern Leben* (1868–72), while Charles Alphonse Brot's 1835 novel *Jane Grey. Episode de l'histoire d'Angleterre* was put on the stage in 1857.[31] In 1863 came Jean Marie Dargaud's *Histoire de Jane Grey en cinq actes*. Operatic composers were equally attracted to the story, although nothing has entered the repertoire. Donizetti considered Jane as a possible subject when his *Maria Stuarda* was banned in Italy in 1834. In 1836 Nicola Vaccai's *Giovanna Gray Tragedia lirica in tre parti* was played in Milan, but without success.[32] Antonio d'Antoni's opera was never performed. Later operatic composers who have tackled the theme are Henri-Paul Busser and Arnold Rosner.[33] In 1886 Charles Oberthür wrote a cantata and there have been a number of ballads, including one by Arnold Schoenberg.[34] France in particular saw a surge of writing on Jane to parallel Delaroche's painting. In 1831 the *Société libre d'émulation de Rouen* had published a substantial piece on her life and writings.[35] Two years later a short story in the *Musée des Familles* described the events of 12 February 1554 as by the executioners involved.[36] Jane's youthfulness drew particular attention. The *Galerie des Enfans Célèbres, ou Histoire des Jeunes Gens qui se sont Illustres* (1836) by le Comte de Barins was followed by Jane figuring in *La Jeunesse Historique et Célèbre* (1860), *La Galerie des Enfans Célèbres ou Panthéon de la Jeunesse* (1866) and *Les Enfants célèbres, ou Histoire des enfants qui se son immortalisés par le Malheur, la Piété, le Courage, le Génie, le Savoir et les talents* (1870).[37]

Concern with the sentiment of Jane's story could, of course, easily slide into invention, and Jane Grey became a staple figure in 'historical fiction', and remains so. An early instance is the anonymous *Lady Jane Grey, an Historical Tale in 2 volumes* which appeared in 1791. It is full of letters between Jane and individuals real and fanciful, including a 'Lady Laurana de M' who was supposedly imprisoned in the Tower and fell in love with Edward Courtenay. As recently as 2004 these were republished as possibly genuine, despite the publisher having been the William Lane who made a fortune from the Minerva Press 'gothic' novels which Jane Austen satirized.[38] Another example is *The Tablette Booke of Ladye Mary Keyes owne sister to the misfortunate Ladye Jane Dudlie Writt in the Yeare of Oure Lorde Fifteene hundred and Seventie-seven* (1861). Claiming to be a reprint of a 1604 publication, whenever possible it includes genuine historical material and keeps up the fiction (and the cod 'Tudor' spelling) for 337 pages. In fact the book is by Flora F. Wylde and deserves the verdict passed on the 'autobiography' she foisted on her grandmother Flora MacDonald: 'so full of obvious inaccuracies that it could not have been written by the heroine'.[39] Few novelists, however, have been as fevered as William Harrison Ainsworth. Although initially he was praised by Walter Scott, in 1881 *Punch* described him as 'the greatest axe-and-neck-romancer of our time who is quite at the head of his profession'.[40] The impact of historical novels was significantly increased by the addition of plates, and here Ainsworth used George Cruickshank, the illustrator of Dickens. Jane features in Ainsworth's fourth major novel, *The Tower of London* (1840). It is a complicated farrago of nonsense loosely built on the 1553 crisis with the imperial ambassador Simon Renard as only the most Machiavellian of a cast list of villains. Jane is not the leading character but Ainsworth and Cruickshank milk every emotion possible from the procession to the Tower of 'the wisest and most beautiful woman in the kingdom', the 'shudder [that] ran through her frame as she perceived at her feet an axe', the equally fictitious appeal to Mary for the life of Guildford, and an execution where 'the axe fell, and one of the fairest and wisest heads that ever sat on human shoulders fell also'.[41] Where the novel imagined, painters followed. The late Victorian artist, Laselett John Pott, pictured Lady Jane Grey arriving by water at Traitors' Gate, an Ainsworth invention.[42] Pierre Charles Comte's *Le Jugement de Jeanne Grey* showed her in an equally invented confrontation with Bishop Gardiner, Bishop Bonner and John Feckenham, a performance which inspires Guildford Dudley to withdraw his pusillanimous surrender to Rome.[43]

The picture of Jane as an innocent girl steadfast against heartless forces was an interpretation which chimed in well with the morality of the rising middle classes. In their influential *Lives of the Tudor Princesses including Lady Jane Grey and her sisters* [1868] Agnes and Elizabeth Strickland wrote, 'Lady Jane Grey is without doubt the most noble character of the royal Tudor lineage. She was endowed with every attribute that is lovely in domestic life, while her piety, learning, courage and virtue qualified her to give lustre to a crown.'[44] In Tennyson's play *Queen Mary*, a character says of Jane,

> Seventeen – and knew eight languages – in music
> Peerless – her needle perfect, and her learning
> Beyond the churchmen; yet so meek, so modest,
> So wife-like humble to the trivial boy
> Mismatch'd with her for policy!
> [...]
> Seventeen – a rose of grace!
> Girl never breath'd to rival such a rose;
> Rose never blew that equall'd such a bud.[45]

This Jane was also 'packaged' for children. In 1815 the anonymous *History of the Unfortunate Lady Jane Grey and Lord Guildford Dudley* appeared in Whittingham & Arliss's Juvenile Library. Five years later *The Juvenile Plutarch* was published, *Containing Accounts of the Lives of Celebrated Children and of the Infancy of Persons Who Have Been Illustrious for Their Virtues or Talents*. The chapter on Jane announced that 'beauty alone may please at first sight, but it will cease to afford admiration, unless it is adorned by the accomplishments of an improved understanding and animated by a lively virtue and a rational piety. In all these graces the unfortunate Lady Jane Grey was pre-eminently distinguished'; and it concluded by saying that 'she will ever be remembered as a model of female excellence, and doubtless her virtues procured for her 'a crown in the kingdom of heaven, which passeth not away'.[46] 1833 saw the publication of *Historical Tales of Illustrious British Children* and that described Jane as ' the most perfect model of a meritorious young creature of the female sex to be found in history: her example, therefore, is the fittest possible to be held up to the fairest half of the rising generation'.[47]

Jane the moral exemplar was exported to the United States. The American Tract Society and the American Sunday School Union extolled her and she was one of the heroines of *Short Stories from the Lives of Remarkable Women being Narratives of Fact to Correct Fiction, as related to her children by a Mother*.[48] Or again, D. W. Bartlett wrote a *Life of Lady Jane Grey* specifically to inspire American girls 'to imitate the character of the beautiful and illustrious woman whose sad, yet in another sense glorious career [his book] records'.[49] Jane was also held up as a model for American women. 'Miss Leslie from Philadelphia', as she later was known, received her initial education in England, but as the doyenne of advice books for women, she produced this (suitably republican) parlour ballad in praise of modesty:

> Oh not for me! Oh, not for me
> That fatal toy of gems and gold –
> Blood on its ermin'd band I see!
> And thorns are in its silken folds.
> Let me the shaded pathway keep
> Remote from wild ambitions glare,
> Nor lead me to that dizzy steep
> For clouds and storms are gath'ring there.
> [...]
> She died – that glory of her age!
> As never Roman heroine died;
> And Britain's hist'ry has no page
> More dear to British woman's pride![50]

That advice was superfluous. Jane was a standard model for Victorian women. For example, she figured in *Lessons from Women's Lives*, which appeared in 1877 and was immediately seized on as appropriate to be given as a school prize.[51] Two years later she was one of *Fifty Famous Women: Their Virtues and Failings, and the Lessons of their Lives*, and she appeared in 1884 as one of the 'women of letters' in, *Woman's Work and Worth: in Girlhood, Maidenhood and Wifehood* by W. H. Davenport Adams.[52]

That the Jane Grey of advice books and *The Juvenile Plutarch* was far removed from the girl who died on 12 February 1554 hardly needs saying. In no way would the insult 'deformed imp of the Devil' have come from her pen. The reality is that from the moment she was dead 'Jane Grey' became a construct. England's reformers expected little good from the accession of Mary Tudor. The Old Testament told how God had used political misfortune in order to cleanse the ancient Israelites morally; England was now to suffer and emerge purified. Already those who supported Jane had felt the scourge as God frustrated their efforts. Persecution was coming and the challenge would be to stand firm in the faith. Had not Tertullian, one of the Early Fathers, called the blood of martyrs: 'the seedbed of the church'? On Monday 12 February 1554 Jane Grey became the first Protestant martyr.

This interpretation was, of course, equally far from the facts. Jane was guilty. She had admitted this on the scaffold: 'Good people I am come hither to die and by a law I am condemned to the same.' Judicial execution only became martyrdom because of Mary's concern for Jane's everlasting soul. In Christian terms this might be a godly impulse, but the attempt to convert Jane changed the whole public significance of her death. Her staunch resistance to Feckenham, the common belief that if she had embraced Rome she would have been spared, her Tower writings – especially the letter to Harding – and Protestants everywhere could praise God for a saint who had triumphed against the blandishments of Antichrist. Jane had urged Harding to choose 'to die, and gloriously with honour reign with Christ, in whom even in death is life'. That choice she had made, and so joined the 'white-robed army of martyrs'. Leaving Jane in prison might have involved a minimum political risk; beheading her was a crass mistake. Jane dead was Jane victorious. It was a lesson which Mary and her advisers had still not learned two years and one month later when Thomas Cranmer's eleventh-hour withdrawal of his surrender did permanent damage to the Catholic cause. Alive Cranmer had been a spent voice; dying, his words were like a trumpet.

Jane Grey's death was not as momentous as Cranmer's would be, but it was ominous for Mary. It demonstrated that the restoration of Catholicism would not be easy; English reformers had backbone and they now had an icon. John Banks wrote to Henry Bullinger a month after the execution, by which time Jane's father and uncle had followed her to the block.

This family is now overthrown and almost extinct on account of their saving profession of our Saviour, and the cause of the gospel; yet all godly and truly Christian persons have not so much reason to mourn over the ruin of a family so illustrious, as to rejoice that the latest action of her life was terminated in bearing testimony to the name of Jesus.[53]

In Geneva the great Swiss reformer John Calvin celebrated Jane as 'a lady whose example is worthy of everlasting remembrance'.[54] As we have seen, subversive printers in England immediately began the covert distribution of Jane's letters and material was also smuggled in from abroad. In 1555 the exiled Bible translator Miles Coverdale included Jane's letter to her sister in a new edition for the English market of his *Moste frutefull, piththye* [sic] *and learned treatise how a Christian man ought to behaue himself in the daunger of death*.[55] In the early years of Elizabeth Jane's writings continued to appear. Coverdale's treatise with the Katherine Grey letter attached was reprinted in London in 1560 and in the same year Jane's scaffold speech was published in Antwerp, again for the English market.[56] In 1564 Coverdale included the letter to Katherine in his *Certain most godly, fruitful and comfortable letters*.[57] By then the first edition of Foxe was on sale and in his sermon to the 1563 parliament Alexander Nowell, the dean of St Paul's, could cite 'for your and our better example, the end and death of the Lady Jane'.[58]

A further edition of *An Epistle of the Ladye Iane* came out in 1570, but by then publishers were becoming less interested in the iconic Jane.[59] The 1560s had brought limited religious reform and the hope of some stability, so that the threat of renewed Catholic persecution had receded. What is more, John Foxe's lengthy account of the 'sorrowful adversity' of Princess Elizabeth when imprisoned during Mary's reign and her 'miraculous protection of God ... in so many straits and distresses' had elevated the new queen in Jane's place. It was also the case that the claim of Jane's two sisters to be Elizabeth's next heirs was politically contentious – promoting it put John Hales in the Tower in 1565. Not until the next century could a vignette of Jane's execution appear alongside one of Elizabeth being taken to the Tower, Protestant martyrs together.[60] Given this, only Jane's unobjectionable 'effectual prayer' and her letter to her sister Katherine remained in circulation.[61]

Interest in a Protestant Jane re-emerges in the years before the Civil War. In 1615, the 1554 *An Epistle of the Ladye Iane* reappeared as *The Life, Death and Actions of the Most Chast, Learned and Religious Lady, the Lady Iane Gray.*[62] The anonymous editor described the text as 'coming, in an old ancient printed copy, into my hands, as it were half forgotten by the world'. But despite this and despite the piece needing, so he said, his 'best art and industry' to 'polish and cleanse it', he had decided to publish it to 'awaken the sleepy world from her fantastic lethargy to behold in that which we call the weaker sex a strength matchless and invincible'.[63] Given that the letter to Harding and the dialogue with Feckenham are reproduced in full, the desired 'awakening' was probably awakening to the Rome-ward implications of changes then being imposed on the Anglican church. The book certainly touched a chord, for it was reissued in 1629 and in 1636 at the height of Laudianism. During the Interregnum the puritan emphasis on the value of the testimony of past saints ensured that the Presbyterian minister Samuel Clarke would include her in *The Second Part of the Marrow of Ecclesiastical History; Containing the Lives of Many Eminent Christians, Which have Lived Since the Primitive Times to This Present Age* (1650). This interest in Jane continued after the Restoration as Charles II surreptitiously, and James II openly, espoused policies which appeared to undermine the Protestant hegemony.[64] In 1678, the year of the Popish Plot, Samuel Crossman reworked his earlier *The Young Man's Monitor* as *The Young Man's Calling*, adding 'remarks' on Jane, Edward VI, the young Elizabeth I and James I's son Henry, 'excellent young persons ... famous for piety and virtue'. Crossman was active in agitating over the Plot and his section on Jane included her Tower writings and a vignette of her standing up to Feckenham.[65] In 1688, the year in which the Catholic James was ousted by his daughter Mary and her husband William, the *Conference between Lady Jane Grey and F[ather] Fecknam a Romish priest* was reissued. In 1701 a version of her letter to Katherine – allegedly translated from the Greek – was included as one of the 'predictions' in a collection of prophecies.[66] In 1714 Edward Young, a rising poet and associate of Addison and Steele, wrote *The Force of Religion or Vanquished Love*. In it Guildford's human (and amorous) regrets are contrasted with Jane's spiritual beauty and piety, but the main concern is the evil of Catholicism. Mary is 'incensed Maria', 'fierce Maria'. Indeed, 'ill content that they should only bleed', she refines her cruelty by sending a priest to the couple and to Suffolk, offering life if all three will convert. The men crumble, but like Isabella in *Measure for Measure* Jane is steadfast: 'the martyr triumphed in her breast'. 'My victory's complete, and tell your queen I thank her for the blow'.[67] The poem went through three editions in less than two years and a London bookseller cashed in by rushing out *The Life, Character and Death of the Most Illustrious Pattern of Female Vertue, the Lady Jane Gray, who was Beheaded in the Tower at Sixteen Years of Age, for her Stedfast Adherence to the Protestant Religion.*[68]

The theatre too exploited Jane topically.[69] In the early 1680s John Banks, a lawyer-cum-playwright, wrote *The Innocent Usurper or the Death of the Lady Jane Grey*. This has the duke of Northumberland attempting to oust Mary because she is 'a fierce bigot', and declaring that the Dudleys were to replace the Tudors. Jane Grey, however, stands against him, declaring that disinheriting Mary is 'a horrid act'.[70] Given a current context of the campaign to bar the Catholic James from the throne and then the Monmouth rebellion, a play about 1553 offered an apposite warning against upsetting divine right, even in order to exclude a Catholic ruler. In the event the play was delayed until the 1692–3 season, and then it was banned. William and Mary had replaced James in 1689 'by divine right' on the fiction that James II had resigned the crown, so nothing was less welcome than a drama exploring the issue of dynastic change. The principal theatrical treatment of Jane came early in the next century from the pen of Nicholas Rowe. *The Tragedy of Lady Jane Gray* opened at Drury Lane on Wednesday 20 April 1715, for a (then) lengthy initial run of ten performances. The sensitivities which had banned Banks's play were now reversed. William was praised for making the decisive break with Catholicism, with George I coming in on a mission to continue the exclusion of the papist James III. The earlier attempt to bring in the Protestant Jane Grey in place of the Catholic Mary was, thus, apt to a degree. The Prologue spelled out the message.

> The only love that warmed her blooming youth
> Was husband, England, liberty and truth.
> For these she fell, while with too weak a hand,
> She strove to save a blind ungrateful land.
> But thus the secret laws of fate ordain,
> William's great hand was doomed to break that chain
> And end the hopes of Rome's tyrannic reign.

And the audience left with the Epilogue ringing in their ears:

> If from these scenes, to guard your faith you learn,
> If for our laws you show a just concern,
> If you are taught to dread a popish reign,
> Our beauteous patriot has not died in vain.[71]

The play was dedicated to George I's daughter Caroline of Ansbach, the Princess Royal, and clearly pleased since Rowe was appointed poet laureate three months later. Its continuing success was then guaranteed by James III's invasion of Scotland in September 1715 and his subsequent defeat. Over the next sixty years, *The Tragedy of Lady Jane Gray* was played in London forty more times.[72] It was also quickly in print and went through nineteen London editions in the century (six by 1733) – plus ten published elsewhere.

The threat of a Catholic restoration retreated during the eighteenth century, but books on Jane remained a staple of residual anti-popery. In 1807 the Reverend Legh Richmond, a prominent evangelical, included *Some Account of Lady Jane Grey* in his eight-volume *Fathers of the English Church*, which revived interest in the way she and others likeminded had held their beliefs.[73] In 1824, the early stirrings of what would become the Oxford Movement and Anglo-Catholicism were countered by the Church of England Tract Society's republication of *The Life and Death of Lady Jane Grey*; the Religious Tract Society followed suit in 1830 and in 1831 circulated her letters.[74] Women in particular were seen to need role models to guard against the dangers of Anglo-Catholicism and Rome itself. Thus in a single decade, Jane featured in *The Last Hours of Christian Women, or an Account of the Death of some Eminent Christian Women of the Church of England from the period of the Reformation* (1851), followed by *Ladies of the Reformation: Memoirs of Distinguished Female Characters, Belonging to the Period of the Reformation in the 16th Century* (1855), and *Women of the Reformation: Their Lives, Faith and Trials* (1861).[75] Children, too, had to be warned. Anne Lydia Bond wrote a *History of England for the Use of Young People* in which the illustration at the head of the chapter on Queen Mary showed likenesses of Jane, Cranmer, Latimer and Ridley beside the stake, the block and the axe.[76] In *Little Arthur's History of England* (1835), Maria Callcott called Jane 'beautiful, virtuous, and wise, and above all, a Protestant', and that in a book which went through seventy editions and sold 80,000 copies in the century.[77]

Since Victorian days Jane has continued and continues to be the subject of numerous biographies, semi-biographies and novels, principally but not only in Britain and North America. Some of these continue with a Protestant message, but what now fascinates the overwhelming majority is the personality of Jane and her macabre fate. Over a score of titles were published in the twentieth century and more since.[78] She has figured in comics, in magazines and in strip cartoons as well as in a variety of *objets* such as statuettes, plates and cigarette cards.[79] With the advent of first cinema and then television came opportunities to go beyond literature, fine art and illustration by attempting to animate the past. Jane has appeared as a minor character in adaptations for film and TV of Mark Twain's novel *The Prince and the Pauper* and in serials such as *Elizabeth R* (1971), but three attempts have been made to tell her story in its own right.[80] The earliest was the silent film *Lady Jane Grey, or the Court of Intrigue*, released in 1923 and starring Nina Vanna in the role of Jane.[81] *Tudor Rose* followed, issued by Gaumont Pictures in 1936 with a cast studded with established and rising stars including Cedric Hardwicke, John Mills, Martita Hunt and Sybil Thorndike.[82] The seventeen-year-old Nova Pilbeam played Jane to acclaim, although her career was not to progress much further, in marked contrast to John Mills who played Guildford Dudley. The personal interest is on the way a forced marriage (which Jane resisted) grew into friendship, even love, as she and Guildford Dudley shared the experience of the Tower, which is a great deal to build on perhaps a month of supervised encounters in the Tower garden.[83] *Lady Jane*, directed by Trevor Nunn, is the third of the films and the longest – perhaps too long (142 minutes) – released by Paramount in 1986. With a brilliant cast and a feature film debut for Helena Bonham-Carter as Jane, the movie is in essence romantic invention, based on the novel of the same name by A. C. H. Smith.[84] Again the focus was on a heroine and hero imprisoned together, this time enhanced by their equally fictitious concern for social and religious reform. Using modern media to tell Jane's story with a balance of imaginative reconstruction and historical veracity is a challenge yet to be met.

28

ENVOI

THE pages of history are asterisked with names which defy the erosion of time. Jane Grey is one such, but strangely so. Truth to tell she counted for little. She was important for barely nine months, she ruled for only thirteen days. She contributed little to writing and nothing to ideas. She founded no dynasty and left almost no memorabilia. Then what is it, keeps the story of Jane alive while many more significant figures in history are recalled only by scholars? For many years Jane was a saint in the Protestant pantheon, but martyrs are now out of fashion – and so too ideal Victorian maidens. In the West, growing secularization ensures that relatively few people even understand the issues which meant so much to her. And yet her name still lives. Something is due to a memorable sobriquet: 'the nine days queen' – not any Jane, that Jane. Romance, too, is part of the explanation; along with Anne Boleyn, Katherine Howard and Mary Queen of Scots, Jane completes a quartet of Tudor queens who died on the scaffold. Undeniable, too, there is the macabre attraction of the girl sacrifice. She died Jane Dudley, but is universally remembered as Jane Grey, Ariadne chained to the rock. All this and more. But the fundamental justification for remembering Jane is the justification for remembering Anne Frank centuries later. They speak for the multitude of brutality's victims who have no voice.

'If my faults deserve punishment, my youth at least, and my imprudence were worthy of excuse; God and posterity will show me favour.'

NOTES

The Scene

1 See below pp. 14–5.
2 *Cal. S. P. Spanish*, xi.73: 7 Jul. 1553, Ambassadors to Charles V.
3 *Chronicle of Queen Jane*, p. 10.
4 R. C. McCoy, 'From the Tower to the tiltyard', in *Historical Journal* 27 (1984), 425–35.
5 See below p. 163.
6 M. Hale, *The Prerogatives of the King*, ed. D. E. C. Yale, Selden Society, 92 (1976), 78.

1 The Year of Three Sovereigns

1 Nichols, *Lit. Rems.*, i.clxxi–clxxvi.
2 Folger Library MS Lb256, 501; HMC *Molyneux*, p. 610. This is wrongly dated 1553.
3 *Cal. S. P. Domestic, Edward*, 800; Tytler, *Edward and Mary*, ii.155.
4 HMC *Middleton*, p. 521.
5 See below, p. 37.
6 *Cal. S. P. Spanish*, xi.9: 17 Feb. 1553, Scheyfve to Charles V.
7 Nichols, *Lit. Rems.*, i.clxxvi.
8 Haynes, *State Papers*, i.145.
9 Loach, *Edward VI*, pp. 160–2.

10 Haynes, *State Papers*, i.146; Nichols, *Lit. Rems.*, i.clxxvii–viii.
11 *Cal. S. P. Spanish*, xi.32: 10 Apr. 1553, Scheyfve to Charles V; Machyn, *Diary*, pp. 33–4.
12 See below, pp. 137sqq.
13 Haynes, *State Papers*, i.149.
14 Vertot, *Ambassades*, ii.26–7.
15 Bindoff, in *History Today* 3.
16 *Vita Mariae*, p. 244.
17 See below, p. 145.
18 Wriothesley, *Chronicle*, ii.100.
19 *Chronicle of Queen Jane*, pp. 6–7.
20 See above, p. 3.
21 *Cal. S. P. Spanish*, xi.8–9: 17 Feb. 1553, Scheyfve to Charles V; Machyn, *Diary*, pp. 30–1.
22 *Cal. S. P. Spanish*, xi.81: 11 July, Charles V to Scheyfve.
23 Nichols, *Lit. Rems.*, i.cccxix–cccxx.
24 Henry died at midnight, 28 January, Edward was proclaimed at 9 a.m. on 31 January, i.e. 57 hours (Nichols, *Lit. Rems.*, i.cclxvi; Jordan, *Edward VI*, i.51–2). Edward died 8/9 p.m., 6 July, Jane was proclaimed at 5/6 p.m. 10 July, i.e. 92 hours (Loach, *Edward VI*, p. 167; Machyn, *Diary*, p. 35).
25 *Cal. S. P. Spanish*, xi.71: 4 Jul. 1553, Scheyfve to Charles V, but see Alsop, in *Albion* 24/4.

2 In Search of Jane Grey

1 Nicolas, *Memoirs*, p. xiii.
2 Battista Spinola, 10 July, 1553, quoted in Davey, *Jane Grey*, p. 253.
3 Vertot, *Ambassades*, ii.57.
4 Ascham, *The Schoolmaster*, p. 36.
5 Chaloner, in *De Republica*, pp. 296–7.
6 Grafton, *Abridgement* (1562), fo. 156.
7 Godwin, *Annales*, p. 264. The term Godwin used was 'not admire-able'.
8 Pollini, *L'Historia*, p. 351.
9 NPG D21393.
10 Ibid., 4451.
11 S. E. James, 'Lady Jane Grey or Queen Kateryn Parr?', in *Burlington Magazine*, 138 (1996), 20–4.
12 Strong, *Portraits*, i.78–9; ii. plates 147, 148.
13 Yale Center for British Art; *Lost Faces*, pp. 79–83.
14 If the sitter was a Dudley wife and the miniature is a wedding memento, the acorns suggest Amy Robsart, who married Robert Dudley in 1550 at the precise age of 18 (Robert, *robur*, Latin for oak). Other identifications are advanced by Mr Christopher Foley and in Susan James *The Feminine Dynamic in English Art, 1485–1603* (Farnham, 2009)
15 Nicolas, *Memoirs*, p. cxxxii*.
16 Jane was born in 1537; see below, p. 36.
17 Hans Eworth, Fitzwilliam Museum, Cambridge.
18 J. S. Edwards, 'A new face for the lady', in *History Today* 55 (2005), 44–5, but see n. 20 below.
19 It is also arguable that the costume dates from the later 1550s.
20 A possible identification from outside the family is Jane Dormer, the future Duchess of Feria and one of Mary Tudor's great favourites, though again the appearance of age would be a problem. *Lost Faces*, pp. 86–7. Dr Edwards now finds this 'convincing'.
21 *First Special Exhibition of National Portraits*, Victoria and Albert Museum

(April 1866); catalogue no. 193; NPG 6804; Herbert Norris, *Costume and Fashion* (1938–50), iii(2). I am indebted to the advice of Mr Christopher Foley.
22 *Mary Grey*, anon Chequers; *Katherine Grey* Marcus Gheeraerts (ex Christie).
23 Strong, *Portraits*, ii. plate 145; Cust, in *Walpole Soc.* 6, 15–35.
24 Jane's father Henry Grey and Fitzalan's first wife Katherine Grey were brother and sister.
25 Strong, *Portraits*, i.79. No detailed examination of the painting has been made but I am told that the cartellino is illegible.
26 *Jane Grey*, anon. (Syon House); ibid., anon (Audley End); *Portrait of a Lady* (Berry-Hill Galleries, N.Y, ex Metropolitan Museum); Roy Strong, *Portraits of Queen Elizabeth* (Oxford, 1963), plate 3; Philip Mould, *Fine Paintings*, ed. Bendor Grosvenor (2008), p. 8.
27 *Lost Faces*, pp. 85–6.
28 Henry Grey, duke of Kent, who acquired the portrait for Wrest Park in 1701, belonged to the Greys of Ruthin. The families divided in 1440 and, *pace Lost Faces*, p. 85, it seems unlikely that the Dunham Massey portraits were copies of the Wast Hill painting.
29 Lavender, not wheat, *pace Lost Faces*, pp. 82, 86.
30 *Lost Faces*, pp. 85–6.
31 NPG D10931.
32 *Cal. S. P. Domestic, Edward*, 157; *Epistolae Tigurinae*, pp. 3–7; translations in *Original Letters*, pp. 5–11.
33 BL, Harley MS 2342, fo. 74ᵛ; see Plate 26.
34 Commendone, *Accession*, pp. 45–8; Rosso, *I successi*, fos 53 ff.
35 Commendone, *Accession*, p. 45.
36 Pollini Girolamo, *Storia Ecclesiastica*, pp. 279–82; *L'Historia*, pp. 355–8.
37 *Nicolai Sanderi, De origine ac progressu Schismatis Anglicani liber*, ed. Edward Rishton (Cologne, 1585).
38 Pollini, *L'Historia*, p. 354. This is an addition to *Storia Ecclesiastica*, p. 278.

39   See below, p. 248. But Northumberland was condemned on 18 August, so Pollini is premature to say it triggered the letter.

40   Foxe, *Acts and Monuments* (1563), pp. 917, 923.

41   Pollini, *L'Historia*, p. 357.

42   For this and the following see Foxe, *Acts and Monuments* (1570), p. 1581.

43   BL, Harley MS 2342 fos. 78–80.

44   See below, p. 266.

45   Foxe, *Acts and Monuments* (1563), p. 919.

46   Cf. 'for I will wash my hands guiltless thereof, but only for that I consented to the thing which I was enforced into'. *An Epistle*, sig. Bvii[v].

47   *Original Letters*, p. 303.

48   Ibid., pp. 293–4. Banks did not know Jane personally but shows knowledge of the family: see pp. 21, 72.

49   STC 7279. Day was apparently backed by William Cecil: Arnold, *Burghley*, pp. 66–8.

50   STC 7279.5.

51   Some of the moveable type used to set the work had been used by Scoloker.

52   *An Epistle*, sig. Biii[v], Bv[r]; *Here in this Booke*, sig. Bi[v].

53   Foxe, *Acts and Monuments* (1563), pp. 917–18; *Here in this Booke* dates the dialogue with Feckenham 'ij days before she suffered death': sig. Bii[v] (as Foxe). *An Epistle* says four: sig. Bii[v]; Foxe has the dialogue end with Jane saying 'God the Lord defend [prohibit]!' *Here in this Booke* ends with 'The Lord defend us from these and such like ill words. He would here have had me lean to his church but it would not be. There were many more things whereof we reasoned, but these were chief' (*Here in this Booke*, sig. Bi[v]). *An Epistle* has 'How did king Saul, the Lord define [*sic*]. With these & such like persuasions he would here have had me to have leaned to the church, but it would not be. There were many more things whereof we reasoned, but these were chief' (*An Epistle* sig. Bv[r]).

54   Foxe, *Acts and Monuments* (1563), p. 917; see below, p. 267.

55   See below, p. 268. The famous words which the couple exchanged on parting were introduced in Foxe's first edition with 'these words following were spoken openly'. This agrees with *An Epistle* but *Here in this Booke* simply has 'After this Feckenham took his leave saying …': *An Epistle*, sig. Bv[v]; *Here in this Booke*, sig. B1[v]; Foxe, *Acts and Monuments* (1563), p. 918.

56   As printed in *Here in this Booke* the Harding letter ends with a doxology, sig. Avii. *An Epistle* adds 'Be constant, be constant, fear not for pain: Christ hath redeemed thee and heaven is thy gain', sig. Bii[r], and this is also found in Foxe, *Acts and Monuments* (1563), p. 922, but not in *Here in this Booke*.

57   *Here in this Booke*, sig. Aii[r].

58   Foxe, *Acts and Monuments* (1563), p. 920.

59   *Here in this Booke*, sig. Aiiii[v].

60   Foxe, *Acts and Monuments* (1563), p. 921.

61   *Here in this Booke*, sig. Aii[r], Aiii[v], Aiv[v]; *An Epistle*, sig. Aii (with minor variations).

62   *Here in this Booke* has the heading 'A copy of a letter which the Lady Jane sent to her sister Katherine the night before she suffered death' and ends 'trust in God who only must help you. Yours Jane Dudley'. *An Epistle* has 'An exhortation written by the Lady Jane the night before she suffered in end of the New Testament in Greek which she sent to her sister Lady Katherine', and ends '… must help you. Amen. Your loving sister Jane Dudley'. Foxe has 'A letter written by the Lady Jane in the end of the New Testament in Greek, the which she sent unto her sister Lady Katherine, immediately before she suffered' and ends '… put your only trust in God who only must help you': *Here in this Booke*, sig. Bii, Biii; *An Epistle*, sig. Bvi, Bvii[v]; Foxe, *Acts and Monuments* (1563), p. 918. Davey, *Jane Grey*, p. 334 claims that the Greek Testament was extant in

the (then) British Museum. No such book is recorded in the BL.

63 BL, Harley MS 2342, fo. 59ᵛ–60.

64 Foxe, *Acts and Monuments* (1570), p. 1581.

65 Foxe, *Acts and Monuments* (1563), p. 919, *Here in this Booke*, sig. Biii, Biiiᵛ. It names her maid as 'Mistress Tylney' and states that she gave her book to 'Thomas Brydges the Lieutenant's brother' where Foxe has 'Mistress Ellen' and 'Master Brydges'. According to another account both women were present but the inscription in the prayer book is to Sir John Brydges the lieutenant, and Foxe's use of the surname alone may indicate he was uncertain between the brothers. The text in *Chronicle of Queen Jane*, p. 56a, is independent, but ibid., 58–9 is taken from *Here in this Booke*, sig. Biiiʳ, Biiiᵛ. *Vita Mariae*, Wriothesley, *Chronicle*, and Grey Friars, *Chronicle* do not record the speech; Machyn, *Diary* makes no mention of the execution. Commendone reports it, but not the speech: *Accession*, p. 49. Rosso and Pollini follow Commendone The brother of de Noailles reported as Foxe on 12 Mar. 1553: Vertot, *Ambassades*, iii. 123–5.

66 *An Epistle*, sig. Bviᵛ, Bvii.

3 Jane Grey in Context

1 Pollard, *History*, p. 111.

2 Lawrence Humphrey, President of Magdalen College, Oxford: 'twice a martyr—a most true witness to the holy faith and free from any charge against the realm.' Foxe, *Acts and Monuments* (1563), p. 923.

3 Zentralbibliothek Zürich, RP 17–19.

4 *Epistolae Tigurinae*, translated as *Original Letters*.

5 *Cal. S. P. Venetian*, v.532.

6 *Cal. S. P. Spanish*, xi.37–196.

7 See below, pp. 144–5.

8 See below, p. 248.

9 Vertot, *Ambassades*, ii.26, 55, 57.

10 See below, pp. 155–6, 182.

11 Vertot, *Ambassades*, ii.50–94; Harbison, *Rival Ambassadors*, pp. 343–51.

12 *Cal. S. P. Venetian*, v.934, p. 533.

13 *A Chronicle of England during the Reigns of the Tudors, from 1485 to 1559*, ed. W. D. Hamilton (Camden Soc. n.s. xi, xx, 1875, 1877).

14 Grey Friars, *Chronicle*.

15 Machyn, *Diary*.

16 *Chronicle of Queen Jane*.

17 The MS was used by Stow, and Nichols supplies gaps from that source and from letters.

18 Cf. *Chronicle of Queen Jane*, p. 82: 'Note, to ampliefy yt', and the gaps left to be filled in.

19 Ibid., p. vi; Challis, *Coinage*, pp. 315, 318, 321.

20 Ascham, *The Schoolmaster*, p. 36; see below, p. 00.

21 Florio, *Historia*. For the following see Yates, *Florio*, pp. 3–78; Wyatt, *Italian Encounter*, pp. 98–101.

22 Hooper: February, 1555; Ridley: October 1555; Cranmer: March 1556.

23 For the following see Bostoen, in *The Bookshop of the World*, pp. 119–30.

24 At death he owned 90 books in Italian. Ibid., p. 123.

25 The patron is not named. Boesten suggests Jane's uncle Lord John Grey (d.1564) or her sister Katherine (d.1568), and Queen Elizabeth's hostility to the Greys would clearly account for the failure to publish.

26 This would explain how Radermacher came to have other writings by Florio.

27 See below, pp. 29–30.

28 Grafton, *Abridgement*; *Tudor Proclamations*, ii.16.

29 Stow, *Chronicles/Annales* (1592).

30 Holinshed, *Chronicles*.

31 P.V., *Narratio Historica Vicissitudinis rerum, quae in inclyto Brittaniae regno acciderunt Anno domini 1553, Mense Julio* (? Marburg/Wittenberg, 1553). It starts with the plot to remove Somerset.

(Erroneously attributed to Peter Martyr (Peter Vermiglio); see Denys Hay, 'The *Narratio Historica* of P. Vincentius, 1553' in *EHR* lxviii (1948), 350–6.)

32   Ibid., sig. Diii (wine), Bviii, Bviii^v (poison).

33   De Guaras, *Relation*, p. 114.

34   Commendone, *Accession*. The original is in Latin.

35   *Cal. S. P. Venetian, 1534–54*, p. 485. He became a cardinal in 1565.

36   e.g., the detail that Jane rebuffed the executioner. His text was completed while Anne of Cleves was alive [d.1557]. Commendone, *Accession*, pp. 3, 72.

37   *Cal. S. P. Venetian, 1534–54*, pp. 406–7, 411; Contile, *Historia*. Usually identified as a pirated version of the Rosso text (see below), but the plausible link with Commendone via Soranzo casts doubt on this. It has been attributed, incorrectly, to Federigo Badoaro.

38   Rosso, *I successi*.

39   Pollini, *Storia Ecclesiastica*. Elizabeth protested to the Grand Duke of Tuscany, so the enlarged (and even more offensive) second edition, *L'Historia Ecclesiastica della Rivoluzion d'Inghilterra, divisa in libri quattro ne' quali si tratta di quello ch'e avvenuto in quell'isola da che Arrigo Ottava cominciò a pensare di ripudiar Cataerina ... infino a quest'ultimi anni di Lisabetta* (Rome, 1594), was published outside the duke's jurisdiction. Bernardo Davanzotti, *Scisma d'Inghilterra* (Rome, 1602) was marginally less abrasive and possibly something of an olive branch: Wyatt, *Italian Encounter*, pp. 128–30.

40   Stephen Perlin, *Description des Royaulmes d'Angleterre et d'Escosse* (Paris, 1558), translated in *The Antiquarian Repertory* iv (1809), 503–12.

41   Ibid., p. 512.

42   C. Bémont, 'Les révolutions d'Angleterre en 1553 et 1554, racontées par un fourrier de l'empereur Charles-Quint', in *Revue Historique* 110 (1912), 56–76.

43   BL, Add. MS 48093; *De Rebus Gestis Mariae Anglorum Reginae Commentario-*

lus, ed. and trs. D. MacCulloch, in *Camden Miscellany* xxviii (1984), pp. 181–301. Wingfield took events to 5 May and ended his work before Philip of Spain arrived, but cf. ibid., p. 183.

4   A Damnable Inheritance

1   Tacitus, *Annals* Book 5.

2   For the following see Gunn, *Brandon*.

3   Ibid., pp. 131–2.

4   Gossip had it that this marriage was invalid, making Jane Grey illegitimate: *Cal. S. P. Spanish*, xi.334: 4 Nov. 1553, Renard to Charles V.

5   Gunn, *Brandon*, pp. 131–2.

6   28 Hen. VIII, c.7.

7   Mary, the third and last surviving child, was born in 1545.

8   35 Hen. VIII, c.1.

9   Rymer, *Foedera*, xv.110–17, transcribing National Archives E23/4/1.

10   Anthony Squires, *The Greys* (Hale, 2002).

11   M. Forsyth, *The History of Bradgate* (Leicester, 1974); N. Pevsner, *Leicestershire* (2nd edn, rev. E. Williamson, 1984) pp. 108–9.

12   John Byng, *The Torrington Diaries*, ed. C. B. Andrews (1970), ii.157.

13   W. Burton, *Description of Leicestershire* (1622), pp. 44–5; Nichols, *Leicester*, iii.664; Chandler, *Leland's Itinerary*, p. 279.

14   3159 m^2 against 4050 m^2 and 7035 m^2 respectively.

15   The extensions probably include the outside bays extending on the terrace and the block to the north. It is difficult to reconcile the apparently free-standing building south of the garden with the topography of the site.

16   Nichols, *Leicester*, iii.680.

17   J. Stevenson and A. Squires, *Bradgate Park* (Newtown Linford, 1999), pp. 29–33; Nichols, *Leicester*, iii.681.

18   Ibid., iii.664; Chandler, *Leland's Itinerary*, p. 280.

19   Ibid., pp. 279–81, 283.

20   It appears to have been a staircase.

21   *Original Letters*, p. 406; Ascham, *Works*, i.227.

22   '*qua iam ipsa est 14 annos nata*'. *Original Letters*, p. 276. This is decisive because (a) Aylmer used Arabic numerals and wrote the 4 as a correction of either a badly written 4 or an error; and (b) the letter can be dated between the death of Bucer (28 February) and the elevation of Henry Grey to the dukedom (11 October). I am indebted for this to Dr Alexandra Kess-Hall of the Institut für Schweizerische Reformationsgeschichte of the University of Zurich. It is also important that Aylmer specified annos nata (born 14 years) rather than anno aetatis (in her fourteenth year). *Original Letters*, p. 304. Supporting indications are: (a) Jane was named after her prospective godmother, queen Jane Seymour, who died on 24 October after a difficult confinement and days of high fever ('more than two days': *Register of the Garter*, ed. J. Anstis (1724), i.410, *pace* Loach, *Edward VI*, p. 50), so her agreement to be godmother must have been secured before she went into labour, and probably before she took her chamber in mid-September; and (b) Frances Grey had expected to attend Edward's christening on 16 October and so had been 'churched' by then (*LP*, xii (2).891–3; *SP*, ii.570–1; D. Cressy, 'Purification, thanksgiving and the churching of women', in *Past and Present* 141 (1993), 116). J. S. Edwards has revised his earlier opinion 'in or before June/July 1537' in favour of the second half of 1536, construing 'era di XVII anni solamente' (Florio, *Historia*, p. 68) to mean 17 years old: 'On the birthdate of Lady Jane Grey', in *Notes and Queries* 54 (2007), 240–2; 'A further note on the date of birth of Lady Jane Grey', in *Notes and Queries* 55 (2008), 146–8. This overlooks the statement by John Banks a month after her death that she was 'anno aetatis suae decimo septimo' ['in the seventeenth year of her age'], *Epistolae Tigurinae*, pp. 290–1.

Francis Godwin says of her accession: 'illa annos nata circiter sedecim': *Annales* (1628), p. 193. De Noailles' brother's report on 12 Mar. 1553 was 'nondum decimum-septimum aetatis annum': Vertot, *Ambassades*, iii. 123. Annales (1628), p. 193.

23   The Aylmer letter was probably one of those sent in a batch in May 1551.

24   *Original Letters*, p. 117; Florio, *Historia*, p. 68.

25   The story that she had a nurse, Mrs Ellen, seems apocryphal.

26   For the following see HMC *Middleton MSS*.

27   *Cal. S. P. Domestic, Edward*, 343.

28   HMC *Middleton*, pp. 520–1.

29   Ibid., pp. 394, 396.

30   Ibid., pp. 397–8.

31   *DKR* iv(ii), 245; *Chronicle of Queen Jane*, p. 184. Medley was threatened with confiscation but was never tried. HMC *Middleton*, p. 521.

32   Ibid., p. 521.

33   Ibid., p. 520.

34   Ibid., p. 522; *ODNB*.

35   K. T. Parker, *The Drawings of Hans Holbein* (1983), no. 28. As well as the sitter's apparent age, she appears to hold a walking stick.

36   *Lisle Letters*, v.709.

37   Parker, *Drawings*, no. 56.

38   Holbein was in a circle associated with Anne Boleyn and the duchess was significantly out of sympathy with a court in the throes of accepting the prospective queen. Ives, *Anne Boleyn*, pp. 233–4. Mary died in June 1533.

39   For the problem of the inscriptions, some of which are incorrect and cannot be by Cheke, see E. W. Ives, 'The Queen and the painters: Anne Boleyn, Holbein and Tudor royal portraiture', in *Apollo* 140 (1994), 40–2; S. Foister, *Holbein in England* (2004), pp. 24–7.

40   The caption 'Francis Russell earl of Bedford some time' must postdate 1555 when he inherited, ibid., p. 25. This increases problems about Cheke as the

authority for the names since he was in England and free (but in disgrace) only between October 1556 and his death in September 1557.

41 Plowden, *Jane Grey*, pp. 26, 36; Chapman, *Jane Grey*, pp. 19–21; J. Stevenson and A. Squires, *Bradgate Park* (Newtown Linford, 1994), p. 35.

42 *Notes and Queries* 12 (1855), 451. The story is apocryphal but illustrates the reaction to the marriage.

43 Camden, *Historie*, p. 55.

44 See below, pp. 52, 187.

45 NPG L185.

46 *ODNB*, Gregory Fiennes.

47 Camden, *Historie*, p. 55. In April 1555 the imperial ambassador speculated that Frances could be married to Courtenay, *Cal. S. P. Spanish*, xiii.177. He may have been confusing Frances with Katherine Brandon but she too was married.

48 *Hist. of Parlt. 1558–1603*, iii.449–50; C. J. Berkhout, 'Adrian Stokes', in *Notes and Queries* 47 (2000), 27–8.

49 Robert Brooke, *Ascuns Novel Cases* (1597), f. 109^v. Frances cannot have been in the dark over this: *Reports of William Dalison*, ed. J. H. Baker, Selden Society 124 (2007), p. 25.

50 *Cal. S. P. Dom., 1547–80*, pp. 143, 505: '1st quarter. Royal arms border gobony or & azure'.

51 Chapman, *Jane Grey*, p. 154; Plowden, *Jane Grey*, p. 209. The infant, named Elizabeth, died on 7 February 1556.

52 *ODNB*; *Cal. S. P. Domestic, Mary*, 147: livery of Frances's land to Katherine and Mary. The division of the lands includes Stokes,

53 *Cal. S. P. Domestic, Edward*, 701.

54 Robert Parsons, *A Treatise of Three Conuersions of England* (St Omer, 1603–4), iii.493; Parsons (ibid., ii.493) claimed to have much of his material from Sir Francis Englefield (see below, p. 92). Haynes, *State Papers*, i.29.

55 Jordan, *Edward VI*, i.373, ii.514; 'without the slightest ability or judgement', ibid., i.92.

56 *LP*, xiii(ii) 732. The story of financial incompetence fails to take account of his not yet receiving livery: *LP*, xiii(ii), p. 280.

57 Hayward, *Life and Raigne*, p. 136.

58 Except for the earl of Arundel, 5 years, and Thomas Seymour, 8 years older.

59 *SP*, x.564, xi.60.

60 Nichols, *Lit. Rems.*, i.xcii–xciv.

61 Ibid., i.ccxciii, ccxcvii; *Cal. S. P. Domestic, Edward*, 3, 7, 16.

62 Bernard, in *Nobility*, pp. 212–40.

63 James, *Kateryn Parr*, p. 404.

5 Jane the Person

1 For Thomas Seymour, see Bernard, in *Nobility*, pp. 212–40.

2 Haynes, *State Papers*, i.82; *Cal. S. P. Domestic Edward*, 182; Tytler, *Edward and Mary*, i.138.

3 *Cal. S. P. Domestic, Edward*, 186; Bernard, in *Nobility*, p. 220.

4 *Cal. S. P. Domestic, Edward*, 182, 202; Haynes, *State Papers*, i.85; Tytler, *Edward and Mary*, i.148–9, 154; Bernard, in *Nobility*, pp. 220–1.

5 Bernard, in *Nobility*, p. 221.

6 Nichols, *Lit. Rems.*, i.cxx.

7 *Cal. S. P. Domestic Edward*, 182; Tytler, *Edward and Mary*, i.138–9.

8 For the following, see James, *Kateryn Parr*.

9 Dowling, *Humanism* pp. 236–7 takes a different view of Katherine's education.

10 Susan James suggests that Jane was permanently at Seymour Place until Elizabeth left Katherine. There is no evidence to this effect and it is hard to see how Jane could have developed her strong link to Seymour unless as part of the household: James, *Kateryn Parr*, pp. 317, 323; Haynes, *State Papers*, i.95–7.

11 Ibid., i.99.

12 James, *Kateryn Parr*, p. 323; Tytler, *Edward and Mary*, i.70; *Cal. S. P. Domestic, Edward*, 67 dates this earlier.

13 James, *Kateryn Parr*, p. 329; Tytler, *Edward and Mary*, i.102–3.

14 James, *Kateryn Parr*, p. 411.

15 Ibid., pp. 332–3.

16 Haynes, *State Papers*, i.77.

17 Ibid., i.77–8.

18 Ibid., i.78–9.

19 Ibid., i.79.

20 Ibid., i.77–8, 93.

21 Ibid., i.82.

22 Ibid., i.76.

23 Ibid., i.76; *Cal. S. P. Domestic, Edward*, 182. Frances's letter is dated 2 October: ibid., 158; Tytler, *Edward and Mary*, i.134–5.

24 Davey, *Jane Grey*, p. 155, of. Leicester, *Records* iii, 64.

25 Haynes, *State Papers*, i.98.

26 See below, p. 47.

27 *Cal. S. P. Domestic, Edward*, 182; Tytler, *Edward and Mary*, i.139.

28 Haynes, *State Papers*, i.84.

29 Ibid., i.79.

30 Ibid., i.76.

31 Ibid., i.76–7; *Cal. S. P. Domestic, Edward*, 182; Tytler, *Edward and Mary*, i.140–1. Leicester, *Records* iii.67.

32 *Cal. S. P. Domestic, Edward*, 158; Tytler, *Edward and Mary*, i.134–5; Nichols, *Lit. Rems.*, i.54–7; Haynes, *State Papers*, i.79.

33 Ibid., i.77.

34 *APC*, ii.248–56, 260; Nichols, *Lit. Rems.* i.54–7.

35 'A "journal" of matters of state', pp. 56–7.

36 And only if it could be proved that William Sharington, treasurer of the Bristol mint, had coined illegally.

37 Graves, *House of Lords*, p. 170; *APC*, ii.257.

38 Latimer, *Sermons*, i.228–9.

39 Ibid., i.161, 164.

40 Ibid., i.161–2.

41 Haynes, *State Papers*, i.84.

42 'Forgetting God to love a king/hath been my rod, or else nothing': John Harington, *Nugae Antiquae* (1779), p. 254.

43 Latimer, *Sermons*, i.181–4.

44 *Original Letters*, p. 477.

45 Bernard, in *Nobility*, p. 226.

46 Nichols, *Narratives*, pp. 260–3.

47 E. Dent, *Annals of Winchcombe and Sudeley* (1877), p. 193.

48 *Cal. S. P. Domestic, Edward*, 157; Tytler, *Edward and Mary*, i.133. Jane's letter, dated 1 October 1548, is obviously linked to Frances Grey's letter of 2 October: see above, n. 23.

49 Haynes, *State Papers*, i.78–9.

50 Edward, her eldest surviving son, was born c.1500.

51 *Cal. S. P. Domestic, Edward*, 182; Tytler, *Edward and Mary*, i.140.

52 The only ranking alternatives were the (very difficult) duchess of Somerset and the dowager duchess of Suffolk.

53 *ODNB*.

54 Ascham, *Works*, i(ii), 239–40: 18 Jan. 1551, Ascham to Jane Grey and Aylmer.

55 Ascham, *The Schoolmaster*, pp. 35–6.

56 Ascham, *Works*, i(ii) 239.

57 Ascham, *The Schoolmaster*, p. 36.

58 *Vives and the Renascence Education of Women*, ed. Foster Watson (1912), p. 133.

59 Plowden, *Jane Grey*, p. 62; Megan L. Hickerson, *Making Women Martyrs in Tudor England* (Basingstoke, 2005), p. 165.

60 *Original Letters*, p. 276: May 1551, Aylmer to Bullinger.

61 Ibid., p. 279: 23 Dec. 1551, Aylmer to Bullinger.

62 Madden, *Privy Purse Expences*, p. 199. Possibly also 'another a lace for the neck containing xiiij small rubies and lxx mean pearls'.

63 *Original Letters*, pp. 278–9: 23 Dec. 1551, Aylmer to Bullinger.

64 Aylmer, *An harborowe*, sig. Ni [Strype, *Aylmer*, pp. 195–6].

65 Ibid., sig. Ni^v.

66 Ibid., sig. Ni, Ni^v.

6 Family Priorities

1 *Cal. S. P. Domestic, Edward*, 273, 343.

2 E. Shagan, 'Protector Somerset and the 1549 rebellions: new sources and new perspectives', in *EHR* 144 (1999), 34–43.

3   Hoak, *King's Council*, pp. 55–6, 245, 254; Challis, 'Circulating Medium', pp. 119–20; 2 Feb. 1550, Justice Itinerant of the King's Forests: *Cal. Pat. R. 1550–3*, pp. 15, 27; Steward of royal and duchy lands etc. in Leicestershire, Rutland, Warwickshire and Nottinghamshire and constable of Leicester Castle, 1551: Somerville, *Duchy of Lancaster*, pp. 565, 570.

4   See below, n. 27.

5   HMC *Middleton*, p. 519.

6   *Original Letters*, pp. 276, 404, 422, 432.

7   Ibid., pp. 63, 65–6, 446; Nichols, *Lit. Rems.*, ii.381–3.

8   *Original Letters*, p. 447.

9   Nichols, *Lit. Rems.*, i.clxxvii; *Cal. S. P. Spanish*, xi.9: 17 Feb. 1553, Scheyfve to Charles V.

10   See above, p. 55. Wriothesley, *Chronicle*, ii.60–1; Machyn, *Diary*, pp. 11–12; Nichols, *Lit. Rems.*, ii.362.

11   *APC*, iii: 19 Apr. 1550 to 29 Apr., 5 attendances in 7; 28 May 1550 to 21 Oct., nil. He did attend Edward throughout the 1552 progres and was on a debt commission in December. He was active in local affairs: *Cal. Pat. R., 1550–3*, pp. 391, 395; ibid. *1553*, pp. 356, 362, 414; Leicester, *Records*, iii.52, 65, 67, 456; Nichols, *Lit. Rems.*, ii.436.

12   Ibid., ii.304. *APC*, iii.223, 232, 253, 262, 277, 294–5, 307–8, 324, 362. In December 1551 he took over Somerset's troop of 100 men-at-arms: ibid., ii.381.

13   *Cal. S. P. Domestic*, vi.406, 407.

14   Nichols, *Lit. Rems.*, ii.344; *APC*, iii.379.

15   Ibid., iii.379.

16   Nichols, *Lit. Rems.*, ii.350–2. The Northumberland dukedom was new; the Suffolk title had existed since 1448.

17   Holinshed, *Chronicles* (1808), vi.25.

18   *LP*, vii.153; cf. ibid. xiii(2), 1237.

19   See below, p. 74.

20   Dyer, *Reports*, i.188.

21   *Hist. of Parlt.*, i.405.

22   J. Hurstfield, 'Corruption and reform under Edward VI and Mary', in *EHR* 68 (1953), 23–8; *APC*, iii.479.

23   Fellow of St John's College, Oxford: *Original Letters*, p. 396, but ibid., p. 389 indicates Christ Church. No anglicizing of his name is entirely satisfactory.

24   Ibid., p. 389.

25   For the following see ibid., pp. 392–4.

26   Ibid., pp. 395–6: Edward VI's tutor, the future bishop of Ely.

27   Ibid., p. 399. The letter's contents and place in the correspondence confirm the date as March 1550, but Dorset was raised to no known dignity about this time. He received the Garter in 1547 and became a privy councillor in November 1549, but he gained no first-rank post in the redistribution of offices early in 1550; his dukedom came in October 1551. The likely resolution is that he became one of the six lords attendant on Edward, on the promotion of Lord Wentworth to the post of lord chamberlain on 2 February. A letter in that month confirms that Dorset is 'now daily to attend the king'. HMC *Middleton*, p. 519.

28   *Original Letters*, p. 407.

29   Ibid., p. 400.

30   Bullinger, *Decades*, iv.528.

31   *Original Letters*, 406–7; cf. p. 399.

32   Ibid., p. 443.

33   Florio, *Apologia*, quoted Yates, *Florio*, p. 10.

34   For this and the following see *ODNB* sub nom.

35   *Hist. of Parlt.*, iii.324.

36   Parkhurst, *Ludicra*, p. 50. He had been chaplain to Katherine Parr, and was with her when she died; bishop of Norwich, 1560–75.

37   Heinrich Bullinger, *Der Christlich Eestand* (Zurich, 1540); *Original Letters*, pp. 406, 427.

38   Ibid., p. 393; Jane was at Bradgate when Ascham visited.

39   Ibid., p. 422.

40   Ibid., p. 545.

41 Ibid., pp. 428–9, 434.
42 Ibid., p. 315.
43 Ibid., pp. 434–5.
44 Ibid., pp. 429–32.
45 Ibid., p. 430.
46 Ibid., pp. 4–7; *Epistolae Tigurinae*, pp. 3–5. Written between the death of Bucer 27 February and 12 July 1551 when a follow-up copy was sent; *Original Letters*, pp. 436–7.
47 Parkhurst, *Ludicra*, pp. 50, 51; Foxe, *Acts and Monuments* (1563), p. 923; BL, Egerton MS 2642 fo. 213ᵛ; Strype, *Annals*, ii(ii), 497.
48 *Original Letters*, pp. 276, 277, 422, 423, 429, 432.
49 Ibid., pp. 422, 427.
50 Ascham, *Works*, i(ii), 227.
51 *Cal. S. P. Domestic, Edward*, 794.
52 *Original Letters*, p. 423.
53 Ascham, *Works*, i(ii), 297–8. He also held out the inducement that Jane would inherit considerable wealth following the extinction of the male line of Brandons.
54 Nichols, *Lit. Rems.*, i.lxxviii.
55 Ibid., i.lxvii.
56 Yates, *Florio*, pp. 3–11; Wyatt, *Italian Encounter*, pp. 98–101.
57 Ibid., pp. 212–13.
58 BL, Sloane 3011; Cambridge Univ. Lib. Dd xi.46.
59 Chaloner, in *De Republica*, p. 298.
60 L. Richmond, 'Some appreciation of the Lady Jane Grey and her remains', in *The Fathers of the English Church* (1807), vi.688.
61 *Original Letters*, p. 432.
62 E. Baldwin, *The Life of Lady Jane Grey and of Lord Guildford Dudley her Husband* (1824), title page.
63 J. P. Carley, *The Books of Henry VIII and his Wives* (2004), pp. 14, 16.
64 *Original Letters*, p. 451.
65 Ibid., pp. 5–6; cf. other letters and letters lost, ibid., p. 451, n. 2.
66 Ibid., p. 4 in the handwriting of Aylmer. I owe this to Dr Alexandra Kess-Hall. Perhaps it is significant that Ulm said that he 'speaks Latin with elegance': see above, n. 38.
67 Ibid., p. 447: evidently this was overtaken by events.
68 Ibid., pp. 456, 457.
69 Ibid., p. 433: 29 May 1551, Ulm to Conrad Pellican.

7 A Godly Upbringing

1 E. W. Ives, *Henry VIII* (Oxford, 2007), p. 44.
2 Action against certain accused continued for some months. MacCulloch, *Church Militant*, pp. 63–8, 74–7
3 For the following see James, *Kateryn Parr*.
4 *ODNB*.
5 James, *Kateryn Parr*, p. 333; Latimer, *Sermons*, p. 228.
6 James, *Kateryn Parr*, p. 333.
7 Ibid, pp. 142, 314, 329; see below, pp. 236–7.
8 See above, pp. 60–2.
9 *ODNB*.
10 Ibid.
11 *Hist. of Parlt.*, iii.324–5.
12 *ODNB*: Inscription in St Paul's: 'twice a fighter in the cause of religion' ('*bis pûgil in causa religionis*').
13 A. C. Southern, *Elizabethan Recusant Prose, 1559–1582* (1950), pp. 59–76.
14 *Original Letters*, pp. 406–7; cf. ibid., 399.
15 Baum, 'The godly duke', p. 14.
16 Graves, *House of Lords*, pp. 223–4. The earl of Rutland attended 95% but he was newly come of age.
17 Bernard, in *Nobility*, p. 220.
18 *Cal. S. P. Spanish*, x.6: 14 Jan. 1550, Van der Delft to Charles V; Nichols, *Lit. Rems.*, ii.224. The record is brief: BL, Royal MS 17 Bxxxix fos. 31, 32.
19 Scudamore, *Letters*, p. 97; cf. *Original Letters*, p. 76: 5 Feb. 1550, Hooper to Bullinger: 'The marquis of Dorset, the earl of Warwick and the greater part of the king's council favour the cause of Christ as much as they can.'

20   *Cal. S. P. Spanish*, ix.489: 19 Dec. 1549, Van der Delft to Charles V.
21   Catherine Davies, *A Religion of the Word* (Manchester, 2002), p. 150.
22   *Original Letters*, p. 426; MacCulloch, *Cranmer*, p. 482.
23   Baum, 'The godly duke', p. 3.
24   J. Rivius, *A Treatise against the Folishnesse of Men in Differing the Reformation of their Living*, trans. J. Bankes (London, 1550), sig. a5ᵛ, 6; Baum, 'The godly duke', p. 8.
25   Ibid., p. 7. This is not the case with his presentments in Devon.
26   *ODNB*.
27   Baum, 'The godly duke', pp. 4–5.
28   Ibid., p. 5; *ODNB*.
29   Baum, 'The godly duke', p. 7.
30   *ODNB*.
31   *Original Letters*, p. 5.
32   e.g. November 1549: MacCulloch, *Cranmer*, p. 449.
33   Peter Stephens, 'The Church in Bucer's Commentaries on the Epistle to the Ephesians', in *Martin Bucer*, ed. D. F. Wright (1994), pp. 48, 49. See below, pp. 258, 260.
34   For the following see Wyatt, *Italian Encounter*, pp. 212–13.
35   Michelangelo, *Apologia*, pp. 27–8, quoted Yates, *Florio*, pp. 9–10.
36   *Original Letters*, p. 281.
37   Ibid., pp. 282–3.
38   Ibid., p. 288.
39   Bateson, *Leicester* iii.63; *APC*, iv, 307–8.

8   *Father and Daughter*

1   Foxe, *Acts and Monuments* (1563), p. 1746, adding that once the remark was reported to Mary, Jane forfeited Mary's affection.
2   *Cal. S. P. Venetian*, vi.884, p. 1054: 13 May 1557, Relation of Giovanni Michiel; *C. S. P. Spanish*, xiii.2: 27 Jul. 1554.

3   *Cal. S. P. Venetian*, v.934, p. 533, Relation of Girolamo Soranzo; 'adonnée a la pompe et gourgiasté': Vertot, *Ambassades*, ii.211.
4   *Cal. S. P. Spanish*, xii.7, 'mucho dios es menester para tragar este caliz'.
5   Ibid., xii.7; *Cal. S. P. Venetian*, v.934, p. 533: 18 Aug. 1554, Relation of Girolamo Soranzo.
6   Ibid., v.934, p. 532; ibid., vi.884, p. 1053–4: 13 May 1557, Relation of Giovanni Michiel; cf. A. Baschet, *La Diplomatie Vénétienne* (1862), p. 128; *Cal. S. P. Spanish*, xiii.2.
7   *Cal. S. P. Venetian*, v.884, p. 1054: 13 May 1557, Relation of Giovanni Michiel.
8   Ibid., iv.682. 15 May 1591, Marini Sanuto, 'Diaries'.
9   Ibid., vi.884, p. 1054: 13 May 1557, Relation of Giovanni Michiel.
10   *Cal. S. P. Spanish*, v(i).57: 21 Feb. 1534, Chapuys to Charles V.
11   *Cal. S. P. Spanish*, v(ii).182: 1 Jul. 1536, Chapuys to Charles V; *LP*, xi.7. She also appears to have been threatened with prosecution for treason, but it is hard to see this as other than a threat *in terrorem*.
12   And later a son and a daughter plus neonatal deaths.
13   Prescott, *Mary*, p. 22.
14   Loades, *Mary Tudor*, p. 14.
15   Ives, *Anne Boleyn*, p. 15.
16   For fourteenth- and fifteenth-century interest in establishing a male succession see M. J. Bennett, 'Edward III's entail and the succession to the crown, 1376–1471', *EHR* 113 (1998), 580–609.
17   1 *Mary* I, st.3 c.1 (1554).
18   Loades, *Mary Tudor*, p. 224.
19   *Cal. S. P. Venetian*, ii.1010, p. 433.
20   Loades doubted this, but cf. the July 1525 letter from Katherine to Mary: *Mary Tudor*, pp. 31, 42.
21   *Cal. S. P. Venetian*, v.934, p. 533: 18 Aug. 1554, Relation of Girolamo Soranzo; ibid., vi.884: 13 May 1557, Relation of Giovanni Michiel.
22   Following Dr Aysha Pollnitz, 'Princely education in sixteenth-century Britain' (PhD

thesis, Cambridge University, 2006), rather than Loades, *Mary Tudor*, pp. 31, 33.

23 Dowling, *Humanism*, p. 228.

24 Ibid., p. 228.

25 Ibid., p. 229.

26 Nichols, *Lit. Rems.*, i.9.

27 *Cal. S. P. Spanish*, v(i), p. 224.

28 Loades, *Mary Tudor*, pp. 108–11, 123–33.

29 *LP*, xvii.371; Charles V did not believe Henry would complete any agreed marriage involving Mary: *SP*, x.737: 30 Nov. 1545, Gardiner to Henry VIII.

9   Sister and Brother

1 '*grave passione di cuore*', lit. 'serious affection of the heart'. Alternatively he could have meant palpitations: *Cal. S. P. Venetian*, v.934, p. 533: 18 Aug. 1554.

2 Chandler, *Leland's Itinerary*, p. 317.

3 Bernard, in *Nobility*, p. 213.

4 *Cal. S. P. Spanish*, x.127: Jul. 1550, report of Jehan Dubois.

5 Ibid., xi.47: 30 May 1553, Scheyfve to Charles V; ibid., xi.57: 19 Jun. 1553, ditto. Cf. ibid., x.5: 12 Jun.1550: Mary to Charles V 'whom after God I take as the father of my soul and of my body in all spiritual & temporal matters'.

6 E. Duffy, *The Stripping of the Altars* (1992), pp. 451–3.

7 Foxe, *Acts and Monuments* (1576), p. 1289.

8 *Cal. S. P. Domestic, Edward*, 348.

9 *Cal. S. P. Spanish*, x.161: 17 Aug. 1550, Scheyfve to the Queen Dowager; ibid., x.176: 24 Sep. 1550, ditto.

10 See below pp. 132–3.

11 When this took place is unclear. Mary visited in February 1550 and in August she referred to seeing the king 'not long ago': *Cal. S. P. Spanish*, x.28: 10 Feb. 1550, Van der Delft to Charles V; ibid., x.151: 3 Aug. 1550, Scheyfve to Charles V.

12 Foxe, *Acts and Monuments* (1563), pp. 892–6.

13 Ibid., pp. 890–1.

14 *Cal. S. P. Spanish*, x.212: 27 Jan. 1551, Scheyfve to the Queen Dowager, enclosing Edward's letter to Mary.

15 *APC*, iii.215.

16 Machyn, *Diary*, p. 5.

17 Nichols, *Lit. Rems.*, ii.308–9; *Cal. S. P. Spanish*, x.258–60: 6 Apr., 1551, Scheyfve to Charles V.

18 Nichols, *Lit. Rems.*, ii.309.

19 Nichols, *Lit. Rems.*, i.ccxxvii–ccxxx. His withdrawal as ambassador was only temporary: *ODNB*. Morison was prejudiced, but could have got the story from the bishop of Rochester, one of those consulted; MacCulloch, *Church Militant*, pp. 38–9, 227 suggests Cecil was the source.

20 Edward quoted Psalm 78:59–61: Nichols, *Lit. Rems.*, i.ccxxxix.

21 Foxe, *Acts and Monuments* (1563), p. 898.

22 See below p. 232.

23 Alexander Barclay, the second initially pursued, was won over to reform: MacCulloch, *Cranmer*, pp. 495–6.

24 Loades, *Mary Tudor*, p. 163.

25 Ibid., p. 163; Hoak, *King's Council*, pp. 66–9; Arundel and Derby; *APC*, iii.329.

26 Ibid., iii.333.

27 Ibid., iii.338–40.

28 Ibid., iii.340–1, 352.

29 Ibid., iii.341–6, 348–52.

30 Ibid., iii.351.

31 Ibid., iii.352. 'The Fleet is a prison in London but much less ominous than the Tower': *Cal. S. P. Spanish*, x.390: 26 Oct. 1551: Scheyfve to Charles V.

32 *APC*, iii.508. They were not allowed to return to Mary until she made a special plea in April 1552: ibid., iv.20.

33 War was declared in September but hostilities began in May/June: Nichols, *Lit. Rems.*, ii.331–2, 343.

34 Loades, *Mary Tudor*, p. 167; MacCulloch, *Cranmer*, p. 496. For the diplomatic situation see below, pp. 155–6.

35 'if you should be suffered to break our laws manifestly, were it not a comfort for others to do so': Foxe, *Acts and Monuments* (1576), p. 1291: 24 Jan. 1551, Edward VI to Mary.
36 See Brigden, *London*, pp. 506–11.
37 And as suggested by Charles V: *Cal. S. P. Spanish*, x.68–9: 22 Apr. 1550, Van der Delft to Charles V; ibid., x.284–5: 26 Apr. 1551, ditto.
38 Nichols, *Lit. Rems.*, ii.428, n. 3.
39 For the following see *Cal. S. P. Domestic, Edward*, 776, 777; *Cal. Pat. R., 1550–3*, p. 134; ibid. *1553*, pp. 97–9, 176–7; Loades, *Mary Tudor*, p. 139. Occupation could precede completion of the legalities.
40 *APC*, iv.188. Mary's letter to the council implies that she was reimbursed for all the repairs on her estate: *Cal. S. P. Domestic, Edward*, 777.
41 Colvin, *King's Works*, iii(i) (1975), 254. Loades, *Mary Tudor*, p. 139 suggests that Mary was reluctant to leave St Osyth's and that the government wanted to reduce her access to the coast (as also *Cal. S. P. Spanish*, xi.49: 11 June, 1553, Scheyfve to Charles V). However, one of the new properties was Bungay which had ready access to the sea.
42 For the following: Machyn, *Diary*, pp. 30–1. Corruptions in the original have been removed.
43 If Mary came from Hunsdon in Hertfordshire, the decision to enter London through Bishopsgate and parade along the Cheap was deliberate; if she came from Newhall in Essex that route would be normal.
44 Machyn, *Diary*, p. 31. The presence chamber indicates a grand formal reception, but the imperial ambassador says Mary was received in Edward's bedchamber. *Cal. S. P. Spanish*, xi.9: 17 Feb. 1553, Scheyfve to Charles V.
45 Ibid., xi.35: 28 Apr. 1553, Scheyfve to Charles V.

10 John Dudley: The Career

1 The heir to a peerage would normally have been tried as a commoner, but a new peerage had been created for John by summons, 5 January 1553.
2 See below, pp. 159–61.
3 e.g. Anne Boleyn.
4 Wriothesley, *Chronicle*, i.90–1.
5 *DKR* iv(ii), 233.
6 *Chronicle of Queen Jane*, p. 99; Foxe agrees that he did have a warrant under the broad seal but does not specify the monarch: *Acts and Monuments* (1570), p. 1569. But since Dudley accepted that Mary was the legitimate ruler, his plea makes sense only if referring to Edward.
7 *DKR* iv(ii), 233.
8 *Cal. S. P. Spanish*, xi.171: 16 Aug. 1553, Ambassadors to Charles V.
9 Ibid., xi.186–7: 27 Aug. 1553, Ambassadors to Charles V.
10 Ibid., xi.184–5: 27 Aug.1553, Ambassadors to Charles V.
11 For the career see Loades, *Northumberland*; Beer, *Northumberland*; *ODNB*; *Hist. of Parlt.*, ii.63–6.
12 Hall, *Chronicle*, p. 671.
13 Pollard, *History*, p. 98.
14 Polydore Vergil, *Anglicae Historiae*, ed. D. Hay, (Camden Sec. 3rd ser. lxxiv, 1950), p. 127.
15 S. Gunn, 'The accession of Henry VIII', in *Historical Research*, 64 (1991), 278–88.
16 *ODNB*.
17 'Quelques particularitez d'Angleterre', Bib. Nat. Ancien Saint-German Français 15888, fo. 216.
18 Hall, *Chronicle*, pp. 688–91.
19 Wriothesley, *Chronicle*, i.117.
20 *LP*, ix.886.
21 Ibid., xi.753.
22 Ibid., xii (1).353–4, 457, 601.
23 *SP*, ii.588.

24 *LP*, xvii.163(2), g.220(46). This was a new title, though said to be 'by right of his mother'. Loades, *Northumberland*, pp. 48–9.

25 *Hamilton Papers* ii.no. 232, p. 361.

26 For the following see Margaret Rule, *The Mary Rose* (1982), pp. 30–8.

27 Originally he was to command. *Cal. S. P. Spanish*, ix.127: 24 Jul. 1547: Ambassador to Charles V.

28 William Patten, 'The expedition into Scotland (1548)', in *Tudor Tracts*, ed. A. F. Pollard (1903), pp. 92–4.

29 Ibid., p. 121.

30 *Cal. S. P. Domestic, Edward*, 358. According to Sotherton, Drury was heavily involved. 'The commoyson in Norfolk, 1549', ed. B. L. Beer, in *Journal of Medieval and Renaissance Studies* 6:1 (1976), 96.

31 *Hamilton Papers* i, no. 286, p. 394: 22 Jan. 1543, Lisle to Council.

32 *LP*, xxi(1), 785, 806.

33 *SP*, xi.261; *LP*, xxi(1), 1405.

34 For the above see Loades, *Northumberland* p. 85. E. W. Ives, 'Henry VIII's will: the protectorate provisions of 1546–7', in *Historical Journal* 37 (1994), 905–9; H. Miller, 'Henry VIII's unwritten will', in *Wealth and Power in Tudor England*, ed. E. W. Ives et al. (1978), pp. 88–91, 96–7, 101–2.

35 Nichols. *Lit. Rems.*, i.ccxxvii.

36 'Quelques particularitez d'Angleterre', Bib. Nat. MS Ancien Saint-German Français 15888, fos 214ᵛ–216ᵛ.

37 Loades, *Northumberland*, p. 82; G. Redworth, *In Defence of the Church Catholic* (Oxford, 1990), p. 239.

38 William Patten, 'The expedition into Scotland (1548)', in *Tudor Tracts*, p. 93.

39 See below, p. 116.

40 Troughton, in *Archaeologia* 23, p. 30.

41 Fuller, *Church History*, ii.370. Beaulieu, Papers and Letters on Public Events &c, 1553[1546]–1735, i.1 is different but to the same effect.

42 Knox, *Admonition*, quoted in Nichols, *Lit. Rems.*, i.clxx.

43 *Vita Mariae*, p. 245.

44 A poem from 1535–6 refers to 'the love and devotion with which you and your noble wife adorn the ties of sacred marriage'. *Nugarum*, no. 39, p. 385. This did not prevent Dudley resenting the way his fortune had been carved up. *Lisle Letters*, ii.597, vii.929.

45 *LP*, xxi(1), 1406.

46 Jul. 1552, Dudley to Henry Sidney: Beer, Northumberland, p. 135.

47 S. Gunn, 'A letter of Jane, duchess of Northumberland, in 1553', in *EHR* 114 (1999), 1270.

48 National Archives, PROB 11/37 fos 194–5.

49 Loades, *Northumberland*, p. 224; cf. 'but for a few children which God hath sent me which also helpeth to pluck me on my knees I have no great cause to desire to tarry much longer here'. *Cal. S. P. Domestic, Edward*, 800; Tytler, *Edward and Mary*, ii.155: 3 Jan. 1553, Dudley to Cecil.

50 *Lisle Letters*, v.42–3, 95; *LP*, xiii(i) 337.

51 See below, p. 177.

52 *Cal. S. P. Domestic, Edward*, 630; Tytler, *Edward and Mary*, ii.115–16: 2 Jun. 1552, Dudley to Cecil.

53 See above, p. 104.

54 *Chronicle of Queen Jane*, pp. 25–6.

11   John Dudley: The Black Legend

1 De Guaras, *Relation*, p. 85.

2 Loach, *Edward VI*, pp. 160–2.

3 *Vita Mariae*, p. 245.

4 Pollard, *History*, p. 81.

5 Bindoff, *Tudor England*, p. 165.

6 Loades, *Reign of Mary*, p. 62.

7 G. R. Elton, *Reform and Reformation* (1977), p. 372.

8 Beer, *Northumberland*, p. 148.

9 For an opposite but minority view see Jordan and Gleason, in *Harvard Library*

Bulletin 23, 147–8: 'There was no treason, no hint of vaulting ambition, no clinging to the substance of power during the tortured later months when the serious nature of Edward's illness became only too evident.'

10   Ponet, *Treatis* (1642), p. 62. Alcibiades, an Athenian general (5th century BC) regarded as the archetype of capricious treachery.

11   *Chronicle of Queen Jane*, p. 21 n.

12   Commendone, *Accession*, pp. 4–5.

13   *Chronicle of Queen Jane*, p. 25.

14   Cavendish, *Visions*, p. 121.

15   'A "journall" of matters of state', p. 54; 'Certayne Brife Notes', pp. 124–5.

16   Far from plotting against Thomas Seymour, Dudley warned him about his behaviour. *Cal. S. P. Spanish*, ix.340: 8 Feb. 1549, Van der Delft to Charles V; *Cal. S. P. Domestic, Edward*, 193.

17   *Cal. S. P. Spanish*, ix.19–20: 17 Feb. 1547, Van der Delft to Charles V.

18   Ibid., ix.122: 10 Jul. 1547, Van der Delft to Charles V.

19   Ibid., x.548: 9 Jul. 1552, Scheyfve to Charles V.

20   See below p. 233. The memory of Ket's rebellion endured for a generation. MacCulloch, *Suffolk*, p. 313.

21   J. Berkman, 'Van der Delft's letter', in *BIHR* 53 (1980); *Cal. S. P. Spanish*, x.445: 15 Sep. 1549, Van der Delft to Charles V.

22   For the following see *Chronicle of King Henry the Eighth*, ed. M. A. S. Hume (1889), pp. 185–6; *Cal. S. P. Domestic, Edward*, 358; Tytler, *Edward and Mary*, i.198; 'Certayne Brife Notes', pp. 125–8; *APC*, ii.328–9.

23   *Cal. S. P. Domestic, Edward*, 358; Tytler, *Edward and Mary*, i.198. Somerset specifically tried to counter the accusation about withholding wages. *Cal. S. P. Domestic, Edward*, 376: Tytler, *Edward and Mary*, i.214 n; Pocock, *Troubles*, 27–8.

24   *APC*, ii.330; subsequent meetings were held elsewhere.

25   Ponet, *Treatis* (1642), p. 62. Sir Thomas Arundel and Sir Richard Southwell were Catholics close to Mary.

26   HMC *Salisbury*, i.76.

27   'Certayne Brife Notes', pp. 134–6; cf. Hoak, *King's Council*, pp. 241–58.

28   Ibid., p. 61; Nichols, *Lit. Rems.*, ii.255–6, 268.

29   *Cal. S. P. Domestic, Edward*, 439.

30   Wriothesley, *Chronicle*, ii.41.

31   Nichols, *Lit. Rems.*, ii.273–4.

32   The dukedom of Norfolk was forfeit; the duke of Suffolk was a minor.

33   Deposition Mayor's Court of Norwich, 1 Jul. 1550: *TED*, iii.51. The constant involvement of the council in investigating reports of local unrest shows its positive interaction with the local gentry, not crown weakness, *pace* Jordan, *Edward VI*, ii.56–69, and 'the violence and iniquity of Northumberland's rule', in A. F. Pollard, *England under Protector Somerset* (1900), p. 312.

34   See above, p. 56; Challis, 'Circulating Medium', p. 119, n. 2.

35   Brigden, *London*, pp. 505–7.

36   *Cal. S. P. Domestic, Edward*, 442; Tytler, *Edward and Mary*, ii.21–4. Dudley did not attend the wedding at Sheen either because he was ill or because he was suspicious. *Cal. S. P. Spanish*, x.80–6: 2 May, 1550, Van der Delft to Charles V; ibid., x.98: 6 Jun. 1550, Van der Delft to Charles V; 'A "journall" of matters of state', p. 52.

37   See below, p. 247.

38   *Cal. S. P. Spanish*, xi.46: 30 May 1553, Scheyfve to Charles V; ibid., xi.55: 15 Jun. 1553, Scheyfve to Charles V.

12   *John Dudley: Motives*

1   Tytler, *Edward and Mary*, ii.148; *Nugarum*, no. 83, p. 252, no. 39, pp. 385, 429. Their eldest son became one of Bourbon's pupils; MacCulloch, *Church Militant*, pp. 52–3.

2 This was only three months before 34 and 35 Hen. VIII c.1 restricted access to the vernacular scriptures.

3 *The Examinations of Anne Askew*, ed. E. V. Beilin (Oxford, 1996), p. 96.

4 *Cal. S. P. Spanish*, viii, p. 555: 29 Jan. 1547, Chapuys to the Regent of the Low Countries; cf. ibid., viii, pp. 533–4: 24 Dec. 1546, Van der Delft to Charles V; ibid., ix.221: 5 Dec. 1547, ditto.

5 Beer, *Northumberland*, pp. 69–70; F. A. Gasquet and E. Bishop, *Edward VI and the Book of Common Prayer* (1890), pp. 398, 400, 404–5, 442; MacCulloch, *Cranmer*, p. 406; *Lords' Journals*, i.331; See above p. 71.

6 6 Nov. 1549: *Tudor Proclamations*, i.484; cf. 25 Dec. 1549 stating the Act of Uniformity etc. is not 'the only act of' Somerset: ibid., pp. 485–6; cf. Dudley's remarks to the imperial ambassador in November 1549: *Cal. S. P. Spanish*, ix.476–7: 26 Nov. 1549, Van der Delft to Charles V; cf. Richard Scudamore's comment: Scudamore, *Letters*, pp. 96–7.

7 *The forme and maner of makyng and consecratyng Archebishoppes, Bishoppes, Priestes and Deacons* (Richard Grafton 1549/50), sig. Hiv.

8 Foxe, *Acts and Monuments* (1563), pp. 822–4.

9 *Original Letters*, p. 422; *Cal. S. P. Spanish*, x.222: 13 Feb. 1551, Ambassador to Charles V; cf. 'I have always known the same a most mighty, zealous, and ardent supporter, maintainer, and defender of God's lively word': John Bale, 1552, quoted in MacCulloch, *Church Militant*, p. 53; 'that most faithful and intrepid soldier of Christ': *Original Letters*, p. 82, 27 Mar. 1550, Hooper to Bullinger; 'He is a most holy and fearless instrument of the word of God': ibid., p. 89, 29 Jun. 1550, ditto.

10 Ibid., p. 439.

11 See above. pp. 89–90.

12 *Cal. S. P. Spanish*, x.259: 6 Apr. 1551, Scheyfve to Charles V.

13 Bindoff, *Tudor England*, pp. 160–1.

14 Loades, *Northumberland*, pp.199–200, 268; cf. Beer, *Northumberland*, p. 25; Jordan, *Edward VI*, ii.363.

15 MacCulloch, *Cranmer*, pp. 497–500, 518–34.

16 Ibid., p. 499.

17 *Cal. S. P. Domestic, Edward*, 747; Tytler, *Edward and Mary*, ii.142: 28 Oct. 1552, Dudley to Cecil.

18 *Cal. S. P. Domestic, Edward*, 779; Tytler, *Edward and Mary*, ii.148: 7 Dec. 1552, Dudley to Cecil.

19 MacCulloch, *Church Militant*, pp. 151–4; *Cranmer*, pp. 531–5.

20 Ibid., pp. 500–3, 524–5, 532–4; B. L. Beer, 'Episcopacy and reform in Tudor England', in *Albion* 23.2 (1991).

21 *Cal. S. P. Spanish*, xi.33: 10 Apr. 1553, Jehan Scheyfve, Advices.

22 Tytler, *Edward and Mary*, ii.153: 2 Jan. 1552, Northumberland to Cecil.

23 Loades, *Northumberland*, p. 198.

24 Loades, *Reign of Mary*, p. 99.

25 Machyn, *Diary*, p. 42.

26 *Chronicle of Queen Jane*, pp. 18–19; Grey Friars, *Chronicle*, p. 83.

27 BL, Harley MS 284 fo. 127 (quoted Tytler, *Edward and Mary*, ii.231). Beer, *Northumberland*, p. 162 notes that Dudley mentioned neither the pope nor the mass, but he had accepted the mass the day before and he did endorse 'the true Catholic church' and possibly the Apostolic Succession; de Guaras, *Relation*, p. 107; Commendone, *Accession*, pp. 28–9; BL, Harley MS 284 fo. 127; Jordan and Gleason, in *Harvard Library Bulletin* 23, 172–5, 327–30.

28 *Chronicle of Queen Jane*, p. 25; *Cal. S. P. Spanish*, xi.187: 27 Aug. 1553, Ambassadors to Charles V.

29 MacCulloch, *Cranmer*, p. 594.

30 *Cal. S. P. Spanish*, xi.186: 27 Aug. 1553, Ambassadors to Charles V, saying that Northumberland acknowledged Mary's succession as the hand of God.

31 Jordan and Gleason, in *Harvard Library Bulletin* 23, 340–1.

32   *Chronicle of Queen Jane*, pp. 18–20, ~~pace Loades, Northumberland, p. 268.~~

33   Pollard, *History*, p. 97; *Chronicle of Queen Jane*, p. 25.

34   See below. p. 212.

35   'Relation de l'accusation et mort du duc de Sommersett', Bib. Nat. MS Ancien Saint-German Français 15888, fos 209, 209ᵛ.

36   Robert Parsons said that the emperor was sent a letter and replied, which is impossible in the time, but on 16 August Renard had told Mary that Charles V did not wish Northumberland to be forgiven. Muller, *Stephen Gardiner*, p. 222; *Cal. S. P. Spanish*, xi.168: 16 Aug. 1553, Ambassadors to Charles V. Gardiner did take personal responsibility for the well-being of the duke's soul: Beer, *Northumberland*, p. 158; 'Quelques particularitez d'Angleterre', Bib. Nat. MS Ancien Saint-German Français 15888, fos 217ᵛ–218ᵛ; 'Relation de l'accusation et mort du duc de Sommersett', ibid. fos 209, 210. *Cal. S. P. Spanish*, xi.186: 27 Aug. 1553, Ambassadors to Charles V, says that Gardiner accompanied Dudley to the scaffold. G. Redworth, *In Defence of the Church Catholic* (Oxford, 1990), p. 295 follows, but Loades, *Northumberland*, p. 270 and Beer, *Northumberland*, pp. 158, 161 say the bishop of Worcester, as de Guaras, *Relation*, p. 107, Commendone, *Accession*, p. 29, BL, Harley MS 284 fo. 127 (quoted Tytler, *Edward and Mary*, ii.232) and *The saying of John late Duke of Northumberlande upon the scaffolde* (John Cawood, 1553) in Jordan and Gleason, in *Harvard Library Bulletin* 23, 327–30.

37   Foxe, *Acts and Monuments* (1563) suggests the possibility; ibid. (1570) states it as a fact.

38   BL, Harley MS 787, fo. 61ᵛ: 'most woeful was the news I received this evening by Mr. Lieutenant, that I must prepare myself against tomorrow to receive my deadly stroke.'

39   Ives, *Anne Boleyn*, p. 422.

40   BL, Harley MS 787, fo. 61ᵛ.

41   Wriothesley, *Chronicle*, ii.100.

~~42   Chronicle of Queen Jane, p. 18 implies~~ that the execution was put on hold because the duke asked for the mass; Machyn has the mayor summoned after the postponement: *Diary*, p. 42.

43   *Cal. S. P. Spanish*, xi.187: 27 Aug. 1553, Ambassadors to Charles V.

44   Jordan and Gleason, in *Harvard Library Bulletin* 23, 342–54. By contrast, little use was made of it in England.

45   The following is based on an analysis of 250 letters in *State Papers*, i, iv, v *passim*; e.g. Walter Bucler routinely uses 'God save your Majesty', Edward Carne 'conserve your most excellent Majesty', Stephen Gardiner 'for the preservation of your most noble person long to continue in much felicity', William Paget 'prosperity in all your affairs', and earl of Shrewsbury 'to reign the years of Nestor'.

46   Similar exculpations can be found, e.g. Paget to Henry VIII, 18 Dec. 1545: 'Sir, I beseech your Majesty most humbly at your feet to think (as it hath liked you to do always by your goodness of my simple proceedings) that no man desireth more to serve to your contentation than I, and that I have not this desire for any profit, commodity or estimation (all which you have of your inestimable bountifulness and liberality poured upon me plentifully) but only for my duty's sake, for my conscience's sake, and for that I love you with all my heart, having found you, my good master, most gentle, benign and affable. As God knoweth to whom I pray daily on my knees to send you long life, good health and prosperity in all your affairs': ibid., x.783. It is the frequency of Dudley's anxieties which is notable.

47   *LP* xvii 1194: 12 Dec. 1542, Lisle to Henry VIII.

48   *Hamilton Papers* i, no. 262, p. 344: 21 Dec. 1542, Lisle to Henry VIII.

49   *SP*, iv 239.

50   *Hamilton Papers* I, no. 286, p. 394: 22 Jan. 1543, Lisle to Council.

51 *Hamilton Papers*, no. 339, p. 490: 24 Mar. 1543, Lisle to Henry VIII.
52 *LP*, 20(1) 1237; Haynes, *State Papers*, i.51–2; HMS, *Salisbury*, i.185: 21 Jul. 1545, Lisle to Henry VIII.
53 *SP*, i. 756–7 [*LP*, 20(1)]: 14 Jun. 1545, Lisle to Council. cf. Loades, *Northumberland*, p. 85.
54 Ibid., ii.824: 21 Aug. 1545, Lisle to Henry VIII.
54 Ibid, xi.256: 30 Jul. 1546, Lisle and Wotton to Henry VIII, although clearly written by Lisle.
56 'of force' = open pursuit.
57 *Cal. S. P. Domestic, Edward*, 779; Tytler, *Edward VI and Mary*, ii.150: 7 Dec. 1552, Dudley to Cecil.
58 Haynes, *State Papers*, i.137.
59 *Cal. S. P. Domestic, Edward*, 118 (National Archives, SP10/4/22); Loades, *Northumberland*, pp. 103, 179.
60 *LP*, 20(2) 405. The illness was only temporary.
61 Ibid., 427.
62 Ibid., 391.
63 *LP*, 21(1) 121.
64 *LP*, 19(2) 338.
65 *Cal. S. P. Domestic, Edward*, 123.
66 See above p. 110; cf. Beer, *Northumberland*, p. 76.
67 BL, Add. MS 48126 fo. 7ᵛ. See also a grievance over coining: 'A "journall" of matters of state', p. 60.
68 *Cal. S. P. Spanish*, ix.340; *Cal. S. P. Domestic, Edward*, 193.
69 *APC*, ii.344–5.
70 Loades, *Northumberland*, p. 199.
71 *Cal. S. P. Domestic, Edward*, 732, 734, 747, 750; cf. ibid., 465, 800.
72 Ibid., 789.
73 Ibid., 773.
74 Ibid., 811.
75 'Il avoit eu des accidens de malade dont il se sentoit fort or n'estoit point sans douleur. Il avoit un bras gaste': 'Quelques particularitez d'Angleterre', Bib. Nat. MS Ancien Saint-German Français 15888, fo. 214; *Cal. S. P. Spanish*, ix.383: 28 May 1549, Van der Delft to Charles V.

76 See above p. 109.
77 Loades, *Northumberland*, p. 103, n.70.
78 Ibid., p. 104; Beer, *Northumberland*, pp. 66–8. The trouble in October 1552 was a serious throat infection: ibid., 732, 734. See also *Cal. S. P. Spanish*, ix.122: 10 Jul. 1547, Van der Delft to Charles V; ibid., ix.383: 28 May 1549, ditto; ibid., x.605, 9 Dec. 1552, Scheyfve to Queen Dowager; HMC *Salisbury*, i, no. 380, p. 95; Haynes, *State Papers*, i.119; Loades, *Northumberland*, p. 119.
79 *Cal. S. P. Spanish*, viii.489: 19 Dec. 1548, Van der Delft to Charles V.
80 Scudamore, *Letters*, pp. 91–5.

13 *The Young King*

1 *SP*, i.571.
2 Nichols, *Lit. Rems.*, i.cxcix.
3 For the following, ibid., i.xxxvi–vii.
4 Holbein, National Gallery of Art, Washington, D.C.
5 Fuller, *Church History*, ii.370.
6 *Vita Mariae*, p. 246.
7 J. A. Froude, *The Reign of Mary Tudor* (1909), p. 302.
8 Ives, in *The Reign of Henry VIII*, pp. 1–23.
9 Nichols, *Lit. Rems.*, i.46–7; *Cal. S. P. Domestic, Edward*, 202; Tytler, *Edward and Mary*, i.154–5.
10 *ODNB*.
11 See above p. 124; D. E. Hoak, 'The King's Privy Chamber, 1547–1553', in *Tudor Rule and Revolution*, ed. D. J. Guth and J. W. McKenna (Cambridge, 1982), pp. 87–108. Alford, *Kingship*, pp. 137–40 particularly stresses the element of continuity.
12 See above pp. 56–7; *ODNB*.
13 'Quelques particularitez d'Angleterre', Bib. Nat. MS Ancien Saint-German Français 15888, fo. 216.
14 Nichols, *Lit. Rems.*, i.58.
15 'Quelques particularitez d'Angleterre', Bib. Nat. MS Ancien Saint-German Français 15888, fo. 216ᵛ.

16 Alford, *Kingship*, p. 153.

17 HMC *Salisbury*, i.86–7; cf. 'I never desired to meddle with any of his Highness' money, I can so evil keep my own': *LP*, xxi(1) 553: 6 Apr. 1546, Lisle to Paget.

18 *Cal. S. P. Domestic, Edward*, 800.

19 Nichols, *Lit. Rems.*, i.cxlv–vi.

20 *Cal. S. P. Spanish*, x.258: 6 Apr. 1551, Scheyfve to Charles v; Nichols, *Lit. Rems.*, ii.571. Dr Alford points out that James IV of Scotland was 14 when declared of age. Alford, *Kingship*, p. 171.

21 Nichols, *Lit. Rems.*, ii, *passim*; Hughes and Larkin, *Tudor Proclamations*, i. nos. 372–82. Edward did not record the other proclamations issued in the life of the Chronicle, i.e. 1 and 20 Feb. 1552, and 27 Oct 1552: ibid., nos. 383–5.

22 Challis, *Coinage*, pp. 107–8.

23 *Cal. S. P. Spanish*, x.437: 14 Jan. 1552, Scheyfve to Charles V. ibid. x.493: 30 Mar. 1552, Scheyfve, Advices.

24 Nichols, *Lit. Rems.*, ii.387; *Cal. S. P. Spanish*, x.436–7: 14 Jan. 1552, Scheyfve to Charles V.

25 Scheyfve noted that the king was thoroughly informed.

26 *Cal. S. P. Domestic, Edward*, 555; Nichols, *Lit. Rems.*, ii.347–8; Alford, *Kingship*, pp. 160–1. Hoak, *King's Council*, pp. 138–41 takes this as evidence of Dudley using the king, but Loades, *Northumberland*, pp. 191–2 sees 'more than a touch of recognizable Tudor spirit'. Edward accepted that 'by oversight it chanced, and not thinking the more [signatures] the better'.

27 *APC*, iii.411; Hoak, *King's Council*, pp. 147, 150–1, 155 interprets this as Dudley exploiting procedure, but fails to note the effective revival of the Henrician system: E. W. Ives, 'Henry VIII's will – a forensic conundrum', in *Historical Journal* 35 (1992), 782, 784–7.

28 Nichols, *Lit. Rems.*, ii.337; *Cal. S. P. Spanish*, x.361: 12 Sep. 1551: Scheyfve to Charles V; cf. ibid., x.493, 592: 30 Mar. 1552, 20 Nov. 1552: Scheyfve to Charles V.

29 Jordan, *Edward VI*, ii.422.

30 Hoak postulated training sessions to reconcile Edward's paper of March 1552 with the absence of evidence that Edward attended routine council meetings. But if the paper is a private scheme by the king there is no need to postulate special training sessions. That the council registers never refer to Edward being present is not conclusive, because (a) registers almost never record policy discussions (the part of the agenda he might attend) and (b) Henry VII apart, Tudor monarchs appeared at the council only ad hoc and pro tem, i.e., as Edward said, 'when[ever] [they] would'. Hoak, *King's Council*, pp. 120–1, 132–6.

31 Nichols, *Lit. Rems.*, i.93–143.

32 Ibid., i.181–205.

33 For what follows see Nichols, *Lit. Rems.*, ii.513–38; MacCulloch, *Church Militant*, pp. 30–4; *The Register of the Order of the Garter*, ed. J. Anstis (1724), appendix, pp. xlvi–lii.

34 Nichols, *Lit. Rems.*, ii.475–572; this excludes the minute for his will: ibid., pp. 574–6.

35 Ibid., pp. 489–90.

36 *Cal. S. P. Domestic, Edward*, 588; Nichols, *Lit. Rems.*, ii.491–5; cf. ibid. ii.406. Cecil added four more topics. As it pre-dates the abandonment of the subsidy bill, Edward was writing in advance of parliament. Bills dealing with three of Edward's and one of Cecil's topics were introduced but none passed.

37 Nichols, *Lit. Rems.*, ii.495–8. An act for apparel was one of the Cecil additions, see above, n. 36, and a bill on the subject was introduced into the Commons (whether based on the king's somewhat impractical ideas is not known), but it got nowhere: *Commons' Journal*, p. 20. *Cal. S. P. Spanish*, xi.32: 10 Apr. 1553, Scheyfve, Advices says a bill for apparel was dropped in the March 1553 session.

38 Nichols, *Lit. Rems.*, ii.403; BL, Cotton MS Nero C.x, fo. 841, 'The names of the hole councel'; Nichols, *Lit. Rems.*, ii.498–502.

39 Jordan, *Edward VI*, ii.452. Professor Hoak sees the purpose as providing training for Edward: *King's Council*, pp. 131–6; Alford, *Kingship*, pp. 161–6 sees the provisions as a political rather than bureaucratic measure 'to focus the consideration of public affairs on the person of the king'.

40 It is in draft with deletions and corrections and Edward admits that his paper contradicts arrangements already in place: Nichols, *Lit. Rems.*, ii.501–2.

41 If Dr Alford is correct at n. 39, 'The names of the hole councel' would be a document bridging Edward's exercises and his implementation papers.

42 Nichols, *Lit. Rems.*, ii.456–7, 539–43. The Cecil section dated 'Windsor 23 September' is a shortened version of a position exercise no doubt presented to the council on 19 September: BL, Cotton MS Galba B xii.fo. 230. Edward must have heard about (or even attended) the discussion on the 19th and asked Cecil for a fair copy.

43 BL, Lansdowne MS 1236, fos 19–20; Nichols, *Lit. Rems.*, ii.543–9; *APC*, iv.142–3. Only one routine topic is recorded in the register, which suggests that the rest of the meeting was concerned with the king's paper.

44 Nichols, *Lit.Rems.*, ii.550; for the earlier discussions see ibid., ii.460; *Cal. S. P. Domestic, Edward*, 723; Hoak, *King's Council*, pp. 203–4, 339.

45 Nichols, *Lit. Rems.*, ii.552–5; *APC*, iv.203.

46 F. G. Emmison, 'A Plan of Edward VI and Secretary Petre for reorganizing the privy council's work', in *BIHR* 31 (1958), 203–10.

47 Hoak, *King's Council*, pp. 91–2, 164, but comparison with Paget's 1550 'Advice to the king's council', ibid., pp. 273–5, suggests an overlap with only four of Paget's nine rules.

48 See above p. 116.

49 Nichols, *Lit. Rems.*, ii.547.

50 Ibid., ii.574.

14 'My Deuise for the Succession'

1 Inner Temple, Petyt MS, 47 fo. 317; Nichols, *Lit. Rems.*, ii.571–2.

2 *Chronicle of Queen Jane*, p. 99.

3 Fuller, *Church History*, ii.370. Beaulieu, Papers and Letters, i.1.

4 Bindoff, in *History Today* 3, 647.

5 Jordan, *Edward VI*, ii.515.

6 Nichols, *Lit. Rems.*, ii.574–6, written by Petre and headed 'to be contained in my last will, as parcel thereof'.

7 Ibid., ii.574: 'according to the statute provided in that behalf', i.e. 7 Edward VI c.2. The two documents are also congruent with the 'deuise' laying down the order for the succession and who is to be 'governess' of the realm, and the notes prescribing the extent of discretion over policy and patronage and giving instructions to press on with a number of policies.

8 HMC *Salisbury*, i.108; *Cal. S. P. Spanish*, xi.9: 17 Feb. 1553, Scheyfve to Charles V; ibid., 10: 17 Feb., Scheyfve to the bishop of Arras; Machyn, *Diary*, p. 30; Nichols, *Lit. Rems.*, i.clxxvii–viii; Wriothesley, *Chronicle*, ii.81–2.

9 *Cal. S. P. Spanish*, xi.22: 31 Mar. 1553, Scheyfve, Advices; ibid., 32: 10 Apr. 1553, Scheyfve to the bishop of Arras; ibid., 34: 10 Apr. 1553, Scheyfve, Advices; Wriothesley, *Chronicle*, ii.83; Machyn, *Diary*, p. 33.

10 *Cal. S. P. Spanish*, xi.35: 28 Apr. 1553, Scheyfve to Charles V; ibid., xi.37: 5 May 1553, ditto.

11 Vertot, *Ambassades*, ii.4–5.

12 HMC *Salisbury*, i.121; Haynes, *State Papers*, i.149.

13 BL, Lansdowne MS 3 fo. 23.

14 Haynes, *State Papers*, i.149–50; Nichols, *Lit. Rems.*, i.cxc.

15 *Cal. S. P. Spanish*, xi.40: 12 May 1553, Scheyfve to Charles V.

16 Haynes, *State Papers*, i.150: 15 May 1553, Petre to Cecil; Vertot, *Ambassades*, ii.25.

17 1 Mary st.3 c.1: 'being the very true and undoubted heir and inheritrix' of the crown; 1 Elizabeth c.3: 'rightly, lineally, and lawfully descended and come of the blood royal of this realm'.

18 Ives, in *Historical Research* 81, 258, 261–2, 266. Surrey History Centre MS Cor 3/3: Edward 'considering that ... it should [be] prejudicial to all those that be of the blood royal'.

19 England had never had a queen regnant.

20 35 Henry VIII c.1 reciting 28 Henry VIII, c.7.

21 Ives, in *Historical Research* 81, 268–9.

22 'as concerning the order and disposition of the imperial crown ... and also for a full gift disposition assignment declaration limitation and appointment to whom ... [the crown] ... shall remain and come': 35 Henry VIII c.1; 'declaration, order, assignment, limitation and appointment': Edward, see below pp. 146–7, 167–8.

23 Ives, in *Historical Research* 81, 261–3.

24 28 Henry VIII, c.7, clauses 5 and 6.

25 Ibid., clause 9.

26 Ibid., clause 18.

27 1 Edward VI, c.12, clause 8.

28 Bindoff identified the date 28 March 1553 by reference to the reception of the French ambassadors: *History Today* 3, 647.

29 The alteration to 'Lady Jane and her heires masles' must have been made after 28 May when the report that Edward's condition was terminal destroyed all prospect of VERSION 2 delivering a child while the king was still alive.

30 The final paragraphs of VERSION 1 were also crossed through on the assumption that they were not relevant to a queen regnant, but see n. 32.

31 Nichols, *Lit. Rems.*, ii.572. This subsequent involvement of Edward removes the possibility that the changes producing VERSION 2 were forged.

32 Ibid., ii.572. The signature 'in six several places', indicates that the deleted paragraphs of VERSION 2 had been reinstated. They would be relevant in the event of Jane having no son, and they appear in VERSION 4 which Montagu confirms was prepared 'according to such articles as were signed with the king's proper hand, above and beneath and on every side'. Earlier he had been given 'a bill of articles not signed with the king's hand', indicating that the king added his signature to enforce obedience. None of these documents is extant. Fuller, *Church History*, ii.369, 372.

33 Ibid., ii.370.

34 Pollard, *History*, p. 83; Loach, *Edward VI*, p. 164.

35 Jordan and Gleason, in *Harvard Library Bulletin* 23, 140–1, 148.

36 *Chronicle of Queen Jane*, p. 93.

37 See below p. 192. Diarmaid MacCulloch suggests that this fear explains the support which erstwhile reformist critics gave to Northumberland: *Church Militant*, p. 102.

38 Unless Wingfield was following John Gosnold, SG: *Vita Mariae*, pp. 247, 294. De Guaras, *Relation*, p. 87 and Commendone, *Accession*, p. 5 were writing after the event.

39 e.g. 'letters patent': Wriothesley, *Chronicle*, ii.85 and Jane's proclamation, below at p. 192; 'will': Grey Friars, *Chronicle*, p. 79; Thomas Cranmer to Mary, Dec. 1553 in *Letters*, p. 445; *Vita Mariae*, pp. 247–8. VERSION 4 refers to the will that Edward would be making, but only notes for this survive: *Chronicle of Queen Jane*, p. 98; Nichols, *Lit. Rems.*, ii.574–6. John Baker suggests that technically the document was a will: Dyer, *Reports*, i.xlvii.

40 Note the parallel to the language of Henry VIII's will; cf. also 'having also (thanks be to the living God) our full, whole and perfect memory'.

41 A patent would end 'in witness whereof we have caused this our letters to be made patent'.

42   The document was issued as if a proclamation, i.e. under the great seal on the authority of the sign manual. Henry avoided the authorization problem by choosing to proceed by will, not patent.
43   See above p. 140–1.
44   Fuller, *Church History*, ii.369–74; Beaulieu, Papers and Letters, i.1.
45   Fuller, *Church History*, ii.369.
46   See above p. 105.
47   Fuller, *Church History*, ii.371.
48   Beaulieu, Papers and Letters, i.1ᵛ.
49   The warrant to send out writs is dated 25 June: *Calendar of Patent Rolls, Edward VI* (1924–9), v.419. Decision taken '5 days ago': *Cal. S. P. Spanish*, xi.66, 24 Jun. 1553, Scheyfve to Charles V. Cranmer was ordered to convene Convocation for 19 September: MacCulloch, *Cranmer*, p. 541.
50   E. W. Ives, *The Common Lawyers of Pre-Reformation England* (Cambridge, 1983), pp. 232–4.
51   The lawyers signed on the Thursday following the end of the Law term: Fuller, *Church History*, ii.372–3.Those signing the patent or the engagement to maintain it or both were: Cholmeley CJKB, Portman JKB, Montagu CJCP, Browne JCP, Bradshawe CBExch, Griffin AG, Gosnold SG, Dyer K.Sjt., Bowes MR, Baker Chanc. Exch., North Chanc. Augmentations, Mason and Lucas masters of requests, and Anthony Browne of the Middle Temple. John Cockes, the third master of requests, was imprisoned by Mary, possibly for involvement: *Hist. of Parlt.*, i.663. Bromley JKB did not sign but promised to obey the king and draft the patent: Fuller, *Church History*, ii.372. Two judges did not sign, probably because terminally ill: Edmund Mervin JKB (will dated 24 July, probate 16 November, not reappointed by Mary) and William Coke JCP, present, according to Wingfield, at the meeting with Edward but dead 24 August: *Vita Mariae*, p. 246. Saunders, Broke and Whiddon, king's serjeants, did not sign; the remaining judge, Hales JCP, refused

to do so. The puisne barons of the Exchequer were seemingly not involved.
52   *Vita Mariae*, p. 248.
53   'The Life and Death of Archbishop Cranmer', in Nichols, *Narratives*, pp. 225–6.
54   Edward 'by the advice and consent of his whole council and the chief judges of the realm, gave the crown with the realm to Lady Jane': ibid., p. 225.

15   *King and Minister*

1   BL, Harley MS 284 fo. 127; Tytler, *Edward and Mary*, ii.231.
2   Commendone, *Accession*, p. 48; *State Trials*, p. 766; 'Quelques particularitez d'Angleterre', Bib. Nat. MS Ancien Saint-German Français 15888, fo. 217; 'Relation de l'accusation et mort du duc de Sommersett', ibid., fos 211ᵛ, 212. Cheke and Goodrich were also blamed: ibid., fos 216–7, 225.
3   *Chronicle of Queen Jane*, p. 21.
4   Challis, 'Circulating Medium', p. 142, n. 2; Nichols, *Lit. Rems.*, i.clxvi n., ii.374 n.; *Tudor Proclamations*, i.535; cf. *APC*, ii.375, 469–70.
5   Ibid., iv.120, 129, 130, 211, 269, 288–9. Nichols, *Lit. Rems.*, i.clxvi–viii. Antony Gyllet is clearly a relative of Elizabeth Huggons née Gyllet.
6   *Cal. S. P. Spanish*, x.573: 20 Nov. 1552, Scheyfve to Charles V.
7   *Cal. S. P. Spanish*, xi.8–9: 17 Feb. 1553, Scheyfve to Charles V; ibid., xi.35: 28 Apr. 1553, ditto; ibid., xi.44: 20 May 1553, ditto.
8   De Guaras, 'Relation', p. 87.
9   Commendone, *Accession*, pp. 4, 5.
10   See above, p. 46.
11   Bindoff, in *History Today* 3, 647.
12   Nichols, *Lit. Rems.*, i.clxvii, clxviii. The preference for Clifford over Grey must bury the story that Dudley had his eyes on the crown long term.
13   See below, p. 185.
14   See below, p. 185.

15   *Cal. S. P. Spanish*, x.425: 27 Dec.
1551, Scheyfve, 'Advice'; ibid., x.549: 9
Jul. 1552, Scheyfve to the Queen Dowager;
ibid., x.579: 14 Oct. 1552, Scheyfve,
'Advice'; ibid., xi.13: 21 Feb. 1553,
Scheyfve to Charles V; ibid., xi.40, 12 May
1553, ditto; Nichols, *Lit. Rems.*, ii.465.
16   Pembroke's interest survived through
all the successive redactions of the 'deuise'.
17   Ives, in *Historical Research* 81,
274–6.
18   *Cal. S. P. Spanish*, xi.51: 11 Jun.
1553, Scheyfve to Charles V; *Hist. of
Parlt.*, ii.62; BL, Royal MS 18 C fo. 364.
19   Strype, *Annals*, iv.485.
20   *Cal. S. P. Spanish*, xi.169: 16 Aug.
1553, Ambassadors to Charles V; ibid.,
xi.203: 4 Sep. 1553, ditto.
21   Ibid., xi.49–50: 11 Jun. 1553,
Scheyfve to Charles V.
22   After his suspicions of 28 April
(above at n. 7), Scheyfve's first mention
of a move in favour of Jane is dated 15
June: ibid., xi.55: 15 Jun. 1553, Scheyfve
to Charles V.
23   Ibid., xi.203–4: 4 Sep. 1553, Ambassadors to Charles V.
24   Ibid., xi.169: 16 Aug. 1553, ditto.
25   For the following, Vertot, *Ambassades*, ii.3–7; Harbison, *Rival Ambassadors*, pp. 35–6.
26   'il est venu jusques a nous demander
ce que nous ferions si nous estions en sa
place': Vertot, *Ambassades*, ii.6.
27   Ibid., ii.4.
28   Nichols, *Lit. Rems.*, i.clxxxvi; Petre
wrote that day to the same effect: Haynes,
State Papers, i.149.
29   Scheyfve reported this on 28 April:
Cal. S. P. Spanish, xi.35; his previous communication was dated 10 Apr. 1553: ibid.,
xi.30–4.
30   Ives, in *Hist.Research* 81, 273–4.
31   From Cadiz where American gold
and silver was landed to the bullion market
at Antwerp.
32   Tytler, *Edward and Mary*, ii.180–1.
33   Haynes, *State Papers*, i.121: 16 May
1553, Thomas Chaloner to William Cecil.

34   *Cal. S. P. Spanish*, xi.46–7: 30 May
1553, Scheyfve to Charles V.
35   Ibid., xi.46: ditto.
36   Harbison, *Rival Ambassadors*, p. 37;
Vertot, *Ambassades*, ii.38: 15 June 1553,
Montmorency to de Noailles: 'I pray you
thank [the duke] for my part for the
honest words he has transmitted to me
via Aubespine, making him fully understand the great satisfaction which the
king continues to find in him for the indications that more and more he is inclined
to his service.'
37   *Cal. S. P. Domestic, Edward*, 826.
38   *Cal. S. P. Spanish*, xi.55: 15 Jun.
1553, Scheyfve to Charles V.
39   If the case conference came before
the meeting with de l'Aubespine, the
assurance of French protection could
have been the factor which tipped the
scales in favour of obeying the king.

16   The Will of a King

1   De Guaras, *Relation*, p. 106; Beer,
Northumberland, p. 161; Loades, *Northumberland*, p. 270.
2   See the excuses of Shrewsbury and
Mason: *Cal. S. P. Spanish*, xi.95.
3   Ponet, *Treatis* (1642), p. 64. Something similar is implied in the speech
attributed to Arundel: 'If happily [i.e.
haply] you think it a disparagement to
proclaim Mary queen, having already
acknowledged Jane, showing thereby
your variableness in that kind, I tell you
that this ought not to prevail with you, for
when you have committed an error you
ought to amend it': Arundel, in *Gent.
Mag.* 103, 119–20.
4   *APC*, iv, *passim*. Senior lay councillors
are defined as all with precedence ahead
of the secretaries of state, i.e. earls and
above plus the lord admiral, the lord
chamberlain and the vice-chamberlain
(namely Winchester, Northumberland,
Bedford, Suffolk, Northampton, Shrewsbury, Huntingdon, Pembroke, Clinton,

Darcy, Gates, but omitting Westmorland and Hereford (no attendances after parliament) and Cobham (none after 23 May).

5 Attendances reached ten on only three previous occasions: 6 March, 9 April, 2 May.

6 Median attendance before June was 61%, in June 100%. Adding the treasurer and the comptroller of the household (Cheyne and Cotton) reduces the individual averages from 53% to 46%, 92% to 83% and 100% to 92% for the last week. The above figures contrast with those in Hoak, *King's Council*, p. 111 because (a) they cover only senior counsellors and (b) there was a different pattern of activity in 1553.

7 Winchester, Northumberland, Bedford, Northampton, Shrewsbury, Huntingdon, Pembroke, Clinton, Darcy, Cobham and Gates.

8 See above, p. 148.

9 The council record ends with the meeting of 16 June. According to the imperial ambassadors, the council was meeting in secret without secretaries. *Cal. S. P. Spanish*, xi.57: 19 Jun. 1553, Ambassadors to Charles V.

10 Inner Temple, MS Petyt 47, fo. 316; Nichols, *Lit. Rems.*, ii.572–3. Alternatively, did Edward fear he might not survive to sign the 'declaracion'?

11 Montagu, Baker and John Lucas. Lucas was only a master of requests but his subsequent treatment suggests he was the draftsman. See below pp. 245–6.

12 Vertot, *Ambassades*, ii.40–1. The 'engagement' refers to the 'deuise' as 'to be written in full order' and thus must be prior to 21 June when VERSION 4 was returned by Chancery. The 'engagement' carries the signatures of Winchester, Bedford, Shrewsbury and Cheyne who the ambassadors report were unwilling and also those of Cranmer and Cecil (see below pp. 162–5). Thus their resistance must have been overcome by 18 or at the latest 21 June.

13 *Cal. S. P. Spanish*, xi.57: 19 Jun. 1553, Scheyfve to Charles V.

14 Ibid., xi.66: 24 Jun. 1553, Scheyfve to Charles V; xi.70: 4 Jul. 1553, Scheyfve to Charles V; Vertot, *Ambassades*, ii.40–1.

15 See below, p. 218.

16 26 Jun. 1553: gift to earl of Bedford of lands in Cornwall; ditto earl of Shrewsbury in consideration of service of Coldharbour, etc. and lands in Yorkshire: BL, Royal MS 18 C XXIV fos 368^v, 369^v.

17 26 Jun. 1553: gift to earl of Pembroke of Dunyate, Somerset. BL, Royal MS 18 C XXIV fo. 368^v.

18 Knox, *Admonition*, sig. Cv–Di^v. For Shebna, the treasurer of King Hezekiah who was condemned by God, see Isaiah 22:15–19. According to Holinshed, Winchester helped persuade the guard to march: *Chronicle*, p. 1407.

19 *Cal. S. P. Spanish*, xi.70: 4 Jul. 1553, Scheyfve to Charles V; 1 Jul. 1553; BL, Royal MS 18 C XXIV fo. 373^v: pardon to earl of Arundel of bond in 10,000 marks.

20 Fuller, *Church History*, ii.372.

21 See above, n. 3.

22 See above, p. 159.

23 For the following see Cranmer, *Letters*, ii.443–4; Nichols, *Narratives*, pp. 225–6.

24 The source says 'will', but in the sense of 'desire'. Since Cranmer later signed the 'declaracion', his objection must have been to the engagement. The signatures of Cranmer and Goodrich to the engagement appear to have been crammed in after the peers had signed, but nothing is known of the chancellor refusing. Nichols, *Lit. Rems.*, ii.573 n.

25 Cranmer, *Letters*, ii.445. MacCulloch suggests that the support for canon law in Edward's will was an inducement to Cranmer to sign, but see above p. 136: MacCulloch, *Cranmer*, pp. 539–41.

26 BL, Lansdowne MS 102 fo. 2; Tytler, *Edward and Mary*, ii.192–5: '*Justus adjutoris meus Dominus, qui salvos facit rectos cord[e]*'.

27 BL, Cotton MS Titus B2. fo. 374^r; Strype, *Annals* iv.485–9.

28 The possibility is that Cecil was concerned to rebut charges of disloyalty in John Leslie's *Treatise of Treasons against Q. Elizabeth* (1572).

29 Alford wrote the text submitted but Cecil kept the original autograph. Strype, *Annals* iv.489.

30 Alford, *Burghley*, p. 52.

31 Foxe, *Acts and Monuments* (1570), p. 1568; HMC *Finch*, pp. 1–2.

32 Read, *Cecil*, p. 94. This overlooks Cranmer (see above, n. 23), Montagu and Baker (see below, n. 33).

33 Alford, *Burghley*, p. 57 agrees that Cecil's refusal was to sign the engagement. But confusion or duplicity is inescapable: (a) Cecil says he refused to 'subscribe the book' where the engagement is a single sheet; (b) the witness to the signatures on the engagement was Edward himself; (c) Montagu and John Baker (both councillors) signed the engagement after Cecil; (d) Roger Alford's 'the instrument' must refer to the 'declaracion'.

34 APC, iv.285; Fuller, *Church History*, ii.369.

35 APC, iv.286–9. Since Petre, Cecil and Cheke signed the engagement, they cannot have been excluded from all meetings.

36 *Cal. S. P. Spanish*, xi.54: 15 Jun. 1553, Scheyfve to Charles V; ibid., xi.70: 4 Jul. 1553, Scheyfve to Charles V; Vertot, *Ambassades*, ii.41.

37 See below pp. 232, 235. The remaining absentee was the earl of Cumberland.

38 Four – Cobham, Darcy, Clinton, Rich – were privy councillors and had signed the engagement.

39 Jane, *Proclamation*; *Original Letters*, pp. 272–3; Holinshed, *Chronicles*, iii.1063.

40 Bindoff, in *History Today* 3, 643.

41 Grey Friars, *Chronicle*, p. 78.

42 Troughton, in *Archaeologia* 23, p. 31.

43 'Aske's Examination', ed. Mary Bateson, in *EHR* 5 (1890), 563–4.

44 Statute of Merton.

45 *Cal. S. P. Venetian*, v.934, pp. 535–6: 18 Aug. 1554, Relation of Girolamo Soranzo, accepting the black legend.

46 See above, p. 146.

47 The 'declaracion' clearly reflects the original acts, e.g. the description of Mary and Elizabeth.

48 'whole blood'. Mary and Elizabeth were only of the half blood to each other and to Edward and so could not inherit from him or each other.

49 As deposed by Henry Dudley: *Cal. S. P. Spanish*, xi.173: 16 Aug. 1553, Ambassadors to Charles V, see below p. 194.

17   Preparations

1 De Guaras, *Relation*, p. 88.

2 *Cal. S. P. Spanish*, xi.79, 10 Jul. 1553, Ambassadors to Charles V.

3 MacCulloch, *Cranmer*, p. 542; cf. *Vita Mariae*, p. 249.

4 *Cal. S. P. Spanish*, xi.70: 4 Jul. 1553, Scheyfve to Charles V.

5 Ibid., xi.65: 24 Jun. 1553, Scheyfve to Charles V.

6 Harbison, *Rival Ambassadors*, p. 43.

7 Nichols, *Lit. Rems.*, ii.284–5, 291, 323, 327.

8 *Cal. S. P. Spanish*, xi.44: 20 May 1553, Scheyfve to Charles V, 'The duke of Northumberland continues to send news and has offered his good offices to the princess on several occasions.'

9 Ibid., xi.49: 11 Jun. 1553, Scheyfve to Charles V; ibid., xi.70: 4 Jul. 1553, ditto.

10 *Vita Mariae*, p. 251.

11 De Guaras, *Relation*, p. 89.

12 *Cal. S. P. Spanish*, xi.106: 20 Jul. 1553, Advices from England.

13 J. L. McIntosh, *From Heads of Household to Heads of State: the Pre-Accession Households of Mary and Elizabeth Tudor* (Columbia, N.Y., 2008), ch. 4, paras.1–42.

14 *Cal. S. P. Venetian*, v.934, p. 537: 18 Aug. 1554, Relation of Giacomo Soranzo.

15   *Cal. S. P. Spanish*, xi.74–5: 7 Jul. 1553, Ambassadors to Charles V.

16   Hayward, *Life and Raigne*, pp. 177–8; cf. Pollard, *History*, pp. 88–9; Tittler, *Mary*, p.7; *Chronicle of Queen Jane*, p. 1n; Vertot, *Ambassades*, ii.208; Jordan, *Edward VI*, ii.519.

17   Hayward, *Life and Raigne*, p. 6 (written c.1611–20).

18   Camden, *Historie*, sig. div^r; F. A. Mumby, *The Girlhood of Queen Elizabeth* (1909), p. 81.

19   *Hist of Parlt.*, ii.198–9; N. P. Sil, *Tudor Placemen and Statesmen* (Cranbury, N.J., 2001), p. 83.

20   HMC *Salisbury*, i.93–4; Hayes, *State Papers*, i.117, wrongly dated 1551.

21   See below n. 55; the MS has no date but the outside limits are Thursday 6 July and Sunday 9 July.

22   Colvin, *King's Works*, iv(2), 154–7, 172–5.

23   *Cal. S. P. Spanish*, xi.49: 11 Jun. 1553, Scheyfve to Charles V.

24   Ibid., xi.70: 4 Jul. 1553, Scheyfve to Charles V.

25   Ibid., xi.49: 11 Jun. 1553, Scheyfve to Charles V.

26   Pollard, *History*, pp. 88–9 says that Mary was summoned two days before the death, but this is not supported, as claimed, by *Cal. S. P. Venetian*, 537 and de Guaras, *Relation*, p. 89. *Vita Mariae* says nothing of this.

27   Loades, *Mary Tudor*, p. 165.

28   *Cal. S. P. Spanish*, xi.35: 28 Apr. 1553, Scheyfve to Charles V.

29   R. W. Hoyle, 'War and public finance', in *The Reign of Henry VIII*, ed. Diarmaid MacCulloch (1995), pp. 90–5. Coins of 33.33% fine were issued from 1546 to 1550 (sterling being 92.5% fine); Northumberland would sanction an issue of 25% fine in 1551, but this was prior to a revaluation of all coins to a standard of approximately 92% fine: Challis, *Coinage*, pp. 313–17.

30   Jack, in *Parergon* n.s. 6, 148.

31   D. Hoak, 'The secret history of the Tudor court: the king's coffers and the king's purse, 1542–1553', in *Journal of British Studies* 26 (1987), 220–9; Hoak, *King's Council*, pp. 210–11; S. Gunn, *Early Tudor Government* (1995), p. 151.

32   Brereton, *Letters and Accounts*, pp. 55, 279.

33   Jack, in *Parergon* n.s. 6, 144–5; Beer, *Northumberland*, p. 183; Margaret Audley had married Henry, the second Dudley son, soon after Audley's death in 1544: ibid., pp. 194–5.

34   *APC*, iv.293, 306, 313, 314.

35   *Hist. of Parlt.*, ii.446–7; *Cal. Pat. R., 1553–4*, p. 224.

36   *Cal. S. P. Spanish*, xi.108: 20 Jul. 1553, Advices.

37   *APC*, iv.345; *Cal. Pat. R., 1553–4*, p. 316.

38   *Hist. of Parlt.*, ii.445.

39   *Cal. S. P. Spanish*, xi.66: 24 Jun. 1553, Scheyfve to Charles V.

40   Jack, in *Parergon* n.s. 6, 144. Even in the professional army of Spain pay was regularly substantially in arrears and until Farnese's reforms in the 1590s Spanish troops did not receive rations: G. Parker, *Spain and the Netherlands* (1979), p. 112.

41   Normal costs of an accession included payments for the ceremonial of proclamation and for the printing and circulation of copies of the proclamation. The principal expense was the coronation. Beyond these were the costs of new patents of office and new seals and heraldry: *APC*, iv.426. Payment, however, could be delayed for several years: ibid., iv.261.

42   11 Jul. 1553: payments by Peckham to Thomas Mildmay, Benjamin Gonson, Edward Warner (lieutenant of the Tower), the earl of Oxford and the master of the posts totalling £11,291 6s. 8d.: Jack, in *Parergon* n.s. 6, 146.

43   *APC*, iv.338, 352. However, this may also have included expenditure on Mary's behalf: ibid., iv.417.

44   Ibid., iv.340.

45   Davies in *Econ.HR* ser. 2 xvii.235. In 1546 Henry VIII paid 9d. a day for English horsemen: *SP*, xi.118. In 1549 costs of a troop of mercenary cavalry amounted to 22d. per man per day. The gendarmes had received 13d. a day on their long-term engagements: Jordan, *Edward VI*, ii.20; *APC*, iv.15. Suffolk offered 6d. in 1554; see below p. 263.

46   For the size of the duke's force in 1553 see below pp. 199–200. The army for the invasion of Scotland in 1547 cost £1,000 a day for 14,000 foot and 4,000 horse plus transport to Scotland and back, supplies (deducted) at 2s. 3d. a day: *Col. S. P. Domestic Edward*, 95.

47   Grey Friars, *Chronicle*, p. 80.

48   Hoak, in *Journal of British Studies* 26, 222.

49   John Stow, *Survey of London*, ed. C. L. Kingsford (1908), i.113, 145, 151, 174, 301; ii.182–3. The philanthropic activity of all three shows that they had ample funds at their disposal. For the link with Yorke, see Jordan, *Edward VI*, ii.458–9.

50   Jack, in *Parergon* n.s. 6, 145.

51   *Cal. S. P. Spanish*, xi.55: 15 Jun. 1553, Scheyfve to Charles V.

52   Nichols, *Lit. Rems.*, ii.458.

53   *APC*, iv.49–50, 276–8, effectively repeating those of 16 May 1552. In 1553, Leicestershire (duke of Suffolk) was omitted, no doubt by accident, and Northumberland replaced the earl of Westmorland as lieutenant in the bishopric of Durham. Antony Wingfield (Suffolk) had died and been replaced by Lord Wentworth.

54   *Cal. S. P. Spanish*, xi.44: 20 May 1553, Scheyfve to Charles V and de Noailles (Vertot, *Ambassades*, ii.41: 22 Jun. 1553) state that the lords had been sent home, but this must reflect expectation.

55   HMC *Salisbury*, i.93–4; Haynes, *State Papers*, i.117: endorsed 'The letters of the sudden removing of Queen Mary'. It is not dated, and although the addressee is simply referred to as 'your good Lordship',

the mention of 'the great carefulness and pains by your Lordship there taken for the good order of that country' suggests that the intended recipient was a lord lieutenant who was not apprised of events in London. This is confirmed by a part-completed text intended for Lord Ferrers and Lord Wentworth who were the lieutenants for Staffordshire and Suffolk and were both absent. A similar part draft was for 'counsellors in the North and Wales' which probably means the absentee earls of Derby and Cumberland (for Lancashire and Westmorland) and the deputies of the duke of Northumberland and the earl of Pembroke (for Northumberland, Cumberland, Durham and Wales). It also points out (ibid., 117–18) that the journey is 'too far off for any of her accustomed journeys' and dismisses the excuse which 'some of hers' had produced about sickness in the house. 'We see no likelihood of truth therein', as Mary could easily have moved to Hatfield Castle or Copthall near Romford.

56   Molyneux, in *Arch. Journ.* 30, 276; *Cal. S. P. Spanish*, xi.77–8: 10 Jul. 1553, Ambassadors to Charles V.

57   e.g. ibid., xi.132: 2 Aug. 1553, Ambassadors to Charles V; ibid., xi.135: 2 Aug. 1553, Renard to Charles V etc.

58   Ibid., xi.195: late Aug. 1553, Ambassadors to Mary; cf. ibid., xi.151–2, 155, 166–7, 172–3, 188–9, 194.

59   Ibid., xi.62–4: 23 Jun. 1553, Charles V to Ambassadors.

60   Ibid., xi.66: 24 Jun. 1553, Scheyfve to Charles V; ibid., xi.67: 27 Jun. 1553, ditto.

61   Ibid., xi.71: 4 Jul. 1553, Scheyfve to Charles V.

62   Vertot, *Ambassades*, ii.47; de Noailles makes no mention of an aborted visit on 22 June.

63   Ibid., ii.45.

18   Jane the Queen

1   Strickland, *Tudor Princesses*, p. 136; see below pp. 291–2.

2 Contile, *Historia*, fo. 10ᵛ; Rosso, *I successi*, fos 4ᵛ, 5. Wingfield, however, has it that Jane's mother was 'vigorously opposed' to the match. *Vita Mariae*, p. 245.

3 Commendone, *Accession*, p. 5.

4 Rosso, *I successi*, fo. 5

5 *Cal. S. P. Spanish*, xi.168: 16 Aug., 1553, Ambassadors to Charles V.

6 See above p. 47.

7 Foxe, *Acts and Monuments* (1563), p. 809.

8 I have been unable to verify this from the original. We do not have what she said verbatim.

9 *ODNB*, sub nom Paulet; Chapman, *Portraits* (1960), p. 160 says that the marriage contract was signed 1551; *ODNB*, sub nom Seymour refers to negotiations in 1551.

10 See above p. 153.

11 BL, Royal MS 18 C XXIV fos 340ᵛ, 363ᵛ.

12 *Cal. S. P. Spanish*, xi.40: 12 May 1553, Ambassadors to Charles V.

13 'A description of England and Scotland (Paris, 1558)', in *Antiquarian Repertory* 4 (1809), 503. Various dates have been proposed for the wedding. It took place on Thursday 25 May: Surrey History Centre MS 6729/9/113.

14 *Cal. S. P. Spanish*, xi.40: 12 May 1553, Ambassadors to Charles V; ibid., xi.45–6: 30 May, ditto; Nichols, *Lit. Rems.*, i.cxvi; *Vita Mariae*, p. 245.

15 *Cal. S. P. Spanish*, xi.47: 30 May 1553, Scheyfve to the bishop of Arras.

16 Ibid., xi.53: 12 Jun. 1553, Scheyfve to the bishop of Arras.

17 Commendone, *Accession*, p. 5; Rosso similarly *I successi*, fos 4ᵛ, 5.

18 Wriothesley, *Chronicle*; Grey Friars, *Chronicle*; Machyn, *Diary*.

19 Grafton, *Chronicle*, fo. 156; BL, Harley MS 2342 fos 59ᵛ–60.

20 Grafton issued Jane's proclamation and may well have known Guildford.

21 *Cal. S. P. Spanish*, xi.47: 30 May 1553, Scheyfve to the bishop of Arras.

22 Commendone, *Accession*, pp. 47–8; Stone, *Mary I*, p. 497.

23 Commendone, *Accession*, p. 48; also Stone, *Mary I*, p. 499, Rosso, *I successi*, fo. 56ᵛ.

24 Ibid. The phrase 'come donna & amoreuole di mio marito' is only found in Rosso. For the letter see above pp. 18–19.

25 See below p. 189.

26 *Cal. S. P. Spanish*, xi.113: 22 Jul. 1553, Ambassadors to Charles V.

27 See above pp. 18–19.

28 The following is reconstructed from Commendone, *Accession*, pp. 45–8 and Pollini, *L'Historia*, pp. 354–8 (Stone, *Mary I*, pp. 496–9). The latter is the fuller but as the later of the two was most at risk of 'improvement'.

29 See above pp. 12, 171. However, Mary understood this as 'three days before they went to fetch her from Sion', apparently intending Friday 7 July; see below p. 248.

30 Commendone, *Accession*, p. 45.

31 Colvin, *King's Works*, iv(2), 64.

32 Vertot, *Ambassades*, ii.211.

33 Pollini, *L'Historia*, p. 357; Stone, *Mary I*, p. 498.

34 *Cal. S. P. Spanish*, xi.106: 20 Jul. 1553, anon., 'Advices'.

35 Wriothesley, *Chronicle*, ii.86; *Cal. S. P. Spanish*, xi.106: 20 Jul. 1553, anon., 'Advices'.

36 *Chronicle of Queen Jane*, p. 3. For the entry into the Tower see Battista Spinola, quoted Davey, *Jane Grey*, p. 253.

37 e.g. *Cal. S. P. Spanish*, xi.80: 10 Jul. 1553, Ambassadors to Charles V.

38 BL, Harley MS 611; Davey, *Jane Grey*, pp. 292 ff.

39 HMC *Salisbury*, i.128–9. This is headed 'stuff delivered to the Lady Jane, usurper, at the Tower' and has been construed as a list of items provided for Jane when a prisoner. It is better understood as delivered to Jane on entering the Tower. Cf. BL, Harley 611 fos 17 ff.; Nicholas, *Memoirs* cxxvᵛ–cxxiixᵛ.

40 Presumably a stuffed animal.

41 Otherwise known as barbes. See
Shakespeare, *Merry Wives of Windsor*
Act 4, ii.69–72. Barbes were associated
with mourning.

42 J. R. Planché, *History of British Costume* (1846), p. 250; C. W. Cunnington
et al., *Dictionary of English Costume*
(1965), p. 10.

43 See above pp. 54–5.

44 Pollini, *L'Historia Ecclesiastica*,
p. 357; Stone, *Mary I*, p. 499.

45 Ibid.

46 Pollini, *L'Historia Ecclesiastica*,
pp. 357–8; Stone, *Mary I*, p. 499; Commendone, *Accession*, p. 48 and Rosso,
I successi, fo. 56ᵛ, but reading as Stone
p. 499 instead of 'by me and by act of
parliament'.

47 *Cal. S. P. Spanish*, xi.113: 22 Jul.
1553, Ambassadors to Charles V.

48 BL, Harley MS 523 fos. 11ᵛ, 12ᵛ: 14
Jul. 1553, Hoby to the Council. Hoby's
informant, Don Diego, was Guildford's
godfather.

49 Leo X to Giuliano de Medici.

50 Pollini, *L'Historia Ecclesiastica*,
p. 357; Stone, *Mary I*, p. 498; Commendone, *Accession*, p. 48; Rosso, *I successi*, fo.
56 to the same effect.

19 The Council in London

1 Harold Macmillan.

2 Molyneux, in *Arch. Journ.* 30, 276.

3 Foxe, *Acts and Monuments* (1570),
p. 1567.

4 *Cal. S. P. Spanish*, xi.82–3: 11 Jul.
1553, Ambassadors to Charles V.

5 *Vita Mariae*, pp. 252, 253, 295 n.

6 Foxe, *Acts and Monuments* (1570), p.
1568. This letter too is dated 9 July. Given
the distances involved this is impossible
unless Mary postdated her letter in the
belief that it would have a greater impact
if it arrived on the date it was apparently
written. More probably, the council's letter should be dated 10 July.

7 See below pp. 218–9.

8 Vertot, *Ambassades*, ii.57. The proclamation is about 1860 words long.

9 Once Mary was on the throne there
was every reason to get rid of material
promoted for a traitor. The council
letters survive in a copy dated 10 July,
addressed to the marquis of Northampton as lieutenant for the counties
of Surrey, Northampton, Bedford and
Berkshire (BL, Lansdowne MS 1236
15 fo. 24; Strype, *Memorials* iii.p. 2),
and another drafted the same day
but dated 11 July to the marquis and
his deputies in Surrey, along with the
sheriff, the chief JPs and the 'worship-
ful' of the shire: Surrey History Centre
6729/13/8.

10 *Chronicle of Queen Jane*, pp. 103–5.

11 HMC *Finch*, pp. 1–2; 'Letter of
the Council of Queen Jane Grey' in
Retrospective Review 2nd ser. i.504. of
'the old servitude of the Antichrist
of Rome': Surrey History Culture, MS
Cor 3/3.

12 List compiled from known arrests,
exclusion from the general pardon and
action taken by the privy council.

13 Fitzgerald was the heir to the forfeited earldom of Kildare.

14 *APC*, iv.312, 313, 332, 425.

15 Ibid., iv.416; *Vita Mariae*, p. 270;
Chronicle of Queen Jane, p. 13.

16 *APC*, iv.307, 416.

17 MacCulloch, *Suffolk*, pp. 232–3.

18 'The copie of a Pistel', in *Chronicle of
Queen Jane*, pp. 115–21.

19 Susan Brigden disagrees: *London*,
pp. 523–6.

20 Ibid., p. 521. Stow, *Annales*, p. 1031
says 6 aldermen, 6 staplers and 6 merchant
adventurers, but there were others.
Absentees include a 1552–3 sheriff (John
Maynard), the 1553–4 mayor (Thomas
White) and a 1554–5 sheriff (David
Woodroffe); the latter two were staunch
Catholics.

21 Brigden, *London*, p. 521.

22 See pp. 168, 196.

23 *Cal. S. P. Spanish*, xi.92: 16 Jul. 1553, Ambassadors to Charles V; Strype, *Memorials*, III(i).57.

24 National Archives, C82/973: 14 Jul. 1553, bill signed by Jane appointing Edward Benard sheriff of Wiltshire.

25 Troughton, in *Archaeologia* 35, 23–46.

26 Tittler and Battley, in *BIHR* 57, 136, 137.

27 BL, Lansdowne MS 103, fos 1, 1ᵛ.

28 The list is very rough, with duplication and no pattern to the counties named.

29 The clerk of the crown and the future MP. Clinton had been put in charge of the Tower of London and was preparing to join the force against Mary.

30 BL, Lansdowne MS 103, fos 2, 2ᵛ.

31 *Cal. S. P. Spanish*, xi.74: 7 Jul. 1553, Ambassadors to Charles V; Harbison, *Rival Ambassadors*, p. 47.

32 Vertot, *Ambassades*, ii.52–3.

33 The imperial ambassadors were incorrect in dating this meeting 7 July: *Cal. S. P. Spanish*, xi.77: 10 Jul. 1553, Ambassadors to Charles V.

34 Harbison, *Rival Ambassadors*, pp. 45–6; the text in Vertot, *Ambassades*, ii.50–3 is seriously truncated

35 Harbison, *Rival Ambassadors*, pp. 46–7.

36 For the following see Howard, *Jane Grey*, pp. 248–9 and *Cal. S. P. Spanish*, xi.83–6: 12 Jul. 1553, Ambassadors to Charles V.

37 This takes the deception 'at the audience given us by the council' (ibid., xi.115: 22 Jul. 1553, Ambassadors to Charles V) to refer to the meeting with Cobham and Mason on 12 July, rather than the meeting with seven councillors the next day (see below). An alternative explanation is that Cobham and Mason learned that Charles was recommending that Mary should marry an Englishman and promise to make no religious changes, but this is less likely to have come as a surprise because that compromise had been considered and rejected prior to Edward's

death (see above p. 161): ibid., xi.85: 12 Jul. 1553, Ambassadors to Charles V.

38 Ibid, xi.87, 96, 203: 12 and 19 Jul., 4 Sep. 1553, Ambassadors to Charles V; Wriothesley, *Chronicle*, ii.96.

39 During the interview at Compiègne, news arrived of the fall of Hesdin, 100 miles away, on 17 July.

40 Ibid., xi.123, 173: 29 Jul.and 16 Aug. 1553, Ambassadors to Charles V; Dudley also brought a verbal message, promising support against Charles if needed. Wotton, the ambassador, later confirmed his account of the meeting: Harbison, *Rival Ambassadors*, p. 51.

41 *Cal. S. P. Spanish*, xi.208: 5 Sep. 1552, Renard to Philip.

42 Renard also thought that Dudley took gifts of jewellery: ibid., xi.113: 22 Jul. 1553, Ambassadors to Charles V.

43 The above disagrees with the view of the late Jennifer Loach that Northumberland did offer to cede English territory for French support: 'A close league with the king of France', *Proceedings of the Huguenot Society of Great Britain and Ireland* 25 (1991), 238. I have been unable to compare readings with the French manuscript in Vienna: ibid., 241, n.26. The French translation of Jane's accession proclamation made for de Noailles is not identical to the Grafton text; e.g. it cites the act of 28, not 33 Henry VIII, translates 'common weel' as 'commune volonté', renders the 'good opinion … of our and our sisters and cousin Margaret's good education' as 'bonne opinion … de nous et de nos soeurs et de la bonne education de notre cousine Marguerite' and corrects 'prehenminences' to 'preliminaries'. Vertot, *Ambassades*, ii.63, 65, 66.

44 *Cal. S. P. Spanish*, xi.124: 29 Jul. 1553, Ambassadors to Charles V.

45 The imperial army was based at Hesdin, south of Calais, and between it and the French forces at Amiens; ibid., xi.90: 15 Jul. 1553, anon., 'Advices from a spy'.

46 Ibid., xi.132: 2 Aug. 1553, Ambassadors to Charles V.

47   Instructions to the English ambassa-dors at Brussels on 11 July stressed England's determination to 'conserve and maintain amity': Howard, *Jane Grey*, pp. 248–9.

48   For the following, *Cal. S. P. Spanish*, xi.85, 87: 12 Jul. 1553, Ambassadors to Charles V; ibid., xi.88: 14 Jul. 1553, ditto.

49   Harbison, *Rival Ambassadors*, pp. 49–50 states that the meeting at Pembroke's house took place behind Northumberland's back and is the first sign of a split in Jane's supporters, and that the concocted story of the intercepted letters was launched at this meeting. This is unlikely as the invitation to meet the delegation was issued before Northumberland left, and the meeting was arranged through a council secretary.

50   *Cal. S. P. Spanish*, xi.91: 16 Jul. 1553, Ambassadors to Charles V.

51   HMC *Finch*, p. 1. The Tower resi-dent's statement that Northumberland's leadership was finalized on the evening of the 12th is thus incorrect: *Chronicle of Queen Jane*, p. 5.

52   *Vita Mariae*, pp. 261–2.

53   Commendone, *Accession*, p. 13 only says that Suffolk refused.

54   *Chronicle of Queen Jane*, pp. 5–6.

55   Stow, *Chronicles* (1580), p. 1060.

56   The imperial ambassadors state that first Lord Grey, then Suffolk and Grey together, and then Northumberland, Northampton and Huntingdon were to command. *Cal. S. P. Spanish*, xi.83: 11 Jul. 1553, Ambassadors to Charles V; ibid., xi.86–7: 12 Jul. 1553, ditto.

57   In 1549 Northampton had, against strict instructions, become involved in street fighting in Norwich and been defeated by the rebels; for Suffolk, see above p. 58.

58   *Vita Mariae*, p. 262.

59   See below p. 209.

60   *Chronicle of Queen Jane*, p. 8, but note the problem of when Northumber-land left.

61   *Cal. S. P. Spanish*, xi.86–7: 12 Jul. 1553, Ambassadors to Charles V; ibid., xi.91: 16 Jul. 1553, ditto.

62   Ibid., xi.71: 4 Jul. 1553, Ambassa-dors to Charles V. The number of licenses issued for retainers again indicates no exceptional anxiety. BL Royal MS 18c fos. 341^v, 356, 366^v.

63   Stow, *Chronicles* (1580), p. 1060.

64   Commendone, *Accession*, p. 14, but the further figure of 8,000 horse sent ahead with the earl of Warwick (*recte* Robert Dudley) must be an error for 800; *Cal. Pat. R., 1553–4*, pp. 42–3, 55, 150–1, 157–8, 213, 224.

65   *Cal. S. P. Spanish*, xi.94: 19 Jul. 1553, Ambassadors to Charles V; ibid., xi.103, 20 July to Prince Philip, but with 20 not 12 guns. An Italian writing from London on 20 July gives 2,000 horse and 3,000 foot at least with 14 guns: ibid., xi.107.

66   Contemporary accounts are unani-mous on the importance of Northumber-land's cavalry, e.g. 'in which his chief strength lay': de Guaras, *Relation*, p. 91. Richard Baker, *A Chronicle of the Kings of England* (1643, 1650), p. 334 gives 800 foot, 2,000 horse. He cites no author-ity, but his grandfather Sir John Baker was heavily involved in 1553 and his father was in residence in the Inner Temple.

67   See above, p. 180; HMC *Finch*, i.1–2.

68   *DKR* iv.237–8; Troughton, in *Archaeologia* 23, pp. 36–7.

69   Ibid., p. 39.

70   On 9 July: *Cal. S. P. Spanish*, ix.78: 10 Jul. 1553, Ambassadors to Charles V.

71   Machyn, *Diary*, p. 35; Folger Library, MSS Lb503, Lb24 (HMC *Molyneux*, App. p. 610); the lords also fortified their houses in London and the city authorities introduced 'watch and ward': Wriothesley, *Chronicle*, ii.87; *Cal. S. P. Spanish*, xi.87: 12 Jul. 1553, Ambassadors to Charles V. Earlier the ambassadors reported that mili-tary supplies and equipment (including the guns of the Thames forts) had been concentrated or bought up, in part to pre-vent them falling into the hands of Mary's

supporters: ibid., xi.71: 4 Jul. 1553, Ambassadors to Charles V.

72 Grey Friars, *Chronicle*, p. 80.

73 Commendone, *Accession*, p. 13; a continental crown was worth 6s. 4d. Challis, *Coinage*, p. 218.

74 *Cal. S. P. Spanish*, xi.87: 12 Jul. 1553, Ambassadors to Charles V.

75 *ODNB*, sub nom.

76 *Vita Mariae*, p. 262, but Mary's council described a Mr Fortescue (probably Henry, the Essex MP) as treasurer: *APC*, 420; *Hist. of Parlt.* ii.158–8.

77 *Cal. S. P. Spanish*, xi.253: 23 Sep. 1553, Ambassadors to Charles V; the identity of Mewtas is confirmed ibid., xi.261: 30 Sep. 1553, Ambassadors to Charles V.

78 See below, pp. 193, 236: *Tudor Proclamations*, ii.16–17.

20 The March on Framlingham

1 *Cal. S. P. Spanish*, xi.73: 7 Jul. 1533, Ambassadors to Charles V; ibid., xi.89: 14 Jul. 1553, ditto. The news that Dudley had already left reached the ambassadors 'while we were writing'. The 300 horse were probably from the 500 Dudley retainers reported by Scheyfve on 4 July: ibid., xi.71: 4 July to Charles V.

2 The phrase is used in the Council letter of 8 July (see above p. 180) and very probably represents intelligence from Dudley, but cf. below pp. 225–7 for Mary's movements.

3 This was the reason the earl gave for not supporting Mary earlier: *Vita Mariae*, pp. 254, 296 n.26. The earl had served under the duke of Norfolk in the 1544 invasion of France.

4 Wingfield reports that Mary had 60 supporters when she had herself proclaimed on 8 July: *Vita Mariae*, p. 253; on 11 July the imperial ambassadors reported 12 or 14 but a messenger from

Mary reached them on 14 July and reported 500 or 600: *Cal. S. P. Spanish*, xi.83: 11 Jul. to Charles V; ibid., xi.88: 14 Jul. to Charles V; de Guaras, *Relation*, pp. 90–1, between 10 and 14/15 July only 5 or 6 of rank and these 'among the most insignificant of the kingdom', plus 15 or 20 gentlemen and their 'powers'; Tittler and Battley, in *BIHR* 57, 132.

5 *Vita Mariae*, p. 256.

6 For this and the following: *Chronicle of Queen Jane*, pp. 3–8; Wriothesley, *Chronicle*, ii.87; Machyn, *Diary*, p. 36; *Cal. S. P. Spanish*, xi.87–8: 12 Jul. to Charles V; ibid., xi.91: 16 Jul. to Charles V; Commendone, *Accession*, p. 14; *Vita Mariae*, pp. 262–3; Vertot, *Ambassades*, p. 59; *Cal. S. P. Spanish*, xi.107: 20 Jul. 1553, 'Advices from England'; Grey Friars, *Chronicle*, p. 80. MacCulloch, *Vita Mariae*, p. 297 n.46, suggests that the duke left on Thursday 13 July (agreeing with Wriothesley and the imperial envoys, and Wingfield's statement that the duke reached Cambridge on 14 July). However, Machyn reports that the duke left on 14 July (so too Commendone). The subsequent indictments refer to a treasonable assembly at Ware on 14, not 13 July: *Cal. Pat. R., 1553–4*, pp. 42–3, 55, 150–1, 157–8, 213, 224. London to Ware is 25 miles, half a day's ride, so that an assembly there on 14 July is congruent with a morning start on that day as indicated in *Chronicle of Queen Jane*. If the duke left on the morning of the 13th, the indictment date is wrong. He would also have spent 36 hours at Ware waiting for reinforcements (according to the imperial ambassadors on 20 July, 'a couple of days': *Cal. S. P. Spanish*, xi.103: 20 Jul. to Philip). Grey Friars, *Chronicle*, '4 or 5 days beside Ware' cannot be correct. Foxe, with convincing detail, says Cambridge (30 miles further) was reached by supper on Saturday 15 July: *Acts and Monuments* (1586), p. 2086. A morning start from Ware on 15 July allowed ample time to sack Sawston on the way (see below pp. 203–4, 208).

The imperial ambassadors reported on 14 July that Northumberland left London 'yesterday' with the duke of Suffolk (this last certainly an error), but contradicted themselves on 16 July by giving the date as 'two days ago': *Cal. S. P. Spanish*, xi.88: 14 July to Charles V; ibid., xi.91: 16 July to Charles V. The indication in *Chronicle of Queen Jane* that the duke left the Tower on 13 July but London on 14 July resolves some but not all discrepancies. *Vita Mariae*, p. 262 says that the infantry started before Northumberland.

7   *Chronicle of Queen Jane*, p. 8.
8   Ibid.
9   *DKR* iv(ii), 232–40.
10   Ibid., p. 233 pouch 21 m.13 p. 233.
11   *Vita Mariae*, p. 263.
12   *DKR* iv(ii), p. 233 pouch 21 mm. 19–20, p. 233; *Vita Mariae*, pp. 265–6.
13   Ibid., p. 266.
14   See below pp. 212, 241–2.
15   When Robert Dudley's force dispersed is not known.
16   *Original Letters*, p. 243; Commendone, *Accession*, p. 14; *Cal. S. P. Spanish*, xi.103: 20 Jul. 1553, Ambassadors to Philip.
17   *Acts and Monuments* (1570), p. 1569; Holinshed, *Chronicles* (1808), iii.1069.
18   Assuming he left at 8 a.m. on the 14th and arrived at 8 p.m. on the 15th.
19   Nichols, *Narratives*, pp. 191–7; 'Household and privy purse accounts of the Lestranges of Hunstanton', ed. D. Gurney, in *Archaeologia* 25, 439; Brereton, *Letters and Accounts*, pp. 243–4.
20   Some infantry may have been despatched a day earlier: *Vita Mariae*, p. 262.
21   *Vita Mariae*, p. 263.
22   Stow, *Annales* (1580), p. 1060.
23   On 14 July imperial ambassadors expected Northumberland to capture Mary in four days' time, presumably as informed by a messenger who must have left Mary on 13 July: *Cal. S. P. Spanish*, xi.88–9: 14 Jul. 1553, Ambassadors to Charles V.

24   *Vita Mariae*, p. 263; when he left London Northumberland had 600 men plus the guard. Grey Friars, *Chronicle*, p. 80 reports that more than one party of troops left London but the reference may be to Robert Dudley's earlier force or to the artillery train. Holinshed reports supplies still being sent out on 19 July: *Chronicle*, vi.1069.
25   *Cal. S. P. Spanish*, xi.107: Advices from England, dated 18 July.
26   Ibid., p. 107: Advices from England, dated 18 July.
27   Ibid, xi.71: 4 Jul. 1553, Scheyfve to Charles V. Holinshed, *Chronicles*, vi.1070 states that desertion began at Cambridge after Mary was proclaimed.
28   For the following see R. C. Braddock, 'The character and composition of the duke of Northumberland's army', in *Albion* 6 (1974), 342–56, and 'The duke of Northumberland's army reconsidered', ibid. 19 (1987), 13–17; Tighe, in *Albion* 19.
29   *APC*, iv.429–32 and Lansdowne MS, 156.
30   Machyn, *Diary*, p. 36. Foxe, *Acts and Monuments* (1570), p. 1568 states that the guard was unwilling to march against Mary but was persuaded. The imperial ambassadors have the guard swearing allegiance to Jane on 7 July, and the archers of the guard swearing allegiance to the crown on 9 July and being ordered to return the next day to swear to support Edward's settlement, which, if true, means that some at least were given time to choose. *Cal. S. P. Spanish*, xi.77–8: 10 July, Ambassadors to Charles V; de Guaras noted that 'almost all the royal bodyguard' went with the duke: *Relation*, p. 91. After the proclamation of Mary 'most of the guard' is reported as 'gone to my lady Mary', so they were with the duke to the end: *Chronicle of Queen Jane*, p. 13; see also below p. 243.
31   Underhill, *Examination*, in *Tudor Tracts*, pp. 175, 181. Underhill says he was 'of the Band of the Pensioners' and

served in Wyatt's rebellion and at the marriage of Mary and Philip (ibid., pp. 170, 186–93), but he does not figure in the Braddock/Tighe lists (see above, n. 28) and his vacant post as a man-at-arms attendant on her Majesty was granted to Philip Browne on 4 October 1553: *Cal. Pat. R., 1553–4*, pp. 198–9.

32 Machyn, *Diary*, p. 36.

33 De Guaras, *Relation*, pp. 92, 98 calls the army 'a great force ... a powerful force'; *Vita Mariae*, p. 262; *Cal. S. P. Spanish*, xi.94: 19 Jul., Ambassadors to Charles V.

34 *Vita Mariae*, p. 262.

35 De Guaras, *Relation*, p. 95.

36 'Highways from any notable town to the City of London' in Grafton, *Abridgement* (1572), gives London to Woodbridge (12 miles from Framlingham) via Colchester and Chelmsford and to Norwich via Thetford, Newmarket, Barkway and Ware (Cambridge would be a minor detour).

37 Francis Jobson, Northumberland's brother-in-law, was MP for Colchester (*History of Parliament*, ii.444–6; *ODNB*); William Berith, its deputy collector, was 'a great doer for Francis Jobson and a great traveller for the duke': *APC*, iv.311, 313, 317, 323, 418.

38 Wingfield understood Cambridge was a rendezvous for reinforcements from Lincolnshire: *Vita Mariae*, p. 258.

39 See above p. 180.

40 Alsop, in *Albion* 24, 579; de Guaras, *Relation*, pp. 93–4 exaggerates the tonnage.

41 A witness in an Admiralty case of 1555 stated that the object of the fleet was to land troops at Yarmouth 'to keep the country from coming to the queen [Mary]': Alsop, in *Albion* 24, 583.

42 *Cal. S. P. Spanish*, xi.71: 4 Jul. 1553: Scheyfve to Charles V, but his account is confused and much exaggerated.

43 *LP*, 20(2).88; *SP*, i.811; anon., 'The late expedition in Scotland (1544)', in *Tudor Tracts*, p. 41.

44 Surrey History Centre, 6729/314, LM/COR/3/3.

45 Foxe, *Acts and Monuments* (1583), p. 2086.

46 Joshua 1:16–18.

47 Foxe, *Acts and Monuments* (1583), pp. 2086–7.

48 Stow, *Annales*, p. 1064.

49 See below, pp. 165, 235.

50 *APC*, iv.293.

51 Tittler and Battley, in *BIHR* 57, 137.

52 Ibid., 132–5.

53 Ibid., 137–9.

54 *APC*, iv.295.

55 There is no reliable figure for Mary's force. De Guaras, *Relation*, p. 91 claimed 20,000; *Cal. S. P. Spanish*, xi.86: 12 Jul. 1553, Ambassadors to Charles V has 15,000, corrected on 14 Jul. to 5/600 at Kenninghall as on 12 Jul.: ibid., p. 89; Holinshed, *Chronicles*, iii.1067 has 30,000. Wingfield gives no estimate and his stress on Mary's forces growing continuously suggests that no figure could be accurate. For entrenching see *APC 1552–4*, p. 296.

56 *Vita Mariae*, pp. 264–5.

57 *Chronicle of Queen Jane*, pp. 8–9; de Guaras, *Relation*, p. 94. Alsop, in *Albion* 24, 581 doubts that ordnance from the fleet did reach Mary, but see below at n. 59.

58 See below pp. 221, 235.

59 *Vita Mariae*, pp. 258–9, sworn to Mary, 16 or 17 July: *APC 1552–4*, pp. 294, 432.

60 On 16 July orders were given to bring 'such munition and ordnance as remains' in Brooke's ships, and transport was organized on 17 July: ibid., p. 294. The distance was a little over 25 miles. *Cal. S. P. Spanish*, xi.107, 20 Jul. 1533, *Chronicle of Queen Jane*, pp. 5–6, de Guaras, *Relation*, p. 94 and Commendone, *Accession*, p. 14 all mention the movement of artillery from the ships to Framlingham.

61 *APC 1552–4*, p. 295. These were not delivered because the ship had sailed: Alsop, in *Albion* 24, 586.

62   Foxe, *Acts and Monuments* (1583), p. 2087.

21   A Second Front

1   Arundel, in *Gent. Mag.* 103, 119–20.

2   Strype, *Cranmer*, ii.915: Council to Mary. The reference to 'this day' makes the endorsement by William Cecil 'from Baynard's Castle 20 July' incorrect.

3   Ibid., ii.913.

4   The Rich letter contradicts the statement that the council made its mind up on the 18th: de Guaras, *Relation*, pp. 95–6. *ODNB* says Paget was back on the council on February 1553; Hoak, *King's Council*, p. 77 says not.

5   This was clearly before Shrewsbury and Mason made their visits. See below, n. 7.

6   Wriothesley, *Chronicle*, p. 88.

7   *Cal. S. P. Spanish*, xi.95–6: 19 Jul. 1553, Ambassadors to Charles V. It is unlikely that Shrewsbury and Mason saw the ambassadors before the Mayor. An Italian resident present at the proclamation timed their visit to the embassy at 2 p.m.: ibid., xi.108. The ambassadors say that the proclamation came two hours after their visit. De Guaras, *Relation*, p. 96 says between 3 and 4 of the clock; Grey Friars, *Chronicle*, p. 80 says 4 p.m.; Machyn, *Diary*, p. 37 says 5–6 p.m.; Commendone, *Accession*, p. 20 says 4 p.m.

8   De Guaras, *Relation*, p. 96.

9   Wriothesley, *Chronicle*, p. 88; de Guaras implies that the lord mayor etc. needed their maces: *Relation*, p. 96.

10   *Chronicle of Queen Jane*, pp. 11–12; 'covered with gold and precious stones': Commendone, *Accession*, p. 20.

11   *Cal. S. P. Spanish*, xi. p. 108; report by Italian eyewitness.

12   Commendone, *Accession*, p. 21. They left at 9 p.m. and arrived by 7 p.m. on Thursday 20 July: Wriothesley, *Chronicle*, p. 89; *Vita Mariae*, p. 265.

13   Wriothesley, *Chronicle*, p. 89; Grey Friars, *Chronicle*, p. 80; cf. Machyn, *Diary*, p. 37; de Guaras, *Relation*, pp. 96–7.

14   Ibid., pp. 95–6.

15   *Chronicle of Queen Jane*, p. 12. Commendone, *Accession*, p. 19 says that Suffolk gave up after the council sent 1,000 men into the Tower 'by secret ways' to force his surrender. This lacks confirmation and seems improbable.

16   Underhill, 'Examination', in *Tudor Tracts*, pp. 133, 152–3.

17   The male sponsors, Suffolk and Pembroke, were elsewhere so must also have used deputies: ibid., p. 181.

18   *Cal. S. P. Spanish*, xi.113: 22 Jul. 1553: Ambassadors to Charles V; cf. *Chronicle of Queen Jane*, p. 13; Commendone, *Accession*, pp. 20–1.

19   *Cal. S. P. Spanish*, xi.95–6: 19 Jul. 1553: Ambassadors to Charles V; Holinshed, *Chronicles* (1808), iii.1069.

20   Commendone, *Accession*, p. 15.

21   See above, p. 160.

22   *Chronicle of Queen Jane*, pp. 6–7. The phrase 'therewithal the first course for the lords came up' suggests the writer was present.

23   Vertot, *Ambassades*, ii.72. The French is garbled.

24   'packing' = 'an underhand arrangement'. *Chronicle of Queen Jane*, p. 9. But if true, clearly the lords were not confined to the Tower.

25   *Chronicle of Queen Jane*, p. 9 but see n. 24.

26   BL, Lansdowne MS 102 fo. 2; Tytler, *Edward and Mary*, ii.192–5; BL, Cotton MS Titus B2. fo. 374ʳ; Strype, *Annals* iv.488.

27   Commendone, *Accession*, p. 15.

28   *Chronicle of Queen Jane*, p. 7.

29   Arundel, in *Gent. Mag.* 103, 119–20.

30   Commendone, *Accession*, pp. 18–19.

31   Ibid., pp. 15–18.

32   Alford, *Burghley*, p. 51. This major study of Cecil's involvement differs in some particulars from the following: ibid., pp. 50–64.

33 BL, Lansdowne MS 104 fo. 1ʳ [Tytler, *Edward and Mary*, pp. 192–5]. BL, Lansdowne MS 104 fos 3ʳ, 4ᵛ is a copy of instructions left for his wife dated 13 June and later endorsed 'tempore regis Edward VI under imprisonment and in daily expectation of suffering death'. Cf. Read, *Cecil*, p. 96; Alford, *Burghley*, p. 55.
34 BL, Cotton MS Titus B2. fo. 374ʳ; Strype, *Annals* iv.485–9.
35 On 2 Aug. Mary 'reproached' and refused to pardon Shrewsbury. Winchester and Pembroke though they did kiss hands; the latter took the council oath on 8 Aug.: *Cal S. P. Spanish*, xi. 150–1: *APC* iv.313, 425. For the rumour of house arrest see *Chronicle of Queen Jane*. p. 15. 'The Epistle of Poor Pratte' says that Shrewsbury 'beareth himself equal'. i.e. neutral: ibid p. 120. Winchester's reception casts doubt on the letter of protection which Cecil claimed he had been given.
36 *Cal. S. P. Spanish*, xi.236: 14 Sep., Ambassadors to Charles V; Beaulieu, Letters on Public Affairs, i.1.
37 See above, p. 213.
38 Holinshed, *Chronicles* (1808), iii.1068.
39 *Cal. S. P. Spanish*, xi.96, 105: 19 and 20 Jul., Ambassadors to Charles V.
40 For the following see: BL, Add. MS 18738 fo 20, Add. MS 22563 fo 3; Lansdowne MS 3 fo 50; Surrey History Centre LM/COR/3/2, LM/Cor/3/3; Foxe, *Acts and Monuments* (1570), p. 1568; HMC *Finch*, pp. 1–2; *The Retrospective Review*, 2ⁿᵈ ser.(1828), i.504–5; Hoare R. C., *History of Modern Wiltshire* (1843), pp. 266–7.
41 Holinshed, *Chronicles* (1808), iii.1069. This is inserted in a passage quoted from Foxe (1570), p. 1569.
42 *Chronicle of Queen Jane*, p. 9.
43 De Guaras, *Relation*, p. 95; *Cal. S. P. Spanish*, xi.96: 19 Jul., Ambassadors to Charles V.
44 See below p. 237. The date on which council informed Northumberland is uncertain: Strype, *Annals* iv.488. On 19

July Richard Troughton covered 48 miles between Huntingdon and Royston before noon, possibly starting at 4 a.m., i.e. at c.6 mph (including stops), indicating that the 77 miles between Ipswich and London could have been travelled in c.12 hours: Troughton, in *Archaeologia* 23, p. 42.
45 Alford, *Burghley*, pp. 60–1. His new instructions arrived at Stamford on Monday 17 July so (at 6 mph) had been sent on Sunday p.m.: Troughton, in *Archaeologia* 23, p. 37.
46 *Cal. S. P. Spanish*, xi.96: 19 Jul., Ambassadors to Charles V.
47 De Guaras, *Relation*, p. 95.
48 Holinshed, *Chronicles* (1808), iii.1070.
49 Foxe, *Acts and Monuments* (1563), p. 902.
50 See above, pp. 194–5.
51 William Drury, William Waldegrave, Anthony Rouse, George Somerset and Nicolas Hare; for Thomas Cornwallis's reservations see below p. 235.
52 *APC*, iv.296, 307, 416; *Vita Mariae*, p. 254.
53 York: A. G. Dickens, 'Robert Parkyn's Narrative', in *EHR* 62, 77, cf. *Chronicle of Queen Jane*, pp. 113–14; Oxford: C. M. Dent, *Protestant Reformers in Elizabethan Oxford* (1983), p. 13; Wells: Jackson, in *Wilts. Arch. Mag.* 8, 319; Frome, ibid.; Shaftesbury, ibid.; Cornwall: Chris.Skidmore, *Edward VI* (2007), p. 268; Exeter: Cooper, *Propaganda* pp. 22–3; Ipswich: see below p. 235; Worcestershire: Strype, *Annals* IV ii.543; Gloucestershire: ibid.; Boston: Tittler and Battley, in *BIHR* 57, 137; the sheriffs of Essex, Denbigh, and Notts. and Derby were proceeded against, presumably for proclaiming Jane: Grey Friars, *Chronicle*, p. 81 [Robert Corbet]; *Cal. Pat. R.*, 1553–4, p. 430 [Edward Almer]; ibid., 445 [Anthony Neville]; Berwick, or possibly Barwick near Feckenham: Troughton, in *Archaeologia* 23, 36.
54 National Archives, C82/973: 14 Jul. 53, 1553 bill, signed by Jane, appointing

Edw. Benard sheriff of Wilts; Jackson, in *Wilts. Arch. Mag.* 8, 312.

55 De Guaras, *Relation*, p. 91, and see below pp. 235, 237.

56 Coventry was divided: *VCH*, ii.442; Jackson, in *Wilts. Arch. Mag.* 8, 319.

57 Ibid. – identifying 'Thornhill' as William Thornhill of Stalbridge Dorset, the duchy of Lancaster feodary and receiver: *Hist of Parlt.*, iii.445–6.

58 Jackson, in *Wilts. Arch. Mag.* 8, 319.

59 For the following see ibid., 310–22.

60 Sir Nicholas Poyntz and Sir John St Loe, ibid., 310, and below n. 80.

61 They claimed he had done so in 1549: ibid., 320.

62 Surrey History Centre 6729/10/ 139; BL, Add. MS 33230 fo. 21.

63 See below, p. 236.

64 *Chronicle of Queen Jane*, pp. 8, 111.

65 Tittler and Battley, in *BIHR* 57, 136–7.

66 Ibid., 133, 137–9.

67 *Chronicle of Queen Jane*, p. 9.

68 *Vita Mariae*, pp. 263–4.

69 Ibid., p. 266 states that the earl arrived on 20 July, but *APC*, iv.298 indicates that he had written to Mary before 19 July when he was sent instructions to levy Essex forces provisioned for six days. His servants seem to have been recalled before reaching Framlingham: ibid., p. 300.

70 Hoyle, in *Historical Journal* 44, 234.

71 *Cal. Pat. R., 1553–4*, pp. 50, 395.

72 See below, p. 228.

73 *Chronicle of Queen Jane*, p. 8; *Vita Mariae*, pp. 260–1; *Cal. S. P. Spanish*, xi.107: 20 Jul. 1553, Advices.

74 *Cal. Pat. R., 1553–4*, pp. 45, 100; ibid., *1557–8*, pp. 371–4.

75 *Chronicle of Queen Jane*, p. 12; *Cal. Pat. R., 1553–4*, p. 246.

76 *Chronicle of Queen Jane*, p. 12.

77 *Vita Mariae*, p. 261.

78 *APC*, iv.293.

79 Ibid., iv.318.

80 BL, Harley MS 416 fo. 30: John Brydges and Nicholas Poyntz; IT Petyt MS 538.47, fo. 12[r]: John St Loe and Anthony Kingston. Strype, *Memorials* III ii 172–3; Strype, *Cranmer*, p. 913.

81 Bridges: *Vita Mariae*, p. 261; Kingston, Poyntz and St Loe: *Hist. of Parlt.*, ii.469–70, iii.149, 260. Poyntz and St Loe were cousins.

82 Jackson, in *Wilts. Arch. Mag.* 8, 310.

83 Howard, *Jane Grey*, p. 264 incorrectly reads 'reparing to'. I owe confirmation of the correct reading to the kindness of Michael Frost of the Inner Temple Library.

84 In 1549 the stand-off between Somerset at Windsor and the 'London lords' was resolved by Pembroke's forces from the west.

85 Troughton, in *Archaeologia* 23, 42.

86 If on Tuesday Arundel and Pembroke were faced with the need to escalate, this would account for the prepared nature of Arundel's speech the following day; see above p. 217.

22   The Rebellion of Mary Tudor

1 *Chronicle of Queen Jane*, p. 11; Grey Friars, *Chronicle*, p. 80; Machyn, *Diary*, p. 37.

2 *Cal. S. P. Venetian, 1534–54*, 533.

3 Hayward, *Life and Raigne*, pp. 176–7.

4 See below, p. 228.

5 *Vita Mariae*, p. 251.

6 The suggestion that Mary travelled via Hengrave seems without foundation: Loach, *Parliament*, p. 2.

7 See above, p. 329 n. 77.

8 Commendone, *Accession*, p. 7.

9 *Cal. S. P. Venetian,* v.934, p. 537 Relation of Girolamo Soranzo.

10 Prescott, *Mary*, p. 166.

11 See above, pp. 173–4.

12 Loades chooses 5 July: *Mary Tudor*, p. 257.

13 De Guaras, *Relation*, p. 89.

14 *Cal. S. P. Spanish*, xi.70: 4 Jul., Scheyfve to Charles V, giving illness as

the excuse. An Italian then in the service of the imperial ambassador has the even earlier date of 'about 1 July' for Mary's move: ibid., xi.106.

15 *Cal. S. P. Spanish*, xi.109: 20 Jul.; Haynes, *State Papers*, i.118.

16 De Guaras, *Relation*, p. 89.

17 *Cal. S. P. Spanish*, xi.70: 4 Jul., Scheyfve to Charles V. Scheyfve certainly bracketed the warning to Mary from the 'friend' and the details of Edward's will.

18 Commendone, *Accession*, p. 7.

19 Tytler, *Edward and Mary*, ii.186.

20 *Vita Mariae*, pp. 251, 294.

21 *Cal. S. P. Spanish*, xi.74: 7 Jul., Ambassadors to Charles V.

22 *Vita Mariae*, p. 251; *Chronicle of Queen Jane*, pp. 1–2.

23 *Vita Mariae*, pp. 251–2.

24 BL, Lansdowne MS 1236 fo. 29.

25 Tittler, *Mary*, pp. 81–2; Tittler and Battley, in *BIHR* 57, 131.

26 IT, Petyt MS 538/47/13; see p. 222.

27 Tittler and Battley, in *BIHR* 57, 132.

28 Jackson, in *Wilts. Arch. Mag.* 8, 311.

29 Loades, *Mary Tudor*, pp. 153–7; see above, n. 15.

30 See above, n. 23.

31 Loades, *Mary Tudor*, pp. 140–1; *Vita Mariae*, p. 252.

32 Rochester: comptroller of the household; Jerningham: vice-chamberlain and captain of the guard; Waldegrave: keeper of the great wardrobe.

33 See below, p. 237.

34 *ODNB*; *Vita Mariae*, p. 269.

35 Loades points out that organization was not Mary's forte: *Mary Tudor*, p. 177.

36 For the following see Whitelock and MacCulloch, in *Historical Journal* 50:2 (2007), 265–87.

37 *Vita Mariae*, pp. 252–3.

38 Except when at Ludlow.

39 Loades, *Mary Tudor*, pp. 137–8.

40 For the following see *Vita Mariae*, *passim*.

41 *Hist. of Parlt.*, iii.603. Mrs Tonge, née Whyte, but always known by her husband's post of Clarencieux king of arms.

42 Roger Virgoe, 'The recovery of the Howards in East Anglia, 1485–1529', in *Wealth and Power in Tudor England*, ed. E. W. Ives et al. (1978), p. 1. The speaker was Thomas Howard, the 4th duke, 1538–72.

43 BL, Lansdowne MS 1236 fo. 29: 8 Jul., letter to leading gentlemen of the liberty of [Bury] St Edmund.

44 For the following see: *ODNB*; *Vita Mariae*, pp. 255, 296; *Hist. of Parlt.*, ii.60–1, 329–31; iii.535–6.

45 *APC*, iv.429–30.

46 D. Knowles, *The Religious Orders in England*, iii (Cambridge, 1961), 238–9.

47 Whitelock and MacCulloch, in *Historical Journal* 50 at n. 29. According to the imperial ambassador she instituted a regime of four masses a day. *Cal. S. P. Spanish*, ix.100: 16 Jun. 1547, Van der Delft to Charles V; Loades, *Mary Tudor*, p. 143.

48 Whitelock and MacCulloch, in *Historical Journal* 50 at n. 29.

49 *Cal. S. P. Spanish*, ix.100: 16 Jun. 1547, Van der Delft to Charles V. This possibly diminished as controls tightened, see above p. 93.

50 Loades, *Mary Tudor*, pp. 148–9, 159.

51 *APC*, iii.239 and above p. 91.

52 See above, p. 89.

53 Sessions, *Howard*, p. 1.

54 *Vita Mariae*, pp. 254–5.

55 Loach, *Edward VI*, p. 177.

56 MacCulloch, *Suffolk*, p. 84.

57 Ibid., pp. 82–3, 102, 181; *Vita Mariae*, pp. 257, 296.

58 Ibid., pp. 255, 257.

59 *APC*, iii.239; see above p. 91.

60 Foxe, *Acts and Monuments* (1570), p. 1585.

61 Underhill, 'Examination', in *Tudor Tracts*, pp. 171–2.

62 *Hist. of Parlt.*, iii.482.

63 *Hist. of Parlt.*, i.617.

64 A. Fletcher and D. MacCulloch, *Tudor Rebellions* (4th edn 1997), p. 79; Foxe, *Acts and Monuments* (1563), pp. 901–2.

65 Holinshed, *Chronicles* (1808), iii.1069. A reference implying that by 1554 this was common knowledge is made by Knox, *Admonition*, sig. E4.

66 *Tudor Proclamations*, ii.5: 18 Aug., 1553.

67 Foxe, *Acts and Monuments* (1563), p. 901; cf. Knox, *Admonition*, sig. E4.

68 Vertot, *Ambassades*, ii.79–80.

69 Foxe, *Acts and Monuments* (1583), p. 1862; *TED*, i.47–53.

70 See above p. 222.

71 Tittler and Battley in *BIHR* 57, 132–6.

72 *APC*, iv.297, 304, 305, 315, 415.

73 Ibid., pp. 313, 416.

74 Lynn declared on 18 July; Mountford was supplying grain on or before 19 July.

75 See above p. 167.

76 Even to the staunchly Catholic Sir Edward Hastings: Strype, *Memorials* iii(2), pp. 171–2. For Jane see above p. 192–3.

77 *APC*, iv.430; *ODNB*.

78 *Vita Mariae*, p. 259; Whitelock and MacCulloch, in *Historical Journal* 50 at n. 85.

79 *Vita Mariae*, p. 257.

80 Ibid., p. 254.

81 Ibid., pp. 255–6.

82 *Cal. S. P. Dom., 1547–80*, pp. 173–4.

83 *Cal. S. P. Spanish*, ix.172: 16 Aug. 1553, Ambassadors to Charles V; *The Lancashire Lieutenancy under the Tudors and Stuarts*, ed. J. Harland: Chetham Society 49 (1859), 49–50, cf. *Chronicle of Queen Jane*, p. 119.

84 Strype, *Annals* iv(ii).543.

85 See above p. 220–1.

86 See his views on relics, etc., his kindness to the Oxford martyrs, his will and his link with Bishop Jewel: *ODNB*; *Hist. of Parlt.*, iii.622–3.

87 Cooper, *Propaganda*, pp. 21–2.

88 *APC*, iv.417. On 23 August he was told he could have free access to the court: ibid., p. 330.

89 Ibid., p. 305.

90 *Vita Mariae*, p. 252; *Cal. S. P. Domestic, Edward*, 748, 803. Loades, *Northumberland*, p. 221.

91 BL, Royal MS 18C fo. 341^v.

92 See above p. 215.

93 *Chronicle of Queen Jane*, pp. 1–2, 12; the biography has been tampered with. The altercation could have been over precedence, cf. Lord Stourton and Sir John Thynne above p. 220–1.

94 *Chronicle of Queen Jane*, p. 13; *Hist. of Parlt.*, iii.459.

95 For the following see *Vita Mariae*, pp. 258–9.

96 See above pp. 207–8; *LP*, xvi.374 (57); 32 Henry VIII, c.24.

97 For the following see Alsop, in *Albion* 24, 583–6; Stow, *Chronicles* (1580), pp. 1062–3.

23 Every Man for Himself

1 *Cal. S. P. Spanish*, xi.132: 2 Aug. 1553, Ambassadors to Charles V.

2 Vertot, *Ambassades*, ii.79.

3 *APC*, iv.422.

4 *Chronicle of Queen Jane*, p. 13.

5 *Cal. S. P. Spanish*, xi.113: 22 Jul. 1553, Ambassadors to Charles V; BL, Harley MS 523, fo. 11^v [Howard, *Jane Grey*, p. 258]. The duchess of Northumberland was released on or before 29 July, although confined to London: *Cal. S. P. Spanish*, xi.125: 29 Jul. 1553, Ambassadors to Charles V.

6 Ibid., xi.113: 22 Jul. 1553, Ambassadors to Charles V. Underhill, 'Examination', in *Tudor Tracts*, p. 181.

7 Foxe, *Acts and Monuments* (1583), p. 2087; *Chronicle of Queen Jane*, pp. 10–13; Commendone, *Accession*, pp. 21–2; de Guaras, *Relation*, p. 98; *Vita Mariae*, pp. 266–8; Wriothesley, *Chronicle*, ii.90; *Cal. S. P. Spanish*, xi.112: 22 Jul. 1553, Ambassadors to Charles V; Stow, *Annales*, pp. 1035–6.

8 Foxe, *Acts and Monuments* (1583), p. 2087.
9 Stow, *Annales* (1592), pp. 1035–6.
10 The phrase is from Cecil's apologia, see above pp. 163–5.
11 Stow, *Annales*, p. 1036.
12 For the following see *Vita Mariae*, pp. 265–6.
13 See above p. 220.
14 *APC*, iv.294, 297–8.
15 *Vita Mariae*, p. 266; *Cal. S. P. Spanish*, xi.37: 5 May 1553, Scheyfve to Charles V.
16 Stow, *Annales*, p. 1036; *Vita Mariae*, p. 266.
17 Ibid., pp. 266–7.
18 Removed from office October: *ODNB*; Robert Stafford was a committed Protestant and brother-in-law to Dorothy Stafford, see *ODNB*.
19 *Chronicle of Queen Jane*, p. 10.
20 Foxe, *Acts and Monuments* (1583), p. 2087.
21 Commendone, *Accession*, pp. 21–2.
22 Ibid., p. 22; *Chronicle of Queen Jane*, p. 10.
23 *APC*, iv.363; *Cal. S. P. Spanish*, xi.236: 14 Sep. 1553, Ambassadors to Charles V; *Cal. Pat. R., 1553–4*, pp. 75–6, 194–5, 301; ibid., *1554–5*, p. 343. Wingfield refers to 'a book of mulcts' but I have been unable to trace the whereabouts of any such book: *Vita Mariae*, p. 266.
24 See above pp. 96–7.
25 *Chronicle of Queen Jane*, pp. 7, 10.
26 *Cal. S. P. Spanish*, xi.236: 14 Sep. 1553, Ambassadors to Charles V.
27 Foxe, *Acts and Monuments* (1583), p. 2087.
28 Grey Friars, *Chronicle*, pp. 80–1; Wriothesley, *Chronicle*, p. 91; Machyn, *Diary*, pp. 37–8.
29 *Vita Mariae*, pp. 269–71.
30 Ibid., p. 270.
31 Ibid., pp. 270–1.
32 Machyn, *Diary*, p. 38; Wriothesley, *Chronicle*, pp. 91, 92; *Cal. S. P. Spanish*, xi.133: 2 Aug. 1553, Ambassadors to Charles V. For lobbying for the marquis

of Northampton, see ibid., xi.204: 4 Sep. 1553, Ambassadors to Charles V.
33 Ibid., xi.125: 29 Jul. 1553, Ambassadors to Charles V.
34 S. J. Gunn, 'A letter of Jane, Duchess of Northumberland, in 1553', in *EHR* 114 (1999), 1270.
35 Grey Friars, *Chronicle*, p. 81.
36 Beaulieu, Papers and Letters, i.1. An estate with this yield had a capital value in excess of £1000.
37 Richard Grafton. He was also excluded from the Coronation pardon and forced to compound: *ODNB*; *Tudor Proclamations*, ii.16; *Cal. Pat. R., 1553–4*, p. 445; Machyn, *Diary*, pp. 38, 43.
38 Wriothesley, *Chronicle*, pp. 91, 104; Machyn, *Diary*, pp. 38, 43; *ODNB*. This was despite his being conservative in religion: Foxe, *Acts and Monuments* (1563), p. 931.
39 Foxe, *Acts and Monuments* (1570), p. 1563.
40 *Vita Mariae*, p. 246 is incorrect to call them 'puisne judges'; *APC 1552–4*, pp. 305, 308, 311, 322; Machyn, *Diary*, pp. 38, 114, 150; *Hist. of Parlt.*, ii.553–5; Sir Julius Caesar, *The Ancient State, Authoritie, and Proceedings of the Court of Requests*, ed. L. M. Hill (1975), pp. 30, 157, 164. Involvement also accounts for Sir John Baker lying low: *Chronicle of Queen Jane*, p. 15.
41 Ibid., p. 165; *APC*, iv.324; BL, Lansdowne MS 156, fo. 94; *Hist. of Parlt.*, iii.455–6; Underhill, 'Examination', in *Tudor Tracts*, pp. 180–1. See below n. 43.
42 Cranmer, *Letters*, p. 442.
43 BL, Cotton MS Titus B2 fos. 375–6 [Strype, *Annals*, iv.ii.485]; cf. BL, Lansdowne MS 104, fo. 1 [Tytler, *Edward and Mary*, ii.92–3]: 'I refused to make a proclamation and turned the labour to Mr Throckmorton, whose conscience I saw was troubled therewith, misliking the matter.'
44 *Chronicle of Queen Jane*, p. 27. But MacCulloch, *Cranmer*, pp. 544–53 points out that Cranmer's public opposition to

any restoration of the mass effectively forced the government to act.

45   *Vita Mariae*, p. 262 calls him young but cf. *ODNB*; Merriman, *Rough Wooing*, pp. 312–13, 315–16, 374–5; Nichols, *Narratives*, pp. 158, 324.

46   *Cal. S. P. Spanish*, xi.185: 27 Aug. 1553, Ambassadors to Charles V.

47   *Chronicle of Queen Jane*, p. 18.

48   Ibid., pp. 22–4. Palmer had been a strong traditionalist and Foxe interpreted this as Protestant conversion: 'his faith that he had learned in the gospel'; so too Theodore Beza. But although Palmer did not attend mass on 22 August, he had confessed and taken the Catholic sacrament the day before and he was counselled by 'Watson', presumably the future Marian bishop of Lincoln: ibid., pp. 19–21; Foxe, *Acts and Monuments* (1583), pp. 1223–4, 1228, 1408, 1465; Theodore Beza, *Response a la confession du feu Duc Iean de Nortumberlande* (Geneva, 1554) (see Jordan and Gleason, in *Harvard Library Bulletin* 23, 337).

49   *Chronicle of Queen Jane*, pp. 20, 21.

50   *Cal. S. P. Spanish*, xi.187: 27 Aug. 1553, Ambassadors to Charles V. The reference to false written testimony suggests that Palmer still adhered to his initial warnings about Somerset's plans.

51   'on his self will and glory[seeking]', *William, Lord Grey of Wilton*, ed. P. de Malpas Grey Egerton, Camden Society 40 (1847), 16. Somerset later admitted that the setback was less serious than he had thought: *Cal. S. P. Domestic, Edward*, 139.

24   *The Tower*

1   See above p. 26 *Cal. S. P. Spanish*, xi.232–3: 14 Sep. 1553: Charles V to Ambassadors. Renard's erstwhile colleagues took some time to leave England.

2   Ibid., xi.126–7: 30 Jul. 1553, Charles V to Prince Philip; ibid., xi.131–3: 2 Aug. 1553, Ambassadors to Charles V.

3   Ibid., xi.156: 8 Aug. 1553, Ambassadors to Charles V.

4   Ibid., xi.168–9: 16 Aug. 1553, ditto.

5   See above pp. 186–7.

6   Florio, *Historia*, p. 63.

7   *Cal. S. P. Spanish*, xi.168–9: 16 Aug. 1553, Ambassadors to Charles V.

8   Ibid., xi.215–16: 9 Sep. 1553, Ambassadors to Charles V.

9   Ibid., xi.241: 9 Sep. 1553, Ambassadors to Charles V.

10   It sat in the Dean's House in the precinct of St Paul's, Holinshed, *Chronicles* (1808), iv.7.

11   1 Mary St.2 c.16.

12   *Cal. S. P. Spanish*, xi.322, 359: 14 Nov. 1553, Renard to Charles V; Loades, *Mary Tudor*, p. 208.

13   D. C. Bell, *Notices of the Historic Persons Buried in the Chapel of St. Peter ad Vincula in the Tower of London* (1877), pp. 45, 167; Chapel Register (St Peter ad Vincula), 11 February 1587. Jane saw Guildford being taken into the chapel, which indicates that Partridge's house was probably on the west side of Tower Green, between the Queen's House and the Beauchamp Tower and now replaced by later buildings. I am indebted in this to Mrs Bridget Clifford of the Royal Armoury Museum.

14   *Chronicle of Queen Jane*, pp. 24–6.

15   Matthew 10:33. For the significance of this text to Jane, see below p. 255.

16   The procession to the Guildhall, her licence to walk in the garden (see below p. 252) and her walk to the scaffold, possibly also the detail of the actual execution, *Chronicle of Queen Jane*, pp. 32, 33, 56–9.

17   Florio, *Historia*, p. 61.

18   *Chronicle of Queen Jane*, p. 32.

19   For White's Catholicism see *Cal. S. P. Spanish*, xi.332: 1 Nov. 1553, Renard to Charles V.

20   *DKR* iv(ii), 237–8: Sir Thomas White (mayor), duke of Norfolk, earls of Derby, Sussex and Bath, Sir Robert Rochester, Sir Edward Hastings, Sir Nicholas Hare MR, Richard Morgan CJCP, Richard Southwell, Edward Waldegrave, Henry Bedingfield, David

Broke CBE, Edward Saunders JQB, Thomas Moyle and Robert Broke, recorder of London. Sussex was the only one who had initially supported Jane.

21 The record of the sentence on the brothers is missing.

22 Loades, *The Oxford Martyrs* (1990), pp. 119–21; MacCulloch, *Cranmer*, pp. 554–5.

23 Florio, *Historia*, p. 61.

24 BL, Add. MS 26748 fo. 15ᵛ; *Chronicle of Queen Jane*, p. 33. Jane's permission is said to have included walking 'on the hill', but it seems highly unlikely that Jane was allowed to leave the Tower to walk on Tower Hill.

25 Ibid., p. 33; Keay, *Tower of London*, pp. 33, 39.

26 *Chronicle of Queen Jane*, p. 27.

27 See below, p. 265.

28 Florio, *Historia*, p. 62.

29 *Chronicle of Queen Jane*, p. 27.

30 'My hope is, after darkness, light': Foxe, *Acts and Monuments* (1563), p. 922. Clearly written before she knew she was to die. Later editions omit the translation.

31 Florio, *Historia*, p. 62.

32 J. Loach, 'Reformation controversies', in *History of the University of Oxford*, iii, ed. J. McConica (Oxford, 1986), p. 380. News of his defection was known in Strasbourg by 20 November: *Original Letters*, pp. 373–4. In April 1554 Harding was disputing with Ridley: Foxe, *Acts and Monuments* (1563), p. 934; ibid. (1583), p. 1450.

33 *An Epistle*, Aii–Bii; *Here in this Booke*, sig. Aii–Avii; Foxe, *Acts and Monuments* (1563), pp. 920–2.

34 Epistle to the Hebrews 6:4–6, 10:26–7: *Here in this Booke*, sig. Aᵛ; *An Epistle*, sig. Aviiʳ&ᵛ; Foxe, *Acts and Monuments* (1563), p. 921. Jane also cites Matthew 10:33: see pp. 252, 255.

35 *Here in this Booke*, sig. Aviᵛ; *An Epistle*, sig. Biʳ & ᵛ; Foxe, *Acts and Monuments* (1563), p. 922.

36 *Here in this Booke*, sig. Aiiᵛ.

37 The Forty-Two Articles, no. 5.

38 Baruch 6:4. *An Epistle*, Aivʳ & ᵛ; cf. Foxe, *Acts and Monuments* (1563), pp. 920–1; *Here in this Booke*, sig. Aiiʳ & ᵛ truncates this section

39 *An Epistle*, sig. Aivʳ.

40 *An Epistle*, sig Aiiiᵛ; *Here in this Booke*, sig. Aiiiʳ. For 'golden calf', 'whore of Babylon' and 'abominable idol' see respectively Exodus 32, Revelation 17, Matthew 24:15.

41 *An Epistle*, sig. Aviiiᵛ; *The Song of the Three Children* (Greek addition after Daniel 3:23); 2 Maccabees 6:18–31 (Jane calls Eleazar 'that constant father' in the sense of 'father of the church'); ibid. 7:1–39.

42 Matthew 10:39; *An Epistle*, sig. Aᵛ; Foxe, *Acts and Monuments* (1563), p. 921; *Here in this Booke*, sig. Aiv reads 'for my sake and the gospel', which moves the reference to Mark 8.35.

43 Matthew 10:37–8; *An Epistle*, sig. Aᵛ; Foxe, *Acts and Monuments* (1563), p. 291. *Here in this Booke*, sig. Aiv reads 'better than me'.

44 *An Epistle*, sig. Aᵛ–viʳ.

45 Matthew 10:34–5; *Here in this Booke*, sig. Aᵛ; and Foxe, *Acts and Monuments* (1563), p. 921. *An Epistle*, sig. Aviᵛ reads 'daughter against the mother-in-law'.

46 Matthew 10:33. *An Epistle*, sig Avii; *Here in this Booke*, sig. Av; *Acts and Monuments* (1563), p. 921.

47 Matthew 10:28. *An Epistle*, sig. Aviiiʳ&ᵛ; Foxe, *Acts and Monuments* (1563), p. 922. *Here in this Booke*, sig. Avi reads 'fear not them that have power over the body, but only fear him …'.

48 John 15:19. *An Epistle*, sig. Aviiiᵛ; *Here in this Booke*, sig. Avi; Foxe, *Acts and Monuments* (1563), p. 922.

49 *The Life, Death and Actions of the Most Chast Learned and Religious Lady, the Lady Jane Grey* (1615), sig. B3ᵛ.

50 'Friendship is only possible between good men.' The Cicero quotation is in *Here in this Booke*, sig. Aivᵛ but the Spira

reference is misunderstood – 'lamentable case of the spirit of late', ibid., sig. Avi^v; *An Epistle*, sig. Bi^v has the reference to Francis Spira but does not mention Cicero. Foxe omits the name 'Francis'. Foxe, *Acts and Monuments* (1563), pp. 421–2.

51   *A notable and marvellous epistle of the famous doctor Mattewe Gribalde*, translated by E[dward] A[glionby] (Worceter [*sic*] 20 April 1550); cf. Michael MacDonald, 'The Fearefull estate of Francis Spira' in *Journal of British Studies* (1992), i.32.

52   The technical terms are I *exordium*; II *narratio*; III *partitio*; IV *confirmatio*; V *refutatio*; VI *peroratio*.

53   See below, p. 258–9.

54   '*magniloquens*', '*humile*' and '*mediocre*'.

55   *An Epistle*, sig. Bii^v–Bv^v; *Here in this Booke*, sig. Avii^v–Bi^v; Foxe, *Acts and Monuments* (1563), pp. 917–18.

56   See above, pp. 21–2.

57   *An Epistle*, sig. Aiii^v; *Here in this Booke*, sig. Aiii; Foxe, *Acts and Monuments* (1563), p. 920.

58   *An Epistle*, sig. Aiii^v and (with minor differences) *Here in this Booke*, sig. Aiii; Foxe, *Acts and Monuments* (1563), p. 920.

59   See above, p. 73.

60   W. P. Stephens, 'The Church in Bucer's Commentaries on the Epistle to the Ephesians' in *Martin Bucer: Reforming Church and Community*, ed. D. F. Wright (Cambridge, 1994), p. 49.

61   Florio, *Historia*, p. 70; cf. the fact that her father intended to flee to Scotland to enjoy liberty of conscience, ibid. p. 52. This could be one of the 'many more things whereof we reasoned' (*Here in this Booke*, sig. Bi^v; *An Epistle*, sig. Bv^r), but it could be a gloss by Florio, who held a number of unorthodox opinions.

62   The prayer is first found in Foxe, *Acts and Monuments* (1563), pp. 919–20.

63   'too puffed up/too pressed down' echoes Proverbs 30:9 which is not by Solomon [ibid., 30:1].

64   The latter part quotes from 1 Corinthians 10:13.

65   An Epistle to the Hebrews 12:5–11.

66   The Forty-Two Articles, no. 17.

67   Florio, *Historia*, p. 60.

68   W. P. Stephens, 'The Church in Bucer's Commentaries on the Epistle to the Ephesians' in *Martin Bucer: Reforming Church and Community*, ed. D. F. Wright (Cambridge, 1994), p. 48.

25   Nemesis

1   On 28 October 1553. *Cal. S. P. Spanish*, xi.320: 29 Oct. 1553, Renard to Philip II.

2   *Chronicle of Queen Jane*, p. 32.

3   Ibid., pp. 34–5.

4   For the following see Loades, *Conspiracies*; Harbison, *Rival Ambassadors*, pp. 89–136.

5   Ibid., pp. 94–5, 112ff.; *Cal. S. P. Spanish*, xi.441: 17 Dec. 1553, Renard to Charles V.

6   Foxe, *Acts and Monuments* (1563), p. 1730.

7   Loades, *Conspiracies*, p. 23.

8   *Chronicle of Queen Jane*, p. 122; *Cal. S. P. Domestic, Mary*, 84.

9   The confession is lost but known through the imperial ambassador: *Cal. S. P. Spanish*, xii.87: 8 Feb. 1554, Renard to Charles V.

10   *Chronicle of Queen Jane*, p. 37.

11   *Cal. S. P. Domestic, Mary*, 84: Bowyer was interrogated within days of the events. His later confession is not always congruent: ibid., 781.

12   It also disproves the duke's claim that he acted on news of Warner's arrest. Bowyer's itinerary shows that the brothers left London at 7 p.m. on a journey of 90 miles.

13   *Cal. S. P. Domestic, Mary*, 84.

14   *Cal. S. P. Spanish*, xii.81: 5 Feb. 1554, Renard to Charles V. The servant was hanged. Machyn, *Diary*, p. 44 says that the undersheriff of Leicestershire was hanged on 6 February for carrying

Suffolk's letters. Stow, *Annales* (1592), p. 1050 says it was a servant of Suffolk and 'late-undersheriff', on 7 February.

15 *DKR* iv(ii). 245–6, Dyer, *Reports*, i.10.

16 Holinshed, *Chronicles*, iv.14. The encounter with Huntingdon came out at Suffolk's trial and is best explained as above: *Chronicle of Queen Jane*, pp. 60–1.

17 Holinshed, *Chronicles*, iv.14.

18 *Cal. S. P. Spanish*, xii.85: 8 Feb. 1554, Renard to Charles V; William Dugdale, *The Antiquities of Warwickshire* (1730), p. 80b. Commendone, *Accession*, p. 40 says that Suffolk left the tree because of cold and lack of food.

19 I am indebted for this information to Rose, Lady Daventry and to Mr Martin Dunne.

20 Loades, *Conspiracies*, p. 100; Wriothesley, *Chronicle*, ii.110.

21 Stow, *Annales* (1592), p. 1053; *Chronicle of Queen Jane*, pp. 53–4; Wriothesley, *Chronicle*, ii.111. The delay was probably until Wyatt's assault had been repelled. Machyn, *Diary*, p. 54 has Suffolk arrive on 6 February, Grey Friars, *Chronicle*, p. 88 on 8 February.

22 *Chronicle of Queen Jane*, p. 63; Loades, *Conspiracies*, p. 96; Holinshed, *Chronicles*, iv.14.

23 cf. the transfer of Armour to Leicester: Somerville, *Duchy of Lancaster*, p. 573.

24 Bowyer says Enfield Chase, but Gardiner specified Cheshunt. *Chronicle of Queen Jane*, p. 184. Either was well off the normal route.

25 Ibid., p. 184; *Cal. S. P. Domestic, Mary*, 54. A genuine loyalist would have gone to London, only 11 miles away. *Hist. of Parlt.*, iii.667–8.

26 *Cal. S. P. Spanish*, xii.55: 29 Jan. 1554, Renard to Charles V.

27 *Chronicle of Queen Jane*, p. 61. Suffolk probably cited his brother's influence in mitigation, confident that Thomas had evaded capture. Suffolk was tried on 17 February; Thomas was only sent up from Oswestry on 15 February and arrived

21 February: ibid., pp. 60, 63. Renard said Suffolk was warned by de Noailles but this is an instance of his paranoia about France: *Cal. S. P. Spanish*, xii.54: 29 Jan. 1554, Renard to Charles V.

28 'She is the mercifulest prince, as I have truly found her, that ever reigned': *Chronicle of Queen Jane*, p. 29.

29 Ibid., p. 61; *Cal. S. P. Spanish*, xii. 55–7: 29 Jan. 1554, Renard to Charles V.

30 Commendone, *Accession*, pp. 38–9.

31 *Cal. S. P. Spanish*, xi.332, 359: 1 Nov. 1553, Renard to Charles V; ibid., xi.359: 14 Nov. 1553, ditto.

32 The Lords' Journal is not extant. The repeal bill passed on 8 November 1553.

33 Foxe, *Acts and Monuments* (1563), pp. 906–16.

34 *Cal. S. P. Spanish*, xi.366: 17 Nov. 1553, Renard to Charles V.

35 Ibid., xi.393, 395: 28 Nov. 1553, Renard to Charles V, also reporting that the Queen believed that the duke's marriage with Duchess Frances was invalid because of his initial commitment to marry Katherine Fitzalan, the current earl of Arundel's sister; see above p. 34.

36 Ibid., xi.444: 20 Dec. 1553, Renard to Charles V. Renard reported on 17 December that Thomas and John Grey were among those planning to stop Philip of Spain: ibid., 441.

37 Graves, *House of Lords*, p. 24.

38 See above, p. 59.

39 *Chronicle of Queen Jane*, p. 55.

40 *Cal. S. P. Spanish*, xii.85: 8 Feb. 1554, Renard to Charles V.

41 Commendone, *Accession*, p. 44.

42 *An Epistle*, sig. Bii^v: four days before Jane's death; *Cal. S. P. Spanish*, xii.87: 8 Feb. 1554, Renard to Charles V. Foxe, Florio and *Here in this Booke* do not mention a reprieve and place the dialogue with Feckenham two days before the execution, i.e. on Saturday 10 February. The anomaly could be explained by this being the second visit: *Here in this Booke*, sig. Avii^v; *Acts and Monuments* (1563), p. 917; Florio, *Historia*, p. 68.

43 Loades, *Conspiracies*, p. 28; *Cal. S. P. Domestic, Mary*, 42; *Tudor Proclamations*, ii.27; cf. *Chronicle of Queen Jane*, p. 185.

44 Holinshed, *Chronicles*, iv.23; *Chronicle of Queen Jane*, p. 123.

45 Ibid, p. 186.

46 Proctor's twice-printed account of Wyatt's Rebellion states that on 27 January the sheriff of Kent claimed that the object was to make Jane queen, but Proctor, a committed Catholic controversialist, stated that he was not quoting verbatim: Proctor, *Wyat's Rebellion*, pp. 218–19. The story was repeated by George Cavendish and was perpetuated through Cooper's *Chronicle*, 'I claimed and proclaimed from place to place / The title to be just of my daughter Jane': Cavendish, *Visions*, p. 150.

47 *Cal. S. P. Spanish*, xii.87: 8 Feb. 1554, Renard to Charles V; ibid., xii.95: 12 Feb., ditto.

48 Ibid., xii.120: 17 Feb. 1554, Renard to Philip.

49 Commendone, *Accession*, p. 44.

50 Florio, *Historia*, p. 67.

51 See above, p. 159.

52 Knox, *Admonition*, sig. E2ᵛ, E3. The colophon (sig. I3) has the date 20 July 1554, which is confirmed by the reference to gallows in London streets and the marriage to Philip (sig. E3, 3ᵛ). This establishes that Knox was not referring to heresy burnings.

53 *Chronicle of Queen Jane*, p. 54. None of this seems relevant to his ostensible text, 2 Corinthians 6:1–10.

54 What follows is a reconstruction on the basis of *Here in this Booke*, sig. Aviiᵛ–Biᵛ; *The Epistle* Biiᵛ–Bvᵛ; Commendone, *Accession*, pp. 44–5; Pollini, *L'Historia*, pp. 358–9; Foxe, *Acts and Monuments* (1563), pp. 917–18.

55 Ibid., p. 917.

56 Commendone, *Accession*, p. 44.

57 Pollini, *Storia Ecclesiastica*, p. 352; *L'Historia*, pp. 358–9.

58 Florio, *Historia*, pp. 69–70.

59 Commendone, *Accession*, p. 44.

60 Florio, *Historia*, p. 71.

61 *An Epistle*, sig. Bᵛ.

62 Ibid.

26 The River of Jordan

1 Florio, *Historia*, p. 73.

2 Ibid., p. 120 dates the letter 10 February.

3 De Lisle, *Sisters* (2009), pp. 151–2, 172; Mary Grey's books do indicate an interest in advanced Protestant writing: *ODNB*.

4 Plowden, *Jane Grey*, p. 144.

5 *Here in this Booke*, sig. Bii.

6 *An Epistle*, sig. Bviᵛ; *Here in this Booke*, sig. Biiʳ ᵃⁿᵈ ᵛ reads 'delight your flesh only'.

7 *Here in this Booke*, sig. Biiᵛ.

8 *An Epistle*, sig. Bviiʳ ᵃⁿᵈ ᵛ. The passage is garbled in *Here in this Booke*, sig. Biiᵛ.

9 *Here in this Booke*, sig. Bii. Jane assumes that the treason verdict had destroyed her rights, making Katherine the senior heir. She echoes Matthew 6:20: 'Lay up for yourselves treasures in heaven where neither moth nor rust doth corrupt and thieves do not break in nor steal.'

10 It appears not to have survived.

11 BL, Harley MS 2342. Brydges was born in 1492 and had been one of those Jane had called on for support: see above p. 223.

12 Ibid., fos. 78–80.

13 Florio, *Historia*, p. 71.

14 Commendone, *Accession*, p. 49; Rosso, *I successi*, fo. 57ᵛ; Florio, *Historia*, pp. 134–5 repeats the story but on the authority of Rosso.

15 There is no evidence that pages have been removed from Harley MS 2342. I owe this information to Dr Andrea Clarke of the British Library.

16 Nicolas, *Memoirs*, pp. xciv–c.

17 On this conjecture, Commendone and the related Italian sources only mistook the recipient of the epigrams. The confusion over Jane's final writings was

noted by J. H. Froude, *The Reign of Mary Tudor* (1910), p. 112.

18   For the following: *Chronicle of Queen Jane*, pp. 54–6. For his execution, Suffolk left the Tower about 9 a.m.: Foxe, *Acts and Monuments* (1570), p. 1637.

19   Commendone, *Accession*, p. 49.

20   Stow, *Annales* (1580), p. 1089.

21   *Chronicle of Queen Jane*, p. 55.

22   See above pp. 173, 245–6; BL, Lansdowne MS 156 fo. 94.

23   See above p. 91; *Chronicle of Queen Jane*, p. 14; *Hist. of Parlt.*, i.513–5.

24   i.e. the Develin Tower: *Chronicle of Queen Jane*, p. 55.

25   The story that then and earlier he had wept greatly is based on a misreading by Stow: ibid., p. 55, but cf. Holinshed, *Chronicles* (1808), iv.22.

26   Grafton, *Abridgement*, p. 156.

27   *Chronicle of Queen Jane*, p. 55; Stow, *Annales*, p. 1089.

28   Holinshed, *Chronicles* (1808), iv.22.

29   Florio, *Historia*, p. 75.

30   'O Guildford, Guildford, the foretaste is not so bitter that you have tasted and that I shall soon taste as to make my flesh tremble, but that is nothing compared to the feast that you and I shall this day partake of in heaven': Howard, *Jane Grey*, p. 378, quoting Florio, *Historia*, p. 76.

31   See above, p. 249; but not Jaoob: *Chronicle of Queen Jane*, p. 25.

32   BL, Harley MS 2342 fos 74–77.

33   For the following see: *Here in this Booke*, sig. Biii$^{r\&v}$ [*Jane and Mary*, pp. 56–9]; *An Epistle*, sig. Bvii^v, Bviii; Commendone, *Accession*, pp. 49, 72; Rosso, *I successi*, fos 57–8; Pollini, *L'Historia*, pp. 358–9; Foxe, *Acts and Monuments* (1563), p. 919.

34   BL, Harley MS 2342 passim; Nicolas, *Memoirs*, p. 54.

35   Ives, *Anne Boleyn*, p. 357.

36   The scaffold speech is quoted from *Here in this Booke*, sig. Biii$^{r\ \&\ v}$. *An Epistle of the Ladye Iane* reads 'only for that I consented to the thing which I was enforced into': sig. Bvii^v.

37   Davey, *Jane Grey*, p. 343, but no source is cited and I have been unable to verify.

38   Commendone, *Accession*, p. 49.

39   Ibid. There are more po-faced versions. 'She said that his company had caused her more hours of thought and reflection and that death itself did not bring her any fear': Pollini, *L'Historia*, p. 359; 'God, I beseech him abundantly reward you for your kindness toward me, although I must needs say it was more unwelcome to me, than my instant death is terrible': Godwin, *Annales*, p. 297.

40   It was a perquisite of the executioner.

41   Davey, *Jane Grey*, p. 346. I have been unable to verify this. François de Noailles reported 'une grande abondance de sang'. Vertot, *Ambassades*, iii.126.

27   Afterlife

1   S. Bann, 'Delaroche, Napoleon and English Collectors', in *Apollo*, clxii. no 524n.s. (Oct. 2005), 24.

2   The afterlife of Jane Grey is a huge subject. What follows is only indicative.

3   Mainly derivatives of the de Passe and the Wrest Park likenesses.

4   For what follows see Strong, *Painting the Past*.

5   e.g. Samuel Wale, *The Execution of Lady Jane* (1770); Angelica Kauffmann, *Lady Jane giving her table-book to Sir John Gage* [*sic*] (*c*.1790); Giovanni Battista Cipriani, *The Duke of Northumberland and Suffolk praying Lady Jane Grey to accept the crown* (1786); William Martin, *The Death of Lady Jane Grey* (1787); William Osborne Hamilton, *The Resignation of Lady Jane Grey* (1788); Robert Fullerton, *The Lady Jane, the Night before her Execution* (1793).

6   Strong, *Painting the Past*, p. 129; *Lady Jane Grey prevailed upon to accept the Crown* (Woburn Abbey).

7   Cast by Elkingtons; cf. C. H. Feler, '*Lady Jane Accepting the Crown*' on the frieze of Middlesex Guildhall.

8 *Jane Grey and Roger Ascham*, NPG D7387.

9 *Lady Jane Grey Preparing for Execution* (the New York Historical Society); Flagg to Reed, 16 Jun., 1834.

10 Strong, *Painting the Past*, p. 125.

11 Cavendish, *Visions*, p. 131.

12 John Wight, 1562, J. Tisdale, 1562–3, possibly J. Sampson, 1560.

13 Chaloner, in *De Republica*, pp. 296–9. See above pp. 15, 66.

14 Ibid., p. 299.

15 Ibid., p. 297.

16 Ibid., p. 298. Chaloner also claims that others involved in Jane's death received divine punishment.

17 Michael Drayton, *England's Heroicall Epistles* (1597), p. 72 (*recte* 100).

18 Philip Henslowe, *Diary*, ed. R. A. Foakes (2nd edn, 2002), pp. 218, 219. Those involved were Thomas Heywood, Thomas Dekker, Henry Chettle, Wentworth Smith and John Webster.

19 *The Famous History of Sir Thomas Wyat*, sig. A3ᵛ. Jane is executed first and her head brought on stage, thus eliciting a response from Guildford.

20 Ibid., sig. G3.

21 Hayward, *Life and Raigne*, p. 174.

22 Burnet, *History*, pp. 458, 459, 764.

23 BL, Egerton MS 2009/171.

24 James Cawthorn, in Alexander Chalmers, *The Works of the English Poets*, xiv (1810), 244–5.

25 George Keate, *Epistle from Lady Jane Grey to Lord Guildford Dudley* (1757).

26 *A New Opera-Epilogue to the Tragedy of Lady Jane Grey acted for the benefit of Mistress Sterling* (Dublin, 1730).

27 Lady Jane Grey, *Tres epistolae, quarum duae sunt anecdotae* (Tartu, 1810); Lady Jane Grey, *Fragmens littéraires de Lady Jeanne Grey ... par E. Frère* [Rouen] (1832); Lady Jane Grey, *Joannae Graiae litterae ad H. Bullinger* [Zurich] (1840).

28 Anon., *The Life and Death of Lady Jane Grey* [Philadelphia] (1835).

29 Eduard Sommer, *Johanne Gray. Trauerspiel in fünf Acten* [Dresden] (1832).

30 *Magasin Théâtral* xxxvii (Paris, 1844).

31 Christian Barth, *Bilder aus dem innern Leben* (Heidelberg, 1868–72), vol. 5; Eugène Nus and Charles Alphonse Brot, *Jane Grey, drame historique* (1857).

32 Libretto by Carlo Pepoli.

33 Henri-Paul Busser (1891); Arnold Rosner (New York, 1982).

34 Charles Oberthür, *Lady Jane Grey, A Historical Cantata*, words by E. Oxenford (1886); Louis Niedermeyer, setting of 'Jane Gray' by Pacini Émilien; Felix Petyrek, 'Jane Grey' Opus 1; Anton Strelezki, *Lady Jane Grey, Danse à l'antique pour piano* (1902); Arnold Schoenberg, *Zwei Balladen*, Opus 12 Nr. 1 'Jane Grey' (1920) setting of Heinrich Ammann; Felix Zemlensky, *Jane Grey. Zwei Balladen*, no. 1.

35 Edouard Frère, 'Notice sur la vie et les écrits de Lady Jeanne Grey Reine d'Angleterre', in *Bulletin de la Société libre d'émulation de Rouen*, Séance Publique, 6 Juin 1831, pp. 45–77.

36 Frédéric Soulié, *Musée des Familles* (Oct. 1833).

37 Michel Möring, *La Jeunesse Historique et Célèbre* (1860); François Tulou, *Galerie des Enfans Célèbres ou Panthéon de la Jeunesse* (1866); Michel Masson, *Les Enfants célèbres, ou Histoire des enfants qui se sont immortalisés par le Malheur, la Piété, le Courage, le Génie, le Savoir et les talents* (1870).

38 J. D. Taylor, *Documents of Lady Jane Grey* (New York, 2004).

39 *ODNB*.

40 *Punch's Fancy Portraits* (1881), no. 50.

41 Harrison Ainsworth, *The Tower of London* (1840), pp. 32, 341, 423.

42 Laselett John Pott, *Lady Jane Grey on the way to the Tower of London*.

43 *Le Jugement de Jeanne Grey* (1857), formerly in the collection of the duc de Morny.

44 Strickland, *Tudor Princesses*, p. 94.

45 Tennyson, *Queen Mary*, Act III Scene 1 (1875).

46 *The Juvenile Plutarch* (1820), pp. 44–5, 52.

47 A. Strickland, *Historical Tales of Illustrious British Children* (1833); cf. Anon., *A Memoir of the Life of Lady Jane Grey Addressed Chiefly to Young Persons* (1834).

48 American Tract Society: *The Life and Death of Lady Jane Grey* (1827–76); American Sunday School Union: *The Execution of Lady Jane Grey* (Philadelphia, 1848); *Short Stories from the Lives of Remarkable Women* (New York, 1861), pp. 14–23.

49 D. W. Bartlett, *Life of Lady Jane Grey* (Philadelphia, 1886).

50 Eliza Leslie, 'Lady Jane Grey', in S. C. Hall, *The Juvenile Forget Me Not: A Christmas and New Year's Gift, Or Birthday Present* (1833), pp. 210–12.

51 Sarah J. Hale, *Lessons from Women's Lives* (1877), pp. 190–6.

52 Anon., *Fifty Famous Women: Their Virtues and Failings, and the Lessons of their Lives* (1879); W. H. Davenport Adams, *Woman's Work and Worth: in Girlhood, Maidenhood and Wifehood* (1884).

53 *Original Letters*, p. 303: 15 Mar. 1554, John Banks to Bullinger.

54 Ibid., p. 716: 13 Nov. 1554, John Calvin to John Grey.

55 M. Coverdale, *A moste frutefull, piththye* [*sic*] *and learned treatise, how a Christian man ought to behaue himself in the daunger of death*, 2nd edn, 1555, conjecturally printed in Antwerp (a translation from Otto Werdmüller, *Kleinot gnannt der Tod*, 1st edn, London 1550).

56 Ibid., London 1560 (a further edition Hugh Singleton 1574); *The ende of the Ladie Jane Dudlie on the Scaffolde* (Antwerp, 1560).

57 *Certain most godly, fruitful, and comfortable letters*, ed. M. Coverdale (London, 1564).

58 *A Catechism written in Latin by Alexander Nowell*, ed. G. E. Corrie (Parker Society 44, 1853), p. 229.

59 Anon., *An Epistle of the Ladye Iane* (1569–70).

60 Anon., *The History of the life, bloody reign and death of Queen Mary* (1682) frontispiece.

61 An edition of *An Epistle* is conjecturally dated 1570; Werdmüller with the letter to Katherine was reprinted in 1574 and 1595. Thomas Bentley, *The Monument of Matrons, conteining seven severall Lamps of Virginite* (1582), pp. 98–102 has the letter and the prayer.

62 Anon., *The Life, Death and Actions of the Most Chast, Learned, and Religious Lady, the Lady Iane Gray* (1615, 1629, 1636).

63 Ibid., sig. A2, A2^v.

64 Peter Heylin, *Ecclesia Restaurata* (1667).

65 Samuel Crossman, *The Young Man's Calling* (1678), pp. 100, 306–27.

66 'Lady Jane Grey's Letter to her Sister', in *The Strange and Wonderful Predictions of Mr. Christopher Love* (?1701), pp. 61–4.

67 Edward Young, *The Force of Religion or Vanquished Love* (1714).

68 Anon., *The Life, Character, and Death, of the Most Illustrious Pattern of Female Vertue, the Lady Jane Gray* (1714).

69 Jean Marsden, 'Sex politics and she-tragedy: reconfiguring Lady Jane Grey', in *Studies in English Literature* 42/3 (2002), 501–22.

70 John Banks, *The Innocent Usurper or the Death of the Lady Jane Grey* (1694).

71 Rowe, *Jane Gray* A1^v and Epilogue.

72 *London Stage*, and four times before 1820.

73 Legh Richmond, *Fathers of the English Church* (1807).

74 *The Life and Death of Lady Jane Grey*, Church of England Tract Society, 11 (1835); cf. Religious Tract Society (1841); 'England in the 16th century or a History of the reigns of the house

of Tudor', in *Church of England Magazine* 19 (Jul.–Dec. 1845); 'LJ Reading – Bradgate Palace', in *British Heroes and Worthies*, Religious Tract Society (1871).

75 Henry Clissold, *The Last Hours of Christian Women, or An Account of the Death of some Eminent Christian Women of the Church of England from the period of the Reformation* (1851); James Anderson, *Ladies of the Reformation: Memoirs of Distinguished Female Characters, Belonging to the Period of the Reformation in the 16th Century* (1855); Ellen O. Clayton, *Women of the Reformation: Their Lives, Faith and Trials* (1861); cf. Annie Wittenmyer, *Women of the Reformation* (1885).

76 Anne Lydia Bond, *History of England for the Use of Young People*, p. 163.

77 Maria Callcott, *Little Arthur's History of England* (1835), p. ii.85.

78 e.g. Ida Taylor, *Lady Jane Grey and her Times, or Nine Days a Queen* (New York, 1908); Richard Davey, *The Nine Days' Queen* (1909); Kate Dickinson Sweetser, *Ten Girls from History* (1912); Hattie Longstreet Price, *The Story of the Janes* (1928); Nora Cranfield, *A Bid for a Throne* (1934); Jack Lindsey (alias Muriel John St Clair), *The Tudor Pawn* (1938); Alice Harwood, *She had to be Queen* (1948), alias *The Lily and the Leopard* (1949); Katherine Wigmore Eyre, *Another Spring: the Story of Lady Jane Grey* (1949); Philip Lindsay, *There is No Escape* (1950); Marguerite Vance, *Lady Jane Grey, Reluctant Queen* (1952); Hester Chapman, *Lady Jane Grey* (1962); Ursula Bloom, alias Loyania Prole, *My Love, my Little Queen* (1961, 1985) and *The Ten-day Queen* (1983); Gladys Malvern, *The World of Lady Jane Grey* (New York, 1964); Pamela Barrow, *Traitor Queen* (1974); Margaret Mullally, *A Crown in Darkness* (1976); Maureen Peters, *Destiny's Lady* (1978); Karleen Bradford, *The Nine Day Queen* (1986); Mary Luke, *The Nine Days Queen* (1986); A. C. H. Smith, *Lady Jane* (1986, 1988); Derek Bourne-Jones, *Brief Candle: a Poetic Study* (1991); Deborah Meroff, *Coronation of Glory* (Canada, 1998); Alison Plowden, *Lady Jane Grey, Nine Days Queen* (2003); Faith Cook, *Lady Jane Grey, Nine Day Queen of England* (New York, 2004); Irene Howat, *Ten Girls who Didn't Give In* (2004); Ann Rinaldi, *Nine Days a Queen* (2005); Alison Weir, *Innocent Traitor* (2006); Edward Charles, *The Shadow of the Lady Jane Grey* (2007); Leanda de Lisle, *The Sisters who would be Queen* (2009).

79 Christopher Logue, 'Real Life Stories' no. 80 in *Girl* (comic; 14 Sep. 1955); J. Mainwaring, *British History in Strip Pictures* (1953); *June and School Friend*, Second Book of Heroines, *The Teenager Queen* (strip cartoon; 1971).

80 *Elizabeth R.*, BBC (1971).

81 British and Colonial Kinematograph Co., directed by Edwin Greenwood.

82 Also Miles Malleson, Leslie Perrins, Felix Aylmer, Gwen Ffrangcon Davies; Gaumont, directed by Robert Stevenson; released in the USA as *Nine Days a Queen*.

83 See above, p. 252.

84 A. C. H. Smith, *Lady Jane* (1986, 1988).

BIBLIOGRAPHICAL
ABBREVIATIONS

T HE following lists the abbreviated and full titles of works referred to.
Unless otherwise stated, both here and in the notes the place of publication is
London.

Alford, *Burghley*	Stephen Alford, *Burghley: William Cecil at the court of Elizabeth I* (New Haven, 2008)
Alford, *Kingship*	Stephen Alford, *Kingship and Politics in the Reign of Edward VI* (Cambridge, 2002)
Alsop, in *Albion* 24	J. D. Alsop, 'A regime at sea: the navy and the 1553 succession crisis', in *Albion* 24(4) (1992), 577–90
APC	*Acts of the Privy Council of England*, ed. J. R. Dasent (1890–1907)
Arundel, in *Gent. Mag.* 103	'A life of Henrye Fitzallen laste Earle of Arundell of that name', ed. J. G. Nichols, in *Gentleman's Magazine*, 103/2 (1833), 11, 118, 210, 490
Ascham, *The Schoolmaster*	Roger Ascham, *The Schoolmaster*, ed. L. V. Ryan (Ithaca, N.Y., 1967)
Ascham, *Works*	Roger Ascham, *The Whole Works of Roger Ascham*, ed. J. A. Giles (1864–5)
Aylmer, *An harborowe*	John Aylmer, *An harborowe for faithfull and trewe subjectes agaynst the late blowne Blaste [by J. Knox] concerninge the gouernment of wemen* (Strasbourg, 1559)
Baum, 'The godly duke'	B. S. Baum, 'The godly duke of Suffolk: noble Protestantism in Edwardian England' (unpublished paper cf. B.S. Baum, 'The mid-Tudor polity of Edward VI, Jane Grey and Mary I' (Oxford M.St., 2004)

Beaulieu	MSS of Lord Montagu of Beaulieu
Beer, *Northumberland*	B. L. Beer, *Northumberland: the Political Career of John Dudley, Earl of Warwick and Duke of Northumberland* (Kent, Ohio, 1973)
Bernard, in *Nobility*	George Bernard, 'The downfall of Sir Thomas Seymour', in *The Tudor Nobility* (Manchester, 1992), pp. 212–40
BIHR	*Bulletin of the Institute of Historical Research*
Bindoff, in *History Today* 3	S. T. Bindoff, 'A kingdom at stake, 1553', in *History Today* 3(9) (1953), 642–8
Bindoff, *Tudor England*	S. T. Bindoff, *Tudor England* (Harmondsworth, 1950)
BL	British Library
Bostoen, in *The Bookshop of the World*	Karel Bostoen, 'Editing, printing, publishing and selling the life and death of Lady Jane Grey in 1607', in *The Bookshop of the World: the Role of the Low Countries in the Book-Trade 1473–1941*, ed. Lotta Hellinga et al. ('t Goy-Houten, 2001), pp. 119–30
Brereton, *Letters and Accounts*	*Letters and Accounts of William Brereton of Malpas*, ed. E. W. Ives. Record Society of Lancashire and Cheshire 116 (Old Woking, 1976)
Brigden, *London*	S. Brigden, *London and the Reformation* (Oxford, 1989)
Bullinger, *Decades*	Henry Bullinger, *The Decades of Henry Bullinger*, ed. T. Harding. Parker Society Publications (Cambridge, 1852)
Burnet, *History*	Gilbert Burnet, *The History of the Reformation of the Church of England* (1880)
Cal. Pat. R.	*Calendar of Patent Rolls*
Cal. S. P. Dom., 1547–80	*Calendar of State Papers Domestic, 1547–80*
Cal. S. P. Dom., 1601–3	*Calendar of State Papers Domestic, 1601–1603 with additions, 1547–65*
Cal. S. P. Domestic, Edward	*Calendar of State Papers Domestic, Edward VI*, ed. C. S. Knighton (1992)
Cal. S. P. Domestic, Mary	*Calendar of State Papers Domestic, Mary I*, ed. C. S. Knighton (1998)
Cal. S. P. Spanish	*Calendar of Letters ... and State Papers ... between England and Spain,*

	ed. G. A. Bergenroth et al. (1862–1954)
Cal. S. P. Venetian	*Calendar of State Papers ... in ... Venice*, ed. Rawdon Brown et al. (1864–1940)
Camden, *Historie*	William Camden, *The Historie of the Most Renowned and Victorious Princesse Elizabeth* (1635)
Cavendish, *Visions*	George Cavendish, *Metrical Visions*, ed. A. S. G. Edwards (Columbia, S.C., 1980)
'Certayne Brife Notes'	'Certayne Brife Notes', ed. Simon Adams et al., in *Religion, Politics, and Society in Sixteenth-Century England*, ed. Ian W. Archer et al. Camden 5th ser. 22 (Cambridge, 2003), pp. 123–36
Challis, 'Circulating medium'	C. E. Challis, 'The circulating medium', in *The Price Revolution in Sixteenth-Century England*, ed. P. H. Ramsey (1971)
Challis, *Coinage*	C. E. Challis, *The Tudor Coinage* (Manchester, 1978)
Chaloner, in *De Republica*	Thomas Chaloner, 'Deploratio acerbate necis Heroidis praestantissimae Dominae Janae Grayae Henrici Ducis Suffolchiae filiae, quae secure percussa, animo constantissimo mortem oppetiit', in *De Republica Anglorum instauranda libri decem*, published posthumously (London, 1579)
Chandler, *John Leland*	John Leland, *John Leland's Itinerary: Travels in Tudor England*, ed. J. Chandler (Stroud, 1993)
Chapman, *Jane Grey*	Hester W. Chapman, *Lady Jane Grey, October 1537–February 1554* (1962)
Chapman, *Portraits*	Hester W. Chapman, *Two Tudor Portraits: Henry Howard, Earl of Surrey and Lady Katherine Grey* (1960)
Chronicle of Queen Jane	*The Chronicle of Queen Jane, and of Two Years of Queen Mary*, ed. J. G. Nichols. Camden Society 48 (1850)
Colvin, *King's Works*	H. M. Colvin et al., *The History of the King's Works* (1963–82)
Commendone, *Accession*	Giovanni Francesco Commendone, *The Accession, Coronation and Marriage of Mary Tudor*, ed. C. V. Malfatti (Barcelona, 1956)

Commons, *Journal*	*Journal of the House of Commons*
Contile, *Historia*	Giulio Raviglio Rosso, *Historia delle cose occorse nel regno d'Inghilterra, in materia del duca di Notomberlan dopo la morte di Odoardo VI*, ed. Luca Contile (Venice, 1558)
Cooper, *Propaganda*	J. P. D. Cooper, *Propaganda and the Tudor State* (Clarendon, 2003)
Cranmer, *Letters*	*Miscellaneous Writing and Letters of Thomas Cranmer*, ed. J. E. Cox. Parker Society Publications (Cambridge,1846)
Cust, in *Walpole Soc.* 6	L. Cust, 'The Lumley inventories', in *Walpole Society* 6 (1918), 15–35
Davey, *Jane Grey*	Richard P. B. Davey, *The Nine Days' Queen, Lady Jane Grey and her Times*, ed. M. Hume (1909)
Davies, in *Econ. HR* ser. 2 xvii	C. S. L. Davies, 'Provisions for armies, 1509–50: a study in the effectiveness of early Tudor government', in *Economic History Review* ser. 2.17 (1964–5), 234–48
de Guaras, *Relation*	Antonio de Guaras, 'A most true relation', in *The Accession of Queen Mary*, ed. R. Garnett (1892)
de Lisle, *Sisters*	Leanda de Lisle, *The Sisters who would be Queen: the Tragedy of Mary, Katherine and Lady Jane Grey* (2009)
DKR iv(ii)	*Reports of the Deputy Keeper of Public Records*, iv: Appendix ii: Baga de Secretis (1843)
Dowling, *Humanism*	M. Dowling, *Humanism in the Age of Henry VIII* (Beckenham, 1986)
Dyer, *Reports*	James Dyer, *Reports from the Lost Notebooks of Sir James Dyer*, ed. J. H. Baker, Selden Society 109, 110 (1994)
EHR	*English Historical Review*
Ellis, *Letters*	H. Ellis, *Original Letters, Illustrative of English History* (1824–46)
An Epistle	Lady Jane Grey, *An Epistle of the Ladye Jane, a righte vertuous woman* (1554)
Epistolae Tigurinae	*Epistolae Tigurinae 1531–1558*, ed. H. Robinson. Parker Society Publications (Cambridge, 1848)
Florio, *Apologia*	Michelangelo Florio, *Apologia di M. Michel Agnolo Fiorentino: ne la*

quale si tratta de la vera e falsa chiesa
(Basel, 1557)

Florio, *Historia* Michelangelo Florio, *Historia de la vita e de la morte de l'illustriss. Signora Giovanna Graia gia regina eletta e publicata in Inghilterra e de la cose accadute in quel Regno dopo la morte del Re Edoardo VI* (Middelburg, 1607)

Foxe, *Acts and Monuments* John Foxe, *Acts and monuments* (1563–83)

Fuller, *Church History* Thomas Fuller, *The Church History of Britain* (1842)

Godwin, *Annales* Francis Godwin, *Annales of England* (1630) (Latin version 1616)

Grafton, *Abridgement* Richard Grafton, *An Abridgement of the Chronicles of England* (1562–3)

Graves, *House of Lords* Michael A. R. Graves, *The House of Lords in the Parliaments of Edward VI and Mary I: an Institutional Study* (Cambridge, 1981)

Grey Friars, *Chronicle* *Chronicle of the Grey Friars of London*, ed. J. G. Nichols. Camden Society 53 (1852)

Gunn, *Brandon* S. J. Gunn, *Charles Brandon, Duke of Suffolk, c.1484–1545* (Oxford, 1988)

Hall, *Chronicle* Edward Hall, *Chronicle*, ed. H. Ellis (1809)

Hamilton Papers *The Hamilton Papers: Letters and Papers Illustrating the Political Relations of England and Scotland in the XVIth Century*, ed. J. Bain (Edinburgh, 1890–2)

Harbison, *Rival Ambassadors* E. H. Harbison, *Rival Ambassadors at the Court of Queen Mary* (Princeton, 1940)

Haynes, *State Papers* *A Collection of State Papers ... left by William Cecil*, ed. Samuel Haynes and William Murdin (1740–59)

Hayward, *Life and Raigne* John Hayward, *The Life and Raigne of King Edward the Sixth*, ed. B. L. Beer (Kent, Ohio, 1993)

Here in this Booke Lady Jane Grey, *Here in this Booke ye haue a godly Epistle* (1554?)

Hist. of Parlt.   *The House of Commons, 1509–1558*, ed.
                                               S. T. Bindoff. History of Parliament
                                               (1982)

Hist. of Parlt. 1558–1603   *The House of Commons, 1558–1603*, ed.
                                               P. W. Hasler. History of Parliament
                                               (1981)

HMC   Historical Manuscripts Commission
HMC *Finch*   HMC, *Manuscripts of Allan George Finch,
                                               Esq.* (1913)

HMC *Middleton*   HMC, *The Manuscripts of Lord
                                               Middleton* (1911)

HMC *Molyneux*   HMC, *Seventh Report*, MSS of
                                               W. M. Molyneux (1879)

Hoak, *King's Council*   Dale Hoak, *The King's Council in the
                                               Reign of Edward VI* (Cambridge,
                                               1976)

Holinshed, *Chronicles*   Raphael Holinshed, *Chronicles of
                                               England, Scotland, and Irelande* (1577),
                                               ed. H. Ellis (1807–8)

Howard, *Jane Grey*   George Howard, *Lady Jane Grey, and her
                                               Times*, ed. F. C. Laird (1822)

Hoyle, in *Historical Journal* 44   R. W. Hoyle, 'Agrarian agitation in
                                               mid-sixteenth-century Norfolk: a
                                               petition of 1553', in *Historical Journal*
                                               44 (2001), 223–38

Ives, *Anne Boleyn*   E. W. Ives, *The Life and Death of Anne
                                               Boleyn* (Oxford, 2004)

Ives, in *Historical Research* 81   E. W. Ives, 'Tudor dynastic problems
                                               revisited', in *Historical Research* 81
                                               (212) (2008), 255–79

Ives, in *The Reign of Henry VIII*   E. W. Ives, 'Henry VIII: the political
                                               perspective', in *The Reign of Henry
                                               VIII: Politics, Policy and Piety*, ed.
                                               Diarmaid MacCulloch (Basingstoke,
                                               1995), pp. 1–23

Jack, in *Parergon* n.s. 6   Sybil M. Jack, 'Northumberland, Queen
                                               Jane and the financing of the 1553
                                               coup', in *Parergon* n.s. 6 (1988),
                                               137–48

Jackson, in *Wilts. Arch. Mag.* 8   J. E. Jackson, 'Charles, Lord Stourton,
                                               and the murder of the Hartgills', in
                                               Wiltshire Archaeological Magazine 8
                                               (1864), 242–341

James, *Kateryn Parr*   S. E. James, *Kateryn Parr: the Making of
                                               a Queen* (Aldershot, 1999)

Jane, *Proclamation*   Lady Jane Grey, *Jane, by the grace of God
                                               quene of England*, (1553)

Jordan and Gleason, in
Harvard Library Bulletin 23

W. K. Jordan and M. R. Gleason, 'The saying of John late duke of Northumberland upon the scaffold, 1553' in *Harvard Library Bulletin* 23 (1975), 139–79, 324–55

Jordan, *Edward VI*

W. K. Jordan, *Edward VI* (1968–70)

'A "journal" of matters of state'

'A "journal" of matters of state', ed. Simon Adams et al., in *Religion, Politics and Society in Sixteenth-Century England,* ed. Ian W. Archer et al. Camden Society 5th ser. 22 (Cambridge, 2003), pp. 52–122

Keay, *Tower of London*

Anna Keay, *The Elizabethan Tower of London: the Haiward and Gascoyne Plan of 1597* (2001)

Knox, *Admonition*

John Knox, *A Faythfull Admonition to the professors of the truth in England* (1554)

Latimer, *Sermons*

Hugh Latimer, *Sermons,* ed. G. E. Corrie, Parker Society Publications (Cambridge, 1844)

Leicester, *Records*

Leicester, *Records of the Borough,* ed. M. Bateson (1899–1905)

Lisle Letters

Lisle Letters, ed. M. St Clare Byrne (Chicago, 1981)

Loach, *Edward VI*

Jennifer Loach, *Edward VI,* ed. George Bernard and Penry Williams (1999)

Loach, *Parliament*

Jennifer Loach, *Parliament and the Crown in the Reign of Mary Tudor* (Oxford, 1986)

Loades, *Conspiracies*

David Loades, *Two Tudor Conspiracies* (Cambridge, 1965)

Loades, *Mary Tudor*

David Loades, *Mary Tudor: a Life* (Oxford, 1989)

Loades, *Northumberland*

David Loades, *John Dudley, Duke of Northumberland, 1504–1553* (Oxford, 1996)

Loades, *Reign of Mary*

David Loades, *The Reign of Mary Tudor: Politics, Government and Religion in England, 1553–58* (1979)

London Stage

The London Stage, parts 2 to 5, ed. E. L. Avery, A. H. Scouton, G. W. Stone and C. B. Hogan (Carbondale, Ill., 1960–8)

Lords' Journals	*Journals of the House of Lords* (1846)
Lost Faces	*Lost Faces: Identity and Discovery in Tudor Royal Portraiture*, ed. B. Grosvenor (2007)
LP	*Letters and Papers, Foreign and Domestic, of the Reign of Henry VIII*, ed. J. S. Brewer et al. (1862–1932)
MacCulloch, *Cranmer*	Diarmaid MacCulloch, *Thomas Cranmer, a Life* (1996)
MacCulloch, *Church Militant*	Diarmaid MacCulloch, *Tudor Church Militant: Edward VI and the Protestant Reformation* (1999)
MacCulloch, *Suffolk*	Diarmaid MacCulloch, *Suffolk and the Tudors: Politics and Religion in an English County 1500–1600* (Oxford, 1986)
Machyn, *Diary*	Henry Machyn, *The Diary of Henry Machyn: Citizen and Merchant-Taylor Of London, from A.D. 1550 To A.D. 1563*, ed. J. G. Nichols, Camden Society 42 (1848)
Madden, *Privy Purse Expences*	F. Madden, *Privy Purse Expences of the Princess Mary* (1831)
Merriman, *Rough Wooings*	Marcus Merriman, *The Rough Wooings: Mary Queen of Scots, 1542–1551* (East Linton, 2000)
Molyneux, in *Arch. Journ.* 30	J. More Molyneux, 'Letters illustrating the reign of Queen Jane', in *Archaeological Journal* 30 (1873), 273–8
Muller, *Stephen Gardiner*	J. A. Muller, *Stephen Gardiner and the Tudor Reaction* (1926)
Nichols, *Lit. Rems.*	Edward VI, *Literary Remains of King Edward VI*, ed. J. G. Nichols. Roxburghe Club (1857)
Nichols, *Leicester*	John Nichols, *The History and Antiquities of the County of Leicester* (1795–1815)
Nichols, *Narratives*	J. G. Nichols, *Narratives of the Days of the Reformation, Chiefly from the Manuscripts of John Foxe the Martyrologist*. Camden Society 77 (1859)
Nicolas, *Memoirs*	N. H. Nicolas, *Memoirs and Literary Remains of Lady Jane Grey* (1832)
NPG	National. Portrait Gallery

Nugarum	Borbonius [Nicolas Bourbon], *Nugarum Libri Octo* (Lyons, 1538)
ODNB	*Oxford Dictionary of National Biography* (Oxford, 2004)
Original Letters	*Original Letters Relative to the English Reformation*, ed. H. Robinson. Parker Society Publications (Cambridge, 1846–7)
Parkhurst, *Ludicra*	John Parkhurst, *Ludicra sive Epigrammata Juvenilia* (1573)
Plowden, *Jane Grey*	Alison Plowden, *Lady Jane Grey: Nine Days Queen* (Stroud, 2003)
Pocock, *Troubles*	Nicholas Pocock, *Troubles Connected with the Prayer Book of 1549*, Camden Society 37 (1884)
Pollard, *History*	A. F. Pollard, *History of England from the Accession of Edward VI to the Death of Elizabeth (1547–1603)* (1910)
Pollini, *L'Historia*	Girolamo Pollini, *L'Historia Ecclesiastica della Rivoluzion d'Inghilterra, divisa in libri quattro ne' quali si tratta di quello ch'e avvenuto in quell'isola, da che Arrigo Ottava cominciò a pensare di ripudiar Cataerina … infino a quest'ultimi anni di Lisabetta* (Rome, 1594)
Pollini, *Storia Ecclesiastica*	Girolamo Pollini, *Storia Ecclesiastica della Rivoluzione d'Inghilterra* (Bologna, 1591)
Ponet, *Treatis*	John Ponet, *A Short Treatis of Politique Power* (1556, repr.1642)
Prescott, *Mary*	H. F. M. Prescott, *Mary Tudor* (1952)
Proctor, *Wyat's Rebellion*	John Proctor, *The History of Wyat's Rebellion* (1554, 2nd edn 1555), reprinted in *Tudor Tracts*, pp. 198–257
Read, *Cecil*	Conyers Read, *Mr. Secretary Cecil and Queen Elizabeth* (1955)
Rosso, *I successi*	Giulio Raviglio Rosso, *I successi d'Inghilterra dopo la morte di Odoardo Sesto, fino all giunta in quell regno del Sereniss. Don Filippo d'Austria Principe di Spagna con Dna Maria di Lancastro, Reina di quell Regno* (Ferrara, 1560)
Rowe, *Jane Gray*	Nicholas Rowe, *The Tragedy of Lady Jane Gray* [sic] (1715)
Rymer, *Foedera*	T. Rymer, *Foedera*, ed. T. D. Hardy (1869–85)

Scudamore, *Letters*	'The letters of Richard Scudamore', ed. S. Brigden, in *Camden Miscellany 30*, Camden 4th Series 39 (1990), pp. 67–148, 504–9
Sessions, *Howard*	W. A. Sessions, *Henry Howard, the Poet Earl of Surrey: a Life* (Oxford, 1999)
Somerville, *Duchy of Lancaster*	R. Somerville, *History of the Duchy of Lancaster* (1953)
SP	Record Commissioners, *State Papers: King Henry VIII* (1830–52)
State Trials	*State Trials*, ed. William Cobbett (1809)
STC	Short Title Catalogue
Stone, *Mary I*	Stone, J. M., *The History of Mary I* (1901)
Stow, *Chronicles*	John Stow, *A Summarie of Englyshe Chronicles* (1565)
Stow, *Annales*	John Stow, *The Chronicles of England* (1580), later *The Annales of England* (1592)
Strickland, *Tudor Princesses*	Agnes and Elizabeth Strickland, *Lives of the Tudor Princesses including Lady Jane Gray and her sisters* (1868)
Strong, *Painting the Past*	Roy Strong, *Painting the Past: the Victorian Painter and British History* (2004)
Strong, *Portraits*	Roy Strong, *Tudor and Jacobean Portraits* (1969)
Strype, *Annals, Memorials, Cranmer, Aylmer*	John Strype, *Annals of the Reformation, Ecclesiastical Memorials, Memorial of Cranmer, Life of John Aylmer*, in *Works* (Oxford, 1820–40)
TED	*Tudor Economic Documents: Being Select Documents Illustrating the Economic and Social History of Tudor England*, ed. R. H. Tawney and E. Power (1924)
Tighe, in *Albion* 19	W. J. Tighe, 'The gentlemen pensioners, the duke of Northumberland, and the attempted coup of July 1553', in *Albion* 19 (1987), 1–11
Tittler, *Mary*	R. Tittler, *The Reign of Mary I* (1991)
Tittler and Battley, in *BIHR*	R. Tittler and S. L. Battley, 'The local community and the Crown in 1553: the accession of Mary Tudor revisited', in *BIHR* 57(136) (1984), 131–9
Troughton, in *Archaeologia* 23	'The petition of Richard Troughton', ed. F. Madden, in *Archaeologia* 23 (1831), 18–49

Tudor Proclamations	*Tudor Royal Proclamations*, ed. P. L. Hughes and J. F. Larkin (1964–9)
Tudor Tracts	*Tudor Tracts*, ed. A. F. Pollard (New York, 1964)
Tytler, *Edward and Mary*	P. F. Tytler, *England under the Reigns of Edward VI and Mary* (1839)
Underhill, 'Examination'	'The examination and imprisonment of Edward Underhill', in *Tudor Tracts*, pp. 170–98
VCH	*Victoria County History*
Vertot, *Ambassades*	*Ambassades de Messieurs de Noailles en Angleterre*, ed. R. A. de Vertot and C. Villaret (Leyden, 1763)
Vita Mariae	*De Rebus Gestis Mariae Anglorum Reginae Commentariolus*, ed. and trs. Diarmaid MacCulloch as 'The "Vita Mariae Angliae Reginae" of Robert Wingfield of Brantham', in *Camden Miscellany* 28, Camden Society 4th ser. 29 (1984), 181–301
Whitelock and MacCulloch, in *Historical Journal* 50	Anne Whitelock and Diarmaid MacCulloch, 'Princess Mary's household and the succession crisis, July 1553', in *Historical Journal* 50(2) (2007), 265–87
Wriothesley, *Chronicle*	Charles Wriothesley, *A Chronicle of England during the Reigns of the Tudors, from* AD *1485 to 1559*, ed. W. D. Hamilton. Camden Society n.s. 11, 20 (1875, 1877)
Wyatt, *Italian Encounter*	Michael Wyatt, *The Italian Encounter with Tudor England: a Cultural Politics of Translation* (Cambridge, 2005)
Yates, *Florio*	Frances Yates, *John Florio: the Life of an Italian in Shakespeare's England* (Cambridge, 1934)

INDEX

Edward VI (*cont'd*)
  see also 34, 35, 51, 57, 65, 81, 93–4, 111,
    138, 153–4, 159–60, 164–6, 174–5, 189
Elizabeth, Princess, 9, 34, 35, 38–9, 44, 48,
    51, 54–5, 64, 65, 70, 84, 99, 113, 139–40,
    143, 148, 153, 155, 156, 167–8, 173,
    232, 262, 265, 288
Elizabeth of York, 79
Ellen, lady in waiting, 275–6
Elton, G.R., 108
Ely, bishop of *see* Goodrich, Thomas
Empson, Richard, 98
Englefield, Francis, 92, 228–9, 231, 235
Erasmus, 70, 72, 81
Essex, 220
European 'War of the English Succession',
    threat of, 182, 197
Euston Hall, Suffolk, 226, 232
Eworth Hans, 16, 38
Exeter, 220
Exeter, bishop, of *see* Veysey, John
Exeter, dean of, *see* Haddon, James
Exeter, marchioness of, *see* Blount, Gertrude
Exeter, marquis of, *see* Courtenay, Henry
Exton, Rutland, 234

Feckenham, John, 17, 21–22, 257–8, 266–70,
    271, 272, 274, 275–7, 285, 287
Ferdinand of Aragon, 82
Fetherstone, Richard, 82
Fiennes de Clinton, Edward lord Clinton, 94,
    111, 148, 194–5, 201, 203, 218, 242, 243
  see Fitzgerald, Katherine (*wife*)
Fiennes, Gregory, 38
Fitzalan Henry, earl of Arundel, 3, 16, 34, 56,
    91, 94, 110, 119, 161–2, 187, 189, 197,
    213, 214, 215, 217, 218, 223–4, 227,
    235–6, 242, 243–4, 266
  see Arundell, Mary (*wife*)
Fitzalan, Katherine, 34
Fitzgerald, Elizabeth, widow of Anthony
    Browne, wife of Edward Fiennes de
    Clinton, lady Clinton, 94
Fitzgerald, Garret, 193
Fitzroy, Henry, duke of Richmond, 8, 82, 143
Fitzwilliam, William, earl of Southampton, 35
Flagg, George Whiting, 279
Florio, Michelangelo, 22, 27–8, 62, 65, 73,
    249, 252–3, 255, 258, 263. 268, 269, 275
Fontainebleau, 103
Fortescue, Edward, 201
Foxe, John, 18–19, 20–3, 77, 162, 203,
    219–20, 232, 279, 288

Fradelle, Henri Jean-Baptiste Victoire, 279
Framlingham, Suffolk, 9–10, 30, 93, 199, 202,
    203, 206, 208, 209–10, 211, 215, 226,
    234, 235, 237, 242, 243, 246, 247, 274
France, 12, 98, 100, 102–3, 106, 155–7,
    180–2, 196, 264, 283–4
France, admiral of, 102, 103
France, diplomacy, 26, 57, 138, 159, 161,
    180–2
Francis I, 80–81, 85, 103, 121–2
François, dauphin of France, 81, 156
French ambassadors, *see* de Boisdauphin,
    René de Laval; de Noailles, Antoine
Frome, Somerset, 220
Froude, J.A., 128

Gardiner, Stephen, 104, 115, 118, 184, 241,
    264, 268, 285
Garter King at Arms, 214
Gates, John, 10, 129–31, 147, 150–1, 173,
    202, 242, 243, 244, 246, 249
Gates, Henry, 10, 221–2, 242, 243, 244, 246
George I, 290
Gleason M.R., 118
Gloucester, bishop of, *see* Hooper, John
Gloucestershire, 220
Glover, Robert, 72
Godwin, Francis, 15
Godwin, Thomas, 15, 111
Golding, Thomas, 221–2
Gonson, Benjamin, 178
Goodrich, Thomas, 47, 72, 114, 165, 218
Gosnold, John, 47–8, 147, 149, 162
Grafton, Richard, 15, 28, 192, 245, 275
Graham, Fergus, 201
Great Yarmouth, Norfolk, 211, 221, 228, 242
Greenwich, 7, 8, 57, 127, 136, 138, 156, 188,
    207, 225
Gresham, John, 179
Greville, Fulk, 37
Grey family, 17, 35, 36–7, 74–5, 151, 168
Grey, Anne, wife of Henry Willoughby, 36, 37
Grey, Elizabeth, wife of Thomas Audley, 37
Grey, Elizabeth, lady Lisle, widow of Edmund
    Dudley, wife of Arthur Plantagenet, 98–9
Grey, Henry, marquis of Dorset, duke of Suffolk
  Career
    advancement, 40, 56– 58, 72, 130
    claims dukedom, 58
    and John Dudley, 56, 71, 105, 185, 216
    and parliament, 43–4, 47, 71, 265
    public role, 43–4, 47, 56, 58–9, 63, 71, 111
    and Thomas Seymour, 41, 42–51, 50–1, 53